INTRODUCTION

~~TO THE~~

LEGAL SYSTEM

2018–2019

MARTIN PARTINGTON

OXFORD
UNIVERSITY PRESS

OXFORD
UNIVERSITY PRESS

Great Clarendon Street, Oxford, OX2 6DP,
United Kingdom

Oxford University Press is a department of the University of Oxford.
It furthers the University's objective of excellence in research, scholarship,
and education by publishing worldwide. Oxford is a registered trade mark of
Oxford University Press in the UK and in certain other countries

Tenth edition 2015
Eleventh edition 2016
Twelfth edition 2017

Impression: 1

Published in the United States of America by Oxford University Press
198 Madison Avenue, New York, NY 10016, United States of America

British Library Cataloguing in Publication Data
Data available

Library of Congress Control Number: 2017963303

ISBN 978-0-19-881886-1

Printed in Great Britain by
Bell & Bain Ltd., Glasgow

About the author

Martin Partington is Emeritus Professor of Law and Senior Research Fellow at the University of Bristol.

He has over 50 years' experience as a law teacher, researcher, and writer on a variety of legal subjects (including administrative justice, legal education, and the English legal system), a (part-time) legal practitioner, a legal policy adviser, and a law reformer. He taught at the Universities of Bristol and Warwick, the London School of Economics, and Brunel University.

He has been associated with a wide range of bodies and institutions including, at different stages in his career and for different lengths of time: the Hillfields Advice Centre in Coventry; the Legal Action Group; the Training Committee of the Institute of Housing; the Management Committees of Citizens' Advice Bureaux in Coventry, Paddington, and Uxbridge; the Education Committee of the Law Society; the Lord Chancellor's Advisory Committee on Legal Aid; the Independent Tribunal Service for Social Security Appeal Tribunals; the Judicial Studies Board (both the main Board and its Tribunals Committee); the Council on Tribunals; the Civil Justice Council (and its sub-committee on Alternative Dispute Resolution); the Committee of Heads of University Law Schools; the Socio-Legal Studies Association; and the Socio-Legal Research Users' Forum.

For a number of years he was Training Adviser to the then President of Social Security Appeal Tribunals and also sat as a part-time Social Security Tribunals Chairman.

He acted as an expert adviser to the Council of Europe, examining Alternatives to Litigation in Disputes between the Individual and the State. In May 2000, he was appointed expert consultee to the Review of Tribunals, set up by the Lord Chancellor and chaired by Sir Andrew Leggatt. He was a member of the Gaymer Review of Industrial Tribunals, 2002.

From 2001 to 2005, he was a Law Commissioner for England and Wales; he was retained as a Special Consultant to the Commission from 2006 to 2008.

In 2002 he was appointed CBE; in 2006 he was elected as a Bencher of Middle Temple; in 2008 he was appointed QC (Hon). In 2015 he was elected a Fellow of the Academy of Social Sciences and awarded the Socio-Legal Studies Association's prize for Contributions to the Socio-Legal Community.

Until recently he was a member of the Executive Board of JUSTICE. He is currently a member of a Civil Justice Council working party on housing dispute resolution. He chairs the Board of the Dispute Service, a company under contract with government to provide tenancy deposit protection and dispute resolution.

This book draws on his lifetime of experience in the law, though it goes without saying that he writes in a personal capacity only.

New to this edition

The 2018–2019 edition of *Introduction to the English Legal System* includes coverage of:

- the implications of Brexit;
- redrawing of parliamentary constituency boundaries;
- progress with the government's *Transformation of our Justice System* reform programme;
- reform of the youth criminal justice system;
- the Lammy report on discrimination in the criminal justice system;
- civil justice reform, including establishment of the Business and Property Courts of England and Wales;
- new ideas for controlling the costs of civil litigation;
- significant changes to the fees policy for administrative tribunals;
- further proposals for reform of the regulation of the legal professions and claims management companies;
- research into alternative business structures;
- review of the impact of legal aid cuts;
- proposals relating to the use of Alternative Dispute Resolution.

Preface to the 2018–2019 edition

Although it is only a year since I completed the last edition of this book, I have had to to revise and update the whole text, both to reflect new developments and to address comments I have received from readers. Three matters are noted here.

1. *Transformation.* Government proposals to transform the work of courts and tribunals (*see Chapters 4, 5, 6, 8,* and *11*) continue apace. Legislation to implement some of the proposed changes has been delayed but is expected to be on the statute book during the coming year.

2. *Regulation.* There is continuing debate about the shape of the regulatory framework that underpins the work of professionally qualified lawyers and others who deliver legal services, which is aimed at promoting innovation in the delivery of legal services to the public (*Chapter 9*).

3. *Alternative dispute resolution.* Proposals for encouraging greater use of ADR have been set out in a consultation paper from the Civil Justice Council. (*Chapter 10*).

I have retained an outline of how the EU makes law, on the assumption that UK lawyers will still need to know the bases on which the EU operates. (*Chapter 3*).

Those starting to study law should note that by the time they finish their studies and start looking for law or law-related jobs, things are likely to be very different from what they are now. I will endeavour to keep readers posted on relevant developments in my blog.

The aims of the book remain the same—to provide all those coming new to the study of law, whether at A-level, degree level, or postgraduate conversion level, with an overview of the context within which law is made and practised in England and Wales; to encourage readers to start to think more broadly about the role that law plays in society; to provide a text that is as approachable as possible; and, more generally, to create a resource for those teaching citizenship in schools. The importance of better public understanding of law and legal institutions cannot be overstated. I hope this book will make a contribution to this better understanding.

The increasing amount of material available on the internet is reflected in the large number of websites listed (with description) in the Online Resources. Please send me information about new websites that you find interesting but that are not mentioned there; similarly, please let me know of links that no longer work. I have continued to develop 'Spotlight on the Justice System'—my personal blog on new developments in the English legal system, which is also available via the Online Resources and at www.martinpartington.com.

I would like to thank my editor Natasha Ellis-Knight and others involved in the production of this book at Oxford University Press for all their support. I would also like to thank Nick Wehmeier for all his work on the Online Resources and the blog, and Clare Weaver and her team for their outstanding promotional work.

I remain responsible for all errors and omissions.

The book is dedicated to my children Adam and Hannah—my original 'target readership'—and above all to Daphne for her insistence that I retain a sense of balance in my life.

Bristol, 8 December 2017

Guide to the Online Resources

www.oup.com/uk/partington18_19/

The Online Resources that accompany this book provide students and lecturers with ready-to-use teaching and learning materials. These resources are free of charge and are designed to maximize your learning experience.

Student resources

Author blog with podcasts—www.martinpartington.com

Martin Partington's regularly updated blog, which accompanies this book, is intended to help you keep up to date with key developments in the law. The blog offers:

- Access to important developments in law and on-going changes in legal policy
- The author's views and ideas on topical debates in the English legal system
- Interesting and engaging podcasts, which capture the author's discussions with leading lawyers on the more controversial issues affecting the English legal system
- The opportunity to post your thoughts, communicating with the author directly. I look forward to hearing from you!

Multiple-choice questions

The best way to reinforce your understanding of the English legal system is through frequent and cumulative revision. As such, a bank of self-marking multiple-choice questions is provided for each chapter of the text. These include instant feedback on your answers and cross-references to the textbook.

Questions for reflection and discussion

Questions are included for each chapter to test your understanding of the topics covered, and also to help you reflect on the key challenges and debates.

Flashcard glossary

Interactive flashcards containing key terms and concepts are provided to test your understanding of legal terminology.

Video resources

Accompanying video resources allow you to further reinforce your understanding of the English legal system.

Web links

Annotated web links allow you to easily research topics of particular interest.

Outline contents

Contents

PART IV THE DELIVERY AND FUNDING OF LEGAL SERVICES

PART V CONCLUSION

List of boxes and diagrams

Boxes

Diagrams

Table of Cases

Table of Legislation

UK Bills

US Legislation

UK Statutory Instruments

Non-statutory Codes of Practice

EU Legislation

Treaties

Directives

Regulations

International Treaties and Conventions

PART I

INTRODUCTION

1

Aims, themes, and structure

1.1 Aims

When I was first asked to write this book, my instructions were that it should: be genuinely introductory; be not too long; be relatively uncluttered by footnotes; be accessible to the more general reader; and, at the same time, offer an approach to thinking about the English legal system and its place in society not found elsewhere.

It is now nearly 20 years since the book originally appeared. However, the fundamental aims of this 13th edition remain the same. Written for all those coming new to the study of law, it:

- provides an introductory account of the English legal system, examining how it has developed in recent years and how it is likely to change in future; and

- considers how principles that underpin the legal system relate to some of the most difficult issues facing the modern world. (For example, how should the government's need to protect civil liberties be balanced with its need to manage risks associated with terrorism?)

The book is primarily about the *English* legal system (which includes for the present the legal system in Wales). There is a quite different system in Scotland and a rather different system in Northern Ireland. There are times when it is not sensible to refer just to 'England'; thus I use the phrases 'Great Britain' or 'United Kingdom' where they seem more appropriate. Nonetheless, the focus of the book is on the English legal system.

This does not mean that the book is only about institutions located in England and Wales. The English legal system is subject to important external factors, notably the European Union (at least until the process of Brexit is complete) and the Council of Europe.

Many who study law in England come from other countries. I hope you can both learn from the issues discussed here, and relate the questions raised to the situation in your home countries. Many of you come from other common law countries—whose legal systems are based on the principles of the English legal system, in particular that judges have power to make law; others come from civil law countries, whose legal systems are founded on principles of law and the codification of law developed in

Roman times.[1] Are the legal systems with which you may be more familiar fitted to their purpose? Are there lessons to be learned from the English experience? What do you think the English should be learning from experience elsewhere?

1.2 Themes

Although an introductory book, I address three themes inadequately considered in other books with the same or similar titles:

- *The holistic approach.* Many books on the English legal system are rather 'practitioner-oriented'; they focus primarily on those parts of the system in which professionally qualified lawyers practise law. The *holistic* approach adopted here is designed to introduce you to activities and functions often ignored elsewhere. I have done this, not just to be different, but also to ensure that you start to appreciate the enormous variety of professional contexts in which the legal knowledge and skills you are setting out to acquire can be used. All students should be encouraged to think about law and legal practice beyond the boundaries of the legal profession. This approach also benefits those of you who are studying law for its own inherent interest, without necessarily intending to become practising lawyers.

- *Change and evolution.* Many other introductory accounts are somewhat descriptive and 'static' in approach, providing a snapshot of the system at the moment of writing. I think it is essential that you understand just how dynamic and subject to change the English legal system now is. The pace of change is so rapid that the professional world today's new students will enter in five years' time will be significantly different from what it is now. Thus a recurring theme is change and the forces that have shaped and are shaping the English legal system.

- *Constitutional function.* The English legal system is often portrayed as being independent of the British system of government. Indeed, one important claim made for law and its practice is that it is 'independent' of government. Yet the government of the country is based in law; the institutions of law derive their power and authority from the system of government. There is a symbiotic relationship between law and government. The legal system is simultaneously independent of and part of the system of government of the country. Understanding the constitutional function of the English legal system and the relationship of the legal system to other branches of government is another theme underpinning the discussion in this work.

---

[1] The distinction between common law systems and civil law systems is not discussed in this book; a helpful introduction can be found in Merryman, J. H., *The Civil Law Tradition: An Introduction to the Legal Systems of Europe and Latin America* (3rd edn, Stanford, CA, Stanford University Press, 2007).

1.3 Structure

Having set out the themes that underpin the book, the structure of the book is as follows.

Titled *Law, Society, and Authority, Part II* contains two chapters that raise fundamental issues about the social functions of law and the legitimacy of law. It is impossible to study law without asking: what is the purpose of law? What impact does law have on society? Thus *Chapter 2* considers the role law plays in the way in which society is ordered, exposing the different and often conflicting functions inherent in the phrase 'law and order'. Having concluded that law makes an important contribution to the ordering of society, *Chapter 3* considers how law is made, who makes it, and whence those who make the law get their authority for making it and imposing it on society. The role of Parliament, the senior courts, and key European institutions are discussed.

Part III considers the institutional framework within which law is developed and practised. I start, in *Chapter 4*, with an account of the role of government in shaping the institutions and practice of law. Primary attention is paid to the Ministry of Justice, but I also consider the role of other government departments. In *Chapters 5* to *8* I look at the four legal systems which, for the purpose of this book, make up the English legal system. Most English legal system books draw a simple distinction between criminal and civil justice. I offer a more nuanced delineation of the constituent justice systems: criminal justice, administrative justice, family justice, and civil and commercial justice. In each chapter, a 'holistic' approach is adopted. Thus I consider not only the work of the formal legal institutions such as courts, but also the informal or other processes that do not catch the public eye (and, indeed, which are often not properly understood by professional lawyers) but which form an essential part of the framework of the English legal system when seen in the round.

In *Part IV* I look at the delivery and funding of legal services. *Chapter 9* considers the role both of those professionally qualified to practise law and of other groups who provide legal services but who are not formally qualified as solicitors and barristers. It sets out the key changes currently being made to the ways in which the legal profession works and is regulated. It considers adjudicators and other dispute resolvers who play a very significant role in the working of the legal systems. And it reflects on the contribution made by law teachers, both those working in universities and others working in private colleges and other contexts in the formation of legal professionals. *Chapter 10* reflects on how legal services are (and should be) paid for, and considers in particular the enormous changes being made to the funding of civil litigation following changes to the system of legal aid.

A short concluding *Part V* rounds out the discussion in the book by asking why the English legal system is currently undergoing so much transformation. What are the principal drivers for these changes? Will the changes undermine the system? Or will they help to adapt it to meet better the demands placed upon it in the twenty-first century?

1.4 Questions

Use the self-test questions in the Online Resources to test your understanding of the topics covered in this chapter and receive tailored feedback: www.oup.com/uk/partington18_19/.

1.5 Web links

Check the Online Resources for a selection of annotated web links allowing you to easily research topics of particular interest: www.oup.com/uk/partington18_19/.

1.6 Blog items

See Spotlight on the Justice System, at www.martinpartington.com/category/chapter-1-2/.

PART II

LAW, SOCIETY, AND AUTHORITY

2

Law and society: the purposes and functions of law

2.1 Introduction: understanding the role of law in society

A primary aim of this book is to enable you to understand the institutional framework within which rules of law are made and used. This book does not analyse specific rules of law, for example, 'What is the legal definition of murder?' or 'When is a contract legally binding?' Nonetheless, it is impossible to make any sense of the institutional framework without having some idea of the *social purposes* or *social functions* of law. The aim of this chapter is to get you to start thinking about these issues.

To do this, I distinguish between what I call the macro and the micro functions of law. Macro functions of law are those relating to the *general* role law plays in the running and ordering of society. Micro functions—which derive from those macro functions—relate to more *specific* uses to which law is put. The distinction becomes clearer as the discussion proceeds.

2.2 Macro functions of law: law and orders

If you ask, 'What is the role of law in society?', a common response would be 'to maintain order'. Much public debate and political rhetoric links law and order. There are two problems with this response.

First, it is extremely ambiguous. There is no single concept of order, but rather a variety of orders in relation to which law may play a role. These include:

- public order;
- political order;
- social order;
- economic order;
- international order; and
- moral order.

Secondly, the relationship between law and each of these types of order is extremely complex. The ability of law to shape these different orders is not unconstrained, but is subject to wider political and social forces. The law is not a neutral force which simply contributes to the organization of society, but is otherwise detached from that society. The relationship between law and orders in any given society cannot be understood without understanding the political, social, and economic ideologies that underpin that society. The role that law plays in one society differs sharply from that which it plays in another.

The ambiguities surrounding the concept of order, and the complexity of the relationship between law and orders, are considered further in the following paragraphs.

2.2.1 Law and public order

Many argue that a—possibly the—primary function of law is the *preservation of public order*. But maintaining public order is not exclusively a task for law; many other factors, such as pressure from family or friends or work colleagues, play an important part. Nonetheless, the fact that law sets the boundaries of acceptable behaviour and prescribes sanctions for breaches of those boundaries (which is in essence the function of criminal law) makes a significant contribution to preserving public order.

The preservation of public order, however, immediately raises another but not necessarily consistent function for law: the *protection of civil liberties and human rights*. The ability of people to argue freely about their beliefs is crucial in a democratic society. Limits may need to be set to the freedom of individuals to advance unpopular views, for example, those that are obscene or defamatory or that incite racial or religious hatred. Nevertheless, within those limits, freedoms of speech and thought must be protected by law.

Until recently, the British had no formal statement of human rights, comparable to the Bill of Rights enshrined in the Constitution of the United States. Rather, they relied on long-standing principles of law allowing people to indicate dissent, for example, by peaceful demonstrations or marches. Since October 2000, when the Human Rights Act 1998 came into effect, a more formal code of human rights has applied in the United Kingdom (*see Box 2.1*). Protection of human rights and civil liberties can therefore be identified as another function of law.

Box 2.1 Legal system explained

European Convention on Human Rights

In outline, the European Convention on Human Rights protects the right to:

- life (art 2)
- liberty and security (art 5)

Box 2.1 Continued

- a fair trial in civil and criminal matters (art 6)
- respect for private and family life (art 8)
- freedom of thought, conscience, and religion (art 9)
- freedom of expression (art 10)
- assembly and association (art 11)
- marry (art 12)
- effective remedy for violation of rights (art 13)
- property and peaceful enjoyment of possessions (Protocol 1, art 1)
- education (Protocol 1, art 2)
- vote in elections (Protocol 1, art 3)
- freedom of movement (Protocol 4, art 2)
- appeal to a higher court in criminal matters (Protocol 7, art 2)
- compensation for wrongful conviction (Protocol 7, art 3)

In addition, the Convention prohibits:

- torture (art 3)
- inhuman or degrading treatment or punishment (art 3)
- slavery and forced labour (art 4)
- arbitrary and unlawful detention (art 5)
- punishment without law (art 7)
- imprisonment for debt (Protocol 4, art 1)
- expulsion of a state's own nationals (Protocol 4, art 3)
- the collective deportation of foreigners (Protocol 4, art 4 and Protocol 7, art 1)
- the death penalty (Protocol 6, art 1)
- discrimination in the enjoyment of the rights and freedoms secured by the Convention (art 14, Protocol 12, art 1)

With the exception of the prohibition on torture, which is an absolute right, it is possible for states to 'derogate' from these rights in times of emergency (art 15). Governments may also limit the political activities of foreigners (art 16). It is also possible for governments to limit these rights so long as any limitation applies to everyone in the state (art 18).

Find the full text of the Convention at www.echr.coe.int/documents/convention_eng.pdf.

In recent years, there has been some doubt as to whether the UK would remain subject to the European Convention since the government had indicated that it wanted to repeal the Human Rights Act 1998 (which incorporated the Convention into UK law) and replace it with a UK Bill of Rights. For the moment, this issue is not on the political agenda.

But this protective function cannot always be consistent with the preservation of public order. There are occasions when the preservation of public order results in restrictions on civil liberties. Conversely, the protection of civil liberties can on occasion limit the ability of public authorities to control public order.

In highly repressive societies, the use of law to preserve public order becomes so dominant that civil liberties and other fundamental freedoms are destroyed. In more tolerant societies where dissent is permitted, there must be a balance. There is sharp debate about the extent to which law's function is to preserve public order, as opposed to protecting other rights and freedoms. Human rights groups, such as *Liberty* and *Justice*, which seek to defend human rights and civil liberty, may not always persuade governments to change their minds on proposals relating to the development of law. But their ability to challenge and criticize government is fundamental in a democratic system based on the rule of law. The law's function in relation to the maintenance of public order is, thus, highly contingent upon the nature of the society in which law operates.

The enactment of the Investigatory Powers Act 2016 provides an excellent example of the difficulties in getting the balance right between ensuring government can control matters relating to public security and ensuring that the liberty of the individual is properly protected (*see Box 2.2*).

Box 2.2 Reform in progress

Balancing freedom and security: Investigatory Powers Act 2016

The Investigatory Powers Act creates a new legal framework for use by UK security and intelligence agencies, law enforcement, and other public authorities who need to obtain communications data. This covers the interception of communications, the retention and acquisition of communications data, and equipment interference for obtaining communications and other data. It is not lawful to obtain such data other than as provided for by the Act. The Act also makes provision relating to the security and intelligence agencies' retention and examination of bulk personal datasets.

Debate on the Bill, which was also the subject of pre-legislative scrutiny (*see 3.3.1.1*), showed how hard it is to balance the need of the state to intercept and acquire information about communications between those who would wish to do harm to society, while at the same time protecting rights of individual privacy.

Much debate focused on the limits that should be placed on those who wished to exercise the powers set out in the Act, and who should be the final decision taker when really controversial decisions had to be taken.

Links to the Act and material relating to the Act can be found at services.parliament. uk/bills/2015-16/investigatorypowers.html.

2.2.2 Law and political order

Another primary function of law is to underpin the political order—the constitutional function of law. In this context, the United Kingdom is an oddity. It is one of a very few countries that does not have a written constitution. Many important practices within the British Constitution derive from unwritten 'conventions', rather than from written rules of law (*see Box 3.2*). Some crucial aspects of the way the system of government is organized in the United Kingdom fall outside the scope of law altogether, based more in political theory than in legal rules. In view of this, some argue that support for constitutional arrangements should not be regarded as one of the macro functions of law.

Nevertheless, despite the lack of a written constitution, it is right to include this topic here. It emphasizes the fact that, although the United Kingdom has no written constitution, a great deal of fundamental law regulates the way in which its political system operates. Many of the UK's constitutional arrangements are enshrined in law.

To give some examples:

- Legislation providing for the devolution of powers from the government in London to, respectively, the Scottish Parliament and the Welsh Assembly has created a new legal framework for regulating the relationship between the government in London and governments in Edinburgh and Cardiff.

- The Human Rights Act 1998 has significantly affected the practice of government. Legislation must be compliant with the provisions of the European Convention on Human Rights, which are incorporated in that Act.

- Following the passing of the Freedom of Information Act 2000, which came into effect in 2005, there is law that determines the extent to which governments can operate openly or in secret.

- The Supreme Court was created in 2009 (to replace the judicial functions of the House of Lords).

- Many other examples can be given: the introduction of fixed-term Parliaments; the detailed law relating to the running of elections; or the law regulating the relationship between central and local government.

Given this rapidly growing body of law, many commentators now argue that the British should take the last step and adopt a written constitution, drawing all these constitutional provisions into a single document.

The argument against a written constitution is that it permits changes to the constitutional settlement to be made more easily than in countries with written constitutions. An important consequence of the Scottish independence referendum held in September 2014 was that there was further change to our constitutional arrangements (*see 3.3.1.7*). There will be significant constitutional consequences arising from Brexit. Such changes can be made without the need for special parliamentary procedures.

2.2.3 Law and social order

Law also impacts upon a country's 'social order'. Defining the nature of social order is extremely complex; there are widely varying opinions. However, it is clear that in the United Kingdom, as in many other democratic countries, there are substantial differences between individuals. These may arise from differences of ability, or differences of income or wealth, or differences of birth or class. These differences are reflected in many rules of law, in particular those that define concepts of property and contract. The present social order is supported by law which protects the rights of those with property and the economic power to enter and enforce contractual arrangements. Much criminal law also seeks to protect property rights. On this analysis, the relationship between law and social order may be seen as conservative, in the sense that it seeks to conserve established social arrangements.

However, as with the role of law in relation to public order, there are other ways of thinking about the relationship between law and social order. Many people assert that a fundamental purpose of law is to promote a more dynamic social order, designed to ensure that society is not locked into historic structures that sustain inequality, but is based on principles of equality and the prevention of social exclusion.

How to attack inequality is the subject of fierce debate. Some argue that equality can be achieved only if there is a complete removal of the differences between people—so that, for example, everyone in employment receives more or less equal pay, there is equality in the amounts of wealth capable of being held by individuals, and so on.

Others take the view that equality in this sense is neither the right nor a sensible way to promote a new social order. They argue that the focus should be on *equality of opportunity*, for example, in the provision of education or health care or employment.

Many modern rules of law have the promotion of equality of opportunity as a prime objective. Thus in the United Kingdom, there is law designed to combat discrimination based on grounds of gender, ethnicity and race, disability, or age. This was given a new focus by the enactment of the Equality Act 2010 (*see Box 2.3*). This is driven not by simplistic notions of political correctness but by the very practical belief that our collective good is enhanced by ensuring that all citizens play a full part in the economic and social life of the nation. To give a simple example, if women are excluded from the workforce, 50 per cent of the available talent is thereby excluded.

Box 2.3 Legal system explained

Equality Act 2010

The Equality Act 2010 replaces previous anti-discrimination laws. It covers nine 'protected characteristics' which cannot be used as a reason to treat people unfairly. As every person has one or more of the protected characteristics, the Act potentially protects everyone against unfair treatment. The protected characteristics are:

- age;
- disability;
- gender reassignment;
- marriage and civil partnership;
- pregnancy and maternity;

Box 2.3 Continued

- race;
- religion or belief;
- sex;
- sexual orientation.

The Equality Act 2010 sets out the different ways in which it is unlawful to treat some-one, such as direct and indirect discrimination, harassment, victimization, and failing to make a reasonable adjustment for a disabled person. The Act prohibits unfair treat-ment: in the workplace; when providing goods, facilities, and services; when exercis-ing public functions; in the disposal and management of premises; in education; and by associations (such as private clubs).

In addition to anti-discrimination legislation, a great deal of social, welfare, and educational policy-making seeks to assist in the promotion of a new social order. Law gives legitimacy to those policies. There is nothing new about this. Since the development of the Welfare State in the middle of the nineteenth century, it has been accepted that it is right that governments should seek, to varying degrees, to promote equality, for example by taxing the better off relatively more than the poor. The law clearly plays a central part in implementing these policies.

However, the mere fact that policies have been developed and enshrined in Acts of Parliament does not mean that a new social order is thereby automatically created. The evidence is that in modern Britain there remain very marked inequalities—whether based on class, education, employment, health, or other life opportunities. While there may be aspirations towards equality, the social reality is that equality—however defined—has not yet been fully realized.

The claim that law has a role to play in the promotion of equality is one that is frequently made. It was advanced by those who promoted the first Race Relations Act in 1965, and was also used in debate on the Equality Act 2010. Promotion of equality can thus be included as one of the macro functions of law. However, law also plays a role in maintaining the existing social order, for example through the protection of rights in property. This function may conflict with law's role in promoting greater equality. This leads some to argue that law has another, more political, function—namely, supporting the existing social order as opposed to promoting a new social order. As with the tension between the preservation of public order and the protection of civil liberty, there are tensions between the role of law in the preservation of the existing social order and its role in the promotion of a new social order.

Similarly, claims are made that a function of law is to promote social justice. The extent to which law and the legal system, by themselves, can deliver social justice is limited. Social justice is more a political concept than a legal one. Law may be able to support steps taken to achieve social justice and thus promote a new social order;

but it would be unrealistic to claim that law can achieve this in isolation from other non-legal factors that underpin modern society.

Even if the ability of law directly to foster social justice or equality is limited, there is nevertheless an important claim for law: that it has a role to play in protecting the weak against the powerful. This became a very important function for law as the concept of the Welfare State developed, not just in the United Kingdom but across the developed world.

2.2.4 Law and economic order

The relationship between law and economic order raises matters similar to those considered in the relationship between law and social order. The dominant economic philosophy in the United Kingdom, indeed throughout the Western world, is market capitalism.[1] The development of capitalism has been dependent on the recognition of legally enforceable rights in private property, whether in land or other forms of security. Law defines ownership rights in property as well as laying down procedures for the transfer of those ownership rights from one person to another. The law enables different property rights (e.g. tenancy or trust) to co-exist in the same piece of property. And the law provides mechanisms for the enforcement of those rights. Concepts of property developed in law have been crucial to economic development.

Similar arguments apply to contract. Recognition of the legally enforceable bargain (contract), breaches of which can be litigated in the courts, has been an essential tool in the development of the modern market capitalist economy. As with its function in the maintenance of the social order, so too can law be seen as instrumental in the creation and underpinning of the economic order.

Nevertheless, there are other ways in which law is now used to regulate the economic order. It has long been recognized that market economies are bad at delivering certain socially desirable outcomes. Without regulation, those operating factories or machinery might do so without proper regard for health and safety, as happened in the nineteenth century. A great deal of modern law creates regulatory frameworks within which capitalist entrepreneurs must operate. Currently, there is widespread discussion about how the banks should be regulated. Here, too, regulation is justified on the ground that it fills gaps left by market failure.

Indeed, it has long been recognized that untrammelled capitalist activity contains its own contradictions. There is an inexorable tendency for capitalists to accumulate market position and, if possible, dominate that position through the exercise of monopoly power. However, the shift from competition to monopoly poses a fundamental threat to the operation of the market. Thus legal mechanisms are used to promote competition and to limit the development of monopolistic positions.

---

[1] Differences between different models of capitalism—e.g. the Anglo-American model, the European model, or the Japanese model—are not considered here. It should not be assumed that the operation of capitalism is the same in all countries.

It is also inevitable that those with greater bargaining power will seek through contract to impose their wishes on parties with weaker bargaining positions. A great deal of modern law is designed to level the playing field. Thus a vast body of consumer law is designed to soften the binding nature of contractual relationships by giving rights to consumers in situations where the bargaining power between the supplier of goods or services and the consumer of those goods or services is unequal. For example, there are legal requirements that those who sell insurance policies or other expensive financial products must allow the purchaser a 'cooling-off period' within which the purchaser may change his or her mind. Housing law regulates the relationship between landlords and tenants. Employment law regulates the relationship between employer and employee. More generally, there are measures enabling the consumer to challenge terms in contracts thought to be 'unfair'.

As with law and public order and law and social order, in relation to economic order the law performs functions that are to a degree in conflict. Law has helped to legitimate the tools essential to the commercial context within which market capitalism is able to flourish. At the same time, law is used to curb the excesses of market behaviour that can arise from unregulated operation of market capitalism.

2.2.5 Law and international order

Another function of law is support for international order. This is an extremely complex and controversial subject not considered in detail here. Some argue that there is really no such thing as international law; rather that maintenance of international order is sustained by international relations and diplomatic pressure. But in many respects, international bodies and politicians like to point to legal authority for what they are trying to achieve. Consider the following examples:

- Recent incursions by the United Nations into the world's trouble-spots have been justified in part by reference to the legal framework of the United Nations Charter and its executive bodies, in particular the Security Council.

- Attempts to deal with genocide and 'crimes against humanity'—a particular curse of the modern age—are being made through special War Crimes Tribunals that have been established by the United Nations and which sit in The Hague and elsewhere.

- In other areas, such as the regulation of world trade or the protection of the environment, the regulation of the use of the sea, or space, there is an increasing tendency not only to enter treaties—which historically was common practice—but also to create special institutions and mechanisms for enforcement, like courts or tribunals, which are independent of particular national governments.

- The conduct of war has long been subject to international legal constraints, for example the Geneva Convention on the treatment of prisoners of war. Similarly, other constraints on behaviour in time of war, such as the prevention of torture, have been proscribed in instruments of international law.

- One of the most pressing of current social issues, the protection of those seeking asylum in one country because of a well-founded fear of persecution in another, is essentially shaped by principles of international law.

These are important and controversial issues. Even though the focus of this work is on the rather more parochial subject of the 'English legal system', we cannot ignore the global context in which countries now operate. Legal instruments and institutions have played a significant part in this development; the role of law in the wider international context should not be forgotten.

2.2.6 Law and moral order

Another macro function of law is to provide support for the moral ordering of society. This is also extremely controversial. Some theorists argue that there should be little, if any, distinction between law and morality; that the law should clearly and deliberately mirror those issues of morality which people think 'ought' to inform the way we should behave. Others draw a clear distinction between law and morality. They argue that the mere fact that many people believe that certain forms of behaviour or activity are morally wrong (e.g. engaging in homosexual activity, or tax avoidance[2]) should not mean that such behaviour should be defined as unlawful.

There are clear dangers and considerable difficulties in seeking to equate law and morality, not least because of the problems of determining what the common morality is on any given issue. Nevertheless, many rules of law are founded on a moral view of society. Perhaps the clearest example is the moral imperative not to kill people, reflected in rules of criminal law which outlaw such activity. Even here, though, there may be tension between the moral and the legal. Many of those who accept the moral principle that it is wrong for one human being to kill another would nevertheless accept that the law could permit some forms of euthanasia or assisted suicide to prevent pain and distress for those who are dying.

In general, it may be suggested that rules of criminal law which reflect some common morality, however defined, may be more acceptable and effective in regulating behaviour than those rules which do not. Even so, there are some behaviours that many might regard as undesirable—drinking cheap alcohol or being under the influence of drugs in the streets—but which should not simply because of that be defined as criminal.

We should also note that ideas about what behaviours should be regulated by criminal law change. For example many of the criminal offences that 200 or 300 years ago led to draconian punishments such as transportation or even the death penalty now seem very trivial, and are either not criminal at all or dealt with much less severely. Today, many argue that a less criminalized approach to the use of soft drugs might lead not only to more equitable treatment of drug users, as compared with those who use

---

[2] Tax avoidance is technically legal, as opposed to tax evasion which is clearly illegal.

alcohol or nicotine, but also to reductions in other forms of criminality resulting from the need for drug users to break the law to obtain the money to buy their drugs. On the other hand, there are powerful political arguments that any relaxation in the government's approach to drug use would 'send the wrong signal' to the community at large.

In a different context, much of the law that seeks to regulate relationships between individuals is also based in concepts of morality—for example, the law relating to marriage. (The debate on the decision to legally recognize homosexual marriage threw the relationship between law and morality into sharp focus.) This is another context in which law provides at least some support for the moral order, a function reinforced by the principle of the protection of family life found in Article 8 of the European Convention on Human Rights.

Related to the relationship between law and moral order is the relationship between *law and religious order*. Despite the decline in religious belief in England, there are still many who argue that religion—both formal and informal—remains an important facet of society at large. However, and in contrast with discussion about the relationship between law and morality, it is not now often argued that law should be directly supportive of religion. Indeed many would argue, whether in general principle or because of their own religious (or anti-religious) beliefs, that law should *not* be used to support the religious order. Questions of spirituality and religious belief should fall within that private sphere of activity in which the law should not intervene.

Nevertheless, the historical role played by religion in the development of modern England cannot be wholly ignored. At its most basic, its calendar and major holiday festivals are based in the Christian tradition, rather than that of other religious groupings. There are a number of legal privileges that attach exclusively to the Church of England; there are others that apply to religious groups more generally. Thus it is arguable, though not often seen in this light, that present-day law still plays a residual part in the support of religious order, in particular the Christian religious order.

This is controversial, not least because of the rise in a number of countries of various forms of religious fundamentalism. These are often accompanied by degrees of intolerance towards others that are quite unacceptable in a modern pluralistic society. Indeed, it may be the case that, in order to protect social pluralism, the law should be used more to protect the ability of those of different religious beliefs to hold and practise their religion, another issue embraced in the European Convention on Human Rights (*see Box 2.1*).

2.3 Other macro functions

In addition to the ways in which law may interact with the maintenance of and challenges to different types of order, law plays a number of other macro functions in society.

2.3.1 The resolution of social problems

The response of politicians and their officials to many issues perceived as social problems is to pass laws seeking to deal with those issues. This is the expected political response. Only rarely do politicians concede that there may be enough law, and that what is needed is better understanding of or enforcement of existing law. Even more rarely are politicians willing to accept that a possible solution to a problem might be to repeal existing rules of law or to develop the law in such a way as to 'decriminalize' the activity in question. Their mindset assumes that a function of law is 'to solve social problems'. Indeed, whole careers are devoted to the promotion of legislation allegedly designed to address particular social issues—even if, as often happens, there is a perfectly satisfactory law already available, or where changing the law is not really a solution to the problem. Recent debate about the (in)ability of law to regulate anti-social behaviour is a good example.

One obvious consequence of creating legal provisions to solve social problems is that people—ever mindful of their own self-interest—respond to new legal frameworks in ways not predicted by the law-makers. Tax law offers numerous instances where laws designed to achieve one objective (increased taxation) are thwarted by taxpayers who rearrange their affairs to avoid new tax burdens. A hidden but often inevitable consequence of using law to solve social problems is, therefore, that the new law results not in the solution of existing social problems but rather in the creation of new social problems. The process of dealing with one issue leads to the creation of another, which in turn has to be 'solved' later.

2.3.2 The regulation of human relationships

Another important function of law is the regulation of the nature and extent of human relationships. The definition of and the formalities relating to the creation of marriage and civil partnerships are determined by legal rules. Law provides a framework for the distribution of assets on the breakdown of marriage and civil partnership. Law sets boundaries to the scope of sexual relationships, prescribing, for example, the minimum age of sexual consent, and making certain sexual relationships within the 'prohibited degrees of consanguinity' (incest and other close relationships) unlawful. The law also sets down a framework for the treatment of children and other family members.

2.3.3 The educative or ideological function of law

A further function of law, almost irrespective of its impact in particular cases, is an educative one; it contributes to the shaping of the 'ideology' of a nation. To give a simple if significant example, there is no doubt that attitudes to drinking and driving have changed dramatically over the last 25 years. In part, this is the result of powerful advertising, demonstrating the devastating impact that drink-drive accidents can have on victims and their families. But the change in attitude has also been the result of changes in the law contributing to a climate of opinion in which drinking and driving is no longer regarded as socially acceptable behaviour. Another example is the contribution law made to the elimination of smoking in public places.

A third example is law, mentioned earlier, outlawing various forms of discrimination. When such laws come into effect, those who argue for their introduction often accept that the law cannot, on its own, alter the attitudes of mind that lead to the discriminatory behaviours that result in the creation of those laws. However, those who sponsor such laws see them as not only creating certain legal rights that may be enforceable by individuals, but also sending a more general message to society at large that discriminatory behaviour is not acceptable.

More generally, countries that embrace the principle of the rule of law are, in effect, asserting that the powers of officials of the state must be limited and that the individual citizen should have both the right and the opportunity to challenge decisions where they are thought to be wrong or in some respect unfair.

The decision by the British government to introduce the Human Rights Act 1998, incorporating the European Convention on Human Rights directly into English law, is another example of legislation that not only creates legal rights which individuals may seek to enforce through the courts, but also sends an important educative signal about the limits within which people, particularly those who work within government, must behave. In this sense, therefore, another macro function of law relates to the education of the public's social attitudes and responsibilities.

2.4 Micro functions of law

Turning from the 'macro' to the 'micro' level involves consideration of rather more specific functions for law, many of which derive from the 'macro' functions identified earlier. A number of examples are offered; this does not purport to be a comprehensive list. You may be able to think of other functions not identified here. You may also be able to identify other examples to illustrate the particular functions which are set out in the following paragraphs.

2.4.1 Defining the limits of acceptable behaviour

Most people have some awareness of the *criminal law*. A major objective of this branch of the law is to prescribe the limits of socially acceptable behaviour. The criminal law prohibits many kinds of activity about which there would be widespread agreement, such as murder and violent crime. It also outlaws a wide range of other activities about which there may be more debate, such as the use of particular types of drugs. The following points may be made in this context:

- Not all behaviour that may be regarded by many as undesirable is characterized in legal terms as criminal. Thus there is no law preventing a person over the age of 18 from drinking alcohol. However, where the consequences of that conduct may impinge on others, the law often steps in. There is strict law making it unlawful for persons who have been drinking alcohol or taking drugs to drive.

- Human conduct is regulated in many ways in addition to the use of law. Codes of morality, religious principles, pressures of friends and family all constrain the ways in which people behave.

- Different countries set the boundaries of their criminal law in different places: what is criminal in one country is not necessarily criminal in another.[3] Although there is a great deal of commonality between different bodies of criminal law, in important respects the boundaries of criminal law are *culturally determined*, set by the demands of the specific society. There are particularly important distinctions in societies with different religious traditions or moral backgrounds: laws applying in Islamic countries are in many respects quite different from those in countries founded on the Judaeo-Christian tradition.

- The boundaries of the criminal law are *dynamic*. Activity which has historically been regarded as criminal is not necessarily regarded as criminal forever. The prohibition of the sale of alcohol in the United States during the 1920s is a good example.

However, the function of law in regulating human behaviour is not exclusively through the criminal law. Areas of *civil law* have a similar function. For example, if a party to a contract breaks that contract, rules of law allow the party affected to claim compensation from the person in breach. The law of negligence prescribes situations in which a person who has negligently injured another has to compensate that other for the injury. In short, law defines the scope of obligations that exist between individuals and provides remedies for breach of those obligations. Although the objective of civil law is not to punish an offender, in the sense used in considering criminal law, nevertheless rules of civil law clearly signal that a contract cannot be breached with impunity, nor can one person act negligently in relation to another. In this sense, the rules of civil law also send the message that certain types of behaviour are unacceptable or undesirable.

2.4.2 Defining the consequences of certain forms of behaviour

Law does not simply define forms of behaviour that are unacceptable. It also prescribes consequences. In the case of criminal law, these are the punishments that attach to a finding of guilt. Similarly, in the area of civil law, law prescribes the remedies that the person affected by a breach of contract or a negligent act may obtain from the perpetrator.

In some situations the same facts may generate a variety of legal consequences. For example, a road accident may be caused by a person driving a car carelessly or recklessly. This may result in the police seeking to get that person prosecuted through the criminal courts; if found guilty, this may result in the imposition of a fine or even imprisonment. If the accident causes damage to another, that other person may seek compensation by bringing an action in the civil courts for damages in negligence against the driver. The driver may argue that the accident occurred because her car

---

[3] This has the important practical consequence that, if a person commits a criminal act in one country and flees to another country where that act is not criminal, this is often the basis for successfully resisting extradition proceedings—official proceedings to bring the alleged miscreant back to the country where the original act took place where he or she may be subject to criminal proceedings.

was improperly serviced, and may therefore bring a civil action for breach of contract against the garage. Three different legal consequences have arisen from the same incident.

2.4.3 Defining processes for the transaction of business and other activities

A rather different function of law is to define procedures by which certain transactions must be carried out. Some of these are quite straightforward, such as those relating to the making of simple contracts. In other cases, particularly where there is concern to prevent fraud, considerable formality may be required. Many of these relate to transactions dealing with the transfer of property rights. For example, the process of buying and selling houses is subject to a number of formal legal requirements, known collectively as the rules of conveyancing. There are detailed rules relating to the creation of leases. There are special rules for the creation of wills. Similarly, there are detailed requirements for the creation of trusts or settlements of property. These are all designed to protect valuable assets and prevent fraud.

One of the problems with prescribing formal requirements is that, whatever the law states, in practice people attempt to carry out these transactions in ignorance of the rules. The law must then develop supplementary principles to prevent injustice occurring, notwithstanding the existence of procedural irregularity. Many of the principles of the law of equity have developed in response to this problem.

2.4.4 Creating regulatory frameworks

A great deal of modern law seeks to regulate those who provide services to the public. For example, much law now regulates the professional activities of lawyers, doctors, architects, nurses, or estate agents. There is a vast regulatory framework designed to control the activities of those who provide financial services to the public, to prevent fraud and other breaches of trust. Another branch of regulatory law relates to the promotion of health and safety in the workplace and other contexts.

A consequence of the privatization of formerly nationalized industries has been the creation of an extensive body of law designed to regulate the activities of companies now in the private sector (such as telecommunications, utilities—gas, water, and electricity—and transport), including the promotion of competition and the regulation of prices. And specific areas of economic activity are subject to the most detailed legal regulation designed to promote standards and give the consumer value for money. The regulation of the housing market through housing law is a prime example.

A different form of regulatory law, but one that has been in existence for many years, is planning law regulating the use to which land in the United Kingdom can be put. Law that seeks to regulate industry in order to protect the environment is another example. In this context, the law operates at an international as well as a national level.

Another area of activity which has seen the development of new regulatory frameworks is found in the context of major scientific discoveries. For example, a consequence of greater understanding of our genetic codes has led to thinking about how this new knowledge might relate to the development of new kinds of clinical therapy, or new forms of treatments—e.g. to combat hereditary disease. These raise complex moral issues as well as practical challenges which resulted in the establishment of new regulatory procedures.

Regulatory law also serves another purpose. It defines the categories of persons able to make representations to government about a particular policy or decision. For example, again in the context of planning law, the relevant law determines who may challenge decisions of the planning authorities and who may appear to make their case at any public inquiry resulting from a planning decision.

Complaints are frequently heard that the burden of regulation is too great; governments often assert that they are trying to cut back on regulation. But in practice there is no escaping regulation. For example, politicians often say that they want to protect consumers. How do they do that? Through regulation!

2.4.5 Giving authority to agents of the state to take actions against citizens

Another function of law is to give power to state officials to take action against members of the public. There are numerous examples: the powers of the police to stop, search, question, arrest, and caution members of the public is one; the power of doctors to detain in mental hospitals those diagnosed as suffering from acute mental illness is another; the power of social workers to remove children from families where they are thought to be at risk and to place them in the care of the local authorities is a third. Similarly, agents of both central and local government are given power to take money away from members of the public through taxation.

A rather different example is the power given to government and other agencies of the state to acquire land compulsorily in the public interest.

2.4.6 Preventing the abuse of power by officials

In contrast to the previous heading, much law is designed to prevent abuses of power by public servants. For example, the police are required to operate within a framework of powers prescribed by the Police and Criminal Evidence Act 1984, which limits their powers of arrest, search, and questioning, considered further in *Chapter 5*.

The essence of administrative law, discussed in *Chapter 6*, relates to the importance of officials acting within a framework of law which prescribes their power; not allowing officials to use discretionary powers in an abusive way; and giving people the opportunity to take advantage of certain procedural safeguards—for example, a right to put their case—before adverse decisions about them are taken. These are further examples of rules of law setting boundaries to the power of state officials.

2.4.7 Giving power/authority to officials to assist the public

The law also sets down a vast range of requirements for agencies of the state to provide services or other goods to the public. At the most general level, all public expenditure has to be legitimated by special Acts of Parliament known as Appropriation Acts. These give general authority for the expenditure of public money on the whole range of programmes run by government.

More specific bodies of law deal with the details. Social security law is one example, setting out as it does the entitlements to social security benefits which have been created by government. Many other examples could be given: entitlement to free education is one, free treatment within the National Health Service is another. All these activities, of the social security, education, and health authorities, are underpinned by detailed legal frameworks.

2.4.8 Prescribing procedures for the use of law

In addition to prescribing procedures for conducting different types of transaction, there is another important body of law—procedural law—which seeks to control the ways in which courts and other adjudicative bodies operate. This body of law may set limits to the evidence that can be brought in different types of cases. It also prescribes the way in which different types of proceedings, whether in the courts or other legal fora, are to be conducted.

2.5 Key points

It is not claimed here that these examples of the macro and micro functions of law in society are exhaustive. Readers should ask themselves whether there are other functions for law and whether they should be regarded as macro or micro in character. There is a huge literature on the relationship of law and society of which the foregoing is only a very limited summary. However, a number of points can be noted:

1. All the functions of law, whether macro or micro, are *contingent* upon the stage in the development of that society and the pressures and challenges facing that society. While many of these functions of law are common to very many societies, others are not.

2. The laws that exist and the ways in which they are used are dependent on the ideology and politics of the particular country. For example, current notions of social justice and equality in the United Kingdom have developed in the light of particular socio-political and economic theories. They will change in the future. The list of functions proposed here should not, therefore, be regarded as set in concrete; it reflects broader changes in the social and political ideas and ideals of that society.

3. The functions of law are by no means always consistent with each other: preservation of social order may, on occasion, be in sharp conflict with the function of protecting civil liberties; the role of law in advancing equality or social justice may be in conflict with its role in supporting current social and economic orders.

4. It should be remembered that there are still activities that are not currently the subject of legal regulation. Governments frequently claim that they are seeking to limit the encroachment of law. Interestingly, however, when a new technology arrives that actually enables activities to occur outside conventional regulatory frameworks—the rise of the internet and new communications technologies are good examples—politicians and others quickly become agitated.

5. There are many mechanisms, outside law, that are used to regulate and alter people's behaviour. Much of the practice of economics is based on the assumption that, if financial incentives are right, behaviours change. An interesting example is the proposal that problems of global pollution and global warming must be tackled not just by laws saying what should or should not be done, but also by getting financial incentives right—higher taxes paid by those who pollute, for example.

6. More fundamentally, there are significant issues about the way in which we order our society that are either not touched on at all by law or only in relatively insignificant ways. For example, one of the major social issues of our time relates to the extent to which groups in the community are excluded from the mainstream of social life, whether through lack of money or other material resources, such as housing. To be sure, there are legislative provisions relating to the provision of social security benefits or to the provision of accommodation to the homeless. However, the entitlements contained in these bodies of law are not absolute but are highly contingent on legal tests being met. Those claiming benefits or access to housing have a substantial list of conditions that they must satisfy before they can be helped. The fact that the rhetoric of law employs concepts such as liberty or justice does not mean that substantive law actually delivers social justice to all citizens of the United Kingdom.

7. Perhaps the most important point to stress is that although the discussion has, perhaps, been somewhat abstract, the issues considered are central to many of the most serious challenges facing the United Kingdom. One obvious example is how governments should respond to terrorist attacks, such as the recent attacks in Manchester and London. How should this be handled? By giving the Home Secretary new powers to detain people for longer periods without being charged for any offence, or new powers to deport those felt to be promoting religious intolerance? By allowing courts to receive evidence obtained as the result of covert surveillance? Or will these developments undermine freedoms essential to British values and the British way of life?

8. Finally, it should be stressed that the functions of law set out here are those which, in theory, have the impact on society suggested. Whether or not laws have their intended impacts can only be tested by empirical research on law. In thinking about the impact of law on society, consideration must be given to the developing body of empirical research on law.

2.6 Questions

Use the self-test questions in the Online Resources to test your understanding of the topics covered in this chapter and receive tailored feedback: www.oup.com/uk/partington18_19/.

2.7 Web links

Check the Online Resources for a selection of annotated web links allowing you to research easily topics of particular interest: www.oup.com/uk/partington18_19/.

2.8 Blog items

See Spotlight on the Justice System, at www.martinpartington.com/category/chapter-2/.

Suggestions for further reading

ABEL-SMITH, B., and STEVENS, R., *In Search of Justice: Society and the Legal System* (London, Allen Lane, 1968)

GENN, H. (and others), *Law in the Real World* (London, Nuffield Foundation, 2006)

PARTINGTON, M. (ed), *Law's Reality: Case Studies in Empirical Research on Law* (Special research issue of the Journal of Law and Society, 2008)

Other suggestions can be seen in the Further Reading listed in the **Online Resources**.

3

Law-making: authority and process

Chapter 2 considered a number of functions that law plays in the ordering of society. Here we consider how law is made in the United Kingdom. Before getting into any detail, we ask: what gives the law-making institutions their authority? What gives law-makers their legitimacy?

3.1 Introduction: power, legitimacy, and authority in the law-making process

One of the macro functions of law identified in *Chapter 2* was support for the political order. Law provides much, if not all, of the legal framework within which power is exercised. But simply stating that constitutional principles provide governments or other executive agencies with the power to make law begs a more fundamental question: from where do these constitutional legal principles derive their authority?

The answer is far from easy. Different societies base claims for the legitimacy of their law-makers on different theoretical foundations. In broad terms, however, law-makers may be said to derive their authority from two principal sources:

(1) the basic constitutional framework or constitutional settlement that operates within that country; and

(2) the underlying political ideology of that country.

The reasons why people are more or less willing to accept these as bases for the exercise of power are complex. One is that most people, while accepting that certain services such as education and health need to be provided, do not want to run them themselves. They are happy to let politicians and bureaucrats get on with the job. Furthermore, once a government has established a claim to exercise power, particularly coercive power, it invariably creates the machinery—police, security services, and the like—to enforce the law which results from the exercise of that power.

But it should always be remembered that even the most fundamental of constitutional arrangements fail if significant groups within a particular society find that constitutional basis unworkable. The fact that in some countries in the world there have been civil wars, that in others there have been *coups d'état*, demonstrates the point. The destruction of the Berlin Wall, the collapse of apartheid in South Africa, and more recently events in countries in the Middle East, can all be cited as modern examples.

Even countries that now enjoy the most stable and secure of constitutional arrangements, such as the United Kingdom or the United States, can trace their present situation to resistance to or rebellion against historically unacceptable constitutional arrangements.

In the United Kingdom, and in many other developed countries, that consent is more taken for granted than actively sought (save on particular issues which are the subject of referendums (*see Box 3.1*)). In these countries, free and regular elections are the primary mechanism through which continuing consent to govern is implied. What concerns many people today, particularly in countries where democratic process is well established, is that voter apathy weakens the legitimacy of law-making institutions.[1] This leads some to argue that voting in elections should be made compulsory; this is already the law in Australia, for example. Whether or not this step is taken, it is vital that cynicism regarding politicians should not prevent citizens from participating in this fundamental constitutional process. It is also important that electoral processes are as efficient and corruption-free as possible.[2]

Box 3.1 Legal system explained

Referendums

Referendums are a mechanism for giving the electorate a chance to vote on a specific question of policy. In countries, such as the United Kingdom, where referendums are neither mandatory nor binding, there nonetheless exists an unwritten convention that important constitutional changes are put to a referendum and that the result will be respected. Although rare, there have been a number of important referendums in recent years:

- In 2011, there was a referendum on whether the system of voting in General Elections should be changed from 'first past the post' to one involving an element of proportional representation. Even though proportional representation is used in a number of contexts already, including elections to the Scottish and Welsh Parliaments, the idea was rejected by the electorate in 2011.
- In 2014 Scotland held a referendum on whether it should leave the United Kingdom; although this was defeated, it led to a commitment by the Westminster government to devolve further power to the Scottish Parliament.
- In 2016 there was a referendum on whether the United Kingdom should leave the European Union. The majority was in favour of leaving, reversing a referendum on the same subject held in 1975. This has set in train a process whose detailed outcome is, at the time of writing, still far from clear.

---

[1] See www.democracymatters.org.uk/ for an alliance of organizations anxious to encourage citizen engagement in the democratic process.

[2] The Electoral Registration and Administration Act 2013 made technical changes to the electoral process. For more detail, see my blog, www.martinpartington.com.

Box 3.1 Continued

Advocates of referendums argue that certain decisions are best taken out of the hands of representatives in Parliament and determined directly by the people. Critics argue that in a representative democracy, it is the job of politicians to take these decisions. Voters in a referendum are not sufficiently informed to make decisions on complicated or technical issues, being swayed by strong personalities and expensive advertising campaigns. They also argue that voter apathy may result in low turnout so that in reality the results of referendums do not reflect general public opinion. Although legally a referendum result is not binding on a government, nevertheless to ignore the outcome would usually be politically unthinkable.

Lastly, the authority and legitimacy of a country's law-making institutions must not be squandered. Recent scandals concerning the expenses claimed by Members of Parliament (MPs) represented a serious challenge for the UK Parliament. The Parliamentary Standards Act 2009 was enacted to try to address the issue. It created the Independent Parliamentary Standards Authority and the Parliamentary Standards Commissioner, whose task is to monitor the propriety of MPs' expense claims and other financial interests.

3.1.1 Constitutions and constitutionalism

One basis for the authority given to the law-makers can therefore be found in a country's constitution and its related principles of constitutionalism. What are these?

In most countries there exists a *written constitution* or other form of 'basic law' that defines the powers of the law-making institutions of the country. The constitutional arrangements of the United Kingdom are unusual; there is no formal written constitution. Many of the most important constitutional principles are found not in any written document but in unwritten practice, known as *constitutional conventions* (*see Boxes 3.2 and 3.3*).

Box 3.2 Legal system explained

Constitutional conventions

There is a substantial literature on constitutional conventions and the extent to which they have changed over the years. Some examples of constitutional conventions may be noted, as follows.

Constitutional monarchy. The theoretical Head of State remains the monarch. The principle of constitutional monarchy means that the Queen takes no active part in the running of the country. Although the parliamentary year starts with the 'Queen's

Box 3.2 Continued

speech' and although bills are given 'royal assent', the Queen does not intervene in the politics of the law-making programme. The Queen is kept informed about what is happening in Parliament and, through audiences with the Prime Minister of the day, is briefed about significant developments. It would be surprising if, on occasion, she did not offer her views on particular issues. But the monarch is not the source of political decision-taking or law-making.

Prerogative powers. Nevertheless, there are still certain functions of government that are based not in legislative authority, but on the historic exercise of power by the monarch. These are known as 'prerogative powers'. The most dramatic and controversial example is the power to go to war. This is exercised by ministers not under the authority of an Act of Parliament, but by exercise of prerogative powers. (In practice these days, governments do not go to war without ensuring that Parliament has at least had an opportunity to debate the merits of such action.) The Home Secretary's 'prerogative of mercy' to reduce a sentence imposed by the courts after a criminal trial is another example. The ability to enter into international treaties is a third example. The government's argument that it could start the process of quitting the EU by use of the prerogative was rejected by the Supreme Court in January 2017, on the ground that the prerogative could not be used to take away rights created by Parliament when it enacted the European Communities Act 1972. (*See R (Miller) v Secretary of State for Exiting the European Union* [2017] UKSC 5, noted in my blog at February 2017.)

Cabinet government and collective responsibility. The very existence of the Cabinet—the central committee of ministers chaired by the Prime Minister, which decides the government's legislative programme—is another aspect of the British Constitution based in convention, rather than legislation. The related doctrine of collective responsibility, whereby ministers who do not agree with the policy of the government as determined in Cabinet are supposed to resign, is also based in constitutional convention, not constitutional law.

Individual ministerial responsibility. Another constitutional convention is that ministers should take ultimate responsibility for what goes on in their departments. This means that they must answer questions in Parliament or select committees about the work of their departments. On occasion this may also lead ministers to resign, where something has gone very seriously wrong, though in practice this is now a rare occurrence.

These unwritten principles are nevertheless supplemented by an increasing number of statutory provisions that have constitutional effect (*see 2.2.2*). Devolution of powers to government in Scotland and Wales, human rights, and freedom of information have required legislation which has transformed the constitutional legal landscape. The Constitutional Reform Act 2005 went further, significantly changing the role of the Lord Chancellor, making the Lord Chief Justice the head of the judiciary, and creating the new Supreme Court.

A key outcome of the referendum on Scottish devolution was the promise that further powers would be devolved from the government in Westminster to the Scottish Parliament. Provision for this is in the Scotland Act 2016. (Information on the Bill is available on my blog: www.martinpartington.com.)

One noteworthy feature of the Act is that it enshrines in law a constitutional convention, which, as noted earlier, are usually unwritten rules of constitutional practice (*see Box 3.3*).

Box 3.3 Reform in progress

Legislating a constitutional convention

During the debate on what became the Scotland Act 1998, Lord Sewel indicated in the House of Lords (HL Deb vol 592 col 791) that 'we would expect a convention to be established that Westminster would not normally legislate with regard to devolved matters without the consent of the Scottish Parliament'.

Section 2 of the Scotland Act 2016 inserts a new subsection (8) into section 28 of the 1998 Act so it is recognized in statute that, although the sovereignty of the UK Parliament is unchanged by the legislative competence of the Scottish Parliament, the UK Parliament will not normally legislate for devolved matters in Scotland without the consent of the Scottish Parliament. A similar provision has been enacted relating to Wales—see section 2 of the Wales Act 2017.

For further details see www.legislation.gov.uk/ukpga/2016/11/contents/enacted; and www.legislation.gov.uk/ukpga/2017/4/introduction/enacted.

There have been a number of important constitutional changes made in recent years, for example the creation of the Supreme Court (*see 8.13.1*) or the introduction of fixed-term (five-year) Parliaments (*see Box 3.4*). The relative ease with which important changes to the structure of government in the United Kingdom may be made arises from the fact that the United Kingdom does *not* have a written constitution.

Box 3.4 Reform in progress

Fixed-term Parliaments Act 2011

One peculiarity of the British system of government used to be that the duration of the Westminster Parliament—i.e. the length of time a government lasts following a general election—was not fixed. The Septennial Act 1715, as amended by the Parliament Act 1911, limited any Parliament to five years. If not dissolved at the end of the five-year period, it automatically expired. These provisions gave the Prime Minister of the day considerable flexibility on when he or she 'goes to the country'—a decision that may well be determined by the state of the public opinion polls.

Box 3.4 Continued

The Coalition government enacted the Fixed-term Parliaments Act 2011. This set down fixed days for polls for parliamentary general elections. The polling day for elections will usually be the first Thursday in May every five years. The first such polling day was 7 May 2015. Under the legislation, the Prime Minister has power to alter, by statutory instrument, the polling day for parliamentary general elections, but only to a day not more than two months earlier or later than the scheduled polling day.

The holding of early parliamentary general elections outside this time frame can be triggered either by a vote of no confidence in the government following which the House of Commons did not endorse a new government within 14 days, or a vote by at least two-thirds of all MPs in favour of an early election. The ease with which this can be achieved was revealed when Prime Minister Theresa May decided to hold an early election in June 2017. Where such an early election occurs, the next scheduled election after that will be five years from the previous first Thursday in May, i.e. in May 2022.

British *constitutionalism*—the principles which underpin the constitution—rests on three principal concepts: the *sovereignty of Parliament*, the *rule of law*, and the *separation of powers*. Definitions of these concepts have, over the years, been fiercely contested. For present purposes:

- The *sovereignty of Parliament* asserts that the ultimate legal authority for law-making in the United Kingdom is Parliament.

- The *rule of law* insists that power should not be exercised by persons acting by or on behalf of the state without their being able to point to legal *authority* for their actions. Further, the processes by which decisions are reached should be fair. The Constitutional Reform Act 2005 gives statutory recognition to the concept of the rule of law.

- The *separation of powers* suggests that, to prevent any particular arm of government from becoming too powerful, there should be separation between the legislative (law-making), executive, and judicial arms of government. Thereby each branch of government is subject to *checks and balances*. This in turn leads to the proposition that the judges in particular, and lawyers in general, must act independently of government—a principle clearly recognized in the Constitutional Reform Act 2005.

These principles relate to the central issues of power: who may exercise it, how it can be controlled, and how those who exercise power can be called to account.

3.1.2 Political ideology

Stating these constitutional principles still leaves unanswered the question: what is the theoretical basis on which power to make law may be asserted by political institutions?

To answer this it is necessary to consider the underlying political ideology of the country.

In the United Kingdom, and many other countries, the currently dominant political ideology is *representative democracy*, expressed principally through the holding of regular elections. Democratic theory suggests that society is unable to function effectively if everyone retains their unique power to control their own life or the lives of others. Instead, political parties set out their ideas for the policies they would like to deliver in election manifestos. By electing MPs who are members of those political parties to *represent* the views of electors, individuals pass to those elected some of the control or *sovereignty* that gives them the authority to govern on behalf of the people. In practice, that authority extends not just to issues set out in manifestos, but to the much wider range of issues that inevitably arise during the course of any period of government.

Those in power are also subject to the principle of *accountability*. Thus politicians are regularly called to account when general elections are held. The electoral process gives those elected to political office their authority to make laws on behalf of the citizens of the country. But they know that if their actions are not approved of by the electorate they will be defeated at the next general election. They are also subject to accountability through the *checks and balances* that exist, both within Parliament (such as parliamentary debates or questions to ministers) and outside (including the essential part played by the press and other mass media in exposing things that go wrong within government).

3.1.2.1 Principles in practice

The application of these principles is not as clear in practice as theory might imply:

- First, in the British system, the work of Parliament is strictly controlled by the political party that forms the government of the day. There are very few issues on which MPs vote independently of their party. There is the occasional backbench revolt; and the occasional 'free vote' on a matter of conscience where the party 'whip' is not applied. But these are the exception, not the rule.

- Secondly, all legislation in the United Kingdom passes through not only the elected House of Commons, but also the non-elected House of Lords. Although the House of Lords rarely exercises the power it theoretically has to delay bills from becoming law, on many occasions the House of Lords amends, often very substantially, legislation coming to it from the House of Commons. The threat of delay may also lead to significant amendment or even the dropping of legislative proposals. While there is in the Commons a clear link between the democratic process of election and the outcomes of the legislative process, in the Lords this is not so.

- Thirdly, knowing the extent to which the electoral process actually represents the will of the people is very difficult. In the United Kingdom, the 'first past the post' voting system has meant that nearly all recently elected governments have attained power with significantly less than 50 per cent of the popular vote. This leads many, particularly those in the smaller parties who struggle to get elected under the present system, to argue that a fairer voting system would incorporate proportional representation, with seats in Parliament distributed in proportion to votes cast. The primary argument against this apparently attractive proposition is that this tends to lead to coalition governments, in which small minority parties acquire a disproportionately powerful position. Nevertheless, proportional representation has been introduced in the United Kingdom in the context of elections of members to the European Parliament and elections to the devolved Parliaments in Wales and Scotland. In 2011 the Liberal Democrat party tried to get a change to the voting rules, but the public rejected the idea in a referendum.

- A fourth issue said to weaken the democratic process is a decline in the percentage of the population voting in elections. This has led to procedural changes making it easier for people to vote by post. There have also been suggestions that there should be electronic voting systems in supermarkets. There have even been calls to make voting compulsory, as happens in some other countries.

- Fifthly, there are important sources of law other than Parliament. Under the British system of separation of powers, judges in the higher courts have power to make new rules of law. They do this through the development of rules of 'common law'—long-standing principles of law developed over the years, in some cases centuries, by the judges (*see 3.4*). Yet judges are not elected; they do not get their authority from any theory of representative democracy. The legitimacy for their law-making is found in other constitutional principles, in particular the separation of powers. The judges are recognized to be both a part of the machinery of government and, at the same time, independent of it.

3.2 The law-making institutions in the UK and Europe

With these points in mind, we take a closer look at the functions of a number of the law-making institutions that exist in the United Kingdom and consider: (1) the British Parliament and central government; and (2) judges and the courts. Later in the chapter we discuss the impact of Europe on the law-making process in the United Kingdom and how this is likely to change following Brexit.

3.3 The British Parliament and central government

The principal law-making body in the United Kingdom is the British Parliament. Its legislative programme is at the heart of the law-making process. By no means all legislative measures are the subject of detailed parliamentary scrutiny (*see Box 3.5*), but the vast bulk of legislative measures derive their authority from the parliamentary process. Even the European measures that the British government is currently required to put into law have to have the stamp of parliamentary approval.

Box 3.5 Legal system explained

Statute law: the classification of legislative measures

The vast bulk of new law brought into effect in England is statute law, that is, law that has been enacted by Parliament following debate in the House of Commons and the House of Lords, or law made under the authority of statutes. Statute law comes in a variety of forms:

- primary legislation;
- secondary legislation;
- tertiary legislation; and
- (though not strictly statute law) 'quasi-legislation' or 'soft law'.

Primary legislation comprises the *Acts of Parliament* that are passed by Parliament. Most Acts are 'Public General Acts', which apply generally in England. They also apply in Wales if they relate to matters not devolved to the Welsh Assembly Government. They often apply in Scotland, though not on matters devolved to the Scottish Parliament. (Each Act contains a section detailing the precise extent of its coverage.) Some are 'Local or Personal Acts' applying only in particular localities or to specific people (*see further Box 3.6*).

Primary legislation is supplemented by a vast body of *secondary legislation*—regulations and orders made under the authority of an Act of Parliament. These are known generically as *statutory instruments*. There are typically over 3,000 of these made each year, running to many thousands of pages of text. They are not subject to detailed parliamentary scrutiny, though in many cases statutory instruments cannot be made by the government without consultation with specialist advisory committees (*see Box 3.9*).

Besides primary and secondary legislation, there is a huge amount of *tertiary legislation*—legislative instruments, made under the authority of an Act of Parliament, but which are subject to no parliamentary scrutiny at all. For example, in housing law, numerous powers are given to ministers to issue 'directions' or other instruments, drafted in the form of legislation and which effectively have the force of law, but which are simply issued by the government department in question. Similar examples are found in many other areas of government.

There is, lastly, a fourth category of instrument, sometimes referred to as *quasi-legislation* or *soft law*, which comprises statements of good practice or guidance. These may be made under the authority of an Act of Parliament and are in some cases subject to parliamentary approval. But, as with tertiary legislation, they get no detailed parliamentary discussion. Examples include the Highway Code or the codes of practice relating to police behaviour made under the Police and Criminal Evidence Act 1984 (*see Chapter 5*). Many other examples could be given.

Box 3.5 Continued

There is a practical problem with tertiary and quasi-legislation. It is not published through the National Archive—the official outlet for legislative publications. An important issue of principle flows from this. It is frequently asserted that because legislation is published by a single authoritative source, 'everyone is deemed to know the law'. Such a claim is simply not sustainable in the case of such instruments.

Box 3.6 Legal system explained

Acts of Parliament: Public General Acts and Local and Personal Acts

Most Acts of Parliament are Public General Acts (*see Box 3.5*).

Local and Personal Acts (together called 'Private Acts') apply only to a local area (say a town), to a specific institution (say a body such as a university), or to a particular individual. The procedure by which Local and Personal Acts become law is quite different from the procedure by which Public General Acts become law. The detail is not considered here, but in essence such Acts use a procedure involving committees of the House, not the full House of Commons.

Private Acts must be sharply distinguished from Private Members' Acts (*see Box 3.7*).

The legislative process has undergone significant change in recent years—an example of the often-understated dynamism that characterizes many developments in the English legal system. The discussion here focuses on the process of enacting an Act of Parliament. Apart from the inherent importance of the subject, there is a good practical reason why lawyers need to know about this. There are now circumstances—albeit limited—in which what was said about a bill as it passed through Parliament may be used in court when dealing with a question of statutory interpretation (*see Pepper v Hart* [1993] AC 593 (HL); *see further 3.4.2*).

3.3.1 Primary legislation

All Acts of Parliament start as bills. Bills are accompanied by an Explanatory Note, drafted by the bill's sponsors, which sets out the background to the bill and explains what it is trying to achieve. (Since 1999, Explanatory Notes have also been published alongside new Acts of Parliament.) These notes are key to any public understanding of legislation. They are written in plain language and explain the policy and legal context to non-lawyers. All bills and notes are published on the internet. Four distinct types of bill may be identified:

(1) Government bills, designed to advance the political programme of the party in government. They are sponsored by government ministers and absorb the bulk of parliamentary time spent on legislation.

(2) Law reform bills, arising from recommendations made by law reform agencies, such as the Law Commission (*see further 4.2.6*). These are less politically controversial.

(3) Consolidation bills, which bring together into a single place a wide range of legislative provisions scattered through many Acts of Parliament and thus difficult to find. These measures do not introduce new law but tidy up and re-present what is already on the statute book. Failure to consolidate adds to the complexity of carrying out legal research, since printed versions of Acts of Parliament that have been substantially amended can be very misleading. New computer technology makes it easier to keep texts of statutes up to date. In the United Kingdom this is achieved in part by commercial legal information providers such as Westlaw, in part by government through its Statute Law Database. This does not reduce the need for regular consolidation bills. A special procedure enables these bills to reach the statute book without going through the full parliamentary process discussed later.

(4) Private Members' bills, which are a special type of bill introduced by backbench MPs (*see Box 3.7*).

Box 3.7 Legal system explained

Private Members' Acts

Private Members' Acts start as bills introduced by backbench MPs who are not members of the government. They are subject to special rules. The most important is that they cannot contain any provision that would result in the expenditure of public money.

The backbenchers who bring these bills forward are selected following a ballot—a process that takes place early in each parliamentary session. Private Members' bills are debated only on Fridays—a day when the pressure of government business is usually less. Twenty private members are able to introduce their measures following the ballot; those near the top of the list have a greater chance of seeing their bills introduced into law. For a bill to have any chance of success it must either be supported by the government, or at least not actively resisted by the government.

The Housing (Homeless Persons) Bill 1976 is a good example: as originally drafted it would have given a range of legal rights to the homeless that the government regarded as wholly unacceptable. In that case, the government offered the bill's sponsor, the late Stephen Ross, an alternative bill, which he took forward. With this government support the bill passed into law.

Private Members' bills can be used to introduce measures on which there are fierce divisions of opinion, but where those divisions are not the subject of party political debate. An example is the Abortion Act 1967, which was a very important, obviously controversial, measure introduced by David Steel, to which none of the main political parties wished to tie their political reputations. The willingness of a private member

Box 3.7 Continued

to take such an issue forward means that the political parties, in particular the government party, can to an extent distance themselves from the issue.

Over the last 15 years or so, about eight out of 20 Private Members' bills have reached the statute book each year. There are three other means by which backbenchers may attempt to introduce legislation: 'presentation bills', Ten Minute Rule bills, and bills from individual members of the House of Lords. The numbers of such bills passing into law are tiny and are not considered further here.

3.3.1.1 Preparatory stages

Before being presented to Parliament, many bills start the process of becoming law by being included in the political manifesto of the party that won the last general election. Political parties want power to turn their ideas into legislative form. Issues that involve a good deal of specialist know-how are frequently the subject of consultation with persons or other agencies outside government. There are various ways in which this is carried out.

Commonly, ideas for new policies and related changes in the law are floated in *green papers*, so called because years ago they were published with green covers. (These days, image-conscious governments produce green papers with multi-coloured covers.) They set out policy proposals and ask the public for comments on them. The government often attempts to steer responses by indicating its preliminary view on what should happen.

Following initial consultation, further and firmer statements of the government's policy objectives may be published in *white papers* (which are also no longer white) that summarize responses to consultations and set out what the government plans to do.

It used to be the case that all bills had to be presented first to Parliament. However, the wisdom of this principle became subject to increasing criticism.

As the result of important procedural changes introduced in 1997, a number of bills are now published in draft and circulated for comment and criticism by those most likely to be affected, prior to their formal introduction into Parliament. They are usually the subject of an inquiry by one of the select committees of the House of Commons or the House of Lords, occasionally a joint committee of both Houses, which involves taking evidence—oral and written—from those likely to be affected by the proposed legislation. The reports arising from these inquiries can lead to changes being made to the bill before it is introduced formally into Parliament. (The Investigatory Powers Bill 2015 was subject to this procedure.) On occasion, a draft bill is abandoned completely.

3.3.1.2 The Queen's speech

Each session of Parliament opens, usually in May, with the Queen's speech. (Following the 2017 General Election, the Queen's Speech was delivered in June.

With Brexit as the dominant legislative issue, it was decided that the parliamentary session should run for two years until May 2019.) Written by the government, the speech sets out the legislative priorities for the coming parliamentary session. Getting a slot in the Queen's speech is a key objective for ministers seeking to introduce a bill into Parliament. Without it, their legislative ambitions cannot be advanced. The only exception is emergency legislation needed to deal with an important but unexpected issue. The contents of the Queen's speech are determined by a Cabinet committee.

3.3.1.3 Parliamentary stages

Once a bill's policy objectives have been determined by government, those policies are transformed into legislative form—the bill—by specially trained lawyers known as parliamentary counsel. Most measures designed to advance the political objectives of the government are presented first in the House of Commons; less controversial measures (including consolidation bills) may start in the House of Lords. *Diagram 3.1* sets out the different stages.

The *first reading* is purely formal. The House orders the bill to be printed. No further progress can be made until it has been printed.

At the *second reading*, the minister responsible sets out the main policy objectives; the opposition parties set out their objections. This is followed by comments from other MPs. At the end of the debate, there is a summing-up by a government minister. It is rare for a government bill to be defeated at this stage, though this happened to the Shops Bill 1986, designed to deregulate Sunday trading. If a bill requires either the raising of taxation or the expenditure of public money, Parliament also has to pass (respectively) a ways and means resolution or a money resolution.

The *committee stage* involves detailed scrutiny of the text. This is carried out by one of several *public bill* committees of MPs, which range in size from 16 to 50. These committees have power to take written and oral evidence from officials and experts outside Parliament. They consider the clauses of the bill, as drafted, consider amendments proposed to those clauses, and determine whether or not such amendments should or should not be accepted. This is a highly 'political' stage in the legislative process. Not only do opposition members put down amendments that they have thought of, but

Diagram 3.1   Passage of a bill

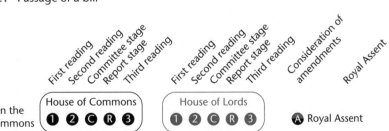

A bill can start in the House of Commons or the House of Lords and must be approved in the same form by both Houses before becoming an Act of Parliament.

members of public bill committees are also subject to intense lobbying from groups outside Parliament, seeking to persuade them to put down amendments that reflect their interests. (These groups also exert pressure in other ways, through press releases, interviews on TV and radio, and so on.)

Given that the governing party always has a majority on the committee, and that MPs from the government side are instructed to vote as the whip tells them, the government usually either gets its way or makes only those concessions which it is prepared to accept. Nevertheless, bills are frequently amended and often emerge from the overall process significantly changed from the form in which they were first advanced. Very occasionally, where a bill is being rushed through Parliament or involves significant constitutional change, the committee stage takes place in the whole House.

The *report stage* is where what happened to the bill in committee is reported to the main House. This gives the government the chance to undo anything that the committee may have done to the bill which the government does not like. It is often the point at which amendments which the government itself wishes to bring into the bill (perhaps following debate in committee) are introduced.

Lastly, the *third reading* is a more formal stage in which the bill in its amended form is brought together but no more amendments are made. The bill then goes to the House of Lords, where it begins a similar process.

The progress of a bill through Parliament is regulated by a *programme order*, formally approved by Parliament following the second reading. This sets out the dates by which each stage of the bill must be completed. One effect of programme orders is that, not infrequently, substantial parts of a bill may pass into law without any debate.

3.3.1.4 The House of Lords

Procedure in the House of Lords is broadly similar to that in the Commons. The major differences are:

(1) the committee stage is taken on the floor of the House. There are no separate committees of peers which report back to the House as a whole;

(2) there is no programme order, and thus debate on amendments is not restricted; and

(3) amendments can be made at the third reading stage.

These potentially can be, and on occasion are, a source of delay. In theory the House of Lords could wreck or seriously delay legislation. But peers are aware that, given their status as a non-elected legislative body, the ultimate decision on legislation must lie with the elected House of Commons. While they do not in practice wholly destroy bills, there have been a number of occasions in recent years where they have secured significant amendments or even caused a bill to be withdrawn. (For a case study on the work of the House of Lords, *see Box 3.8.*)

Box 3.8 Reform in progress

House of Lords consideration of the Constitutional Reform Bill 2004

In June 2003, the then Labour government decided it wanted to abolish the post of Lord Chancellor, establish a new mechanism for the appointment of judges, and create a new Supreme Court. This generated considerable controversy, not least among the senior judiciary who feared that such a step could undermine the conventional constitutional balance of power between the judicial and executive branches of government. It was also discovered that, in any event, simple abolition of the office of Lord Chancellor without legislation was not technically possible.

There followed a period of public consultation on the three principal elements of reform, and the government published summaries of the responses on 26 January 2004. The Supreme Court and judicial appointments issues were also considered by the Constitutional Affairs Committee of the House of Commons, which reported on 3 February 2004. One of its recommendations was that the Constitutional Reform Bill would be 'a clear candidate for examination in draft'. A number of speakers in the House of Lords on 12 February 2004 made the same point.

Nevertheless, the government decided to introduce the Constitutional Reform Bill into the House of Lords without prior discussion. It became clear that, such was the degree of opposition to the bill, it stood little chance of being passed by the House of Lords. However, the Lords was also conscious that to deny progress to what the government regarded as an important measure would be a risky step to take.

The compromise was to 'rediscover' a procedure—not used in relation to a government bill for about 90 years—of referring the bill to a specially constituted select committee of the House of Lords. The Committee spent nine days hearing evidence and a further 11 days deliberating. It made numerous drafting changes to the bill, though on the two main issues—abolition of the post of Lord Chancellor and creation of the Supreme Court—the committee remained divided.

The effect of the process was that people outside Parliament had a chance to comment on the bill. The Committee also made detailed changes to the bill, as public bill committees of the House of Commons do.

Although the select committee did not agree on everything, the bill, as amended, was recommitted to the House of Lords, from which it finally emerged as the Constitutional Reform Act 2005.

One of the most important features of the select committee's report is that it published the hitherto unpublished agreement reached by the Lord Chancellor and the Lord Chief Justice on the guarantees needed to ensure the continuing independence of the judiciary. For further information about the concordat, as the agreement is known, *see 4.2.3.*

Once the Lords' stages are complete, there is a further process in the Commons and the Lords for all the amendments to be agreed to produce a single version of the text. Particularly towards the end of the parliamentary year, this can lead to dramatic horse-trading (called, unbelievably, 'ping-pong') between Lords and Commons, especially where measures are very controversial. In the last resort, the House of Lords has power under the Parliament Act 1911 to delay a Commons bill (though not a money bill) for up to one year. If there is an ultimate impasse, then the view of the elected legislature, the House of Commons, prevails. The most recent occasion on which the Parliament Act was invoked was in relation to the passing of the Hunting Act 2004.

Carry forward enables a bill to be carried forward from one parliamentary session to the next. However, bills that are not enacted before a general election is held cannot be carried forward to the new Parliament, even if the new government is formed by the same political party as the outgoing government. In such cases, the bill must start the parliamentary process afresh.

3.3.1.5 Royal assent and commencement

Lastly comes *royal assent*. This has not been withheld since 1707, but, reflecting the fact that the United Kingdom is a constitutional monarchy, remains a formal step that has to be completed. It is at this point that the *clauses* in the bill become the *sections* in the Act.

The mere fact that an Act has completed the legislative process does not mean it becomes effective at once. Commonly, new administrative arrangements have to be made before an Act can become operational. In such cases, the legislation is effective only when a *commencement order*—a special type of statutory instrument (*see 3.3.2*)— is made. (The Easter Act 1928 has still not been brought into force.) It is essential that those who wish to use new rules of law discover whether or not statutory provisions are in force. This can involve difficult detailed research. However, the availability of statutes online, through legislation database services such as Westlaw or LexisNexis and the government Statute Law Database, has made it easier to discover whether new legislation is in force.

3.3.1.6 Reports of debates

The debates on all the parliamentary stages are the subject of verbatim reporting in the Official Reports of the Houses of Parliament (known collectively as *Hansard*). Thus it is possible to research what was said and by whom at each stage of the parliamentary process. These reports also detail how MPs voted. These reports are available online.

3.3.1.7 English votes for English laws

An important outcome of the referendum on Scottish devolution was that the Prime Minister, David Cameron, pledged to introduce the principle of English votes for English laws. This would mean that for legislative proposals that would only affect England (or in some cases England and Wales), MPs from other parts of the UK would have their rights to vote restricted. Finding a way of putting this principle into practice proved to be extremely controversial.

Changes to parliamentary procedure to bring the principle into effect were agreed on 22 October 2015. The changes are extremely complex. I published a detailed note on the changes at www.martinpartington.com; look in the October 2015 archive. The

House of Commons Procedure Committee will at some stage undertake a review of how these procedures are operating in practice.

3.3.2 Secondary legislation

Because of the time needed to ensure the passage of legislation through Parliament, modern Acts of Parliament tend to contain the essential principles of legislation only. The detail is filled in by *secondary legislation* made under the authority of the Act, but which is not subject to the full parliamentary scrutiny that a bill faces. Secondary legislation is technically known as *statutory instruments*, which come in two forms, *regulations* (the most common) and *orders*.

Underpinning the creation of secondary legislation are a number of controls designed to ensure that governments only introduce measures for which they have authority.

(1) Regulations are subject to formal vetting by the Joint Committee on Statutory Instruments.

(2) Many categories of statutory instruments also have to be shown in draft to particular bodies or organizations detailed in the 'parent' Act. There are governmental advisory committees which have the specific task of commenting on and vetting proposed regulations (*see Box 3.9*). Some parent Acts require the government not just to consult with a specific nominated body, but with 'such bodies as appear to have an interest in the legislation'. This is code for requiring the government to discuss the content of proposed delegated legislation with a range of interested groups.

(3) There is the potential for some parliamentary input, though this rarely happens. All regulations are subject either to a *negative resolution procedure* or to an *affirmative resolution procedure*. (Two particular types of statutory instrument, commencement orders—which bring Acts of Parliament, or parts of Acts of Parliament into effect—and orders in council, are not subject to any parliamentary procedure.) The *negative resolution procedure* is the more common. It means that, once laid before Parliament, a new regulation becomes effective on the date stated in the regulation, *unless* Parliament passes a resolution stating that the regulations should be annulled. Given that regulations are introduced by government and that (usually) the government has a majority in the House of Commons, annulment happens very infrequently.

By contrast, the *affirmative resolution procedure* means that a regulation laid before Parliament cannot become effective unless Parliament adopts a resolution that states *positively* that the regulation should become effective. This process does not give the House of Commons much control over the detail, since debate is permitted only on the underlying issues, not specific details. But affirmative resolution debates give some opportunity for opposition parties to make broad political points about the regulation in question. An example is found in the annual uprating of social security benefits. The relevant regulations are subject to the affirmative resolution procedure. Debate on whether the new amounts should be 50p more or less is not permitted; but general debate about social security provision and social welfare policy is allowed.

(4) In an extreme case, the validity of a statutory instrument may be challenged in the courts and, if found to be *ultra vires* (outside the legal framework provided by the parent Act), will be declared by the courts to be a nullity. (*See 6.3.4.*)

Box 3.9 Legal system explained

Case study: consultation on regulations: the case of social security

An example of the use of a specialist committee to review delegated legislation is found in the work of the Social Security Advisory Committee, which looks at draft regulations relating to social security. It not only considers the proposals, but also consults on them with a wide range of bodies and pressure groups outside government. It reflects on these comments before making its own report to the government. The government then decides whether or not to accept the advice of its Committee.

When it brings forward the final version of the regulations, the government is required to publish a special report which not only reproduces the report from the Advisory Committee, but also details why the government has (or more often has not) followed the advice of the Committee.

This represents a particular form of accountability which to some extent replaces normal parliamentary debate; arguably it is more relevant since most of those consulted have a specialist interest in and knowledge of the area. This is a model that, it has been forcefully argued, should apply in other regulation-making contexts.

For more information go to www.gov.uk/government/organisations/social-security-advisory-committee.

3.3.3 Amending legislation

The process of amending legislation is usually done by passing a new Act that alters an Act already on the statute book. Thus time for amending legislation must find a slot in the legislative programme. On occasion, ministers have sought to make their lives easier by providing that provisions in an Act of Parliament can be amended by statutory instrument, thereby avoiding Parliament. These provisions are called 'Henry VIII clauses', reflecting the propensity of that monarch to ride roughshod over Parliament. However, they are not regarded with favour. (At the time of writing, the European Union (Withdrawal) Bill 2017 is being heavily criticized for the wide powers it proposes for ministers to amend European legislation which has to be brought into UK statutes.)

One consequence of the passing of amending legislation is that it makes it harder to find out what the current law is on a particular subject. The Statute Law Database provides details of how and when legislation has been amended. It is not yet complete, in the sense that not all legislation on the statute book is currently in the database; but its scope is expanding. Commercial legal databases such as Westlaw, LexisNexis, and Justcite also contain statutes as amended.

3.3.4 Regulatory reform

Over the last 20 years, it has been accepted that where legislation imposes unnecessary regulatory burdens on business or individuals, they should be able to be removed without waiting for a full parliamentary legislative slot. The first Act to move in this direction was the Deregulation and Contracting-Out Act 1994. It provided that, subject to detailed safeguards, ministers could lay orders before Parliament that had the effect of amending legislation. The power was used 48 times to remove burdens that might not otherwise have received parliamentary time.

The Regulatory Reform Act 2001 gave ministers wider powers to lay orders before Parliament to amend legislation, again so long as any such amendment removed burdens. This Act was replaced by the Legislative and Regulatory Reform Act 2006, which came into force at the start of 2007. Further detailed amendment is found in the Enterprise and Regulatory Reform Act 2013.

The passage of all these bills was very controversial. MPs and commentators outside government argued that the powers could allow ministers to make significant legislative change without exposing their arguments to parliamentary scrutiny. Many of their fears were, frankly, overstated; ministers' powers to amend legislation are significantly circumscribed (*see Box 3.10* for further detail). Perhaps because of these procedural complexities, the most recent legislation removing regulations—the Deregulation Act 2015—went through the normal parliamentary process.

Box 3.10 Legal system explained

Legislative and Regulatory Reform Act 2006: scope of the Act

The Act gives ministers power to make any provision by an order, called a legislative reform order, that would remove or reduce any burden, or remove or reduce the overall burdens, to which any person is subject as a direct or indirect result of any legislation. Burdens are defined as: a financial cost; an administrative inconvenience; an obstacle to efficiency, productivity, or profitability; or a sanction, criminal or otherwise, which affects the carrying on of any lawful activity. Each of these concepts is defined further in the legislation. Ministers can only use their power to reform an area where there is already a legislative framework. It could be used to replace one statutory regime with another where this removes or reduces burdens. But it cannot be used to introduce an entirely new regulatory regime. So, for example, it would not be possible to create an entirely new legislative framework relating to a new area of consumer protection, employment rights, or environmental protection simply because there are considered to be good policy reasons for doing so.

Box 3.10 Continued

Ministers are also given power to amend the powers of regulators so that their functions comply more closely with defined Principles of Good Regulation. These are that regulatory activities should be carried out in a way that is transparent, accountable, proportionate, and consistent, and should be targeted only at cases in which action is needed.

Save where a minister wants simply to restate existing law, he or she must meet six conditions:

(1) There are no non-legislative solutions that will satisfactorily remedy the difficulty that the order is intended to address.
(2) The effect of the provision made by the order is proportionate to its policy objective.
(3) The provision made by the order, taken as a whole, strikes a fair balance between the public interest and the interests of the persons adversely affected by the order.
(4) The provision made by the order does not remove any necessary protection.
(5) The provision made by the order will not prevent any person from continuing to exercise any right or freedom that he or she might reasonably expect to continue to exercise.
(6) The provision made by the order is not constitutionally significant.

The Act sets out the procedures ministers must follow. First, the minister must consult on his proposals. He must then lay a draft order and an explanatory document before Parliament. The order must be made by statutory instrument in accordance with the negative resolution procedure, or the affirmative resolution procedure (*see 3.3.2*), or the super-affirmative resolution procedure. The minister's recommended procedure applies unless either House of Parliament requires a higher level of procedure.

Super-affirmative procedure

The super-affirmative procedure affords greater parliamentary scrutiny than the ordinary affirmative resolution orders procedure. First, the minister must lay a proposed legislative reform order before Parliament in draft, together with a full explanatory document. Following a 60-day period of parliamentary consideration, during which time the proposal is referred automatically and simultaneously to two parliamentary committees, the committees make their first reports to their respective Houses. If the reports are favourable, the next stage is for the minister formally to lay a draft order in each House, along with an explanation of any changes made to the original draft proposal. If the minister accepts any changes proposed to the draft order by the committees or others between this stage and the final vote on the order, he must formally withdraw the draft order he has laid and replace it with another which incorporates the changes. The ability to make changes (minor or otherwise) to the draft order is a key feature of the order-making power, which is not available to statutory instruments dealt with in the usual way.

Box 3.10 Continued

> The final procedural stages for parliamentary scrutiny of draft regulatory reform orders are set out in standing orders. The Commons committee produces a report on the draft order within 15 days. The Lords committee has no set time period but usually reports within the same time period. Each House then considers the relevant committee report on the draft order (this is the main feature that makes this form of parliamentary consideration 'super-affirmative').

3.3.5 Post-legislative scrutiny

This idea, which had been floating around academic circles for many years, is fairly simple. After a period following the enactment of a new Act of Parliament, is it not sensible to ask: is the Act working as it was intended to do?

The House of Lords Constitution Committee considered it in 2004. Things moved forward significantly when the then Labour administration asked the Law Commission to think how it could be turned into a practical reality. Its report was published in 2006; the then government's response was published in 2008. The Law Commission's report and the government's response can be accessed at: https://www.lawcom.gov.uk/project/post-legislative-scrutiny/.

Since then there has been a programme of post-legislative scrutinies.[3] The key features of the programme are:

- not all Acts of Parliament are subject to scrutiny;
- where there is scrutiny, the review is undertaken by the relevant departmental select committee—it is a process driven by backbench MPs, taking evidence and reaching conclusions as they do in other inquiries they undertake;
- the scrutiny process is started by the preparation within the government department concerned of a memorandum on the Act of Parliament under review which is presented to the select committee, who then invite wider observations and inputs from people and bodies outside government on the Act's operation.

It is not thought that the impact of such scrutinies has been very dramatic. Certainly no legislation has been repealed as a result of scrutiny.

3.3.6 The use of parliamentary time: a comment

Given the domination of the parliamentary timetable by the government machine, it is sometimes asked whether the amount of time spent debating proposals in relation

---

[3] For an example of a post-legislative scrutiny exercise, see the Justice Select Committee's inquiry into the operation of the Freedom of Information Act. The Ministry of Justice's memorandum which formed the basis for the inquiry, the evidence taken by the committee, and its final report can all be found at www.parliament.uk/business/committees/committees-a-z/commons-select/justice-committee/inquiries/parliament-2010/foi//.

to which the outcome is totally or largely predictable is worthwhile. Elected MPs do not, in general, have any detailed control over the content of Acts of Parliament; indeed, there is no guarantee that all clauses in bills are subject to considered debate. The vast bulk of legislation—secondary legislation—reaches the statute book with no consideration by MPs at all.

Nevertheless, it should be remembered that much of the detail of the parliamentary process was developed in an age when the party machine and the discipline over the parliamentary party provided by the whips were not as they are today. The ability of a government with an overall majority to dominate the legislative process is perhaps the best reason for retaining the detailed process that currently exists. This arises from the very political theories, noted earlier, that underpin the British Constitution and its system of government. Although ministers may be able to achieve their desired goals in the end, the process ensures that they will have been subject to challenge by elected MPs. Without these procedures it would be far harder for ministers seeking to defend a particular measure to claim legitimacy for their legislative acts. Where the government lacks an overall majority, as in the current (2017) Parliament, legislative outcomes may be less certain.

3.4 Judges and the courts

It should be stressed at the outset that only judges in the higher courts—the Supreme Court, the Court of Appeal, and the High Court—have authority to make law (*see further Chapter 8*). There are three principal ways in which English judges develop English law:

- *Development of the common law.* England is a 'common law' country. This means that many of the principal doctrines of law have been established, not by Parliament, but through cases determined in the higher courts. Many examples of judicial law-making can be given:
  - the fundamental law of contract, on which much economic activity is based;
  - the law of negligence, which relates (among other matters) to dealing with the aftermath of accidents and other forms of injury; and
  - the development of the principles of *judicial review*, which is the basis on which judicial control of the administrative arm of government is achieved.
- *Statutory interpretation.* Courts play a crucial role in the interpretation of the statutes that Parliament has enacted.
- *Procedural law.* Courts also make important contributions to the development of procedures that the courts must follow.

3.4.1 Development of the common law

It seems odd today, but judicial power to make law was, for many years, not acknowledged. Judges said their power was merely to 'discover' basic principles of the common law. No one seriously believes this now; judges do make law. There is, however, often unease about the theoretical basis for this power. Certainly it cannot derive from any theory of representative democracy; judges are not elected. Rather, the power of the judiciary depends on the doctrine of the *separation of powers*, that to prevent dictatorial powers from being asserted by any one branch of government there must be checks and balances in the constitution. Judges have the primary task of ensuring adherence by ministers and other agents of the state to the principles of the rule of law. This cannot be achieved without an independent judiciary (*see further Box 3.11*).

Box 3.11 Legal system explained

Independence of the judiciary

The key claim made for the judges, indeed for adjudicators of all kinds (*see Chapter 9*), is that they must not only be, but also be seen to be, independent. Judicial independence relates centrally to the constitutional function of judges in interpreting and applying law outside the constraints of internal government departmental policies. Judges and adjudicators not perceived as independent are fatally compromised in the eyes of the public, particularly by those whose disputes are being resolved by them. One of the strong claims for adjudicators in the English legal system is that, with rare exceptions, they both appear to be independent and do in fact act independently. This is not to say that they may not bring their own views of the world into play when reaching decisions or determining facts. But claims of corruption of those who hold judicial office—which would undermine judicial independence—are not heard in England.

The Constitutional Reform Act 2005 made judicial independence, for the first time, subject to statutory protection. Section 3 states, in part:

(1) The Lord Chancellor, other ministers of the Crown, and all with responsibility for matters relating to the judiciary or otherwise to the administration of justice must uphold the continued independence of the judiciary ...

(2) The following particular duties are imposed for the purpose of upholding that independence.

(3) The Lord Chancellor and other ministers of the Crown must not seek to influence particular judicial decisions through any special access to the judiciary.

(4) The Lord Chancellor must have regard to—

(a) the need to defend that independence;

(b) the need for the judiciary to have the support necessary to enable them to exercise their functions;

(c) the need for the public interest in regard to matters relating to the judiciary or otherwise to the administration of justice to be properly represented in decisions affecting those matters.

Occasionally you hear government ministers criticizing the senior judiciary. There have also been cases where the Press have been not simply critical but abusive of the

---

Box 3.11 Continued

judiciary. In two important lectures delivered by the recently retired Lord Chief Justice, Sir John Thomas, he noted the importance of an independent judiciary in supporting the rule of law, and argued that abuse of the judiciary could undermine its constitutional standing. On such occasions, he made it clear that the Lord Chancellor should remember his/her obligations under section 3 of the Constitutional Reform Act, 2005.[4]

The law-making powers of the judiciary are supported by two other fundamental principles: the hierarchical structure of the courts, and the doctrine of precedent.

3.4.1.1 The hierarchical structure of the courts

The idea of courts being arranged within a hierarchical framework is quite straight-forward. The courts are organized on the basis of seniority (*see Diagram 3.2*); the higher the level of seniority, the greater the authority of the court. Thus the decisions of the Supreme Court (formerly the House of Lords) are the most authoritative; those of the Court of Appeal are next; those of the High Court are third. Decisions of courts at lower levels are not regarded as precedents, though very occasionally the judgment of a county court judge on a novel point of law may get reported (*see Box 3.12* on the importance of law reporting).

Box 3.12 Legal system explained

Law reporting

The ability of the courts to develop principles of common law or to give authoritative interpretations of statutory principles relies on the publication of law reports, which contain reasoned judgments prepared by judges in particular cases, and from which general principles of law are then drawn.

Decisions as to which cases get reported are not, in general, taken by members of the judiciary themselves, but by editorial teams responsible for the publication of law reports. Many sets of law reports are now published. The publication of law reports is

---

[4] See https://www.judiciary.gov.uk/announcements/lionel-cohen-lecture-by-the-lord-chief-justice-the-judiciary-within-the-state-governance-and-cohesion-of-the-judiciary/; and https://www.judiciary.gov.uk/announcements/michael-ryle-memorial-lecture-by-the-lord-chief-justice-the-judiciary-within-the-state-the-relationship-between-the-branches-of-the-state/.

Diagram 3.2 An outline of the court structure in England and Wales

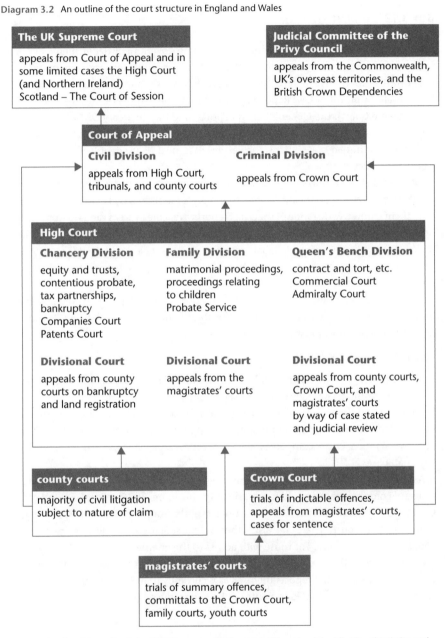

The UK Supreme Court

appeals from Court of Appeal and in some limited cases the High Court (and Northern Ireland) Scotland – The Court of Session

Judicial Committee of the Privy Council

appeals from the Commonwealth, UK's overseas territories, and the British Crown Dependencies

Court of Appeal

Civil Division

appeals from High Court, tribunals, and county courts

Criminal Division

appeals from Crown Court

High Court

Chancery Division

equity and trusts, contentious probate, tax partnerships, bankruptcy Companies Court Patents Court

Family Division

matrimonial proceedings, proceedings relating to children Probate Service

Queen's Bench Division

contract and tort, etc. Commercial Court Admiralty Court

Divisional Court

appeals from county courts on bankruptcy and land registration

Divisional Court

appeals from the magistrates' courts

Divisional Court

appeals from county courts, Crown Court, and magistrates' courts by way of case stated and judicial review

county courts

majority of civil litigation subject to nature of claim

Crown Court

trials of indictable offences, appeals from magistrates' courts, cases for sentence

magistrates' courts

trials of summary offences, committals to the Crown Court, family courts, youth courts

Source: Judicial and Court Statistics 2010 (see www.justice.gov.uk/downloads/publications/statistics-and-data/courts-and-sentencing/judicial-court-stats.pdf). This diagram is, of necessity, much simplified and should not be taken as a comprehensive statement on the jurisdiction of any specific court. It also omits any reference to the Court of Justice of the European Union and the European Court of Human Rights.

Box 3.12 Continued

not seen as a function of government (though some government departments do, in fact, publish the text of decisions in specialist areas, such as taxation and immigration).

The most authoritative of the generalist sets of law reports are those published by the Incorporated Council of Law Reporting, which publishes: Appeal Cases (decisions of the Supreme Court), the Queen's Bench Reports, and the Chancery Division Reports. The Council also publishes the *Weekly Law Reports*. There is a requirement that if a case is reported in these reports, that is the version that must be used, at least in the High Court and Court of Appeal.

Other sets of law reports are published by commercial publishers. The most widely available generalist set is the *All England Law Reports*, published by LexisNexis. In addition, there is now a wide range of specialist reports available in areas ranging from local government to housing, from education to family law, from criminal appeals to judicial review. Many sub-specialisms in legal practice now have their own sets of law reports. Law reports are also reported in some broadsheet newspapers; the most widely used are those reported in *The Times*.

Maintaining a complete library of all sets of reports is very expensive, only possible for the best-endowed university libraries, the libraries of the Law Society and the Inns of Court, and the most prosperous law firms.

Legal electronic databases

In addition to reports in paper format, more and more law reports are now published in electronic format. For many years, LexisNexis provided full-text versions of decisions from a range of the most senior courts. Initially, their use was limited by the refusal of judges to take into account judgments that appeared only in the Lexis format. This has now changed. Other companies, such as Westlaw and Justcite, also offer extensive legal databases.

A great deal of source legal material is also available free online. The Supreme Court/House of Lords has placed all judgments since 14 November 1996 online; Her Majesty's Courts and Tribunals Service website carries reports from the Court of Appeal and Administrative Court. There are also other online sources available (*see the Online Resources, list of websites*). For those with access to the internet, the costs of obtaining the report of a particular case are limited to the costs of going online and printing the text. The provision of the reports themselves is currently free. To facilitate use of these sources, 'neutral citation' of judgments has been introduced (*see Box 3.13*).

Box 3.13 Legal system explained

Neutral citation of judgments

Since 11 January 2001 every judgment of the Court of Appeal and of the Administrative Court, and since 14 January 2002 every judgment of the High Court, has been prepared and issued as approved with single spacing, paragraph numbering (in the margins),

Box 3.13 Continued

and no page numbers. In courts with more than one judge, the paragraph numbering continues sequentially through each judgment and does not start again at the beginning of each judgment. A unique reference number is given to each judgment.

Each Court of Appeal judgment starts with the year, followed by EW (for England and Wales), then CA (for Court of Appeal), followed by Civ (for Civil) or Crim (for Criminal), and finally the sequential number. For example: *Smith v Jones* [2001] EWCA Civ 10.

In the High Court, abbreviated as HC, the number comes before the divisional abbreviation and, unlike Court of Appeal judgments, the latter is bracketed: (Ch(ancery)), (Pat(ent)), (Q(ueens) B(ench)), (Admin(istrative)), (Comm(ercial)), (Admlty (Admiralty)), (TCC (Technology and Construction Court)), or (Fam(ily)) as appropriate. For example, [2002] EWHC 123 (Fam) or [2002] EWHC 124 (QB) or [2002] EWHC 125 (Ch).

Paragraph numbers are referred to in square brackets. Thus paragraph 59 in *Green v White* [2002] EWHC 124 (QB) would be cited: *Green v White* [2002] EWHC 124 at [59]; paragraphs 30–35 in *Smith v Jones* would be *Smith v Jones* [2001] EWCA Civ 10 at ––. Page numbers are not given.

This 'neutral citation' is the official number attributed to the judgment and must always be used at least once when the judgment is cited in a later judgment. It is designed to facilitate the use of websites so that any confusion caused by differences in pagination that occur when information is downloaded to different computers with different printers is avoided.

There have been occasions on which this hierarchical structure has been challenged, most notably by the late Lord Denning when, as Master of the Rolls, he was the senior judge in the Court of Appeal. He argued that, since most appeals ended in his court and did not proceed to the House of Lords/Supreme Court, his court should have similar law-making power to the top court. His arguments did not prevail, though they provoke a broader question: do we need all the levels of court, in particular all the levels of appeal, that currently exist?

3.4.1.2 The doctrine of precedent

This is also a simple idea, though not always easy to apply in practice. The essence of precedent is that a principle of law, established in one case, must be applied in a similar situation in a later case. Such law continues to be applied until either another court decides that the case was incorrectly decided, or for some other reason cannot be allowed to stand; or until a court higher in the hierarchy overturns the decision; or until Parliament decides to change the law by passing a new Act of Parliament that overrules or alters the rule laid down by the court.

There have long been arguments for and against the use of precedent. Against, it is argued that precedent introduces unnecessary rigidity into the law, thereby preventing legal doctrine from developing as society develops. In favour, the use of precedent is said to bring certainty to the law by enabling people to know how issues in the future will be resolved. The principle of law in one case that forms the precedent is known by the Latin phrase *ratio decidendi*. Any part of a judgment that does not form part of the *ratio* is not part of the precedent, and thus not relevant in later cases. These are referred to as *obiter dicta*.

There are many reasons why these apparently straightforward ideas can be exceptionally hard to apply in practice:

(1) The facts on which the *ratio* of one case is based never replicate themselves precisely in a later case. Thus lawyers wishing to argue that a particular precedent does not apply to the later case seek to *distinguish* the two fact situations, thereby, they hope, rendering the earlier decision irrelevant.

(2) Given the large number of reported decisions, there may be situations where a decision in one case was reached in ignorance of other relevant decisions. The argument is then made that the precedent in question was made incorrectly or, again to use the Latin, *per incuriam*.

(3) Because of the large numbers of cases that are now reported, there may be two reported decisions that are simply inconsistent with each other, so that straightforward application of a particular decision to a new situation is not possible.

(4) Since 1966, the House of Lords/Supreme Court has asserted the authority, in very exceptional circumstances, to change its mind and alter a precedent. It may, therefore, on occasion and notwithstanding the existence of clear precedents, decide that earlier cases were wrongly decided and that the law should now be changed.

There are also more technical reasons why the doctrine of precedent is not always simple to apply in practice. It can be very hard to decide what the precedent is. When, in the famous case of *Donoghue v Stevenson* [1932] AC 562, the House of Lords found that a manufacturer of ginger-beer was negligent after it allowed a decomposed snail to enter a ginger-beer bottle, was this a case about not allowing snails to get into ginger-beer bottles? Or was it about not allowing foreign bodies in general to get into manufacturing processes? Or was it about the duty of care that any person—including a professional person giving advice to a client—should demonstrate towards others? In short, what was the 'level of generality' at which the particular instance of snails in ginger-beer bottles was to be treated in future cases?

Even if the principle of law that can be derived from the cases is clear—such as the principle of negligence, that one person owes a 'duty of care' to his or her 'neighbour'—who will be categorized for these purposes as a neighbour? And what will be the standard of behaviour that will result in a conclusion that the 'duty of care' has been broken? If teachers take a party of teenage pupils to the seaside, and one of the pupils is washed out to sea by a freak wave, were the teachers in breach of a duty of care in those circumstances to the pupil who drowned? Or did the fault lie with the pupil who ignored advice and went clambering onto the rocks from which he was swept?

Much of the litigation that arises out of the principles of the law of negligence is not seeking to redefine the principles of the law, but is rather exploring the extent to which those principles should apply in new situations of risk. This is not the place for a detailed analysis of the law of negligence. The point to be stressed here is that, even though at one level the law may be quite clear, the situations to which the law may be applied in future can be far from clear. And the development of the law is in the hands of the senior courts, not legislators.

3.4.2 Statutory interpretation

Statutory interpretation is another way in which courts with authority within the hierarchical structure develop the law. The work of the courts interpreting statutes may not be as dramatic as developing principles of common law, as judges clearly have to work within the texts that have been prescribed by Parliament through the legislative process. Nevertheless, the interpretative process can lead to the clarification of words in statutes, and thus in the implementation of those statutory rules (*see Box 3.14* for an example).

Box 3.14 System in action

Case study: statutory interpretation: the case of Mr Fitzpatrick

Until recently amended, housing law provided that a tenant can pass his or her right to occupy premises on death to a 'member of his family'. Over many years, the question arose: who is a member of the family? In the 1940s, the courts held that the phrase was limited to blood relatives; thus the former mistress of a deceased tenant could not take over the tenancy, despite having lived together with her partner for many years. Later, in the 1960s, the courts held that, with changes in the nature of relationships and society's attitudes, the mistress of a deceased male tenant could in such a circumstance be regarded as a member of the family and thus take over the tenancy.

More recently still, in 1999, the House of Lords decided that the long-standing homosexual partner of a deceased tenant could similarly take over the tenancy. The judges found that, in terms of love and affection and thus the attributes of family, a distinction could no longer sensibly be drawn between a couple of the same sex living together and a couple of different sexes. Reference was made to the provisions of the European Convention on Human Rights protecting family and family life. (See *Fitzpatrick v Sterling Housing Association* [1999] 3 WLR 1113, HL.)

This case illustrates that, even without changing the words, there was scope for developing statute law by interpretation to reflect changes in social practices and attitudes.

The power of the court to interpret statutes increased when the Human Rights Act 1998 came into force. British courts not only interpret legislative provisions, but also test the substance of legislative provisions against the standards laid down in the Human Rights Act 1998, which derive from the Articles of the European Convention on Human Rights (*see 3.5.1.1*). By giving the courts power to declare a statute or provision within a statute to be incompatible with the Convention—effectively requiring ministers to change the law—the Act conferred on the courts a significant new power to develop English law.

One question that may be asked is: why—if Parliament has passed legislation—is there any need for the courts to intervene at all? There are two basic reasons why this needs to happen: the unpredictability of fact situations, and the ambiguity of language.

3.4.2.1 The unpredictability of fact situations

However detailed statutory provisions may be, they can only set down rules at a certain level of generality. There will always be those whose particular circumstances are not captured *precisely* by the legislative provisions. In such cases the facts need to be determined by the courts—in itself not always a straightforward task—and, once this has been done, a judgment reached as to whether or not the relevant legislative provision applies. Particularly where legislative provisions seek to impose some burden or penalty on the citizen, there is a general judicial policy that this should not happen unless those provisions quite clearly 'bite' on the individual circumstances concerned. To give an example: the 'tax avoidance industry' engages in the detailed analysis of tax legislation to see whether arrangements can be made to enable those who might otherwise have to pay tax quite legitimately to avoid paying it.[5]

Many apparently pedantic points taken in some criminal trials are, similarly, the result of the principle that a person should not be convicted of a crime unless the facts found by the court are clearly caught by the relevant statutory provisions.

3.4.2.2 The ambiguity of language

The other justification for the role of the courts is that the meaning of language is not itself precise. There may be ambiguities arising from the way particular rules have been drafted. There may be differences in the meaning of words chosen. Some statutory provisions are deliberately drafted using words such as 'reasonable' or 'fair' that do not have a precise meaning and that therefore give scope to officials and others for the exercise of discretion or judgment. There may be changes in the meaning of a word (*see Box 3.14*) resulting from broader developments in society.

There is, in the literature on statutory interpretation, a set of principles—rather inaccurately described as 'rules'—designed to be of assistance. These include:

- the literal rule;
- the golden rule;
- the mischief rule; and
- the 'unified common approach'.

---

[5] The distinction between tax avoidance, which if successful is lawful, and tax evasion, which is clearly unlawful, should be noted. In recent years, governments have become increasingly adept in their attempts to thwart tax evaders. Tax incentives—schemes that attract tax advantages and are part of the government's fiscal policy, for example tax relief on pension premiums—are quite different.

The *literal rule* is what it implies. The words of a statute should be given their literal meaning. However, this does not solve the problem of linguistic ambiguity—words may have more than one literal meaning.

The *golden rule* suggests that the courts should use the literal rule unless this would lead to manifest absurdity.

The *mischief rule* asks the judge to consider what was the legislative purpose of the Act—what was the 'mischief' the Act was trying to deal with. Any question of interpretation should be resolved in such a way as not to thwart that purpose. The problem with this view is: does it not undermine the independence of the judiciary? If the mischief rule is rigidly adhered to, does this not result in the judges losing their independence and doing the government's job for it? On the other hand, if legislative intention is wilfully ignored by the judges, how does that square with the constitutional principle that the primary law-making authority should rest with the democratically elected Parliament, not the unelected judiciary?

It will be quickly appreciated that these principles are not consistent with each other; they offer great scope for reaching different conclusions. The reality is that different judges favour different approaches; indeed individual judges are themselves not consistent.

The *unified common approach* is the label now used to suggest that judges should adopt a broader, less specific approach. It implies that judges should start by considering the literal meaning of the words; but if they are really not clear or would lead to absurd results then the judge should consider what the purpose of the Act was and interpret the Act so as to advance that purpose.

The inference should not be drawn from this discussion that the bases on which the judiciary interprets legislation are so varied that there is no principle at all. Reading reported judgments in decided cases reveals that judges in the higher courts go to great lengths to try to ensure that their decisions are founded in rationality and principle. But that there are different approaches cannot be denied, and the inevitable consequence is that there is some inconsistency of outcome. The ability of different judges to arrive at different decisions in individual cases is seen most clearly in cases that go to appeal, when judges are quite frequently divided in their views.

3.4.3 Procedural law

A third way in which judges make law is by the development of new procedures. A number of examples may be briefly mentioned.

- The day-to-day practice of litigation is regulated by rules of procedure that are drafted by the judiciary—in Rules Committees—acting under legislative authority. Many rules of court are supplemented by practice directions, also made by the judiciary (*see Chapters 6, 7, and 8*).

- Rules of evidence—what evidence is or is not admissible in a court of law—have to an important degree been developed by the judiciary, though supplemented by very important statutory provisions, for example the Police and Criminal

Evidence Act 1984, the Civil Evidence Act 1991, or the Criminal Justice Act 2003 (*see Chapter 5*).

• A number of powers of the court are asserted on the basis of what it claims as its 'inherent jurisdiction'—the High Court's powers of wardship over children may be given as an example (*see Chapter 7*).

• The most important judicial development of the last 50 years has been the shaping of the rules and practice relating to judicial review, which goes to the heart of the powers of the judiciary to render government departments and other public bodies legally accountable for their actions (*see Chapter 6*).

3.5 European law-making institutions and their impact on the UK

So far, the discussion has considered the law-making process in the United Kingdom as though it was a completely domestic process. But no student of the modern English legal system can ignore the impact of international law in general, and European law in particular, on the United Kingdom. European law-making institutions and their practices and procedures are poorly understood. The following pages offer a brief introduction to the law-making functions carried out in Europe, the role of the courts in Europe, and their overall impact on the United Kingdom.

Before proceeding, you must always remember that, when talking about European law-making, two completely separate institutions are involved which are frequently confused: the Council of Europe and the European Union. While the UK government is in the process of exiting the European Union, this in no way affects the relationship between the UK and the Council of Europe.

3.5.1 The Council of Europe

The Council of Europe was established in 1949. Its primary aim was to prevent a repeat of the human rights outrages of the Second World War period. More recently it has engaged in assisting countries of the former Eastern Bloc to develop institutional arrangements to support their moves towards democracy. The Council has 47 member countries and is based in Strasbourg.

3.5.1.1 European Convention on Human Rights

The Council of Europe's most significant achievement, insofar as its impact on English law is concerned, was the creation of the European Convention on Human Rights. This document, drafted with considerable input from British lawyers, is a charter of fundamental rights and freedoms agreed by all the member states of the Council of Europe. In common with all international treaties, the Convention could not come into effect until it had been ratified by a specified number of governments. This happened in 1953. The Convention has been amended a number of times since then. The current version, amended by Protocol 14, came into effect in June 2010 (*see Box 2.1*). Two more protocols, 15 and 16, have been made by the Council, but they are not yet in force as they have not been ratified by a sufficient number of member states.

Ensuring adherence by member states to the standards set out in the Convention is the responsibility of the European Court of Human Rights, which has power to decide cases raising alleged breaches of the European Convention by member states of the Council of Europe.

Normally, treaties seek to regulate relationships between nation states. They may provide that one country may take action against another where there is an alleged breach of an international treaty obligation. The European Convention on Human Rights is unusual. In it, provision is made for *individuals* to take proceedings to the European Court of Human Rights where it is alleged that a government is in breach of its obligations under the treaty. In the case of the United Kingdom, the right of individuals to take proceedings against the British government for alleged breaches of the Convention was accepted by the British government in 1966.

3.5.1.2 The impact of the Council of Europe

The impact of the Council of Europe on the law-making process in the United Kingdom has been indirect. The European Convention on Human Rights sets out a list of rights—principles against which the actions of governments may be tested (*see Box 2.1*). Where cases are taken before the European Court of Human Rights in Strasbourg that result in a decision that a rule of British law or some practice of the British government is contrary to the provisions of the Convention, this leads to a requirement that the British government change the law to bring it into line with the Convention, as interpreted by the Court. In over 50 years, there have only been around 30 decisions of the Court adverse to the British government, though many more cases have been taken to but rejected by the Court (for an example, *see Box 3.15*).

Box 3.15 System in action

Case study: prisoners' voting rights[6]

The UK government believes that all prisoners should be denied the right to vote while they are in jail. However, in *Hirst v United Kingdom (No 2)* ((2006) 42 EHRR 41) the European Court of Human Rights (ECtHR) found that this blanket ban was incompatible with the European Convention on Human Rights. (A number of other cases had also reached this conclusion.)

Given the clear ruling of the ECtHR, in 2012 the UK government—after considerable delay and with major misgivings—published a draft Voting Eligibility (Prisoners) Bill. This bill was subject to pre-legislative scrutiny by a Joint Committee of the House of

---

[6] Up-to-date information can be found in my blog at www.martinpartington.com.

Box 3.15 Continued

Commons and the House of Lords. In December 2013, it published a thoughtful report on the issue. It stated that:

'It is not possible to reconcile the principle of the rule of law with remaining within the Convention while declining to implement the judgment of the Court.'

The Committee identified a number of principles which it argued should be taken into account, including:

- 'In a democracy the vote is a right, not a privilege: it should not be removed without good reason ...'
- 'There is a legitimate expectation that those convicted of the most heinous crimes should, as part of their punishment, be stripped of the power embodied in the right to vote ...'
- 'There are no convincing penal-policy arguments in favour of disenfranchisement; but a case has been made that enfranchisement might assist prisoner rehabilitation by providing an incentive to re-engage with society.'

The Committee concluded that 'the Government [should] introduce a Bill at the start of the 2014–15 session, which should provide that all prisoners serving sentences of 12 months or less should be entitled to vote in all UK parliamentary, local and European elections'. No bill was published.

Since then, more cases have been taken to the European Court of Human Rights. Thus, in *Firth and others v United Kingdom* [2014] ECHR 874, a Chamber of the Court held that—failing a legislative response to its earlier rulings—the United Kingdom remained in breach of the European Convention on Human Rights. However, the Chamber refused to award any damages to the applicants, on the grounds that this ruling was enough.

The decision also included a dissenting judgment from Judge Nicolaou, who did not think that there had been a breach of the European Convention. In another dissenting judgment, Judge Wojtyczek indicated his view that the line of decisions developed by the European Court might not be correct; in his view the whole issue should have been revisited by the Court.

There undoubtedly remains in the UK a view that prisoners should not have the vote. However, there is also no doubt that, pending any revision of the ECtHR's approach, the present position of the UK government is at odds with the European Convention as interpreted by the ECtHR. The final outcome of this impasse is still unclear.

3.5.1.3 Human Rights Act 1998

Following enactment of the Human Rights Act 1998, most of the articles of the European Convention on Human Rights became directly enforceable in the English courts. It is arguable that the Human Rights Act 1998 did not really change UK law but simply made it easier to use because cases can now be brought in the United Kingdom without the need to go to Strasbourg.

The Human Rights Act 1998 has had two principal effects on the law-making process in the United Kingdom.

First, in presenting bills to Parliament, ministers must declare that in their opinion proposed legislation complies with Convention provisions. Policy-makers within government have become conscious of the need to ensure that policies are Convention-compliant. New legislation is scrutinized for compliance by the Parliamentary Joint Committee on Human Rights. To that extent the Act has had significant impact.

Secondly, under section 4 of the Human Rights Act 1998, British courts have power to declare a provision of UK law to be incompatible with the provisions of the Convention. This formula was adopted to preserve the notion of the sovereignty of Parliament. This is in effect a direction to the government of the day that a particular statutory provision must be amended in order to comply with the provisions of the European Convention on Human Rights. Although not declaring an Act of Parliament, or a provision in an Act, unlawful, any such judicial ruling puts pressure on ministers to introduce changes so that the incompatibility is removed. In this sense, the legislative freedom of ministers is reduced.

Legal arguments based on the Human Rights Act 1998 have been advanced in a significant number of cases in the upper courts (High Court, Court of Appeal, and Supreme Court). However, the extent to which these arguments have been upheld in the courts has so far been relatively limited. A major exception to this generalization has been in the area of counter-terrorism, where getting the right balance between protecting personal freedom and introducing measures to try to ensure security from terrorist attack is exceptionally difficult.

For example, following the bombing of the Twin Towers in New York City in September 2001, the Labour government of Tony Blair sought to extend significantly, to 90 days, the length of time terror suspects could be detained without a criminal charge being brought against them. The House of Lords ruled in *A and Others v Secretary of State for the Home Department* [2004] UKHL 56 that this was contrary to the provisions of the European Convention on Human Rights. A further attempt to introduce a similar provision was defeated in the House of Commons in 2006. The Coalition government decided, in the Protection of Freedoms Act 2012, that the normal period of detention without charge of those suspected of terrorism should be 14 days.

One feature of the Human Rights Act 1998 is that it provides that, in interpreting its provisions, English judges must take account of the jurisprudence developed by the European Court of Human Rights in Strasbourg. One possibly unexpected consequence is that judges in the court in Strasbourg now take more notice of what British judges say on human rights issues and their interpretation of the Convention than they did before the Human Rights Act was enacted.

3.5.1.4 The authority of the Council of Europe

The authority of the Council of Europe to make rules of law which have an effect in the United Kingdom stems from the international treaty, which set out the constitution of the Council and the powers of the European Court of Human Rights. These documents came into effect in the UK following exercise of its prerogative power to sign up to international treaties. Members of the Council are appointed by governments who have signed up to be members of the Council. There are no public elections for membership of the Council of Europe.

In this respect, the Council and the Court are like other international bodies to which the UK has signed up.

3.5.1.5 The European Court of Human Rights

The European Court on Human Rights, also based in Strasbourg, is the ultimate arbiter of whether there has or has not been a breach of the European Convention on Human Rights. In the UK, and since the passing of the Human Rights Act 1998, it is clear that any allegation of breach of the European Convention on Human Rights must now be determined first in the English courts. Nevertheless, there remains a residual right for parties to go to the European Court of Human Rights.

Paradoxically, some now claim that the Human Rights Act 1998 has to an extent undermined the legitimacy and authority of the European Court of Human Rights. They argue that if issues under the European Convention on Human Rights can be argued in the UK Supreme Court, there should be no need for a further tier to appeal to the European Court. On the other side, there are still those who strongly defend the right of the European Court to be the ultimate authority in the interpretation of the European Convention, not least because this ensures that consistent standards are applied throughout all the member states of the Council of Europe.

The Council of Europe itself has recognized that there is a need to reform the relationship between the European Court of Human Rights and member states, though this is more for the practical reason that the Court has a huge backlog of cases which has led to quite unacceptable delays. In 2012, an important conference was held in Brighton, which set out the framework for a programme of reform to the Court (*see Box 3.16*).

Box 3.16 Reform in progress

Reforming the European Court of Human Rights: the Brighton Declaration

The question of the relationship between the English legal system, in particular the UK Supreme Court, and the European Court of Human Rights has generated a lot of political controversy—much of it deriving from the decision in the case involving the terror suspect Abu Qatada. The British government wanted to deport him to Jordan for trial. The European Court feared that evidence obtained by torture could be used against him. This would be contrary to the European Convention on Human Rights. The European Court decided that he could not be deported until this question had been resolved. The political fallout from this very controversial case has been significant, with many people demanding that the United Kingdom no longer acknowledge the jurisdiction of the European Court.

Box 3.16 Continued

In April 2012—during the UK Presidency of the Council of Europe—a conference was held in Brighton to consider proposals for the reform of the Court, designed to rebalance the relationship between Strasbourg and national supreme courts.

In outline, the Brighton Declaration made proposals for:

- amending the Convention to include the principles of subsidiarity and the margin of appreciation; this should give more power to domestic courts to decide matters without intervention from Strasbourg;
- amending the Convention to tighten the admissibility criteria, so that trivial cases can be thrown out and the focus of the Court can be on serious abuses;
- reducing the time limit for making claims from six months to four;
- improving the selection process for judges;
- setting out a roadmap for further reform.

The full text of the Brighton Declaration is at wcd.coe.int/ViewDoc.jsp?id= 1934031.

Some progress in achieving these goals has been made. (See my blog, October 2017.) Nevertheless, despite a number of changes, the principal problem facing the Court—delay—seems to be as intractable as ever. In my view, the final implementation of any effective reform proposals will take a considerable time to complete.

There has been controversy in the United Kingdom about the impact of the Human Rights Act. In 2011, the then Coalition government proposed that the Human Rights Act might be repealed and replaced by a new British Bill of Rights. An Independent Commission on a UK Bill of Rights was asked to look into the matter. It reported at the end of 2012. Its conclusions were not clear-cut.

Since then, the issue has slipped down the political agenda and will certainly not be revived before the Brexit negotiations are complete.

3.5.2 The European Union

The European Economic Community was established in 1957 by the Treaty of Rome. It became the European Community (EC) in 1967. The United Kingdom joined the Community in 1973, and confirmed that decision following a UK-wide referendum in 1975. It has now started the process of leaving the Union, following the referendum on the issue held in 2016. Despite the fact that once the Brexit process is complete, law made by the EU institutions will no longer directly impact on the UK, I think that anyone studying law should have at least some understanding of how the EU works. The following paragraphs offer a short introduction to the EU and its institutions.

3.5.2.1 The development of the EU

The Treaty of Rome gave the Community a number of tasks including: establishing a common market and progressively approximating the economic policies of the

Member States. Originally there were only six members of the Community. In 1986, the Single European Act made further provision for the establishment of the common market, now referred to as the 'internal market'. This is defined as an area without internal frontiers, in which the free movement of goods, persons, services, and capital is ensured. The Single Market Act also brought a number of new policy areas into the Community's competence, including, for example, a specific environmental competence.

The Maastricht Treaty (1993) established the European Union, which had a three-pillar structure: the European Community was the first pillar; the common foreign and security policy the second pillar; and justice and home affairs (covering immigration and asylum, civil judicial cooperation, and police and judicial cooperation in criminal matters) the third pillar. Further changes were made by the Treaty of Amsterdam (1997) and the Treaty of Nice (2001), including to the competences of the Union.

The European Union entered a period of expansion which prompted calls for a new treaty. After long discussion, and a failed attempt to establish a European-wide constitution for the European Union, the Lisbon Treaty was signed in 2007. This treaty renamed and amended the original treaties, collapsed the three-pillar system into a single European Union, and incorporated the Charter of Fundamental Rights into the EU Treaties. There are currently 28 countries in the EU, with more beginning the process of accession to the Union. The UK is in the process of leaving.

The fundamental purpose of the European Union remains the creation of a free market for the provision of goods and services in all EU countries. To achieve this, the European Union seeks to provide a framework within which trade between the member countries of the European Union can take place fairly. For example, there are policies on the promotion of competition and the regulation of anti-competitive practices; there are policies to liberalize industries, such as telecommunications or the airlines, to allow greater freedom of consumer choice; it has policies on agriculture and fisheries designed to promote those two industries and promote European food security. It prescribes EU-wide standards for the manufacture of goods, both to protect consumers and to try to ensure that industry overheads are broadly similar. It also sets common standards for social security provision for workers, as well as entitlements for citizens of one country in the European Union to work in other countries of the Union. There are specific rules relating to employment protection, including safety at work and the prohibition of discriminatory employment practices. The laws of the European Union are designed to promote those policies.

In recent years, the European Union has developed other wider areas of activity, for example, the promotion of human rights and supporting measures for social cohesion. In response to criticism about the inability of the European Union to intervene in situations of conflict that might seem to warrant a Europe-wide approach, it has sought to develop a common foreign and security policy and a common defence policy. It is seeking to develop supra-national responses to challenges posed by climate change and environmental degradation. There have been important initiatives in the area of justice and home affairs. And, of course, the European Union has been seeking ways to resolve the financial problems that exist in the euro-zone.

Powerful voices within the EU would like to see yet further expansion and integration of policies and institutions on a trans-European scale. This has been one of the reasons why eurosceptics (not just in the UK but in other European countries as well) have been resisting what is sometimes referred to as the European project.

3.5.2.2 Law-making in the EU

The law-making processes of the European Union are extremely complex. They are not at all like the parliamentary processes we are familiar with in the United Kingdom. While suggestions for law-making come from a variety of sources, under the European Treaties, the European Commission has the exclusive right to initiate proposals for legislation. Whether or not its proposals become law and, if so, on what terms, depends on the outcome of complex negotiations and consensus-building between the Commission, the Council of Ministers,[7] and the European Parliament. (*See Box 3.17* for a summary of the EU legislative process.)

Box 3.17 Legal system explained

The legislative process in the EU

(1) *Legislative proposal from the European Commission.* The European Commission prepares legislative proposals on its own initiative or at the request of other EU institutions or countries, or following a citizens' initiative, often after public consultations. The final proposal is forwarded simultaneously to the European Parliament, Council, and national parliaments and, in some cases, to the Committee of the Regions and the Economic and Social Committee.

(2) *First reading in European Parliament.* The President of the European Parliament refers the proposal to a parliamentary committee, which appoints a rapporteur who is responsible for drawing up a draft report containing amendments to the proposed text. The committee votes on this report and any amendments to it tabled by other members. The European Parliament (EP) then discusses and votes on the legislative proposal in plenary on the basis of the committee report and amendments. The result is the EP's position. The EP can accept the proposal without any changes or make amendments. In rare cases the President can request the Commission to withdraw its proposal. The EP's first reading position is forwarded to the Council.

---

[7] Although in the formal descriptions of the European Union there is only one Council of Ministers, there is in fact a substantial number of Councils of Ministers reflecting the different portfolios of those ministers, for example agriculture, foreign policy, economic matters, trade matters, and the like. The supreme Council of Ministers comprises the leaders of the governments of the European Union, brought together to determine the most fundamental issues affecting the Union. Initially, decisions of the Council of Ministers had to be unanimous; a single vote against a proposal would result in its not being adopted. As the European Union has expanded, the principle of unanimity has been replaced in a large number of policy areas by the principle of qualified majority, which enables measures to be introduced despite the opposition of some ministers.

Box 3.17 Continued

(3) *First reading in Council.* Preparatory work in Council runs in parallel with the first reading in the EP, but Council may only formally conduct its first reading based on Parliament's position. Council can: accept the EP position, in which case the legislative act is adopted; or adopt changes to the EP's position, leading to a Council's first reading position, which is sent to the EP for a second reading.

(4) *Second reading in the EP.* The EP has three (with a possible extension to four) months to examine Council's position. The Council position goes first to the responsible committee, which prepares a recommendation for the EP's second reading. Plenary votes on the recommendation including possible albeit limited amendments. There are four possible outcomes to a second reading: the EP approves Council's position and the act is adopted; the EP fails to take a decision within the time limit, in which case the act is adopted as amended by Council in its first reading; the EP rejects Council's first reading position, in which case the act is not adopted, and the procedure is ended; the EP proposes amendments to Council's first reading position and forwards its position to Council for a second reading.

(5) *Second reading in Council.* Council has three (with a possible extension to four) months to examine the EP's second reading position. It is also informed about the European Commission's position on the EP's second reading amendments. The Council either approves all the EP's amendments, in which case the legislative act is adopted, or it does not approve all the amendments. In the latter case, the President of the Council, in agreement with the Parliament President, convenes a meeting of the Conciliation Committee.

(6) *Conciliation.* Within six (with a possible extension to eight) weeks of the Council's refusal to adopt the EP's second reading position, the Presidents of the Council and European Parliament convene the Conciliation Committee, with equal numbers of MEPs and Council representatives. The Conciliation Committee has six weeks (with a possible extension to eight) to decide on a joint text based on the second reading positions of the EP and Council. If the Conciliation Committee does not approve a joint text, the proposed legislative act falls, and the procedure is ended. If the Conciliation Committee approves a joint text, the text is forwarded for a third reading to the EP and the Council.

(7) *Third reading in Council and Parliament.* The joint text is sent simultaneously to the EP and Council for approval. There is no specific order in which the co-legislators must decide. They have six (or eight if jointly agreed) weeks to decide and they cannot modify the text. In the EP, the vote on the joint text is preceded by a debate in plenary. If Parliament and Council approve the joint text, the legislative proposal is adopted. If one or both rejects it, or does not respond in time, the legislation falls, and the procedure is ended. It can only be restarted with a new proposal from the Commission.

Source: www.europarl.europa.eu/aboutparliament/en/20150201PVL00004/Legislative-powers. This site has an excellent slide presentation.

The European Parliament—the only body with directly elected members—plays an important part in the law-making process. Successive treaties (Maastricht (1993), Amsterdam (1997), Nice (2001), and most recently Lisbon (2007) (*see Box 3.18*)) have given the European Parliament increasing amounts of power to control the content of legislative measures. While it still cannot initiate legislative proposals, the majority of European law-making must be approved by a majority of the European Parliament as well as the Council of Ministers. (The poor participation by the British electorate in European elections may be explained, at least in part, by widespread ignorance about the role of the European Parliament and how it has changed.)

Box 3.18 Reform in progress

Principal features of the Lisbon Treaty

The changes introduced by ratification of the Lisbon Treaty are not well understood. The Treaty:

- created the post of President of the European Council, who is elected for two and a half years. This replaced the former system whereby the Presidency of the European Council circulated every six months between the 28 heads of government who are the members of the European Council;
- created the post of High Representative for the Union in Foreign Affairs and Security Policy. The post-holder is also Vice-President of the Commission. The European Union now also has a single legal personality designed to make its international negotiating power more effective;
- gave the European Parliament new powers over EU legislation, the EU budget, and international agreements, designed to ensure the European Parliament is placed on an equal footing with the Council for the vast bulk of EU legislation. It also limits the size of the European Parliament to 751, with no country having more than 96 nor fewer than six Members of the European Parliament;
- made qualified majority voting the default voting method in the European Council of Ministers, save where treaties require a different procedure (e.g. unanimity). This means that qualified majority voting has been extended to many new policy areas, such as immigration and culture. From November 2014, a new voting method was introduced—double majority voting. To be passed by the Council, proposed EU laws require a majority not only of the Union's member countries (55 per cent) but also of the EU population (65 per cent);
- gave national parliaments greater opportunities to be involved in the work of the Union, in particular to monitor the principle of subsidiarity whereby the Union only acts where results can be better attained at Union level;
- explicitly recognized for the first time the possibility of a Member State withdrawing from the European Union.

Source: ec.europa.eu/archives/lisbon_treaty/index_en.htm.

3.5.2.3 The law of the EU

A number of technical points need to be made about the different types of law that are made by the EU institutions.

First, all the institutions of the European Union draw their ultimate authority from the treaties that underpin the establishment of the European Union. There are now two key EU Treaties, which bring together various treaties made since 1957. They are the Treaty on the European Union (TEU, originally called the Maastricht Treaty), and the Treaty on the Functioning of the European Union (TFEU, originally called the Treaty of Rome). These are the basic law or the *primary legislation* of the European Union.

While many of these fundamental provisions of Community law are designed to deal with obligations between states, some have been held by the European Court of Justice to have 'direct effect' on the law of individual Member States in the determination of individual rights and duties. For treaty provisions to have this effect, the content of the provision must be clear; the provision must be self-executing, in the sense that it imposes a specific duty; and the provision must not contain any conditions or qualifications. There are many European Court of Justice decisions that have held particular treaty articles to be of direct effect; for example, Articles 101 and 102 of TFEU, which outlaw anti-competitive agreements, or Article 157 of TFEU, establishing the principle of equal pay between men and women.

Secondly, where a treaty provision is found to be of direct effect, it may be both vertically and horizontally effective. 'Vertical' effectiveness arises when an individual uses a treaty provision to challenge an act of the government or some other public body. 'Horizontal' effectiveness arises where one individual or other body wishes to use EU law to challenge the behaviour of another individual body of similar status.

Thirdly, more detailed legislative measures that seek to implement the detailed policies of the European Union can collectively be described as the *secondary legislation* of the European Union. They are called: regulations, directives, and decisions.

Under Article 288 of TFEU, *regulations* are—like the treaty provisions considered earlier—of 'direct effect', that is to say they automatically become part of the internal law of each of the Member States of the European Union. An example is Regulation 1408/71, which deals with aspects of social security law and the need to insure workers under a scheme of national insurance. As with treaty provisions, regulations may have both vertical and horizontal effectiveness.

Directives are more general in tone. They set down standards towards which Member States are required to aim, but some discretion as to the detail of how that is to be done is left to the Member States. The implementation in the United Kingdom of the Working Time Directive, which regulates the number of hours worked each week, provides a good example. The principle of direct effect may be invoked if there is a complaint that a government has failed so to incorporate the provision into national law. In the United Kingdom, directives are usually brought into effect in statutory instruments. This will cease once the UK has left the EU.

Decisions are rulings on particular matters addressed to either governments of Member States, corporations, or individuals. For example, an argument about whether a particular take-over bid was or was not anti-competitive could be the subject of a decision. Decisions are binding on those to whom they are addressed.

In addition to these forms of secondary legislation, the European Union may also make *recommendations* and *opinions*, but these do not have any direct effect.

3.5.2.4 Enforcement of EU law

One of the fundamental principles of membership of the European Union is that the institutions of the Union, in particular the European Commission in Brussels and the European Court of Justice in Luxembourg, have power to force Member States to obey EU law. This gives the Union power to intervene directly in the law-making processes of Member States. To try to secure the authority of the European Union's law-making powers in the United Kingdom, the UK government did two things. First, prior to the entry of the United Kingdom into the Union (in 1973), Parliament enacted the European Communities Act 1972, which committed the UK government to implementing and abiding by EU law, if necessary without the intervention of the UK Parliament. Secondly, in 1975 it held a referendum (*see Box 3.1*) which sought, and obtained, a majority vote in favour of ratifying the United Kingdom's entry into the Union. The 2016 referendum went the other way. The European Union (Withdrawal) Bill, when enacted, will repeal the European Communities Act, 1972. All the existing rules and regulations made by the EU will become part of UK law.

It was this ability of the European Institutions to make laws which had a direct impact in the UK that led many eurosceptics to argue that the UK should leave the EU, since, in their view, this led to an unacceptable limitation on the powers of the UK Parliament and courts to be the final arbiters of the law which applies in the UK.

One of the currently highly contentious and unresolved issues about the Brexit process is the extent to which, after Brexit, decisions of the European Court of Justice should be taken into account in the UK courts.

3.5.2.5 Where next? A warning

At the time of writing, major questions about the Brexit process remain unanswered. It is likely that there will be many points of detail, not yet decided, that will need to be discussed in future editions of this book. I suppose that there is a possibility that there will be some quite unexpected outcome, particularly if the vote which ministers have promised Parliament at the end of the negotiating period does not go the way the government wants. Thus, those interested in the development of the relationship between the UK and the EU will need to keep abreast of developments. What is stated here is by no means the last word.

3.6 Other sources of law-making

At the end of this lengthy account, other sources of law-making will be mentioned only briefly.

3.6.1 Local and regional government

Local government has long had power to make by-laws—a form of tertiary legislation (*see Box 3.6*)—since by-laws are made under the authority of Acts of Parliament but apply only in the area of the local authority in question.

Under the terms of the Scotland Act 1998, the Scottish Parliament was granted authority to pass legislation in areas within its competence. Following the referendum on Scottish independence, the Scotland Act 2016 devolves more legislative powers. Under the Government of Wales Act 1998, the National Assembly for Wales was given power to pass secondary legislation, again within the scope of its areas of competence. Defined powers to make primary legislation have been granted to the Welsh Assembly government by the Government of Wales Act 2006, expanded by the Government of Wales Act 2014, and further expanded by the Wales Act 2017. The Northern Ireland Act 1998 similarly grants legislative power to the Northern Ireland Assembly (though at the time of preparing this edition the Assembly is not functioning).

3.6.2 Other rule-making agencies

A great deal of rule-making is also undertaken by industry regulators: for example, the Civil Aviation Authority or the regulators of the privatized utilities. The Financial Services Act 2012 created a new regulatory structure consisting of the Bank of England's Financial Policy Committee, the Prudential Regulation Authority, and the Financial Conduct Authority. The rules made by regulatory bodies fall outside the parliamentary framework, though in most cases they are based on legislative authority conferred by Act of Parliament and have the effect of law on those companies that are the subject of their regulation.

3.6.3 Other international institutions and bodies of international law

We have considered the Council of Europe and the European Union in context. Many other international institutions also have an impact on detailed rules of English law. There are many industries, for example aviation and telecommunications, where at least some of the legislative framework results from the provisions of international treaties. Increasing globalization of economic activity combined with increasing pressure to deal with some of the major issues of the day—the environment, genetic engineering, global warming, international trade—ensures that this trend will develop.

Lastly, it is relevant to note the existence of a separate body of private international law—in essence rules of English law, designed to assist in the determination of private law rights and entitlements that have an international dimension.

3.7 Key points

1. Law-making is a central feature of modern government. It is principally based in democratic principles, though by no means all sources of law derive their authority from those principles.

2. Other constitutional principles—in particular the separation of powers—are also engaged.

3. Much legislation is influenced directly or indirectly by international obligations, in particular those arising from the Council of Europe and (for the present) the European Union.

4. There is currently great uncertainty about the legal and political relationships that will exist between the UK and the EU, following the Brexit referendum.

5. The devolution debates, in particular devolution of powers to the Scottish Parliament, have led to changes in who can vote on bills relating solely to England.

6. The making of key rules and regulations is not solely undertaken in Parliament. It also occurs in many contexts outside Parliament.

7. This all makes for considerable complexity that has increased enormously in recent years. It is unlikely that the ordinary person in the street is aware of more than a fraction of the law which in theory affects him or her. It is fanciful to claim that ordinary people can be assumed to know the law.

8. One of the challenges facing modern society is how new technologies can be used to transform this vast mass of legal information into knowledge that can actually be used by the ordinary citizen.

3.8 Questions

Use the self-test questions in the Online Resources to test your understanding of the topics covered in this chapter and receive tailored feedback: www.oup.com/uk/partington18_19/.

3.9 Web links

Check the Online Resources for a selection of annotated web links allowing you to research easily topics of particular interest: www.oup.com/uk/partington18_19/.

3.10 Blog items

See Spotlight on the Justice System, at www.martinpartington.com/category/chapter-3-2/.

Suggestions for further reading

BINGHAM, T., *The Rule of Law* (London, Penguin Books, 2011)

BOGDANOR, V., *The New British Constitution* (Oxford, Hart Publishing, 2009)

CRAIG, P., *The Lisbon Treaty: Law, Politics, and Treaty Reform* (Oxford, Oxford University Press, 2010)

JUSTICE, *Law for Lawmakers: A JUSTICE guide to the law* (JUSTICE, London, 2015) available free at justice.org.uk/law-for-lawmakers-a-justice-guide-to-the-law/

ZANDER, M., *The Law-Making Process* (7th edn, Oxford, Hart Publishing, 2015)

Other suggestions can be seen in the Further Reading listed in the **Online Resources**.

PART III

THE STRUCTURE OF THE LEGAL SYSTEM

4

Shaping the legal system: the role of government

4.1 Introduction: shaping the system

One respect in which the English legal system has changed over the years has been the increased involvement of government in shaping and reforming it. Central government provides substantial levels of funding not only for running courts and tribunals and publicly funded legal services, but also for the huge array of other services which are part of or impact upon the legal system. The police, prison, and probation services are obvious examples. All governments are concerned with keeping levels of public expenditure under control and securing value for money.

The current government's desire to reduce public expenditure is directly affecting the legal system. Some regard any cuts as by definition leading to changes that are retrograde and undesirable. However, this is to assume that all public monies are wisely and efficiently spent. If this assumption is not accepted, then curbs on public expenditure could promote changes that are beneficial to the system. There may be opportunities to improve, as well as threats to existing provision.

This chapter considers the principal government departments that shape the English legal system:

- the Ministry of Justice (MoJ);
- the Home Office;
- the Department for Exiting the European Union; and
- other central government departments.

Lurking behind all of them is the Treasury.

4.2 The Ministry of Justice

The MoJ plays the central role in the development of policy relating to the legal system. It was established in 2007. This was the culmination of a process of constitutional change that started in 2003, when the former Lord Chancellor's Department (LCD) became the Department for Constitutional Affairs (DCA).

There had long been calls for the creation of an MoJ. Many argued that the former split between the LCD/DCA and the Home Office (with the latter largely responsible for criminal justice) prevented the development of coherent justice policy.

There was also concern about the post of the Lord Chancellor. Historically, the Lord Chancellor had always been a member of the (non-elected) House of Lords, not the House of Commons. He was always a qualified lawyer. And he embodied a peculiar position in the government, apparently breaching the principle of the separation of powers, since he was simultaneously a member of the executive (the Lord Chancellor is a member of the Cabinet), the head of the judiciary, and, as Speaker of the House of Lords, a member of the legislature.

When the 2003 changes were made, it was originally intended that the historic post of Lord Chancellor should simply disappear, and that the chief minister should become a Secretary of State, just like any other head of a government department. Closer analysis revealed that this could not be done without legislative change. When first published, the Constitutional Reform Bill contained a clause that would have abolished the post of Lord Chancellor. This became one of a number of issues that were fiercely contested during the passage of the bill through Parliament. In the end, a political compromise was achieved (*see Box 3.8*). It was agreed that the post of Lord Chancellor would be retained, but he would no longer be the Speaker of the House of Lords; nor would he remain the head of the judiciary—this responsibility would pass to the Lord Chief Justice. Nor would the posts of Secretary of State and Lord Chancellor necessarily be held by the same person. In future, the Secretary of State would be exclusively a member of the executive branch of government.

It was also agreed that the officeholder would no longer have to be a member of the House of Lords. But the Constitutional Reform Act 2005 uniquely limits the power of the Prime Minister in relation to the person who may be appointed Lord Chancellor. The convention that the Lord Chancellor should always be a senior barrister is dropped. Instead, the Act states that the Prime Minister must appoint someone 'qualified by experience'. This is defined in section 2 of the Act as experience as a minister of the Crown; as a member of either House of Parliament; as a qualifying legal practitioner; as a teacher of law in a university; or with 'such other experience that the Prime Minister considers relevant'. The present Secretary of State/Lord Chancellor, David Gauke MP, is the seventh to be appointed under the new law.

The MoJ (and its predecessors) is a department that has grown markedly in both size and importance within government. Once, in the 1920s, its Permanent Secretary—the head civil servant—was able to record that not one item of post had been received! For many years the former LCD was seen as a bit odd in the overall government structure. In most government departments, lawyers are used as specialists advising on questions of law, drafting bills and regulations and the like, rather than being closely involved in the development of policy. In the LCD, the Permanent Secretary was required by law to be qualified as a practising lawyer, unlike his counterparts in other departments, who were not required to have specific professional qualifications. This rule was abolished in 1997. Since then, the Permanent Secretary has not been a lawyer.

Over the last 20 years, the MoJ (and its predecessors) has come to operate much more like other large service-delivery departments. It employs around 70,000 people (including probation services) and has a budget of about £9 billion. As is discussed in this chapter, the department radically altered the management of the courts, through the creation of Her Majesty's Courts Service (HMCS) and a new Tribunals Service. In April 2011, these were merged into Her Majesty's Courts and Tribunals Service (HMCTS). It has made major changes to the ways in which the legal profession is regulated. No longer can the MoJ be regarded as at the periphery of government.

4.2.1 Responsibilities

The MoJ's website lists its principal responsibilities for the courts, prisons, probation services, and attendance centres (see www.gov.uk/government/organisations/ministry-of-justice/about). The MoJ also works in partnership with the other government departments and agencies to reform the criminal justice system, to serve the public, and to support the victims of crime. This is, frankly a bland and incomplete list (no mention of civil and commercial justice (*Chapter 8*), administrative justice (*Chapter 6*), family justice (*Chapter 7*), or legal aid (*Chapter 10*)) which undersells its role in government. It disguises the fact that no aspect of the justice system has remained unchanged in recent years. It is the MoJ that has driven that change and that will shape future policy. In short, government injects into the English legal system a dynamism that is often not fully appreciated—both in the sense of its not being understood by those outside the system, and its not being welcomed by those inside. The main policy changes are considered in context in the chapters that follow.

Here we consider those matters that are not considered in other chapters.

4.2.2 Her Majesty's Courts and Tribunals Service

HMCTS is an executive agency of the MoJ. It started operation, as Her Majesty's Courts Service (HMCS), on 1 April 2005, formed by merging the Court Service (created in 1995) and the Magistrates' Courts Service (which had been run separately). The creation of HMCS followed a review of the criminal justice system carried out by Sir Robin Auld in 2001. He argued that a unified court service should be able to offer a more coherent and flexible court system. The separate Her Majesty's Tribunals Service was created in 2006 (*see Chapter 6*). In April 2011, the two services were merged into the single HMCTS.

4.2.2.1 Defining and delivering service standards

In common with other areas of government, HMCTS is required to define and deliver standards of service to the users of the courts and tribunals—whether as claimants, those defending claims, those appearing as witnesses, jurors, other friends and relatives, or general members of the public—standards unheard of only a few years ago. Many of the key tasks required of HMCTS are those of administrative efficiency: dealing with people courteously; dealing with issues expeditiously but fairly; handling matters as economically as possible and seeking to reduce costs; and—in the civil courts—recovering from parties to proceedings the costs associated with the provision of court services.

However, average times for disposing of small claims of under £10,000 are 30 weeks; for cases involving over £10,000 that rises to over a year (go to open.justice.gov.uk/ and following the links to courts/civil cases). In my view, service delivery is not taken as seriously as it should be. The focus of much of the current transformation programme, for both the criminal and civil courts, is on significantly improved efficiency.

4.2.2.2 *Transforming Our Justice System:* investing in IT and proceedings online

For many years HMCTS made some investment in computerization and new information technologies. These enabled some routine proceedings to take place without the need for personal attendance at court. Professional lawyers do not have to waste time attending court on purely procedural matters. While parties to proceedings are still required to attend court for trials, they can similarly 'attend' court from a distance for procedural work. It has become possible to provide evidence through video links, making it easier for witnesses, who may be unable or reluctant to attend a particular court, to appear.

Initially the focus was on increasing the efficiency of the criminal courts. The XHIBIT service, which gives up-to-date information about the progress of criminal cases listed in courts, has operated nationally since March 2006. There has been increased ability to use electronic files, which has reduced the numbers of paper files that have to be brought to court for trials. The government announced that, from 2016, all criminal trials should be conducted using electronic files only. Following a review of the criminal justice system in 2015, a major new programme of efficiency is now being rolled out (*see 5.6*).

On the civil side, HMCTS runs Money Claim Online, which enables persons to bring an action for debt using the internet; Possession Claim Online, which similarly enables certain possession proceedings to be started online; and payments of fines online. But there has long been frustration at the slow progress in the use of e-communications to start and progress disputes. In this context, HMCTS has lagged far behind other complaints and dispute resolution procedures.

There are now signs that things are changing. In September 2016, the government announced a major new programme: *Transforming Our Justice System*. The impact of this policy on each of the four justice systems is discussed in more detail in the following chapters. A considerable financial investment is being made by the Ministry of Justice to deliver this programme. Much of that investment is being achieved by savings being made as a result of a major rationalization of the court estate (*see 4.2.2.3*).

4.2.2.3 Rationalization of the court estate

For a number of years, HMCTS has been taking a hard look at the location of its court buildings and their configuration. This has involved the building of a number of unified court centres where both criminal and civil cases are dealt with. It has also involved closing court buildings. Thus in 2015, it was in the process of closing

93 magistrates' courts and 49 county courts (out of a total of 530 court buildings). Further court closures are in progress.

Court closures are often controversial, as they may involve the abandonment of historic buildings that are much loved locally. It is also argued that reducing the numbers of courts limits access to justice. But it cannot be right to keep buildings that are little used open simply for reasons of nostalgia. And practical alternatives are available.

It is possible to hire short-term accommodation in areas where there is not enough work to justify permanent court buildings. 'Pop-up Courts' are under consideration as a possible new initiative. And there is the untapped potential for remote access to courts using the internet and phone services, once the IT investment has been made. A central feature of the *Transforming Our Justice System* programme is a plan to create an online court for the resolution of a large number of civil disputes (*see 8.14*).

4.2.3 Support for the judiciary: the concordat

One of the reasons why the proposals to create the post of Secretary of State for Justice/ Lord Chancellor were so controversial (*see Box 3.8*) was that the senior judiciary were extremely worried that an office which had historically been a strong defender of the independence of the judiciary might be weakened. The outcome of protracted and often heated discussions between the then Lord Chancellor, Lord Falconer, and the then Lord Chief Justice, Lord Woolf, resulted in publication of a concordat. It sets out how the judiciary-related functions of the Lord Chancellor would in future be carried out.

First, the concordat establishes how the functions of the Secretary of State and the Lord Chief Justice are to be divided. Broadly, the Secretary of State determines fundamental issues, such as the level of resource available to enable the courts and tribunals to operate. These include obvious matters such as pay and pensions and the provision of accommodation. The Lord Chief Justice has responsibility for ensuring the effective deployment of the judicial resources that are available.

Secondly, the importance of the Secretary of State continuing to guarantee the independence of the judiciary was recognized. A section in the Constitutional Reform Act 2005 enshrines the principle in law (*see Box 3.11*).

Thirdly, there was to be greater transparency in a number of areas where this had been lacking. The making of judicial appointments (*see 4.2.5*) is the obvious example. It was important to ensure that judicial appointments would not be subject to political intervention. There were other issues where, in future, there would be greater procedural transparency. These included matters such as the disciplining of judges and dealing with complaints against them.

The principles set out in the concordat were subject to severe test when the creation of the MoJ was announced in 2007. Judges particularly feared that the inclusion of the National Offender Management Service in the overall activity of the new Ministry would result in resources being taken away from courts and tribunals to fund shortfalls in prisons and probation budgets. Eventually, agreement was reached that appropriate levels of funding would be guaranteed.

4.2.4 Managing the judges: the Judicial Office

To reinforce the institutional separation of the judiciary from the executive, a new Judicial Office was established in 2006. Its officials provide administrative support to the Lord Chief Justice. Among their most important tasks is the upholding of the concordat. They support the Lord Chief Justice's responsibilities for the disposition of the judiciary around the court system. In addition, the Office has taken over personnel functions associated with the judiciary and management processes such as appraisal of judicial performance.

For the first time, senior members of the judiciary became involved in the management of judges. Following enactment of the Constitutional Reform Act 2005, a Judicial Executive Board was set up to support the Lord Chief Justice in his executive and leadership roles. The Board receives secretarial support from the Judicial Office. Standing behind the Executive Board, which is a relatively small body of the most senior judges, is the Judges' Council, first established in the nineteenth century. It is a larger body than the Board, and is representative of judges at all the different judicial levels. It has changed its role over the years, and now provides input to the work of the Board. It meets four times a year.

The Judicial Office is also responsible for ensuring that complaints about the judiciary are properly dealt with. This function involves a complex interaction between the Lord Chancellor and the Lord Chief Justice, especially where a serious complaint about a judge is upheld and the question arises whether that individual should remain a judge. Detailed investigation of complaints about judicial conduct is undertaken by the Judicial Conduct Investigations Office. In most cases it can reach a decision about a complaint itself; serious cases may be referred for review by a specially nominated senior judge. In 2016–17, 19 judges were removed from office. This is a tiny percentage (less than 0.1 per cent) of all judicial appointments (*see Chapter 9*).

4.2.4.1 Judicial College

The Judicial Office also has formal responsibility for the work of the Judicial College (formerly the Judicial Studies Board (JSB)). The College is another part of the English legal system that has developed significantly in recent years. For a long time, many judges assumed that they knew all that there was to know about law and legal process, and that therefore judicial training was unnecessary; some regarded it as an impertinence to suggest otherwise. Notwithstanding this complacent view, it is now accepted that judicial training is needed. As early as the 1960s, judicial conferences were convened to address the particular issue of inconsistency in sentencing by the judiciary.

The scope of judicial training was put on a more formal footing in 1979 with the creation of the JSB. Over the following 30 years the Board grew in size and stature to deliver a very considerable programme of judicial training, not only to judges sitting in criminal trials, but also those handling civil trials, and to the chairs of a wide range of tribunals. It also set the framework for the training of magistrates. With the merger of HMCS and the Tribunals Service, the training resources of both were combined and, in April 2011, the JSB was renamed the Judicial College.

The College provides *induction* courses, which must be taken before a judge begins to sit. It also provides a very varied programme of seminars from which sitting judges are required to select a certain number each year to fulfil their *continuing education* requirements.

Besides courses, the College provides written guidance on the running of trials in *Bench Books*—information that judges have with them for easy reference while performing their judicial functions. It has also produced a number of publications offering guidance on the skills needed by judicial officeholders. Its Equal Treatment Advisory Committee has published the *Equal Treatment Bench Book* designed to ensure that parties to proceedings in courts or tribunals feel they have been treated equally and not been subject to any form of discrimination. The College also sponsors one or two more practical books, notably the *Guidelines for the Assessment of Damages in Personal Injury Cases*, aiming to promote greater consistency in determining awards for damages in personal injury cases.

The development of the role of the JSB/Judicial College is a fascinating example of the evolution of policy and practice in the English legal system. It did not stem from ministerial action or the enactment of special legislation. Rather, senior officials in the former LCD, working quietly with influential members of the judiciary, saw this as an important part of the management of a modern judicial system. Pockets of resistance among the judiciary—which undoubtedly existed years ago—have been replaced by an acceptance, reflected in professional life more generally, that continuing education is a proper, indeed essential, part of professional development. Newly appointed judges now expect training; and those in post acknowledge the need for opportunities to reflect on their work.

This is not to say that the model so far developed is perfect. The amount of training that English judges receive is still modest. Unlike the situation in some other jurisdictions, there is no university law school that offers a specialist postgraduate diploma or degree in judicial science, though an Institute for Judicial Studies was created at University College London in 2010. There is always more that can and should be done. Nevertheless, the development of professional judicial studies has been one of the most significant developments in the English legal system in the last two decades. It has not attracted the public attention that it deserves.

4.2.5 Judicial appointments

The process of making judicial appointments has also undergone rapid change. For many years, it was shrouded in secrecy. Appointments were offered to a relatively small circle of barristers, mostly practising in London.

The expansion of the legal profession and the opening of judicial appointments to solicitors were among the factors that meant such an approach was no longer viable. Although written criteria for judicial appointment had been in the public domain for well over 20 years, this was not enough for critics of the system. In recent years, there has been substantial reform.

A key feature of the Constitutional Reform Act 2005 was the creation of the *Judicial Appointments Commission* (JAC), supported by a *Judicial Appointments and Conduct Ombudsman*. The JAC began work in April 2006. One of its aims is to increase judicial diversity. Some interpret this focus on judicial diversity as meaning that those targeted—women, members of ethnic minorities, and people with disabilities—will receive preferential treatment. This is not what the JAC wants or is allowed to do. What it is, quite properly, doing is encouraging all those qualified to apply for judicial appointment to do so. Thus it runs road shows and takes other steps to draw to the attention of members of the legal profession that the process of appointment has changed and is more open.

Important changes were made to the threshold qualification for applying for judicial appointment. The Tribunals, Courts and Enforcement Act 2007 provides that, rather than eligibility for office being based on possession of rights of audience for a specified period, applicants for judicial office have to show that they possess a relevant legal qualification for the requisite period and that, while holding that qualification, they have been gaining legal experience. In respect of many judicial offices, the number of years for which a person must have held such qualification before becoming eligible for appointment has been reduced.

To take the diversity agenda forward, the JAC established an Advisory Panel on Diversity in the Judiciary which, in February 2010, published an important report. Its vision was that by 2020 there should be a much more diverse judiciary at all levels which:

- is as talented, respected, and independent as it was in 2010;
- recognizes the concept of a judicial career;
- seeks and finds talent in more unusual places;
- gives opportunities to a wider range of individuals; and
- is more flexible in its working practices.

To achieve these objectives, the panel made 53 recommendations for improving judicial diversity.

A core feature of the panel's report was that there should be a shift away from the idea of *judicial appointment* that focuses on the individual seeking appointment, towards the idea of a *judicial career* which anyone engaged in the law could be encouraged to consider. This approach is being enhanced following the integration of the courts' and tribunals' services since there are now more opportunities to acquire and develop judicial skills that can be transferred from one part of the justice system to another.

In late 2011 the MoJ proposed further changes to the way in which the JAC functions and the division of responsibilities as between the JAC, the Lord Chief Justice, and the Lord Chancellor. The Crime and Courts Act 2013 gave legislative force to the changes (*see Box 4.1*).

Box 4.1 Reform in progress

Crime and Courts Act 2013: Part 2

Provisions in the Act include:

- changing the rules to allow senior judges to work part-time, intended to help balance work and family lives;
- enabling 'positive action' for appointments—meaning that if two candidates are completely equal in their abilities, a selection can be made on the basis of improving diversity.

The government states that these moves must not change the overriding principle of appointments based on merit, but are intended to promote career progression, and to encourage applications from a wider talent pool to create a judiciary which reflects society.

The Act also contains detailed provisions designed to make the judicial appointments process more efficient. These include:

- having an independent lay commissioner as chair of the selection panel for the post of Lord Chief Justice, rather than a judge;
- increasing JAC involvement in the selection and appointment of the judges who are authorized to sit as Deputy High Court Judges;
- providing the Lord Chancellor with an increased and more effective role in appointing the most senior judges—through the use of pre-selection consultation in appointments to the Court of Appeal and Heads of Division and sitting on the selection commission for the appointment of the Lord Chief Justice and President of the UK Supreme Court;
- reducing the role of the Lord Chancellor in the appointment of less senior judges, by transferring his powers for judicial appointments below the High Court and Court of Appeal to the Lord Chief Justice;
- introducing flexible deployment so judges can move between working in the courts and tribunals systems, to help judicial career development. This was seen as a key step in the report published by the Advisory Panel on Judicial Diversity.

Both the government and many leading judicial figures want to see greater judicial diversity. Annual statistical reports show that some progress towards this objective is being made (*see Box 4.2*). But there is no doubt that there is still a long way to go and achieving the 2020 target in the Advisory Panel's vision seems at present highly unlikely. (*See Chapter 9* for further consideration of the encouragement of greater diversity in the legal profession.)

Box 4.2 Reform in progress

Judicial diversity statistics 2017

The headline findings are:

- 28 per cent (890) of court judges and 45 per cent (806) of tribunal judges were female, similar to the previous year.

Box 4.2 Continued

- Nine out of 38 Court of Appeal Judges were female (24 per cent), also comparable to the previous year, where eight out of 39 (21 per cent) were female.
- Twenty-one out of 97 High Court Judges were female (22 per cent); as at 1 April 2016, 22 out of 106 (21 per cent) were female.
- Around half of all court judges (49 per cent) and just under two thirds of tribunal judges (62 per cent) aged under 40 were female.
- Fourteen out of 66 Deputy High Court Judges (22 per cent) were women.
- Four of the 29 Deputy High Court Judges who declared their ethnicity were BAME.
- 7 per cent of courts (173) and 10 per cent (168) of tribunal judges are BAME.
- BAME representation was highest among those aged under 40, at 10 per cent for courts and 14 per cent for tribunal judges.
- Representation of those with a non-barrister background varied by jurisdiction for both courts and tribunals, with higher proportions of judges in lower courts from a non-barrister background (solicitors and legal executives).
- There has been a continuing reduction in the overall number of magistrates, reducing from 25,104 as at 1 April 2012 to 16,129 as at 1 April 2017, a 36 per cent reduction across the period.
- More than half of magistrates were female (54 per cent—8,712).
- 11 per cent (1,686) of magistrates declared themselves as BAME.
- There were very few magistrates aged under 40 (4 per cent, 635) compared with 86 per cent (13,803) of magistrates who were aged over 50.

The conclusions that may be drawn from these findings is that some progress has been made in the appointment of women as judges; but the numbers of BAME judges remain low. There has been a reduction in the number of non-barrister appointments as court judges.

Further detail is at https://www.judiciary.gov.uk/publications/judicial-statistics-2017/. There is also a progress report from the Judicial Diversity Committee at https://www. judiciary.gov.uk/about-the-judiciary/who-are-the-judiciary/diversity/judicial-diversity-committee-of-the-judges-council-report-on-progress-and-action-plan/. A critical report from JUSTICE, *Increasing Judicial Diversity*, is available at https://justice.org.uk/increasing-judicial-diversity/.

4.2.6 The Law Commission

The Law Commission was established by Act of Parliament in 1965 to keep the law of England and Wales under review. (There are separate Law Commissions for Scotland and Northern Ireland.) It is the most important standing body devoted to questions of law reform. Though independent in character, it falls within the overall responsibility of the MoJ. The Commission is chaired by a Court of Appeal judge, currently Lord Justice Bean. He is supported by four other commissioners, who in turn are assisted by teams of lawyers, research assistants, and a small secretariat.

In carrying out its functions it does not attempt to review all the law all the time. Rather it determines, on a regular basis, programmes of work it intends to carry out.

(At any one time, the Commission is engaged on between 20 and 30 projects, at different stages of development.) In addition, the Commission seeks to *codify* areas of law that have become extremely complex, and to *repeal* legislation that is no longer of practical use. (Since 1965, over 5,000 measures have been removed from the statute book as a result of this work.) The 13th programme was announced at the end of 2017. It contains projects which are responding to technological change, such as: Automated Vehicles, and Electronic Signatures. The general area of property law attracts a number of projects, including Modernising Trust Law for a Global Britain, and Unfair Terms in Residential Leasehold. Three projects will examine how current processes, which affect the public, might be reformed: Administrative Review, Employment Law Hearing Structures, and Simplifying the Immigration Rules. Controversial issues concerning the start and end of life are reflected in proposals to review Surrogacy and A Modern Framework for Disposing of the Dead. In addition to these new projects, the Law Commission will continue to work on items brought over from the 12th Programme of work, including work on Sentencing, and Search warrants.

Its projects are selected on the basis of: importance—how unsatisfactory is the current state of the law; suitability—whether the topic is one of high political sensitivity (which would make it unsuitable); and resources—whether both the financial and human resources are available to enable the job to be done. Selection of topics results from an extensive programme of consultation and negotiation with government departments.

Each project starts with analysis of the existing law, including, where relevant, consideration of how other countries have dealt with the issue in question. It then drafts a preliminary consultation paper setting out a statement of the existing law, explaining why that area of law needs reform, and indicating its preliminary views on how the law might be reformed, on which it seeks comments from members of the public. Having analysed those comments, the Commission develops its ideas into recommendations for the reform of the law. It usually commissions the drafting of a bill designed to capture the outcome of these policy formulations. Drafting is done by Parliamentary Counsel who are specially seconded to the Commission for this purpose.

The mere fact that this stage in the law-making process has been reached does not guarantee that the bill becomes law. It still has to go through the parliamentary process discussed in *Chapter 3*. And no further progress can be made if parliamentary time cannot be found. About two-thirds of the Commission's proposals for reform have reached the statute book (*see Box 4.3*).

Box 4.3 Reform in progress

Law Commission Act 2009 and Protocol

The Law Commission Act 2009 is designed to ensure that government departments take notice of and act upon recommendations arising from the work of the Law Commission. The Act:

Box 4.3 Continued

- requires the Lord Chancellor to prepare an annual report, to be laid before Parliament, on the implementation of Law Commission proposals;
- requires the Lord Chancellor to set out plans for dealing with any Law Commission proposals that have not been implemented and provide the reasoning behind decisions not to implement proposals;
- allows the Lord Chancellor and Law Commission to agree a protocol about the Law Commission's work, designed to provide a framework for the relationship between the UK government and the Law Commission. The Lord Chancellor has to lay the protocol before Parliament.

The protocol was agreed in March 2010. It is intended to increase the number of Law Commission proposals implemented by government and to reduce the time in taking reform forward.

Under the protocol, government departments will:

- give an undertaking that there is serious intention to take forward law reform in any relevant area of law included in the Commission's programme of work;
- keep the Commission up to date on other developments in policy that may impact on its proposals;
- provide an interim response as soon as possible or in any event within six months of the Law Commission publishing its proposals and a full response as soon as possible or in any event within a year.

The Law Commission will:

- consult departmental ministers about potential law reform projects in their areas;
- support all its final reports with an impact assessment;
- take full account of the minister's views in deciding whether and how to continue with a project at agreed review points.

The fifth report on implementation from the Lord Chancellor was published in March 2015. This shows that there has been some improvement in the rate of implementation. The sixth report was published, a year late, in January 2017.

4.2.7 Research

Unlike many other large-spending government departments, the former DCA did not invest heavily in empirical research. Specific policy-related research projects were commissioned from time to time. But policy initiatives too often derived from anecdotal evidence, pressure from influential individual or groups of judges, powerful professional bodies such as the Law Society and the Bar Council, or the ideas or even prejudices of government ministers or Members of Parliament.

The former DCA had a research unit with control over a (modest) budget dedicated to the development of specially commissioned policy-related research. Initially, all the research was carried out by academics or other research agencies on a research con-tract basis. This was later supplemented with an in-house research team.

The creation of the MoJ meant that the very much larger research activity formerly within the Home Office was brought into the new Ministry. The bulk of empiri-cal research published relates to aspects of criminal justice. This is supplemented by research carried out by the Youth Justice Board and the National Offenders Management Service.

Regrettably the Legal Services Research Centre, which did pioneering research on legal and advice services, how people use those services, and gaps in service provisions, has been disbanded following reforms of legal aid (*see Chapter 10*).

It must be right in principle to develop policy that is going to affect large num-bers of people on the basis of hard information rather than soft anecdote. There are, however, significant challenges to the undertaking of empirical research on law, not least the narrowness of vision of many lawyers and their inability to understand the crucial links between the discipline of law and the disciplines of the social sciences. Meeting these challenges requires strong intellectual leadership from the academic community and from policy-makers within government, which has not always been forthcoming.

4.3 The Home Office

The Home Office also has a central role in shaping the institutional framework of the English legal system, particularly in relation to the development of the criminal jus-tice system considered further in *Chapter 5*. Much of the drive for increased efficiency within the criminal justice system, leading to significant changes to the ways in which criminal processes operate, started with Home Office initiatives.

One of the key features of policing in England and Wales is that there is no national police force, but rather 43 different police forces operating throughout the country. Arguments in favour of the creation of a national police force are met by the counter-argument that that would lead to too great a centralization of police power and a lack of local accountability. The Coalition government decided to make police forces more accountable at local level. Part 1 of the Police Reform and Social Responsibility Act 2011 abolished police authorities (which were appointed bodies), replacing them with directly elected Police and Crime Commissioners. The first elections were held on 15 November 2012. A second round took place in May 2016.

It is accepted, however, that issues such as serious organized crime and economic fraud cannot be dealt with effectively by fragmented local forces. In relation to the former, the Serious Organised Crime and Police Act 2005 created the Serious Organised Crime Agency (SOCA), which brought together the National Criminal Intelligence Service, the National Crime Squad, that part of Her Majesty's Revenue and Customs that dealt with drug trafficking, and part of the UK Immigration Service dealing with organized immigration crime. SOCA, however, was criticized for lack of effectiveness.

SOCA was replaced by the National Crime Agency. It started work in October 2013. It brings together border control, economic crime, organized crime, and the work of the Child Exploitation and Online Protection Centre.

Although most of the Home Office's functions relating to the criminal justice system were transferred to the MoJ, it still takes the lead in relation to a number of issues that have an important impact on law-making and the role of law in England and Wales. These include: crime reduction; immigration and nationality; drugs prevention; and race equality and diversity, including anti-discrimination legislation. Particularly controversial areas for which it is responsible include: dealing with internal terrorist threats—which includes the issue of the extent to which people should be able to be detained without charge while inquiries are made; handling claims of asylum-seekers; and anti-social behaviour.

4.4 The Department for Exiting the European Union

One of the consequences of the UK leaving the European Union will be that many arrangements, which had been in place relating to how cross-border disputes and other legal issues should be resolved, will need to be the subject of special negotiation. Preliminary papers have already been published on the following issues which will particularly affect the English legal system:

- Security, law enforcement, and criminal justice, where the UK government is seeking a new partnership arrangement;
- Enforcement and dispute resolution, where the UK government is also seeking a new partnership arrangement;
- Providing a cross-border civil judicial cooperation framework;
- Dealing with ongoing judicial proceedings, in existence at the moment when the UK leaves the EU.

The outcome of discussions on these issues is not known at the time of writing. The Department for Exiting the European Union maintains a list of policy and other documents, with links to their content, at https://www.gov.uk/government/collections/article-50-and-negotiations-with-the-eu.

4.5 Other government departments

A number of other government departments are also associated with the English legal system, some more closely than others.

4.5.1 Attorney-General's Office (AGO)

The AGO exists to support the work of the Attorney-General (A-G) and the Solicitor-General. The A-G occupies an interesting though complex position in government.

Partly, the A-G acts as a kind of in-house lawyer, giving independent legal advice to government; the A-G is also ultimately responsible for the work of the Director of Public Prosecutions and the Crown Prosecution Service (*see Chapter 5*).

One function of great practical importance is that the AGO keeps an eye on sentences imposed in criminal cases, and has the power to appeal where a sentence is, in its view, too lenient. The AGO publishes annual statistics on lenient sentences.

The AGO also publishes a number of important guidance notes on aspects of the criminal justice system, for example on disclosure of evidence to the defence (*see Box 5.10*).

4.5.2 Department for Business, Energy, and Industrial Strategy (BEIS)

BEIS plays a significant role in the development of the English legal system.

For many years, it was responsible for employment law matters. This includes policy relating to employment tribunals (*see Chapter 6*). While some of these functions have moved to the Ministry of Justice, it retains an interest in employment rights as part of its remit on industrial strategy.

BEIS is also responsible for policy on consumer protection. The recent Consumer Protection Act 2015 has expanded consumers' rights, in particular where they download digital content.

BEIS has also been responsible for implementing two instruments from the EU relating to consumer disputes. The first directive creates a scheme for the provision of alternative dispute resolution (ADR). It requires all traders to have a scheme of ADR available and also sets standards for ADR providers. It came into effect on 9 July 2015.

The second regulation provides for the creation of online dispute resolution to enable disputes to be resolved online without the need for any attendance at court. This will be of particular assistance in cases where the trader and the consumer are in different countries. These new procedures have contributed to thinking in the Ministry of Justice and the Civil Justice Council as they consider reforms to the civil justice system under the *Transforming our Justice System* programme to reduce cost and improve efficiency (*see further Chapters 8 and 10*).

More generally, BEIS does much work on regulation, involving detailed consideration of existing rules and regulations, how they might be simplified, and how they can be made more effective without over-burdening industry and commerce. This is a stream of work which underpins many issues relating to civil and commercial justice (*see Chapter 8*).

Finally, BEIS provides the bulk of the funding for Citizens' Advice, a service which helps people resolve their legal, money, and other problems by providing free advice (*see also 9.8.1*).

4.5.3 Ministry of Housing, Communities, and Local Government (MHCLG)

MHCLG is responsible for a wide range of policy, including both planning and housing—both of which involve use of the administrative justice and civil justice systems (*see Chapters 6 and 8*).

The scheme of tenancy deposit protection, put in place by MHCLG under the Housing Act 2004, created processes for the online resolution of disputes about deposits arising between landlords and tenants at the end of a tenancy.

The government has very recently announced (September 2017) that MHCLG will be developing plans for the creation of a new Housing Court. No details on this proposal are currently available, although this is an idea that has been under discussion for many years.

4.5.4 Other departments

The impact of other government departments on the English legal system is less focused than the examples given earlier but is nonetheless important. For example, the Department for Education works closely with the MoJ on issues relating to family justice (*see Chapter 7*) and also on dealing with young offenders (*see Chapter 5*).

One of the great challenges for government as a whole is to ensure that, as far as possible, policy initiatives arising in one department reflect and work with (rather than against) policies arising in other departments. While the principle of a joined-up approach to the delivery of policy is broadly accepted, it is far from easy to deliver this in practice.

4.6 Key points

1. Government plays a central role in the shaping of the English legal system.
2. Political responsibility for these developments has been clarified, with the Secretary of State for Justice/Lord Chancellor answerable to Parliament.
3. There is more transparency, for example on the procedures for making judicial appointments.
4. Progress towards greater diversity in the judiciary is slow.
5. Major changes to the practice and procedures in the courts are being driven by the government's desire to reduce public expenditure.
6. The pace of change is likely to get even faster in the coming years, with major investment in IT transforming the ways in which courts and tribunals work.
7. Many of these changes are enabling new organizations to enter the justice system to supplement the work of courts and tribunals.
8. The institutional changes which will need to be put in place following Brexit have been outlined, but at present there is no detail on exactly how these will be taken forward.

4.7 Questions

Use the self-test questions in the Online Resources to test your understanding of the topics covered in this chapter and receive tailored feedback: www.oup.com/uk/partington18_19/.

4.8 Web links

Check the Online Resources for a selection of annotated web links allowing you to easily research topics of particular interest: www.oup.com/uk/partington18_19/.

4.9 Blog items

See Spotlight on the Justice System, at www.martinpartington.com/category/chapter-4-2/.

Suggestions for further reading

STEVENS, R., *The Independence of the Judiciary: The View from the Lord Chancellor's Office* (rev. edn, Oxford, Clarendon Press, 1997)

WOODHOUSE, D., *The Office of the Lord Chancellor* (Oxford, Hart Publishing, 2001)

Other suggestions are set out in the Further Reading listed in the **Online Resources**.

5

The criminal justice system

5.1 Introduction: criminal justice

Criminal law is central to the relationship between law and society. It seeks to regulate behaviour; it provides sanctions against those who break the rules. It is intimately linked with key social policy objectives, such as the maintenance of law and order and preservation of the peace, security of the individual, and the protection of property. It is also linked to other objectives, especially the protection of human rights and individual freedoms. Indeed, one of the great challenges law-makers face when thinking about the development of rules of criminal law and criminal procedure is how to achieve a proper balance between the provisions of the criminal law and the preservation of liberty and the freedom of the individual. These issues are currently seen in sharp focus in discussions about how we should respond to threats of terrorist activity. Furthermore, the boundaries of the criminal law change over time. They are not always set by the outcome of purely rational debate and argument; they also reflect the preferences and prejudices of politicians. The criminal justice system is that branch of the English legal system in which the criminal law is administered.

Any idea that the criminal justice system can be understood simply by looking at the work of the criminal courts can be quickly disabused by considering the wide range of agencies involved. They include:

- the police service;
- the Crown Prosecution Service;
- the Serious Fraud Office;
- the National Crime Agency;
- other investigating/prosecuting authorities;
- magistrates' courts;
- youth courts and the youth justice system;
- the Crown Court;
- the appeal courts;
- the Criminal Cases Review Commission;
- the National Offender Management Service;
- the prison service;

- the probation service;
- the Criminal Defence Service;
- the Criminal Injuries Compensation Scheme for victims; and
- other victim and witness care services.

Further institutional changes are in progress which are noted in context in this chapter.

Altogether, the criminal justice system affects large numbers of people.[1] It is a big employer. It consumes a great deal of public money: currently over £19 billion a year. Huge sums are spent on policing. The prison service, the probation service, and criminal legal aid also consume large amounts. These sums are not trivial; indeed the United Kingdom spends more on these issues than most other comparable countries.

Given the present government's desire to reduce public expenditure, cost reduction is central to the development of criminal justice policy. This does not necessarily mean that the work of the criminal justice system will be undermined; there may well be ways in which, by doing things differently, expenditure can be saved while efficiency is improved. What is important is that any changes made do not compromise the core values of the criminal justice system, in particular the need for procedures to be fair and for the liberty of the individual to be protected.

At the same time the public must be protected from those who would otherwise be a threat to safety and security. The efficiency of the criminal justice system—to ensure that its social objectives are met, while at the same time reducing expenditure levels— is, as in other areas of social policy, a constant challenge for government.

The criminal justice system has been the subject of much political controversy, many official inquiries, and considerable change. Nearly every year there is new legislation on some aspect of the criminal justice system. To give just a few examples: a Royal Commission on Criminal Procedure reported in 1981; a further Royal Commission on Criminal Justice reported in 1993; and a review of the criminal courts was published in 2001. In the same year, there was also a major review of sentencing policy.

The Cameron-Clegg coalition government introduced major changes to the organization and accountability of the police, with the creation of locally elected Police and Crime Commissioners, as well as cut-backs in the bureaucratic burden imposed on the police. (Her Majesty's Inspectorate of Constabulary estimates that, at present, only around 10 per cent of police are available at any one time for the delivery of frontline services to the public.) In 2017, major reform of the prison system was announced, but the Prisons Bill 2017, which would have brought the policy changes into law, fell when the General Election was called in May 2017. A replacement Bill is awaited.

Some argue that the system is loaded in favour of those accused of criminal activity and against those who are the victims of crime or, more generally, 'the interests of society at large'. This leads to calls for a rebalancing of the system in favour of victims and

---

[1] A longitudinal study carried out by the Home Office showed that 34 per cent of *all* males born in the United Kingdom in 1953 had, by 1993, received at least one conviction for a criminal offence of a more serious nature; the figure for females was 8 per cent. Reported in Taylor, R., *Forty Years of Crime and Criminal Justice Statistics, 1958–1997* (London, Home Office, Research and Development Section, 1999).

witnesses. Others strongly disagree, pointing to the serious miscarriages of justice that have occurred over the years and the need to protect individuals from wrongful involvement in the criminal justice system. In this chapter, each part of the criminal justice system is considered. First, though, we consider the social theories that underpin the system.

5.2 Theories of criminal justice

Just as the social functions of the criminal law are diverse, so too are the different social theories or models that underpin the criminal justice system.[2] From the criminological literature, a number of 'models' of the criminal justice system may be identified. These include:

(1) the *due process* model, in which the primary social goal is said to be 'justice', and the emphasis is on fairness and the rules needed to protect the accused against error and the exercise of arbitrary power;

(2) the *crime control* model, in which the primary social goal is punishment, where the focus is on ensuring that the police are able to obtain convictions in the courts;

(3) a *medical* model, in which the emphasis is on the rehabilitation of the offender, giving decision-takers discretion to achieve this;

(4) the *restorative justice* model, in which the emphasis is on getting the offender to recognize his or her responsibility in committing the offence and to make amends to the victim;

(5) the *bureaucratic* model, in which the emphasis is on the management of crime and the criminal, and the efficient processing of offenders through the system;

(6) a *status passage* model, in which the emphasis is on the denunciation and degradation of the offender, involving a shaming of the offender, reflecting society's views of the offender; and

(7) a *power* model, in which the emphasis is on the maintenance of a particular social/class order, which reinforces the values of certain classes over others.

None of these models offers a uniquely correct interpretation of the criminal justice system. The explanatory power of each model varies, depending on the person looking at the system. The defence lawyer or the defendant will take a different view from the policeman or the prosecutor, the victim, or the Home Secretary. Thinking about these models, however, both highlights the tensions that—perhaps inevitably—exist in this complex sector of the justice system, and also helps to identify assumptions that are all too often left unstated in considering developments in the criminal justice system. You should reflect on how recent developments in criminal justice fit into the models thus identified.

---

[2] The following is derived from the excellent book by King, M., *The Framework of Criminal Justice* (London, Croom Helm, 1981).

5.3 Understanding the criminal justice system

To gain any understanding of the criminal justice system, it is necessary to break the overall structure into more manageable parts. The approach here is to look at the system in three stages:

- pre-trial stages;
- trial stage; and
- post-trial stages.

Each of these is further subdivided.

5.4 Pre-trial stages

Before any alleged criminal gets anywhere near a courtroom, a number of crucial preliminary steps are taken, each of which may affect the outcome of the case, and indeed whether a case ever reaches court at all. The following analysis of the stages that an allegation of criminal activity may go through before trial provides a structure that obviously does not occur as neatly as this in practice; but it should help you to see the overall shape of the criminal justice system more clearly.

5.4.1 The committing, reporting, and recording of crime

It may be obvious that the first step in any criminal process is that some criminal act should have been *committed*. However, by itself, that is not (save in the most exceptional circumstances) sufficient to launch any kind of criminal process. Unless the offence is reported to the authorities, either by the victim or by some other person who has seen the incident or has come to realize that some criminal activity has taken place, no further action will follow (*see Box 5.1* for crime statistics).

Box 5.1 Legal system explained

Crime statistics

There are two principal sources of data on crime. The first are figures for crime recorded by the police; the second are figures derived from the Crime Survey for England and Wales (CSEW).

   As regards the former, there are at least two potential problems:

(1) As with all data, their value is dependent on the quality of the input. There is always the possibility of error in data collection and entry. Some reporting practices may distort patterns of criminality. Indeed, in 2014 there was considerable public concern about the quality of the recorded crime data.

Box 5.1 Continued

(2) The figures relate to reported and recorded crime. Many factors influence reporting and recording. For example, if insurance companies insist on theft from cars or
property being reported, this may lead to an increase in the rate of recorded crime;
conversely, a relaxation in their practices may lead to a reduction in recorded
crime.

It is not argued here that the figures for recorded crime do not reflect trends in criminality in the community. But the simplistic conclusion, often drawn in the media, that
published statistics of recorded crime represent 'the crime figures' is misleading.

The CSEW data are derived from an annual survey in which a sample of the population is interviewed about its experience of crime as well as the criminal justice system.
Although this survey by no means covers the totality of the population, the sample
of over 40,000 people is drawn on the basis of accepted practices for creating social
survey databases. The conclusion to be drawn from the *Crime Survey for England and
Wales* is that a somewhat different picture of criminality and the individual experience
of crime is presented there, compared with the picture presented by the reported
crime statistics. This is illustrated clearly in *Diagram 5.1*, which shows the gap in the
amount of crime estimated by the *Crime Survey for England and Wales* and the numbers
of crimes recorded by the police.

Diagram 5.1   Trends in recorded crime and CSEW, 1981 to year ending June 2017

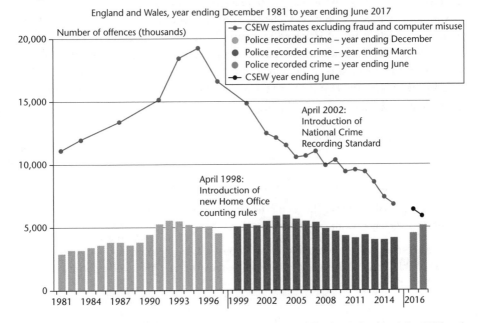

England and Wales, year ending December 1981 to year ending June 2017

Source: Crime in England and Wales, Year Ending June 2017 (London, Office for National Statistics, 2017), p. 3.

The agency to which most crime is reported is the police. But many other agencies also have criminal law enforcement responsibilities. For example:

- local authorities have responsibilities for areas like noise, environmental pollution, and public health;
- central government departments have responsibilities for investigating a wide variety of potential criminal activity—for example social security benefit fraud, tax evasion, and other types of fraudulent commercial activity;
- health and safety agencies have duties to prosecute breaches of health and safety legislation (e.g. unlawful emissions of radioactive material); and
- in rare circumstances, an individual him- or herself may commence a criminal prosecution.

Although the police is the largest single agency to which crimes are reported, the total number of criminal offences committed each year that are dealt with by bodies other than the police exceeds the total number of offences reported to the police. Nonetheless, for present purposes we concentrate on the role of the police. Research shows clearly that, if a victim of crime is unwilling to report a crime and get the police to investigate it, then in all save the gravest situations no effective further action will be taken in relation to that alleged offence.[3] The initial act of reporting is crucial.

Furthermore, if the police are perceived as being unsympathetic in any particular context, then this reduces the likelihood of alleged offences being reported. For example, some years ago the police were perceived as being unsympathetic to female victims of alleged rape. More recently, the same issue arose in the context of the 'grooming' of young girls for sexual purposes. The police changed their practices and this has been reflected in an increase in the number of recorded offences.

Another example is domestic violence. There is a widespread assumption that the police are reluctant to get involved in domestic disputes. Whether or not this perception is correct does not much matter. The number of cases of domestic violence reported to the police is considerably lower than the total number of incidents that actually take place. The Home Office estimates that, on average, a victim experiences 35 incidents of domestic violence before going to the police (*see Box 5.2*).

Box 5.2 System in action

Domestic violence: reform of law and practice

In response to the criticism that domestic violence was not taken seriously enough, the Domestic Violence, Crimes and Victims Act 2004:

- created new police powers to deal with domestic violence, including making it an arrestable, criminal offence to breach a non-molestation order, with a penalty of up to five years in prison;

---

[3] Cretney, A., and Davis, G., *Punishing Violence* (London, Routledge, 1995).

Box 5.2 Continued

- gave stronger legal protection for victims by extending the use of restraining orders—giving courts the power to impose a restraining order where the defendant has been acquitted but the court believes an order is necessary to protect the victim from harassment;
- provided for a code of practice, binding on all criminal justice agencies, so that all victims receive the support, protection, information, and advice they need;
- allowed victims to take their case to the Parliamentary Ombudsman if they feel the code had not been adhered to by the criminal justice agencies;
- set up an independent commissioner for victims to give victims a voice at the heart of government and to safeguard and promote the interests of victims and witnesses, encouraging the spread of good practice and reviewing the statutory code;
- amended the Protection from Harassment Act 1997 to ensure that victims have their say if an application is made to vary or terminate a restraining order that is protecting them from abuse or harassment;
- strengthened the civil law on domestic violence so that cohabiting same-sex couples have the same protection as heterosexual couples, and extended the availability of non-molestation orders to couples who have never lived together or have never been married; and
- created a new offence of familial homicide for causing or allowing the death of a child or vulnerable adult.

Research published in 2008 suggested that the number of domestic violence cases being reported had increased, as had the number of cases going through the courts.

The government has established a number of specialist domestic violence courts. (For a list, see www.cps.gov.uk/publications/equality/vaw/sdvc.html.) Key features of the courts include:

- trained staff with enhanced expertise in dealing with domestic violence, including magistrates specially trained in dealing with domestic violence cases;
- tailored support and advice from independent domestic violence advisers;
- multi-agency risk assessment conferences (MARAC) to provide protection for those most at risk of harm.

Additional provisions designed to protect the victims of domestic violence were included in the Crime and Security Act 2010. Instead of having to go to court to seek an injunction, the Act gives the police power to issue a domestic violence protection notice to a person who has been violent or has threatened violence, breach of which is a criminal offence. These may lead on to the making of a *domestic violence protection order* by a magistrates' court. In addition, the Act created a right to ask whether a prospective partner has a record of domestic violence. (*See also 7.8.*)

See further www.gov.uk/guidance/domestic-violence-and-abuse.

Even if an alleged offence is reported, the police may not think that there is sufficient information to justify the *recording* of the alleged incident. If the matter is not recorded, no further action will be taken. Indeed, even if a crime is both reported and recorded, no effective further action necessarily results. Many reports of petty theft, for example, are not taken further by the police—they do not have the resources to carry out the required investigations.

5.4.2 The investigation stage: police powers

Once a crime has been reported to the relevant agency (still using the police as the main example) the next stage is the investigation. In the case of major incidents this involves the consumption of considerable resources with large numbers of police spending a lot of time on an investigation. In less important cases, the investigation stage may be extremely cursory. (In many cases, the conceptually distinct processes of reporting and investigating are blurred. The police may gain intelligence that a criminal act is being planned. This leads to investigation in advance of the commission of the offence. If the offence is committed, the preliminary intelligence-gathering may also result in the gathering of sufficient evidence to justify the arrest of the person or persons concerned and their being charged with the commission of an offence.)

To enable criminal investigators to do their work, they are given special powers. In the case of the police, these are found in the Police and Criminal Evidence Act 1984 (PACE). The statutory powers of the police are supplemented by important *codes of practice*, which should also be observed by the police (*see Box 5.3*).

Box 5.3 Legal system explained

PACE codes of practice

There are eight codes of practice:

- Code A on Powers of Stop and Search;
- Code B on Search and Seizure;
- Code C on Detention, Treatment, and Questioning of Persons;
- Code D on the Identification of Persons;
- Code E on Tape Recording;
- Code F on Visual Recording of Interviews;
- Code G on the Statutory Power of Arrest by Police Officers; and
- Code H on the Detention and Questioning of those Suspected of Terrorism.

The codes have also been adapted to apply to immigration officers in their work for the UK Border Agency.

Originally, there were just five codes, but they have been revised and added to over the years. Full details of all the current codes including recent amendments are available at www.gov.uk/guidance/police-and-criminal-evidence-act-1984-pace-codes-of-practice. This site also provides a link to a consultation on further amendments to be introduced in 2018.

The principal powers enabling the police to carry out their functions are:

- the power to stop and search;
- the power to arrest and detain;
- the power to question; and
- the power to enter and search premises.

The precise order in which these powers are used in any particular case naturally depends on the circumstances. The extent of police powers, how they are interpreted and applied by the police, and the balance between those powers and the liberty of the individual are constant sources of controversy.

5.4.2.1 Stop and search

The powers of the police to stop and search people or vehicles are contained in section 1 of the PACE. The law provides that a constable must have reasonable grounds for believing that, by exercising his or her powers, stolen goods; an offensive weapon; a knife or other bladed or sharply pointed article; articles adapted for use in burglary, theft, or obtaining by deception; or a vehicle that has been taken without authority will be found.

These general powers are supplemented by many other powers to stop and search to be found in other specific Acts of Parliament—for example relating to terrorism, drugs, firearms, or alcohol at sporting events.

Thus, under section 43(1) of the Terrorism Act 2000 a constable may stop and search a person whom the officer reasonably suspects to be a terrorist to discover whether the person is in possession of anything that may constitute evidence that the person is a terrorist. These searches may only be carried out by an officer of the same sex as the person searched.

Section 60 of the Criminal Justice and Public Order Act 1994 created an extensive power to stop and search 'in anticipation of violence'. However, this power may not be exercised unless a police superintendent has authorized its use in a particular locality. It is this power that causes most difficulty in practice.

In exercising these powers, the police must follow procedures set down in section 2 of the PACE, which, among other things, requires the officer to give his or her name, state why the search is taking place, and record that the stop and search has occurred (unless this is not practicable). The details of what must be recorded, criticized for being overly bureaucratic, were reduced following enactment of the Crime and Security Act 2010.

The language of the legislation gives considerable scope to individual police officers to decide whether or not the conditions for carrying out a stop and search are met. The exercise of the power has been controversial, in particular because of evidence that people from ethnic minorities are significantly more likely to be stopped and searched than those from majority white communities (*see Box 5.4*).

Box 5.4 Reform in progress

Stop and search

Following the widespread riots that swept London and other major cities in the summer of 2011, there were claims that one of the reasons why there was considerable distrust in many communities—especially ethnic minority communities—of the police arose from the use of stop and search powers. In December 2011 the Home Secretary commissioned Her Majesty's Inspectorate of Constabulary (HMIC) to carry out an inspection into the use of stop and search legislation in all 43 Home Office-funded forces in England and Wales.

At the beginning of July 2013, the Home Secretary announced that she wanted to hold a consultation on the use of these powers. There was no suggestion that the powers would be abolished. The consultation was designed to get views from the public about how they should be used.

Just a few days later, HMIC published its report. It was very critical of police practice. The headlines were:

(1) Over a million stop and search encounters have been recorded every year since 2006; but in 2011/12 only 9 per cent led to arrests ... While there is much public debate about the disproportionate use of the powers on black and minority ethnic people, there has to date been surprisingly little attention paid—by either the police service or the public—to how effective the use of stop and search powers is in preventing and detecting crime.

(2) The inspection, which included a public survey of over 19,000 people, found that:

  (a) the majority of forces (30) had not developed an understanding of how to use the powers of stop and search so that they are effective in preventing and detecting crime, with too many forces not collecting sufficient information to assess whether or not the use of the powers had been effective;

  (b) 27 per cent of the 8,783 stop and search records examined by HMIC did not include sufficient grounds to justify the lawful use of the power. The reasons for this include: poor understanding amongst officers about what constitutes the 'reasonable grounds' needed to justify a search, poor supervision, and an absence of direction and oversight by senior officers;

  (c) there is high public support for the use of these powers, but this support diminishes when there is a perception that the police are 'overusing' them; and

  (d) half of forces did nothing to understand the impact that stop and search had on communities, and less than half complied with the requirements of the Police and Criminal Evidence Act 1984 code of practice to make arrangements for stop and search records to be scrutinized by the public.

(3) HMIC concluded that the priority chief officers give to improving the use of stop and search powers has slipped since the publication of the Stephen Lawrence Inquiry Report in 1999.

Box 5.4 Continued

In April 2014, the College of Policing and the Home Office published its *Best Use of Stop and Search* scheme, which police forces have now signed up to. The features of the scheme are:

- data recording—forces will record the broader range of stop and search outcomes, e.g. arrests, cautions, penalty notices for disorder, and all other disposal types. Forces will also show the link, or lack of one, between the object of the search and its outcome;
- lay observation policies—providing the opportunity for members of the local community to accompany police officers on patrol using stop and search;
- stop and search complaints 'community trigger'—a local complaints policy requiring the police to explain to local community scrutiny groups how the powers are being used where there is a large volume of complaints;
- reducing section 60 'no-suspicion' stop and searches by: raising the level of authorization to senior officer (above the rank of chief superintendent); ensuring that section 60 stop and search is only used where it is deemed necessary, and making this clear to the public;
- in anticipation of serious violence, the authorizing officer *must* reasonably believe that an incident involving serious violence will take place rather than *may* take place;
- limiting the duration of initial authorizations to no more than 15 hours (down from 24); and
- communicating to local communities when there is a section 60 authorization in advance (where practicable) and afterwards, so that the public is kept informed of the purpose and success of the operation.

The new scheme can be accessed at www.gov.uk/government/publications/best-use-of-stop-and-search-scheme. In 2016, this was supplemented by a statement of Authorised Professional Practice, available at www.app.college.police.uk/app-content/stop-and-search/.

Information about the HMIC report is available at www.justiceinspectorates.gov.uk/hmic/publications/stop-and-search-powers-20130709/.

The Ministry of Justice publishes annual statistics on race and the criminal justice system, which include an analysis of information about the use of stop and search powers. This shows that members of ethnic minorities are stopped and searched far more than those from the white majority. However, and although somewhat inconclusive, there is some evidence that if the police take a 'softly, softly' approach to stop and search, levels of crime rise. What is clear is that, while the power is an important one, it must be used sensibly if it is not to exacerbate local community feelings and make the task of policing harder.

5.4.2.2 Arrest

Broadly, there are two types of arrest—with warrant, and without warrant:

- An arrest *with warrant* occurs under the authority of a warrant issued by a magistrate. A warrant may be issued after information has been given to the magistrate, on oath, that the person named has or is suspected of having committed an offence.

- There are a number of powers to arrest *without a warrant*. Section 24 of the PACE has been amended by the Serious Organised Crime and Police Act 2005 to provide that the police have a general power to arrest without warrant persons who have committed or are suspected of committing an offence and that it is necessary that the person should be arrested without a warrant. One of the following reasons must be present: (1) to enable the name of the person in question to be ascertained; (2) also the person's address; (3) to prevent the person causing or suffering, or causing loss of or damage to property, or committing an offence against public decency;[4] or causing an unlawful obstruction of the highway; (4) to protect a child or other vulnerable person; (5) to allow prompt and effective investigation of the offence or of the conduct of the person in question; (6) to prevent the disappearance of the person in question.

- The amended law also clarifies the circumstances in which an ordinary citizen may make an arrest. The exercise of the citizen's power of arrest is limited to arresting those committing or suspected of committing an indictable offence.

In addition, there are a number of specific powers to arrest without warrant under particular Acts of Parliament, for example the Mental Health Act 1983. Lastly, there is a common law power to arrest where a breach of the peace is taking place or is reasonably anticipated.

For an arrest to take place without a warrant, the person making the arrest must make it clear, by words or action, that the person arrested is under compulsion. The person arrested must be informed of the ground for the arrest, either at the time of arrest or as soon as possible thereafter, for example where it is not practicable to provide the information before the person to be arrested tries to run away. There is no legal power simply to detain persons for questioning without first making an arrest. (When one hears that a person is 'helping the police with their inquiries', this is an indication that he or she has not been arrested, but is attending the police station 'voluntarily'.)

An arrest is the first stage in a process that may eventually lead to a criminal trial. Research suggests that, despite the legal framework created by the PACE, a very large number of arrests lead to no further action being taken. This raises the question of the extent to which police practice on arrest conforms to the legal rules relating to arrest.

5.4.2.3 Detention

Once a person has been arrested, that person may be detained in a police station to enable further investigation (including questioning of the person) to be carried out. The PACE contains detailed provisions to regulate the time a person can be detained in custody. Under Part IV of the Act (as amended), arrangements must be made for a staff custody officer, usually a police officer, to keep the detention under review. The police have, in general, 24 hours in which they must either charge the arrested person with an offence or release the person, either with or without bail. Exceptionally, authorization for detention without charge for up to 36 hours may be given.

---

[4] This applies only where members of the public going about their normal business cannot reasonably be expected to avoid the person in question.

In the context of responses to terrorist events, there are now special powers to detain those suspected of terrorism offences for longer periods. These are said by the police and other investigating agencies to be needed in order that they can complete essential inquiries. Opponents of these measures argue that they are unnecessarily draconian, and likely to create more problems than they resolve. Currently the period of detention without charge is up to 14 days, though with the possibility of extending the time to 28 days in an emergency (Protection of Freedoms Act 2012, *see 3.5.1.3*). Because powers to detain without either charge or trial are so exceptional, PACE Code H was introduced in July 2006 to regulate police practice in this area.

Once charged, the person may be further detained but must be brought before a magistrates' court as soon as practicable. The magistrates decide whether the person can then be released on bail or remanded in custody.

Part V of the PACE, supplemented by Code C, sets out detailed provisions for the treatment of those who have been detained. Usually, a person detained is entitled to have someone informed of that fact, and to have access to legal advice, which gives the right to consult a solicitor privately at any time. There are powers to delay these rights where this is thought necessary, for example to prevent evidence being destroyed. The statutory rules and code also set out in detail the physical conditions in which people should be detained; these include details about the provision of drinks and refreshment.

The Criminal Justice Act 2003 extended the powers of the police to enable them to take fingerprints and a DNA sample from a person while in police detention following arrest. Fingerprints can now be taken electronically. Thus the police can confirm in a few minutes the identity of a suspect where that person's fingerprints are already held on the national fingerprint database. This prevents persons who may be wanted for other matters avoiding detection by giving the police a false name and address. Fingerprints taken under this provision can also be subject to a speculative search across the crime scene database to see if they are linked to any unsolved crime.

The DNA profile of an arrested person is loaded onto the national DNA database. It can also be subject to a speculative search to see whether it matches a crime scene stain already held on the database. Both these powers can assist the police in the detection and prevention of crime. Currently, the database holds information on just over 5 per cent of the population. A senior judge suggested that all citizens should be required to provide a DNA sample for the national database, arguing that this would help the innocent as much as the wrongdoer; this was fiercely criticized by civil liberty groups. The Coalition government introduced new rules relating to the destruction of DNA data, to reduce the amount of information retained (Protection of Freedoms Act 2012, *see 3.6.1*).

5.4.2.4 Questioning

The power to question suspects detained by the police is the subject of detailed guidance in Code C. The police regard the power to question as crucial. Questioning often leads to the suspect providing a confession. This leads to considerable savings later in the criminal process, as most of those confessing plead guilty.

Two types of confession raise particular problems: 'induced' confessions, and false confessions.

Induced confessions are, as the name implies, confessions that have arisen from the police offering inducements to the suspect to confess—for example, early release on bail or the suggestion that a confession may lead to less serious charges being made against the alleged criminal, or that in some other way the outcome will be less serious than it would otherwise be. Such inducements can colour the reliability of the confession.

Rules of evidence that apply in court are designed to ensure that induced confessions are not made, by preventing the evidence obtained from them from being presented in court. Many police practices, for example the tape recording of interviews or the requirement to issue a formal caution to those who may be charged with an offence, are designed to eliminate improper police behaviour. However, it seems unlikely that the police will never seek to induce a confession, for example in a location where there are no tape recorders. Furthermore, the present form of the 'caution'[5] provides some incentive to people to make statements at an early stage.

False confessions are more problematic. Contrary to common sense and expectation, there have been cases where a person being questioned by the police has confessed to a crime that he or she has not in fact committed. This can arise from the very considerable psychological pressure that people are under when detained in a police station. This was one of the issues that led to the establishment of the Royal Commission on Criminal Evidence and Procedure in 1979.[6]

5.4.2.5 Entering and searching premises

The last general power available to the police (and other crime investigation agencies) is the power to enter and search premises for evidence, and where relevant to seize that evidence. Many specific Acts of Parliament create power to grant warrants to the police for particular purposes, for example investigating drugs offences or theft. Section 8 of the PACE (as amended by the Serious Organised Crime and Police Act 2005) creates a general power enabling magistrates to grant warrants to search for evidence relating to a serious arrestable offence. A warrant may relate to specific premises, or more generally to all premises controlled by an individual. As with other police powers, these statutory provisions are supplemented by statutory safeguards and Code B. Certain types of material are excluded from this provision, for example items subject to legal privilege (principally, communications containing legal advice from a professional legal adviser to his or her client) and certain other categories of excluded material, for example personal records and journalistic records. (There is a procedure whereby a circuit judge may be asked to make an order granting access to such material or, in an extreme case, to grant a warrant to search for this sort of material (see section 9 of and Schedule 1 to the PACE).)

---

[5] 'You do not have to say anything. But it may harm your defence if you do not mention when questioned something which you later rely on in court. Anything you do say may be given in evidence.' This form of words provoked much criticism when introduced, as it was argued that it undermined the right of silence, one of the principal sources of protection for the accused.

[6] See Irving, B., *Police Interrogation: A Study of Current Practice* (Research Study No. 2 for the Royal Commission on Criminal Procedure) (London, Her Majesty's Stationery Office, 1980).

There are also circumstances where the police are empowered to enter and search premises without a warrant: for example, to arrest someone suspected of committing an arrestable offence, or to save life and limb, or to prevent serious damage to property (see section 17 of the PACE).

5.4.3 Comment on police powers

There can be no doubting the powers that the police have over the ordinary citizen. The range of powers may be seen as a sensible code, enabling the police to go about their business of investigating crime and catching suspects. Nevertheless, there are always concerns, backed by specific examples of police malpractice, which reveal that some police act beyond the powers given to them. This in turn means that further controls on police behaviour to prevent the exercise of powers beyond the legally prescribed limits are essential.

Where examples of the planting of evidence or the use of oppressive questioning techniques are demonstrated, some critics argue that use of illegally obtained evidence is endemic to police practice. Others, including the police themselves, argue that such abuses are simply the result of individual 'rotten apples', and that, so long as steps are taken to remove them, the basic activities of the police are undertaken within both the letter and the spirit of the law.

The police who fail to act within the scope of their legal powers may be the subject of internal disciplinary proceedings, or worse. Potentially, the most effective deterrent against breaking the rules arises from the fact that any evidence obtained improperly may not be able to be given in court. As the police know that during the investigative/information-gathering stage these rules of evidence will be applied should a case reach court and be contested, the rules should shape the ways in which evidence is obtained by the police. However, as is noted later, the law of evidence gives judges considerable discretion as to whether or not evidence should be excluded. The practical consequences of bending or ignoring the questioning rules are not always predictable.

As in other aspects of professional and public life, there is now much more formal accountability than was the case some years ago. The overall efficiency of police forces is the responsibility of Her Majesty's Inspectorate of Constabulary and Fire and Rescue Services. The creation of the Independent Police Complaints Commission (from January 2018, the Independent Office for Police Conduct) resulted in new mechanisms for individuals to pursue grievances against the police. In addition, each year a number of cases against the police are brought before the courts by individuals, for example seeking damages for false imprisonment or compensation for damage to property.

Suggestions, made by some, that police activity is characterized by wholesale malpractice and corruption are not justified. Many who have incidental brushes with the police find they operate strictly according to the book and in a perfectly proper fashion. However, it is also true that there are more circumstances than those that hit the headlines in which the police do not behave strictly according to the rule book. The College of Policing was created in part to address public concerns (*see Box 5.5*).

Box 5.5 Reform in progress

The College of Policing

In December 2012, the College of Policing was created, and it is given statutory recognition in the Anti-social Behaviour Crime and Policing Act 2014. It is an independent body with a mission to set standards for the police service on training, development, skills, and qualifications, and to help the service implement these standards. The reason for the creation of the College lies in a number of difficult issues that have affected police forces in recent years which led to falls in public trust in the ability of the police to work effectively and fairly in carrying out its work.

The College has set itself ambitious aims. For example, it is seeking to extend its networks beyond the traditional boundaries of policing—to include the public, further and higher education, the private sector, charitable organizations, and the wider public sector—and make the most of all opportunities to work with others to support policing.

It wants to create open and transparent development opportunities for police officers and staff at all levels. These include:

- being part of a network with local academic institutions to gather evidence and test new approaches;
- participating in a community of practice;
- providing peer support to share experiences;
- working in the College or with one of its partner organizations to gain new skills and knowledge, while sharing learning and experience.

It has recently been proposed that the police service should move towards becoming an all-graduate profession.

One of the first actions of the new College was to develop and publish a new Code of Ethics for the police service (similar in aim to codes of ethical practice which apply to most professional groups). The Code was published in July 2014. See www.college.police.uk/What-we-do/Ethics/Pages/Code-of-Ethics.aspx.

For further information see my blog, www.martinpartington.com, October 2014.

5.4.4 Next steps

On completing the first two stages, the police have a number of choices. They may:

- take no further action, for example where insufficient evidence has been obtained;
- give an informal warning;
- issue a simple caution (for adults) or youth caution (for youths) from a senior police officer—this should only follow an admission of guilt and informed consent by the offender (or his or her parents or guardian in the case of a juvenile);
- exercising powers under the Criminal Justice Act 2003, issue a conditional caution (*see Box 5.6* for more information on cautions);

- refer the papers to the prosecuting authorities for a decision on whether to charge the person with having committed a particular offence, or charge the alleged offender themselves. Under the DPP's *Guidance on Charging*, published in 2013, the majority of charging decisions for less serious offences are still taken by the police. It is estimated that the Crown Prosecution Service is responsible for fewer than 30 per cent of charging decisions.

Box 5.6 System in action

Simple and conditional cautions

Simple cautions provide the police and Crown Prosecution Service with an alternative means for dealing with low-level, mainly first-time offending when specified public interest and eligibility criteria are met.

Guidance from the Ministry of Justice, published in April 2013, notes that simple cautions form part of an offender's criminal record and may be used in future proceedings and, in certain circumstances, may be made available to an employer as part of a criminal record check. Offenders must be made aware of this before agreeing to accept a simple caution. The Youth Justice Board has issued guidance in relation to youth cautions.

Following a review of the use of simple cautions undertaken in 2013, the Secretary of State for Justice announced in September 2013 that such cautions should no longer be available for indictable only offences and certain serious either way offences involving possession of a knife, offensive weapon, or firearm in a public place; offences involving child sex abuse or child pornography; and supplying Class A drugs. Exceptions will be made in certain cases and where a senior officer, as well as the Crown Prosecution Service if necessary, approves of their use.

Conditional cautions may be given where there is sufficient evidence to charge a suspect with an offence which he or she admits, and the suspect agrees to the caution. In such cases, the Crown Prosecution Service usually decides whether a conditional caution is appropriate, which the police administer. Under the Legal Aid, Sentencing and Punishment of Offenders Act 2012, police are given power to issue conditional cautions without reference to a prosecutor.

If the suspect fails to comply with the conditions, he or she is liable to be prosecuted for the offence. A code of practice relating to conditional cautions was published by the Ministry of Justice in April 2013. The conditions that may be used in this context may be:

- reparative (such as writing a letter of apology; repairing damage; paying compensation or undertaking unpaid work in the community, if the public or the wider community are the victim; mediation between the offender and the victim);
- rehabilitative (attendance at drug or alcohol awareness sessions in an effort to halt the causes of the offending behaviour); or
- restrictive (not to approach a particular area or person) if the restriction supports reparation or rehabilitation.

Youth conditional cautions are the subject of guidance from the Youth Justice Board.

In addition to cautions, the police also use penalty notices for disorder, cannabis and khat warnings, and non-statutory community resolution.

Box 5.6 Continued

At the end of 2014, the government announced that it was launching a new pilot scheme that would significantly change the way in which out-of-court disposals are dealt with. The scheme—which did not affect penalty notices for disorder—comprises:

- a new *statutory community resolution*—aimed at first-time offenders.;
- a *suspended prosecution*—designed to tackle more serious offending.

Under this new two-tier framework, offenders would have to take steps to comply with the disposal, rather than just accepting a warning. If they failed to comply, they would risk being prosecuted for the original offence. The pilot scheme was operating in three police areas for 12 months and was to be assessed before a decision was taken on whether to roll out the new framework nationally. To date no such decision has been made.

Cautions are used quite extensively to divert potential cases from the courts, though their use has declined over the last 10 years. They are controversial, because they can lead to an individual having a criminal record without ever having appeared in court.

Sources: Links to the guidance documents and other information on out-of-court disposals can be found at www.gov.uk/government/publications/penalty-notices-for-disorder-guidance-for-police-officers.

For details of the pilot scheme see www.gov.uk/government/news/putting-an-end-to-soft-option-cautions.

Diagram 5.2 Use of out-of-court disposals March 2007 to March 2017

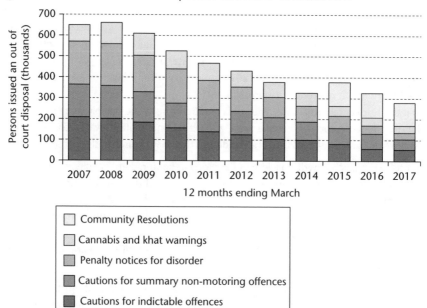

Source: www.gov.uk/government/statistics/criminal-justice-statistics-quarterly-march-2017 Figure 2.

For more information about the use of out-of-court disposals, *see Diagram 5.2*.

In practice, very many reported and recorded crimes are dealt with in the first four of the ways listed earlier. It is statistically much more likely that a case will end at this point and not proceed to formal prosecution. Those who argue that the criminal justice system should be based on the 'due process' model should realize that, in the majority of cases, the formal protections of that model are effectively not available to the accused.

If a person is charged with an offence, a further decision must be taken whether the person charged is to be detained in custody or released on bail (*see Box 5.7*).

Box 5.7 Legal system explained

Bail or custody

A fundamental principle of criminal justice is that a person is deemed to be innocent until proved guilty. It is wrong to deny an innocent person his liberty. Yet the real world suggests some accused of crime are simply too dangerous to be allowed to remain at liberty until any case against them has been determined. They must be remanded in custody, either for their own good or for the good of society at large.

Decisions about whether to release persons on bail (i.e. subject to a requirement that they surrender to custody at a specified time and place) can be taken at any stage in the criminal trial process until the final determination of the last appeal. Thus bail may be granted by the police, magistrates' courts, Crown Courts, the High Court, and the Court of Appeal (Criminal Division). The granting of bail, by whichever agency is involved, is subject to principles laid down in the Bail Act 1976. The Act creates a statutory presumption that bail should be granted unless specified circumstances exist that mean that bail should not be granted. These make it easier to remand in custody persons charged with an offence that may result in a sentence of imprisonment than those charged with one which would not.

In some cases, the presumption is reversed. For example, following the passing of the Criminal Justice Act 2003, there is a presumption that bail will not be granted for a person aged 18 or over who is charged with an imprisonable offence, and tests positive for a specified Class A drug, if he or she refuses to undergo an assessment as to his or her dependency or propensity to misuse such drugs, or, following an assessment, refuses any relevant follow-up action recommended, unless the court is satisfied that there is no significant risk of his reoffending on bail. Also, when deciding whether to grant bail in respect of an offence which appears to have been committed while the defendant was on bail for another offence, courts are required to give particular weight to that fact when assessing the risk that (if granted bail) the defendant may commit further offences.

Under the Legal Aid, Sentencing and Punishment of Offenders Act 2012, the law was further altered, by restricting the court's powers to remand adult unconvicted defendants in custody where it is apparent that there is no real prospect that the defendant would receive a custodial sentence if convicted. A court is still able to remand in custody for the defendant's own protection, or where there was a risk of further offending involving domestic violence.

Box 5.7 Continued

In practice, the vast majority of those against whom criminal proceedings are taken are granted bail. Nevertheless, there are those who argue that bail is granted too readily. In particular, there is disquiet about the numbers of crimes committed by people while they are out on bail. Notwithstanding these fears and the apparent policy of the Bail Act 1976, numbers of those remanded in custody awaiting trial or sentencing or an appeal have increased sharply over the years and have exacerbated the problem of prison overcrowding. This has led policy-makers to consider other options, such as the electronic tagging of defendants so that the authorities can keep track of those persons even though they have not been detained in custody.

There are two types of bail: conditional bail and unconditional bail.

Conditional bail

The police and courts can impose any requirements needed to make sure that defendants attend court and do not commit offences or interfere with witnesses while on bail. Conditions can also be imposed for the defendant's own protection or welfare (where he or she is a child or young person). Common conditions include: not going within a certain distance of a witness's house, or being subject to a curfew. If a defendant is reported or believed to have broken a bail condition, he or she can be arrested and brought before a magistrates' court, which may then place the person in custody.

Unconditional bail

If the police or court think that the defendant is unlikely to commit further offences, will attend court when required, and will not interfere with the justice process, he or she is usually released on unconditional bail.

Breach of bail

Defendants who do not stick to their bail conditions, or fail to attend court on the set date, are in breach of bail. They are liable to be arrested and may have their bail withdrawn. They may be remanded in custody and might not get bail in the future. Failing to appear at court as required is a criminal offence and they can also be prosecuted for this offence.

Time limits on bail

While the rules for the time a person can be held in a police station for questioning are quite strict, the same did not apply to the time a person can be on bail before being charged. In 2015, the then Home Secretary Theresa May announced her intention to limit the time spent on bail to 28 days in the first instance, with power to extend to three months, and then only if one of four defined conditions was satisfied. The issue is dealt with in Part 4 of the Policing and Crime Act 2017.[7]

---

[7] See my blog, www.martinpartington.com, February 2017.

5.4.5 The decision to prosecute

Once the decision to charge a person with an offence has been taken, the case is taken forward by the prosecution authorities. The principal prosecution authority is the Crown Prosecution Service (CPS). The CPS is a public service, headed by the Director of Public Prosecutions (DPP), answerable to Parliament through the Attorney-General. It was established in 1986 under the Prosecution of Offences Act 1985.

Before then, the decision to charge and to prosecute was usually taken by the police themselves. This led to the criticism that, in some cases that had involved miscarriages of justice, the interrelation of investigation and prosecution had resulted in the police inappropriately exercising their powers to prosecute. The Royal Commission on Criminal Procedure 1981 recommended a separation of the investigation and prosecution functions to introduce an element of independence into the latter.

The CPS is a national service, delivered at a local level by 13 areas across England and Wales. Each area is led by a Chief Crown Prosecutor (CCP). A 'virtual' 14th area, CPS Direct, is a telephone service, also headed by a CCP, which provides out-of-hours charging decisions to the police. In addition, three specialist casework divisions (Central Fraud, Serious Crime and Welfare, Rural and Health) deal with the prosecution of cases investigated by Her Majesty's Revenue and Customs, the National Crimes Agency, the UK Border Agency, the Department for Environment, Food and Rural Affairs, the Department for Work and Pensions, and the Department of Health.

The basic procedure is that, after the police have investigated a crime and an alleged offender has been charged, the case papers are passed to one of the CPS lawyers—a Crown Prosecutor—who reviews the papers to decide whether or not to go ahead with the case. The Prosecutor's decision is based on two tests set out in the Code for Crown Prosecutors (*see Box 5.8*), the latest edition of which was published in 2013. There is much public ignorance about these tests.

Box 5.8 Legal system explained

Code for Crown Prosecutors: the decision to prosecute

Crown Prosecutors make charging decisions in accordance with the full code test, other than in those limited circumstances where the threshold test applies. The threshold test applies to cases where it is proposed to keep the suspect in custody after charge, but the evidence required to apply the full code test is not yet available. Where a Crown Prosecutor makes a charging decision in accordance with the threshold test, the case must be reviewed in accordance with the full code test as soon as reasonably practicable, taking into account the progress of the investigation.

The full code test has two stages: evidential, and public interest.

The evidential stage

Prosecutors must be satisfied that there is sufficient evidence to provide a realistic prospect of conviction against each suspect on each charge. They must consider what the defence

Box 5.8 Continued

case may be, and how it is likely to affect the prospects of conviction. A case which does not pass the evidential stage must not proceed, no matter how serious or sensitive it may be.

The finding that there is a realistic prospect of conviction is based on the prosecutor's objective assessment of the evidence, including the impact of any defence and any other information that the suspect has put forward or on which he or she might rely. It means that an objective, impartial, and reasonable jury or bench of magistrates or judge hearing a case alone, properly directed and acting in accordance with the law, is more likely than not to convict the defendant of the charge alleged. This is a different test from the one that the criminal courts themselves must apply. A court may only convict if it is sure that the defendant is guilty.

When deciding whether there is sufficient evidence to prosecute, prosecutors should ask themselves the following:

- *Can the evidence be used in court?* Prosecutors should consider whether there is any question over the admissibility of certain evidence. In doing so, prosecutors should assess: (a) the likelihood of that evidence being held as inadmissible by the court; and (b) the importance of that evidence in relation to the evidence as a whole (*see 5.5.1.2*).
- *Is the evidence reliable?* Prosecutors should consider whether there are any reasons to question the reliability of the evidence, including its accuracy or integrity.
- *Is the evidence credible?* Prosecutors should consider whether there are any reasons to doubt the credibility of the evidence.

The public interest stage

In every case where there is sufficient evidence to justify a prosecution, prosecutors must go on to consider whether a prosecution is required in the public interest. It has never been the rule that a prosecution will automatically take place once the evidential stage is met. A prosecution will usually take place unless the prosecutor is satisfied that there are public interest factors tending against prosecution which outweigh those tending in favour. In some cases the prosecutor may be satisfied that the public interest can be properly served by offering the offender the opportunity to have the matter dealt with by an out-of-court disposal rather than bringing a prosecution.

When deciding the public interest, prosecutors should consider each of the questions set out in what follows so as to identify and determine the relevant public interest factors tending for and against prosecution. These factors, together with any public interest factors set out in relevant guidance or policy issued by the DPP, should enable prosecutors to form an overall assessment of the public interest.

The explanatory text below each question provides guidance to prosecutors when addressing each particular question. The questions identified are not exhaustive, and not all the questions may be relevant in every case. The weight to be attached to each of the questions, and the factors identified, will also vary according to the facts and merits of each case. It is quite possible that one public interest factor alone may outweigh a number of other factors which tend in the opposite direction.

Prosecutors should consider each of the following questions:

(1) *How serious is the offence committed?* The more serious the offence, the more likely it is that a prosecution is required.

Box 5.8 Continued

(2) *What is the level of culpability of the suspect?* The greater the suspect's level of culpability, the more likely it is that a prosecution is required. Culpability is likely to be determined by the suspect's level of involvement; the extent to which the offending was premeditated and/or planned; whether they have previous criminal convictions and/or out-of-court disposals and any offending while on bail or while subject to a court order; whether the offending was or is likely to be continued, repeated, or escalated; and the suspect's age or maturity.

(3) *What are the circumstances of and the harm caused to the victim?* The circumstances of the victim are highly relevant. The greater the vulnerability of the victim, the more likely it is that a prosecution is required. This includes where a position of trust or authority exists between the suspect and victim. A prosecution is also more likely if the offence has been committed against a victim who was at the time a person serving the public. Prosecutors must also have regard to whether the offence was motivated by any form of discrimination against the victim's ethnic or national origin, gender, disability, age, religion or belief, sexual orientation, or gender identity; or the suspect demonstrated hostility towards the victim based on any of those characteristics. Prosecutors should take into account the views expressed by the victim about the impact that the offence has had. In appropriate cases, this may also include the views of the victim's family.

(4) *Was the suspect under the age of 18 at the time of the offence?* The criminal justice system treats children and young people differently from adults and significant weight must be attached to the age of the suspect if they are a child or young person under 18. The best interests and welfare of the child or young person must be considered, including whether a prosecution is likely to have an adverse impact on his or her future prospects that is disproportionate to the seriousness of the offending. As a starting point, the younger the suspect, the less likely it is that a prosecution is required. However, there may be circumstances which mean that, notwithstanding the fact that the suspect is under 18, a prosecution is in the public interest.

(5) *What is the impact on the community?* The greater the impact of the offending on the community, the more likely it is that a prosecution is required.

(6) *Is prosecution a proportionate response?* Prosecutors should also consider whether prosecution is proportionate to the likely outcome, and in so doing the following may be relevant to the case under consideration:

   (a) The cost to the CPS and the wider criminal justice system.

   (b) Cases should be capable of being prosecuted in a way that is consistent with principles of effective case management.

(7) *Do sources of information require protecting?* In cases where public interest immunity does not apply, special care should be taken when proceeding with a prosecution where details may need to be made public that could harm sources of information, international relations, or national security. It is essential that such cases are kept under continuing review.

Source: Adapted from the Code for Crown Prosecutors (London, Crown Prosecution Service, 2013). The full text is at www.cps.gov.uk/publications/code_for_crown_prosecutors/.

Notwithstanding the general approach of the CPS, there are still cases where the CPS comes under heavy criticism, either from the police or from a victim (or his or her family). Particular problems arise in very emotive cases, which may have attracted considerable media publicity, where therefore there is a great pressure to prosecute, but where the evidence to satisfy the tests sketched out earlier may just not be there. In making its decisions, the CPS cannot always reach conclusions that attract universal approval.

One particularly controversial issue relates to assisted suicides. Where a person has assisted a person, often an elderly loved one with a terminal illness, to end his or her life, the question arises whether that person should face prosecution, either for murder or manslaughter. While the law on unlawful killing may be clearly in favour of prosecution, compassion for the victim and his or her assistant may work the other way. In February 2010, the DPP issued specific guidance on when it would and when it would not be in the public interest to bring prosecutions in such cases (see www.cps.gov.uk/publications/prosecution/assisted_suicide.html).

Two other topics have recently been aired: the *right to review*; and *deferred prosecution agreements*.

First, historically, when the CPS decided not to proceed with a prosecution, that was the end of the matter. The courts were clearly unhappy about this. In June 2011, the Court of Appeal, in *R v Christopher Killick* [2011] EWCA Crim 1608, considered in some detail the right of a victim of crime to seek a review of a CPS decision not to prosecute. It concluded that:

- a victim has a right to seek a review;
- a victim should not have to seek recourse to judicial review;
- the right to a review should be the subject of a clear procedure and guidance with time limits.

The CPS created the *Victim's Right to Review Scheme* to give effect to the principles laid down in *Killick* and also to meet Article 10 of the European Union Directive establishing minimum standards on the rights, support, and protection of victims of crime. Between 1 April 2014 and 31 March 2015, the CPS reviewed 1,674 cases, and decisions in 1,464 of those cases were found to be correct. In total, 210 decisions were overturned, which accounts for 0.17 per cent of all qualifying decisions finalized in the period.

The Code for Prosecutors also sets out reasons where a case may be re-opened. These include:

(1) cases where a new look at the original decision shows that it was wrong and, in order to maintain confidence in the criminal justice system, a prosecution should be brought despite the earlier decision;

(2) cases which are stopped so that more evidence (which is likely to become available in the fairly near future) can be collected and prepared. In these cases, the prosecutor will tell the defendant that the prosecution may well start again;

(3) cases which are stopped because of a lack of evidence but where more significant evidence is discovered later; and

(4) cases involving a death in which a review following the findings of an inquest concludes that a prosecution should be brought, notwithstanding any earlier decision not to prosecute.

Secondly, in cases involving serious economic crime, experience in the United States suggests that investigations may be assisted if deferred prosecution agreements can be reached, whereby alleged offenders are charged, but proceedings are suspended while the alleged offender assists the prosecution authorities with the provision of essential information. Such agreements have become possible as the result of a provision in the Crime and Courts Act 2013. The new scheme was started in February 2014. To date, three investigations have been dealt with on this basis.[8]

5.4.5.1 Monitoring

In 1996 an inspectorate was established to monitor the quality and consistency of decision-taking across the country, and to try to ensure the spread of good practice. The inspectorate, originally created by executive action, now operates under the Crown Prosecution Service Inspectorate Act 2000. Much of the work of the inspectorate is undertaken in conjunction with other criminal justice inspectorates (*see Box 5.24*).

5.5 The trial stage

As we have seen, there are many reasons why criminal offences do not all result in an offender being brought before the courts. Even when a case is brought, the public image of what happens is far removed from the typical case. The news media or TV drama series suggest that most prosecutions result in full-scale jury trials in the Crown Court. In fact, the vast bulk of criminal trials are disposed of in the magistrates' court, and the vast bulk of them—both in the Crown Court and in the magistrates' court— are determined on the basis of a plea of guilty. The trial is a statistical rarity.

All prosecutions start in the magistrates' court. Whether they finish there depends on how the case is classified (*see Box 5.9*). The most serious cases—indictable offences— are sent to the Crown Court for disposal. The vast majority of criminal cases—summary cases—are disposed of in the magistrates' court. Cases which are triable either way, i.e. either summarily or on indictment, are determined in the appropriate court, once a decision on the classification of the case has been made.

Box 5.9 Legal system explained

Classification of criminal cases

There are four potential classes of criminal case:

- *Offences triable only on indictment.* These are the most serious cases, such as murder, manslaughter, and rape. If the defendant pleads not guilty, these cases must be tried in the Crown Court, before a jury.

[8] For further detail, see www.sfo.gov.uk/publications/guidance-policy-and-protocols/deferred-prosecution-agreements/.

Box 5.9 Continued

- *Offences triable summarily.* These are all offences created by statute, where the statute provides that they are summary offences. These cases are determined by magistrates. There is no right to trial by jury. There have been some attempts at reclassifying certain offences as summary only, in particular small thefts; but political arguments about 'taking away rights to a jury trial' make change difficult.
- *Offences triable either way.* These are offences, also created by statute, where the Act provides that they may be dealt with either summarily or on indictment. In such cases, the accused currently chooses how he or she wishes to be tried, before magistrates or before a jury. Opting for trial in the Crown Court exposes the accused to the prospect of more serious sentences, as the Crown Court has wider powers of sentence than the magistrates' court, though the latter can commit a case to the Crown Court where it thinks its powers of sentence are inadequate.
- *Summary cases triable on indictment.* In specific cases an accused may have a charge that he or she has committed a summary offence added to a charge that he or she has committed an indictable offence. These can both be dealt with in the same trial in the Crown Court (see sections 40 and 41 of the Criminal Justice Act 1988).

5.5.1 The functions of the courts

Criminal courts have two principal functions:

- dealing with the case, which includes determining guilt where the defendant has pleaded not guilty, as well as deciding on the correct sentence; and
- ensuring that, so far as possible, the trial is fair.

They may also have to deal with other procedural questions, such as whether or not to grant bail or remand a person in custody (*see Box 5.7*).

5.5.1.1 Dealing with the case

In cases where the accused pleads not guilty, the court must hear the evidence, in the light of that evidence reach findings of fact, in the light of those findings determine whether the accused person is or is not guilty of the alleged crime, and, if guilty, pass an appropriate sentence. In the magistrates' courts all these functions are performed by the magistrates. In the Crown Court, finding the facts and deciding guilt are determined by the jury. Before the jury starts its work, it is provided with a summing-up of the case by the trial judge, an exercise designed to help it focus on the issues it must decide.

If a conviction results, then, subject to further pleas in mitigation and reports on the accused from other agencies such as the probation service or social services, sentence is passed by the trial judge.

Many think that the function of the court is to determine the truth about the events that have led to a person appearing in court. In practice, the function of the trial is rather different. The prosecution must prove 'beyond reasonable doubt' that the accused committed the offence alleged. The function of the defence, therefore, is to throw sufficient doubt on what the prosecution is alleging so that the burden of proof is not satisfied. If the burden of proof is not met, the defendant must be acquitted.

Where the defendant pleads guilty, the only issue for the court, again subject to pleas in mitigation made on behalf of the accused and other reports, is to determine sentence.

5.5.1.2 Ensuring the fairness of the trial

Fairness is at the heart of the due process model of criminal justice. A great deal of the law of criminal procedure and evidence is designed to ensure that the accused gets a fair trial. It is in this context that many of the tensions between the 'due process' model and the 'crime control' model may be seen. A number of initiatives have been taken in recent years that have shifted the balance from the former to the latter. The question is whether the balance has now gone too far. The full detail of the relevant law is beyond the scope of this book. However, two examples are briefly considered: evidence, and disclosure.

Evidence. The law on criminal evidence is designed to ensure that only relevant material is put before the court and to prevent material being put before the court that would be unfairly prejudicial to the defendant. Among the rules that exclude evidence in a criminal trial are:

- *the rule against hearsay evidence*: in general, only evidence given by witnesses in court is admitted. What others said to a witness cannot be admitted, as the person who made the statement cannot be challenged (cross-examined) about its veracity. The Criminal Justice Act 2003 relaxed these principles. It provided that witness statements can be used as evidence, subject to a number of safeguards, where the witness is identified but unavailable to testify or the statement is contained in a business document. The court is also given a discretion to admit hearsay evidence where it would not be contrary to the interests of justice for it to be used. In addition, witnesses' previous statements have been made more widely admissible at trial. This enables witnesses to refer to their statement while giving evidence in court and permits greater use of video-recorded statements for crucial evidence in serious cases;

- *the rule preventing the giving of information about an accused person's past record*: in general, the prosecution was not able to disclose to the court evidence about the defendant's history, particularly criminal record, unless that person wished to challenge the veracity of a prosecution witness, say a policeman. Under the Criminal Justice Act 2003, this principle is also relaxed. Judges are given power to let juries hear about a defendant's previous convictions and other misconduct where relevant to the case. The court can exclude evidence of previous misconduct if it thinks that the jury will give it disproportionate weight (in other words, if the relevance of the evidence to the case is outweighed by any prejudicial effect). The starting point, however, is that relevant evidence is admissible. To give an example: if X was being prosecuted for rape, the fact that X had previous convictions for robbery would not be admitted; however, evidence that X had previously been found guilty of other charges of serious assault against women would be. This proposal, which derived in part from a detailed study of the issue by the Law Commission, was extremely controversial. Lawyers' organizations and civil liberty groups argued that a person should be tried only for the crime for which he or she has been prosecuted; to introduce evidence of previous misconduct would undermine the presumption that a person should be regarded as innocent until proved guilty. Those in favour of the proposal argued that, as such evidence will not be admitted generally, but only where it is relevant to the case in question, it should be able to be taken into account.

In some circumstances, there are precise rules of law which relate to the admissibility of evidence. For example, where it is proposed to rely on a confession, section 76 of the PACE requires the prosecution to demonstrate beyond reasonable doubt that the confession was not made by oppression of the person who made it, or as a result of inducements made to the person giving it that might render the confession unreliable.

Section 78 of the PACE also gives the judge/magistrate a general discretion to exclude evidence that would otherwise be admissible and relevant 'where the admission of the evidence would have such an adverse effect on the fairness of the proceedings that the court ought not to admit it'. Evidence obtained by the police in breach of the rules relating to questioning and interrogation can fall into this category.

Disclosure. A separate issue relates to the question of what evidence should be disclosed by the prosecution to the defendant and vice versa. One of the most significant causes of serious miscarriages of justice arises when the prosecution withholds evidence that it has acquired during the process of its investigation but that weakens the case that the prosecution is seeking to build against the accused.

This was a central issue considered by the Royal Commission on Criminal Justice which reported in 1993. As a result of, though not fully accepting, its recommendations, the government introduced a new legal regime relating to disclosure, contained in Parts I and II of the Criminal Procedure and Investigations Act 1996 (*see Box 5.10*). Disputes about whether or not documents should be disclosed are resolved by the court at a pre-trial hearing.

Box 5.10 System in action

Disclosure of evidence

Under the Criminal Investigations and Procedure Act 1996, amended by the Criminal Justice Act 2003, it is provided that:

(1) the investigator (usually the police) must preserve material gathered during the investigation and make available to the prosecutor material falling into defined key categories, plus a list of other material that has been acquired;

(2) the prosecutor must serve on the defence material on which the prosecutor intends to rely to found the case;

Box 5.10 Continued

(3) the prosecutor must also disclose prosecution material that has not previously been disclosed and that might reasonably be considered capable of undermining the case for the prosecution against the accused, or of assisting the case for the accused. There is a continuing duty on the prosecutor to disclose material that meets the new test. The prosecutor is specifically required to review the prosecution material on receipt of the defence statement and to make further disclosure if required under the continuing duty; and

(4) the defence statement must set out the nature of the defence, including any particular defences on which the defence intends to rely. It must also indicate any points of law the defence wishes to make, including any points as to the admissibility of evidence or abuse of process. The judge is required to warn the accused about any failure to comply with the defence statement requirements. There is also a requirement for service of an updated defence statement to assist the management of the trial, requiring the accused to serve, before the trial, details of any witnesses he or she intends to call to give evidence (other than him- or herself) and also details of all experts instructed, including those not called to give evidence. The new obligation on the defence to provide details of the witnesses it intends to call will be accompanied by a code of practice governing the conduct of any interviews by the police or non-police investigators with defence witnesses disclosed in accordance with the requirement.

Any disputes about disclosure are to be resolved by the court in a pre-trial hearing.

The main features of the process are that: (1) it is statute-based; (2) it puts the responsibility on the prosecution to decide what should be disclosed; and (3) it requires the defence to make disclosure of its case before the start of the trial.

The accompanying *code of practice* (made under the authority of Part 2 of the 1996 Act) requires the appointment, in any criminal investigation, of an 'officer in charge', plus a separate 'disclosure officer' who will be responsible for the administration of the investigation, including the operation of the disclosure scheme. The 'investigator'—the police or other officer carrying out the investigation—is made responsible for retaining material gathered or generated by the inquiry. The disclosure officer prepares the schedule of unused material, together with a list of any sensitive material (e.g. relating to national security or information given in confidence). The disclosure officer must send these schedules to the prosecutor, accompanied by copies of any material relating to the unreliability of witnesses or confessions or containing any explanation by the accused for the offence. Once the defence statement is filed, the disclosure officer must look at all the files again and draw attention to any that may assist the defence. The officer must then certify to the prosecutor that, to the best of his or her knowledge and belief, the duties imposed by the code have been complied with. A revised Code was published by the Ministry of Justice in February 2015.

In a decision by the European Court of Human Rights, *Rowe and Davis v United Kingdom* (*The Times*, 1 March 2000), it was held that where the prosecution withheld evidence because it was claimed to be immune from disclosure on the grounds of public interest, the failure to put it before a trial judge so as to permit him to rule on the question of disclosure deprived an accused person of the right to a fair trial.

Box 5.10 Continued

The law places great responsibility on both the investigation and prosecution sides to operate the scheme in accordance with the statutory provisions and code of guidance. There have been two recent reviews of disclosure—in the Crown Courts (2011) and in the magistrates' courts (2014).

In the former, led by Lord Justice Gross, it was concluded that, while the law does not need amendment, those involved in the criminal justice process needed to engage more actively with the operation of the disclosure rules. In particular, the prosecution needs to give early warning of how its case is developing so that the defence can understand the likely parameters of disclosure in the particular case. It is thus important for the defence to engage with prosecutors in this process. It is also essential for the judges to manage the operation of the rules.

The Magistrates' Court Disclosure Review recommended a streamlined procedure in summary cases that are expected to end in a guilty plea, so that a schedule of unused material need not be served in such cases.

The CPS have published a detailed guidance manual on disclosure of material: see www. cps.gov.uk/legal/d_to_g/disclosure_manual/. In addition the Attorney-General's Office has published guidelines on how the disclosure regime should work. This was revised in 2013: see www.gov.uk/government/publications/attorney-generals-guidelines-on-disclosure-2013. In the same year, the judiciary published a protocol on the same topic: see www. judiciary.gov.uk/wp-content/uploads/JCO/Documents/Protocols/Disclosure+Protocol.pdf.

Despite all this, a joint report from HM Crown Prosecution Inspectorate and HM Inspectorate for Constabulary, published in July 2017, showed that the rules and guidance were routinely ignored by police and prosecutors. See www.martinpartington. com, November 2017.

An important innovation in the way the courts work was the creation, in 2004, of a Criminal Procedure Rules Committee, whose task is to create a code of criminal procedure and related practice directions that apply throughout the criminal courts. Modelled on the Civil Procedure Rules Committee (*see 8.4*), it is designed to give judges greater authority to manage the progress of criminal trials. The Rules were published in 2005 and brought together some 50 pre-existing sets of procedural rules. They were consolidated in 2015, but are the subject of regular amendment. The Rules, which govern the practice and procedure of the criminal courts, are designed to change some of the culture of the criminal trial process, in particular through judicial case management (see www.justice.gov.uk/courts/procedure-rules/criminal).

5.5.2 The courts: magistrates' courts

Magistrates' courts have a long history. They have a distinct character as they depend heavily on volunteer/lay persons to determine decisions. Much of the claim to legitimacy for the magistrates is that benches are composed of persons who come from the community affected by the alleged criminal activity (*see Box 5.11* for types of magistrates' courts). Magistrates also play an important role in the Family Court (*see Chapter 7*).

Box 5.11 Legal system explained

Types of magistrates' courts

There are two distinct types of magistrates' courts that operate in England and Wales: *lay justices'* courts, and *district judge* (formerly *stipendiary*) *magistrates'* courts. Lay justices' courts are made up of (usually) three lay persons (i.e. persons with no specific legal qualifications), known as *justices of the peace* (JPs), who sit and determine criminal cases. They receive legal advice on their powers from the *justices' clerk*, a specially appointed official who is legally qualified. JPs provide their services on a voluntary basis; they receive expenses, for example for travel and subsistence, and, where appropriate, can claim a loss of earnings allowance. Apart from that, however, they are unpaid. By far the majority of magistrates' courts are lay justices' courts.

As a result of the Criminal Justice and Courts Act 2015, new single justice procedures can be put in place, whereby proceedings against adults charged with summary-only non-imprisonable offences can be considered by a single magistrate, on the papers. The purpose of this new procedure is to deal more proportionately with straightforward, uncontested cases, involving offences such as failure to register a new vehicle keeper, driving without insurance, exceeding a 30mph speed limit, and TV licence evasion. They would not have to take place in formal courtrooms.

District judge magistrates' courts are run by district judges, who are qualified lawyers and sit on their own, rather than in panels of three. They used to sit only in those areas of the country designated by the government as appropriate for such courts. As the result of a change in the law (section 78 of and Schedule 11 to the Access to Justice Act 1999), they are now able to sit in any magistrates' court in the country, thus giving court managers greater flexibility in the use of this judicial resource.

5.5.2.1 Functions

All criminal trials start in the magistrates' courts. In carrying out their judicial function, there are two distinct types of procedure that they control: *sending for trial* and *summary trials*. In addition, they have responsibility for enforcing non-custodial penalties, especially fines.

5.5.2.2 Sending for trial

Historically, there was a formal stage in a criminal trial, called committal proceedings, designed to ensure that, even though a case was going to be tried in the Crown Court, magistrates were satisfied that there was a case for the defendant to answer. Years ago committal proceedings were fully reported in the press and other mass media; this led to the criticism that such publicity made it difficult to find members of a jury who had not heard about the case. Now committal proceedings have been abolished.

Since January 2001, all indictable only cases have been automatically sent for trial in the Crown Court following the appearance of the defendant before magistrates. For offences triable either way, where it is decided that the trial should be on indictment, committal proceedings have—since 2013—also been abolished. The government estimated that the change would save 60,000 hearings a year.

Under section 49 of the Criminal Procedures and Investigations Act 1996, accused persons must enter a plea—guilty or not guilty—in the magistrates' court. Those who, before this rule came into force, would have been committed to the Crown Court for trial, and who would then have pleaded guilty, are now no longer committed for trial, though they may still be committed for sentence. Despite this change in the rules, over 70 per cent of those appearing in the Crown Court (who by definition pleaded not guilty before the magistrates) plead guilty (i.e. change their plea) when they get to Crown Court.

5.5.2.3 Summary trials

In 2016, over 1,500,000 cases were received by the magistrates' courts. Of these, around 74,600 were sent on to the Crown Court. The rest were dealt with summarily by magistrates. Of these, only 149,423 were listed for trial; thus the vast majority are determined by a plea of guilty. Of the trials, 47 per cent were recorded as effective; 38 per cent were recorded as cracked (e.g. where a last-minute guilty plea was entered); 15 per cent were ineffective.[9] In short fewer than half went ahead as planned.

5.5.2.4 Committals for sentence

In all cases where guilt is established, whether or not there is a trial, the magistrates must impose a penalty. The powers of magistrates to impose sentences are limited. However, where they decide that their powers of sentence are inadequate, they can commit a case to the Crown Court. The number of cases committed to the Crown Court for sentence in 2016 was 32,150. Where custodial sentences were imposed by the Crown Court, around 40 per cent were for six months or less—which the magistrates could have imposed themselves. (For sentencing more generally, *see 5.5.5*.)

5.5.2.5 Fine enforcement

In many cases where the penalty imposed is a fine, the magistrates must follow this up with enforcement proceedings.

5.5.2.6 Youth courts and the youth justice system

A vast amount of criminal activity is carried out by people, mainly male, at a relatively early age. Juvenile delinquency and measures to try to deal with it—not always with conspicuous success—have been high on the policy agendas of governments for many years. There are major tensions between the desire to prevent juvenile crime and deal

---

[9] Figures in this section derived from www.gov.uk/government/statistics/criminal-court-statistics-quarterly-april-to-june-2017. Main tables, Tables M1, M2, and C1. Effective trials are those where the case is disposed of after a full hearing of the evidence.

firmly with those young persons found guilty of criminal activity, and the desire not to blight young lives unnecessarily by giving them criminal records that may prevent them entering the job market or otherwise making a positive contribution to society.

There have also been fierce debates about where the responsibility for youth crime should lie—with individual offenders, with their parent(s), with schools and teachers, or with the wider society, which is said to fail to provide the educational and employment opportunities that might make youth offenders more productive members of society.

The issue was reviewed by the former Labour government in 1997 in the white paper *No More Excuses*.[10] This led to two Acts of Parliament, the Crime and Disorder Act 1998 and the Youth Justice and Criminal Evidence Act 1999. These contained provisions, not only to process young offenders (those under the age of 18) through the criminal justice system more quickly, but also to try to demonstrate to them the effect their actions have on the lives of others.

The Crime and Disorder Act 1998 led to the creation of youth offending teams—multi-disciplinary agencies brought together at the local level to devise effective programmes to prevent offending and reoffending by young people. Their work is kept under review by a *Youth Justice Board*.

The 1998 Act also replaced a non-statutory policy, whereby police could merely decide to caution a young offender, with a new statutory 'final warning'. Once an offender has received one, any further offence leads to criminal proceedings in court.

When dealing with young offenders, magistrates' courts are technically known as *youth courts*. When sitting as a youth court, magistrates are subject to special procedural rules designed to ensure that cases are dealt with as speedily as possible. In 2001, the Home Office published a *Good Practice Guide for Youth Courts*.[11] This evolved from an experiment in two courts that sought to achieve four key objectives:

- effective engagement with defendants and their parents to probe the reasons for offending and to encourage plans to change behaviour;
- changing courtroom layouts to facilitate better communication;
- making the court process more open by lifting reporting restrictions where appropriate, and exercising discretion to allow others such as victims to attend court; and
- giving feedback to sentencers on the outcome of sentences.

The guide is designed to encourage youth courts to respond positively to such initiatives to counter public perceptions that they were not delivering effective justice.

Magistrates also have a special range of sentencing options now brought together in the generic youth rehabilitation order (*see Box 5.12*).

---

[10] (Cm 3809) (London, The Stationery Office, 1997).
[11] *The Youth Court: Changing the Culture of the Youth Court* (London, Home Office, 2001).

Box 5.12 Legal system explained

Youth rehabilitation orders

As a result of the Criminal Justice and Immigration Act 2008, a generic 'youth rehabilitation order' was created. This enables the court to impose one or more of the following:

(1)   an activity requirement;

(2)   a supervision requirement;

(3)   in a case where the offender is aged 16 or 17 at the time of the conviction, an unpaid work requirement;

(4)   a programme requirement;

(5)   an attendance centre requirement;

(6)   a prohibited activity requirement;

(7)   a curfew requirement;

(8)   an exclusion requirement;

(9)   a residence requirement;

(10)   a local authority residence requirement;

(11)   a mental health treatment requirement;

(12)   a drug treatment requirement;

(13)   a drug testing requirement;

(14)   an intoxicating substance treatment requirement; and

(15)   an education requirement.

A youth rehabilitation order may also impose an electronic monitoring requirement, and in some cases must do so. In addition, a youth rehabilitation order may be made with intensive supervision and surveillance, or with fostering.

The Act sets out in detail what each of these requirements involves and when it can be used. The Legal Aid, Sentencing and Punishment of Offenders Act 2012 made detailed amendment to the rules on youth rehabilitation orders.

As a result of the Youth Justice and Criminal Evidence Act 1999, magistrates may refer first-time offenders to a *youth offender panel*. The power to order referral is available only in the youth court. Where a young offender has been tried in the Crown Court, the trial judge may, on conviction, refer the offender to the youth court for sentence in a case where that seems to be appropriate. The youth court may in turn refer the offender to the panel.

Youth offender panels consist of two volunteers recruited directly from the local community, working alongside a member of the youth offending team. The panel aims to agree a programme of behaviour for the young offender to follow. The programme is explicitly based on the theory of 'restorative justice' *(see Box 5.18)*, to ensure that the offender takes responsibility for the consequences of his or her offending behaviour; makes restoration to the victim; and achieves reintegration into the law-abiding community. It must be questioned whether the theory of restorative justice is the only theory behind the new programme; other 'justice models'—including the 'crime control' and the 'bureaucratic'—appear to be in play as well.

In addition to the work of the youth courts, other measures designed to curb anti-social behaviour have also been introduced. These include: local child curfews; anti-social behaviour orders; and acceptable behaviour contracts.

Notwithstanding all these changes, the government announced, in 2017, that there would be further changes to the youth justice system (see *Box 5.13*).

Box 5.13 Reform in progress

Reform of the youth justice system

In 2007, the average monthly number of persons under the age of 18 held in custody was 2,909. Today that average monthly figure is about 900. Generally far fewer young people are brought into the criminal justice system than was the case 10 years ago.

At first sight it might seem that these dramatic falls in numbers—which do not get much publicity—should be a good news story. But the figures mask other problems about the overall state of the youth justice system. Once children and young people are in custody the outcomes are not good. Levels of violence and self-harm are too great and reoffending rates are very high. Sixty-nine per cent of those sentenced to custody go on to commit further offences within a year of their release. This raises questions about what more can be done to ensure that young people do not enter the system in the first place, and if they do are given every opportunity to turn their lives around by receiving appropriate education and training to enable them to start leading productive lives in society.

The government has taken a number of measure to address these problems.

- In 2016, they commissioned Charlie Taylor—a former head teacher and child care expert—to undertake a review of the youth justice system. His report was published in December 2016. The government's response to his report was published on the same day.
- In response to that review, it appointed Charlie Taylor to be the new Chair of the Youth Justice Board—so that he can oversee the reforms he advocated.
- A new Youth Custody Service is to be established as a distinct arm of HM Prison and Probation Service, with a dedicated Director accountable directly to the Chief Executive.
- There has been (yet another) review of the physical estate used for the detention of under 18s. The latest review states bluntly that the time for reports is over—all those who know about this accept that the estate is not up to modern standards. What is needed is action to improve the estate.

Perhaps by comparison with the huge problems facing the prison service more generally—which new proposals for reform of the prison system are designed to address—youth justice is an issue on which it is hard to attract attention from the mass media.

Box 5.13 Continued

But it seems plausible to suggest that if the youth justice system worked more effec-tively, some of the pressures that might arise further down the line could be reduced.

A more recent development is that the President of the Family Court, Sir James Munby, has suggested in a speech that the principle of 'problem-solving' courts should be expanded into the youth justice area. (*See 7.3.1.5.*) Bringing together family justice and criminal justice expertise could enable a more 'holistic' approach to the treatment of young offenders. (*See also Box 5.25.*)

Further details are at www.martinpartington.com February 2017, and November 2017.

5.5.3 The Crown Court

5.5.3.1 Jurisdiction and organization

The Crown Court is where the most serious criminal cases—cases tried on indict-ment—are disposed of. The Crown Court works from 77 court centres, grouped into six circuits: Midland and Oxford; North Eastern; Northern; South Eastern; Wales and Chester; and Western. The 'Old Bailey' is the name given to the Central Criminal Court in London, a Crown Court in the South Eastern Circuit. The Court is divided into three tiers:

- First-tier courts are those in which High Court judges, circuit judges, and recorders sit. They have higher levels of security to deal with the most diffi-cult prisoners. The full range of criminal work, together with High Court civil work (*see Chapter 8*), is dealt with in these courts.

- Second-tier courts are the same, though no civil work is conducted in them.

- Third-tier courts are presided over only by circuit judges or recorders.

The offences dealt with in the Crown Court are themselves divided into three classes, under directions given by the Lord Chief Justice:

- Class 1—Generally heard by a High Court judge, these are the most serious offences, which include treason and murder.

- Class 2—Offences, which include rape, that are usually heard by a circuit judge under the authority of the presiding judge.

- Class 3—Includes all other offences, such as kidnapping, burglary, grievous bod-ily harm, and robbery, which are normally tried by a circuit judge or recorder.

The aim is that the most serious offences should be dealt with by the most senior judges.

The Crown Court also has powers to sentence persons convicted in the magistrates' court where the magistrates have decided that their own powers of sentencing are inade-quate. In addition, the Crown Court hears appeals from decisions of the magistrates' court.

5.5.3.2 Workload

Crown Courts have a substantial workload, though numerically not nearly as great as that of the magistrates' court. Of course, Crown Court cases are by definition more serious than those heard by magistrates.

Cases sent for trial. In 2016, 46,690 triable either way cases and 27,950 indictable only cases were sent for trial in the Crown Court.[12] In 65 per cent of cases the defendant pleaded guilty. Only 32 per cent of defendants were dealt with following a plea of not guilty. Thus a full trial occurs in fewer than a third of cases coming to the Crown Court. Indeed, of these, 34 per cent of trials were 'cracked trials', i.e. cases originally listed for trial, but where the accused changed his plea from not guilty to guilty, most commonly on the day of the trial. Another 15 per cent of trials were 'ineffective' trials, the majority where the defendant was absent or unfit to stand trial, or because a prosecution witness was absent.

Of those pleading not guilty, over a third were acquitted because the prosecution offered no evidence; about a quarter were left unresolved, e.g. because they were 'left on the file'; 4 per cent were acquitted on the direction of the judge. Only around a third of cases actually went to trial before a jury. Of these around 70 per cent resulted in a conviction, around 30 per cent in an acquittal. Of these, the vast majority were by a unanimous decision of the jury. Minority verdicts were given in less than 20 per cent of cases.[13]

Committals for sentence. In 2016, 32,150 committals for sentence were sent to the Crown Court.

Hearing times. In 2016, the average hearing times were:

- for not guilty pleas in indictable cases, 20.0 hours;
- for not guilty pleas in committed triable either way cases, 9.2 hours;
- for guilty pleas (indictable), 2 hours;
- for guilty pleas (triable either way), 1.4 hours;
- for sentence, 0.7 hours.

5.5.4 Issues in the criminal justice trial system

5.5.4.1 Charge and plea bargaining

The high level of guilty pleas in both the magistrates' courts and Crown Courts may suggest that the police and prosecution allow only the strongest cases to come before a court. Even so, it may seem surprising that, in a system in which in theory everyone is innocent until proved guilty, so few accused actually take advantage of the due process model of criminal justice and submit the evidence presented by the prosecution for testing before either the magistrates or a jury.

---

[12] Figures in this section derived from www.gov.uk/government/statistics/criminal-court-statistics-quarterly-april-to-june-2017, Main tables, Tables C.1, C.2, C.5, C.7.

[13] Figures adapted from Cheryl Thomas, *Are Juries Fair?* (*see Box 5.15*).

Of course there are cases where the evidence is so overwhelming that a guilty plea is the only sensible option for the accused. But in less clear-cut cases, at least part of the answer to this puzzle arises from the fact that those within the criminal justice system work quite hard, through various forms of bargaining, to ensure that accused persons plead guilty. This saves considerable amounts of court time (as the statistics for average hearing times set out earlier clearly show) and thus expense and other resources. There are various practices that may occur to assist the accused in deciding what plea to enter.

First, there may be a negotiation between the prosecutor and the defence about the charge to be proceeded with before the courts. If the accused is willing or can be persuaded to plead guilty to a charge that carries a less severe penalty, the prosecution may then decide not to pursue an alternative charge that could arise from the same factual situation, which might attract a more severe penalty.

Secondly, there may be an indication that if a plea of guilty is entered, then, in passing sentence, the judge may reduce the sentence he might otherwise have imposed. Direct negotiations between defence lawyers and judges on sentence, commonplace in the United States, do not take place in the United Kingdom. Further, the decision in *R v Turner* ([1970] 2 QB 321, CA) makes it clear that judges may not indicate the sentence they are planning to impose, nor indicate how that sentence might change were the defendant to plead guilty.

However, at the end of a hearing, section 48(2) of the Criminal Justice and Public Order Act 1994 requires a judge to give reasons for any reduction in the sentence from what would normally be expected for the offence in question taking normal sentencing guidelines into account. The Criminal Justice Act 2003 also requires courts to take into account the stage in the proceedings at which the guilty plea was offered, and the circumstances in which it was made. In practice, judges allow a discount of between 25 and 33 per cent in cases where the defendant pleads guilty: the earlier the plea, the higher the discount. Since 2013, there has been an Early Guilty Plea Protocol, designed to ensure that those accused of offences are encouraged to plead guilty early. A similar protocol operates in magistrates' courts.[14]

The formal legal position is that undue pressure must not be put on defendants to enter any particular plea, as this may lead the innocent to plead guilty to a crime he or she did not commit. Such practices do not fit with the due process model of the criminal justice system. The reality is, however, that justice is frequently negotiated, a practice justified by the added efficiency that it brings to the system, thus fitting the crime control model. The extent to which such practices should be condoned is the subject of considerable debate in the criminal justice literature.

Despite these incentives to plead guilty early, there remains a significant number of cracked trials. These, together with ineffective trials, represent a considerable drain on resources, for two reasons. First, when judges cannot hear a cracked or ineffective case, it is usually too late to give them something else to do. Secondly, cases that collapse at

---

[14] For more detail, see my blog, www.martinpartington.com, October 2013. In 2017, the Sentencing Council published definitive guidelines on the topic, effective from 1 June 2017.

the last minute or cannot go ahead waste the enormous amounts of preparatory work done by the CPS, as well as by the defence, which is costly to the state. Getting the right mix of incentives to ensure resources are not wasted further highlights the tension between the 'due process' and the 'bureaucratic' models of criminal justice.

5.5.4.2 Jury trial

A second issue of considerable current importance relates to the use of juries to determine the facts in Crown Court trials. Three issues can be considered separately: are juries competent to decide cases? To what extent should the accused be entitled to choose trial by jury in those cases where a choice is open to them? Should the classification of indictable offences (for which the right to trial by jury arises automatically) be altered?

The competence of juries. Jury trial is perceived by many as one of the great strengths of the English criminal justice system. There is an enormous literature on juries, asserting their importance as a defender of civil liberty and a bulwark against oppression by the state. Indeed, the use of juries may be said to legitimate decision-taking in the criminal justice system by enabling decisions to be taken by ordinary lay people. This reinforces the independence of the judicial system in this context and thus fits with the constitutional separation of the courts from other decision-making bodies (*see Box 5.14*).

Box 5.14 System in action

Case study: the case of Mr Ponting

There have certainly been historically significant, if rare, cases where juries appear, despite the weight of evidence, to have acted on their conscience to protect civil liberty by finding persons not guilty of crimes which may be said to have significant political overtones. The example of the acquittal of Clive Ponting is often cited. Ponting was a former civil servant, accused of offences under the Official Secrets Act 1911 after he had passed to a Member of Parliament confidential documents relating to the sinking of an Argentinian battleship during the Falklands War in 1982. Despite a ruling from the judge that Ponting had no authorization to pass the documents on, and that there was no other lawful justification for his action, the jury acquitted him. It was assumed that the jury had decided that the moral arguments in favour of his doing what he did outweighed the legal arguments that what he did was unlawful.

Important changes to the constitution and functions of juries have been made over the years. Before 1972, occupation of a house with a prescribed rateable value was one of the criteria for selection. Since then most of the restrictions on jury qualification have gone (with the exception of those relating to mentally disordered persons and certain groups of convicted persons). This has led to profound changes in jury composition, certainly in terms of their class composition. Since 1981, selection for jury service has been by random selection using a computer. Perhaps the most significant change occurred in 1967 when the ability of juries to determine cases on the basis of majority verdicts was introduced.[15] The most recent development is the decision, effective from April 2017, to raise the upper age limit for jurors from 70 to 75.

Despite the arguments in favour of jury trial, which have considerable force, little is actually known about how juries function. Direct research into the work of the jury is not permitted. The only research currently available is through the use of 'surrogate' juries dealing with hypothetical situations, or secondary analysis of data on the outcomes of trials. In 2010, an important study—which had used both these research methods—was published by the Ministry of Justice (*see Box 5.15*).

Box 5.15 System in action

Are juries fair?

Professor Cheryl Thomas sought to discover whether juries were fair, in particular towards defendants from the black and ethnic minority communities who are statistically over-represented in the criminal courts. The research found no evidence of jury bias, though the report also acknowledged that where all-white juries dealt with black defendants, there might be a perception of bias.

The report dealt with some misconceptions about jury verdicts. For example, in rape cases, contrary to popular belief and previous government reports, juries actually convict more often than they acquit (55 per cent jury conviction rate); other serious offences (attempted murder, manslaughter, GBH) have lower jury conviction rates than rape.

Jury conviction rates for rape vary according to the gender and age of the complainant, with high conviction rates for some female complainants and low conviction rates for some male complainants. This challenges the view that juries' failure to convict in rape cases is due to juror bias against female complainants.

Further, the research found that in courts with over 1,000 jury verdicts in 2006–08, the conviction rate ranged from 69 per cent to 53 per cent. There were no courts with a higher jury acquittal than conviction rate. This dispels the myth that there are courts where juries rarely convict.

More worrying was the ability of jurors to understand directions given by judges. The study involved 797 jurors at three courts who all saw the same simulated trial and heard exactly the same judicial directions on the law. Most jurors at Blackfriars (69 per cent) and Winchester (68 per cent) felt they were able to understand the directions, while most jurors at Nottingham (51 per cent) felt the directions were difficult to understand.

Jurors' actual comprehension of the judge's legal directions was also examined. While over half of the jurors perceived the judge's directions as easy to understand, only a minority (31 per cent) actually understood the directions fully in the legal terms

---

[15] See the Juries Act 1974, s. 17. Majority verdicts are subject to an important *Practice Direction* [1967] 1 WLR 1198, and [1970] 1 WLR 916, which regulates their use.

Box 5.15 Continued

used by the judge. Younger jurors were better able than older jurors to comprehend the legal instructions, with comprehension of directions on the law declining as the age of the juror increased.

A written summary of the judge's directions on the law given to jurors at the time of the judge's oral instructions improved juror comprehension of the law: the proportion of jurors who fully understood the legal questions in the case in the terms used by the judge increased from 31 per cent to 48 per cent with written instructions.

Professor Thomas argued that the judiciary should reconsider implementing the Auld recommendations for issuing jurors with written aide-memoires on the law in all cases.

Source: www.justice.gov.uk/downloads/publications/research-and-analysis/moj-research/are-juries-fair-research.pdf.

There have been many suggestions that particular types of case—lengthy and complex fraud trials are given as the prime candidate—are not suitable for jury trial. This has led to alternative proposals being adopted, for example judges sitting with a panel of lay assessors, or such cases being heard by a panel of judges rather than just a single judge.

Part 7 of the Criminal Justice Act 2003 makes provision for the possibility of a trial without a jury where there is a real and present danger of jury tampering, or continued without a jury where the jury has been discharged because of jury tampering (*see Box 5.16* for a case study). The Act also provided a right of appeal to the Court of Appeal for both prosecution and defence. Where a trial is conducted or continued without a jury and a defendant is convicted, the court is required to give its reasons for the conviction.

Box 5.16 System in action

Case study: the case of the Heathrow bullion robbers

Although the law came into force in 2006, it was not until 2010 that, for the first time, a court used the power to hold a criminal trial without a jury. The case involved four persons who had been accused of armed robbery at Heathrow Airport in 2004, involving the theft of more than £1,750,000 in a variety of foreign currencies. An earlier trial had been stopped because there was evidence of jury tampering. In this case, the court accepted the prosecution's argument that there was still a very real threat of jury tampering, which justified the case being tried by a judge sitting on his own.

Despite concerns expressed, this procedure has hardly been used. The CPS has provided a very detailed note setting out the conditions on which they might argue for a trial to proceed without a jury.

Source: www.cps.gov.uk/legal/l_to_o/non_jury_trials/.

While some believe that juries are too ready to acquit defendants, the reality is that far more acquittals are ordered by the trial judge. There are no serious proposals that jury trial should be abolished. Such a step would be politically quite unacceptable, and too great a move from the due process model to the crime control model of criminal justice.

Choice of mode of trial. A quite distinct issue, though also a matter of considerable controversy, is the question of who should have the right to choose jury trial in those cases that are triable either way. Following the Royal Commission on Criminal Procedure's report in 1993, the then government proposed that the decision should be made by the magistrates before whom all such cases initially come, and not left to the discretion of the accused. Two attempts to get such a proposal through Parliament failed, so the government decided not to pursue this issue. Since March 2016, new guidance from the Sentencing Council has required magistrates to be much more robust about retaining such cases, and not referring them to the Crown Court.[16]

Should the classification of indictable offences be altered? There is a quite distinct argument that the present classification of offences allows some cases to be tried by juries where this does not seem warranted by the seriousness of the offence. There have been examples of reclassification happening in recent years. For example, the Criminal Justice Act 1988 reclassified a number of motoring offences as summary only. There have been other attempts to reclassify certain types of minor theft as summary offences, thereby denying those accused of them the right to trial by jury. Proposals for change are always countered by the 'thin end of the wedge' argument, that any step in this direction will encourage governments to take further steps in the same direction, thereby reducing the scope of jury trial still further.

The Criminal Justice Act 2003 contained a provision enabling the sentencing powers of the magistrates' courts to be raised from six to 12 months. This has not yet been brought into effect. However, under the Legal Aid, Sentencing and Punishment of Offenders Act 2012, provision was made (section 85) to give magistrates greater flexibility in the fines that they may impose. Offences are divided into five levels—the least serious are level 1 offences, the most serious level 5. The maximum fine for level 5 offences was generally £5,000 (although there are special circumstances where the maximum is set at a higher level). Regulations brought into force on 15 March 2015 provide that, for offences which attract a level 5 sentence, magistrates have power to impose unlimited fines. Thus where magistrates want to impose higher fines for level 5 offences, they no longer have to send cases to the Crown Court for sentence.

5.5.4.3 Abolition of the dock?

As part of its recent work on reform of the justice system, the Human Rights Group JUSTICE published a paper in 2015 which advocated the abolition of the dock in all but the most serious cases. It was argued that two particular benefits might flow from such a proposal: first, that defendants would be able to participate better in the proceedings

---

[16] See my blog, www.martinpartington.com, January 2016 for details.

being brought against them; secondly, that it would allow more flexibility in how court rooms were used. The suggestions are not yet government policy but could at some point become part of the transformation of the justice system programme.[17]

5.5.4.4 Racial bias in the criminal justice system?

It is clearly essential that those who are subject to proceedings in the criminal justice system feel that they are being dealt with in an even handed way. There have been a number of projects that have tried to establish whether those from the black and minority ethnic (BAME) groups have been treated less favourably than those from other racial/ethnic groups. The topic was examined most recently by David Lammy MP. (*See Box 5.17.*)

Box 5.17 Reform in progress

The treatment of, and outcomes for Black, Asian, and Minority Ethnic (BAME) individuals in the criminal justice system: the Lammy Review

At the beginning of 2016, David Lammy MP was asked by the then Prime Minister David Cameron to review the workings of the criminal justice system, with the object of seeing whether the system worked fairly, in particular in relation to BAME individuals. The final report of his review was published in September 2017.

The bare statistics tell a familiar story, for example:

- BAME individuals are disproportionately represented in the criminal justice system which costs the taxpayer at least £309 million each year.
- The proportion of BAME young offenders in custody rose from 25 per cent to 41 per cent between 2006 and 2016, despite the overall number of young offenders falling to record lows.
- The rate of Black defendants pleading not guilty in Crown Courts in England and Wales between 2006 and 2014 was 41 per cent, compared to 31 per cent of White defendants. (This means they lose the possibility of reduced sentences and it raises questions about their level of trust in the system.)
- The BAME proportion of young people offending for the first time rose from 11 per cent in 2006 to 19 per cent a decade later.
- There was an identical increase in the BAME proportion of young people reoffending over the same period.

Lammy looked at what happens in a number of other countries to see whether we could learn from experience elsewhere. Two specific examples may be noted:

- Taking inspiration from youth justice in Germany, Lammy argues that rigorous assessments of a young offender's maturity should inform sentencing decisions. Those judged to have low levels of maturity could also receive extended support from the youth justice system until they are 21.

---

[17] For the full paper go to justice.org.uk/in-the-dock/.

Box 5.17 Continued

- He also called for 'Local Justice Panels' to be established, taking inspiration from New Zealand's Rangatahi courts, where local people with a direct stake in a young offender's life are invited to contribute to their hearings. These panels would normally deal with first-time offenders given community sentences, include key figures such as teachers or social workers, and hold local services to account for a child's rehabilitation.

Lammy made a number of innovative recommendations for judges, prosecutors, and prisons. For example, he proposed that a 'deferred prosecution' model be rolled out, allowing low-level offenders to receive targeted rehabilitation before entering a plea. Those successfully completing rehabilitation programmes would see their charges dropped, while those who did not would still face criminal proceedings. (Such a scheme has already been piloted in the West Midlands, with violent offenders 35 per cent less likely to reoffend. Victims were also more satisfied, feeling that intervention before submitting a plea was more likely to stop reoffending.)

He recommended that all sentencing remarks made by judges in the Crown Court should be published. He argued that this could help to make justice more transparent for victims, witnesses, and offenders.

He also argued that the UK should learn from the US system for 'sealing' criminal records, claiming ex-offenders should be able to apply to have their case heard by a judge or independent body, such as the Parole Board, where they could prove they have reformed. The judge would then decide whether to 'seal' the record, having considered factors such as time since the offence and evidence of rehabilitation. If the decision went the applicant's way, their record would still exist, but the individual would not need to disclose it and employers would not be able to access it. Lammy hoped this would help the people affected to become more employable.

Lammy accepts that there are other wider social issues that must be addressed as well; but he argues that the recommendations he makes could do much to build greater trust in the criminal justice system, reduce reoffending, and improve outcomes for victims.

Whether or not these recommendations will lead to actual changes on the ground is too early to say. The fact that two prime ministers strongly supported the review might suggest that there would be some political impetus for follow-up. But, given other political priorities, a rapid response from ministers seems unlikely.

The Lammy report is at www.gov.uk/government/news/lammy-publishes-historic-review.

5.5.4.5 Representation

For a discussion of the criminal defence service, *see 10.2.3.*

5.5.5 Sentencing

In the same way that the criminal justice system as a whole may be seen to depend on a variety of conflicting social theories, so too is sentencing policy and practice based on a variety of conflicting theories. The literature on theories of sentencing is extensive. Professor Ashworth has classified the approaches under five main headings:

- desert (retributive) theories;
- deterrence theories;
- rehabilitative theories;
- incapacitative theories; and
- restorative (reparative) theories.

Desert or retributive theories take as their focus the idea that punishment is a natural or appropriate response to crime, at least so long as it is proportionate to the crime committed. It is assumed that a person who commits a crime deserves to be punished; and that society is entitled to see that retribution is exacted from the offender. The problem of determining whether sentences are in fact proportional to the offence is, of course, a matter on which there can be great room for debate—and often is, when the press criticize judges for apparently light (occasionally over-harsh) sentencing.

Deterrence theories offer a slightly different view. Here the perspective is on deterring future offending behaviour by punishing the offender currently before the authorities. Such a theory would then justify harsher penalties being imposed on an offender who has committed the same offence on more than one occasion than would be the case for a first offender. The research literature does not offer great confidence that, in practice, policies of deterrence work. Nonetheless, they are very important politically, and indeed have led to the adoption of mandatory sentences for certain categories of repeat offenders.

Rehabilitative sentencing focuses on the offender and efforts to change his or her behaviour so that he or she can become a full and productive member of society. It may be assumed that offenders are in some way unable to cope with life and thus need professional support to change. It involves elements of diagnosis and treatment; it also implies that particular decisions need to be tailored to the individual offender.

Incapacitative sentencing focuses on the need to identify particular individuals or groups who are likely to do serious harm in the future, and who therefore need to be removed from society ('incapacitated') to prevent such harm occurring. The difficulties of imposing what may be severe penalties on the basis of what may happen in the future are obvious, but arise, for example, in the context of convicted paedophiles.

Restorative approaches concentrate more on the victim and the need for the offender to make amends to the victim. Restorative justice shares with rehabilitative models the belief that such outcomes will encourage the offender to change his way of life, but the focus on the victim is distinctive (*see Box 5.18*). The use of these approaches in youth justice has been noted earlier.

Box 5.18 Legal system explained

Restorative justice

In October 2015, the Restorative Justice Council published an information pack, designed to help magistrates, Crown Court judges, and court staff to understand restorative justice, the benefits it can bring to all parties involved in a crime, and the role that the judiciary can play in the process.

As well as providing information on restorative justice and its use in sentencing, the pack features a checklist for restorative justice, an article about why the judiciary can have confidence in the approach, and the voices of victims and offenders who have taken part in a restorative justice process.

The pack can be downloaded free from www.restorativejustice.org.uk/resources/restorative-justice-and-judiciary-information-pack.

The Criminal Justice Act 2003 sets out a statutory list of the principles and purposes of sentencing, reflecting the approaches outlined earlier (*see Box 5.19*). Given the conflicting nature of these theories, it is not entirely obvious what the purpose of doing this was. As with general theories of criminal justice, different rationales for sentencing practice need to be understood so that not only the present law but also possible alternatives to it can be assessed.

Box 5.19 Legal system explained

Purposes of sentencing

The Criminal Justice Act 2003 listed the following as the purposes to which the court must have regard:

(1) the punishment of offenders;
(2) the reduction of crime (including its reduction by deterrence);
(3) the reform and rehabilitation of offenders;
(4) the protection of the public; and
(5) the making of reparation by offenders to persons affected by their offences.

In relation to young offenders (see 5.5.2.6), the Criminal Justice and Immigration Act 2008 has a different list reflecting a different approach. Here, the court must have regard to:

(1) the principal aim of the youth justice system (which is to prevent offending (or reoffending)) by persons aged under 18;
(2) the welfare of the offender; and

> ### Box 5.19 Continued
>
> (3) the purposes of sentencing, which are:
>
>   (a) the punishment of offenders;
>   (b) the reform and rehabilitation of offenders;
>   (c) the protection of the public; and
>   (d) the making of reparation by offenders to persons affected by their offences.

Determining sentencing policy is extremely hard. Politicians seek to reassure the public that they are taking crime seriously and therefore place emphasis on the deterrent effect of penalties, particularly custodial sentences. They are supported in this by sections of the mass media that make rational discussion of sentencing policy and practice almost impossible. Research tends to show that, in many cases, so-called deterrent sentences do not in general deter. This leads to arguments that there should be more emphasis on rehabilitation and reparation. Certainly, the range of penalties available to the courts has grown in recent years. In particular, new forms of 'community sentence', in which the offender is obliged to undertake some form of reparative work in the community and for the victim, have been introduced. The problem with community sentences is convincing the public that they are not a 'soft option' (*see Box 5.20* for some basic facts on current sentencing outcomes).

> ### Box 5.20 System in action
>
> #### Sentencing: some basic facts
>
> In 2016, around 1.24 million offenders were sentenced, having been found guilty of indictable or summary offences. Of these, the vast majority (74 per cent) were fined. Around 7 per cent were sentenced to immediate custody, with an average sentence length of 16.4 months. (27 per cent of those convicted of indictable offences received an immediate custody sentence.) A smaller but increasing percentage were given Suspended Sentence Orders in the same period. More were sentenced to community sentences than to custody, but their total has been reducing.
>
> *Source*: Criminal Justice Statistics Quarterly Dec 2016, available at www.gov.uk/government/uploads/system/uploads/attachment_data/file/614414/criminal-justice-statistics-quarterly-december-2016.pdf

Current sentencing policy is based on provisions in the Criminal Justice Act 2003, supplemented by the Legal Aid, Sentencing and Punishment of Offenders Act 2012 (*see Box 5.21* for the principal features of the current sentencing regime).

Box 5.21 System in action

Criminal Justice Act 2003: the principal features

Generic community sentences. The Act created a single community sentence under which a range of measures formerly attached to different types of community orders remain available. It also set out the tests that must be met before a community order is made. The statutory tests are supplemented by guidance from the Sentencing Council (*see Box 5.22*).

Short custodial sentences. These were identified as particularly problematic. They were too short to offer the offender any rehabilitation but when the offender came out from prison, there was no further supervision for him or her. Recidivism was common. The 2003 Act offered three alternatives. The first is 'custody minus'. A short prison sentence can be suspended for up to two years while requirements to do some work in the community that is set by the court are satisfied. If the offender breaches any of the requirements, the custodial term is activated. Committing a further offence during the period of suspension also counts as breach.

The other two, 'intermittent custody', where the custodial element would be served intermittently, for example at weekends, and 'custody plus', where those sentenced to less than a year could have a mix of prison and community sentence, were never implemented, and were repealed by the Legal Aid, Sentencing and Punishment of Offenders Act 2012.

Sentences of over 12 months. For offenders serving a sentence of over 12 months (apart from the sentences for dangerous offenders outlined in the next paragraph), release is made automatic at the half-way point. They remain on licence until the end of the sentence.

Sentences for dangerous offenders. The Act introduced a controversial scheme for the sentencing of dangerous adults. These included a sentence of 'imprisonment for public protection'; the period of such sentences was not fixed, but was indeterminate. The court could impose an 'extended sentence' where the maximum term is between two and ten years' imprisonment, which meant that the offender would still be subject to supervision after release from prison. The element of indeterminacy was found not to work well in practice.

Legal Aid, Sentencing and Punishment of Offenders Act 2012: the principal features

The headline provisions are:

- the imposition of a duty on courts to consider making compensation orders for certain types of offence;
- simplifying the provisions setting out the court's duty to give reasons for and to explain the effect of a sentence imposed by the court;
- adding transgender identity to the personal characteristics which will be statutory aggravating factors in sentencing where any offence is motivated by hostility to the victim on this basis. It also provides for a starting point of 30 years for the minimum term for a life sentence for murder aggravated on the grounds of the victim's disability or transgender identity;

Box 5.21 Continued

- making a number of changes in relation to community orders for adults. It clarifies when community orders come to an end and enables a court to impose a fine for breach of a community order;
- amending certain requirements that may be imposed as part of community orders and suspended sentence orders, in particular, curfew requirements and mental health, drug rehabilitation, and alcohol treatment requirements. It also creates new powers to prohibit foreign travel and to impose alcohol abstinence and monitoring requirements as part of an order;
- amending the court's power to suspend a prison sentence by increasing the length of sentences that can be suspended, giving the court discretion not to impose community requirements as part of the sentence and enabling it to impose a fine for breach of a suspended sentence order;
- in relation to the sentencing provisions that apply to youths, enabling a court to impose a penalty for breach of a detention and training order even where the order has finished its term.

As regards dangerous offenders, the new Act requires courts to impose a sentence of life imprisonment for those convicted for the second time of defined serious sexual or violent offences. It also refines the circumstances in which an extended sentence may be imposed.

Such is the complexity of sentencing law that the Law Commission is currently engaged in a pioneering project to create a unified sentencing code. Its preliminary proposals were published in July 2017.

Box 5.22 Reform in progress

Establishment of Sentencing Council

The Coroners and Justice Act 2009 established the Sentencing Council. It is required by statute to consult the Justice Select Committee on any sentencing guidelines it may contemplate making. This is to ensure that there is at least some democratically elected input into the guideline-making process. It publishes guidelines for judges, designed to increase consistency in judicial sentencing practice. It is also developing analyses of the extent to which actual sentencing practice conforms to the guidelines set by the Council. And it has initiated an educational outreach programme to promote a better understanding of sentencing policy in the wider community.

See Annual Reports of the Council, www.sentencingcouncil.org.uk/.

Sentencing practice is frequently the subject of (usually adverse) press comment, much of which is ill-informed. Judges and magistrates are often criticized for sentencing too lightly. Yet there are proportionately many more people in prison in England and Wales than in almost any other European country. Although more community sentences are now handed down than custodial ones, prison overcrowding remains a source of considerable tension in the criminal justice system. Judges are simultaneously told to impose severe sentences where necessary and not to send people to prison unless absolutely essential. Both the design and implementation of sentencing policy is extremely controversial. At least in part this is because there are strongly held assumptions about the effectiveness of particular forms of case disposal that are not borne out either in practice or in the results of research. It is a topic on which rationality is often found to be in short supply.

5.5.5.1 Assets recovery

Orders to recover assets have been possible in specific contexts (e.g. seizing the proceeds of drug trafficking) for some time. The principle was put on a more general basis in the Proceeds of Crime Act 2002. Responsibility for asset recovery is shared between the National Crime Agency and the Crown Prosecution Service. The Serious Crime Act 2015 amends the Proceeds of Crime Act 2002 to make recovery of assets easier.[18] Asset recovery has become a more central aspect of penal policy, particularly in relation to serious organized crime.

5.5.5.2 Rehabilitation of offenders

Notwithstanding the emphasis in much public debate on the need for tough sentencing—which is often equated with use of prison—the fact remains that prison is very expensive, and for many offenders does not act as a deterrent. The former Coalition government developed policy ideas which it was hoped would encourage the a of offenders (*see Box 5.23*).

Box 5.23 Reform in progress

Offender Rehabilitation Act 2014

The objective is to bring down reoffending rates. The Offender Rehabilitation Act 2014 contains the following key reforms:

- creating a new National Probation Service;
- providing that every offender released from custody will receive statutory supervision and rehabilitation in the community;
- putting in place a nationwide 'through the prison gate' resettlement service, meaning most offenders are given continuous support by one provider from custody into the community. This will be supported by ensuring that most offenders are held in a prison designated to their area for at least three months before release;
- creating 21 new rehabilitation providers, designed to get the best out of the public, voluntary, and private sectors, at the local as well as national level;

---

[18] See my blog, www.martinpartington.com, July 2014. For the CPS policy on asset recovery and the new service they launched in 2014 see www.cps.gov.uk/your_cps/our_organisation/asset_recovery.html.

Box 5.23 Continued

- introducing new payment incentives for market providers to focus on reforming offenders, giving providers flexibility to do what works and freedom from bureaucracy, but only paying them in full for real reductions in reoffending.

The proposals to open the delivery of probation services to private sector companies as well as third sector charities are extremely controversial, as they will lead to fundamental, and some argue very harmful, changes in the way in which probation services are delivered. The new scheme came into operation in 2015.

Further information is at www.gov.uk/government/publications/2010-to-2015-government-policy-reoffending-and-rehabilitation/2010-to-2015-government-policy-reoffending-and-rehabilitation#appendix-4-transforming-rehabilitation.

In November 2016, the government published a white paper on prison reform, the precursor to a Prisons Bill which was published in 2017 but which fell when the 2017 General Election was called. A replacement Bill is currently awaited. Here too the policy focus is on trying to create an environment in prison in which rehabilitation can take place.

5.6 *Transforming our Justice System*: criminal justice

The need for improved efficiency in the criminal justice system has long been recognized. But this was given much more urgency in 2014 when Lord Justice Leveson was asked to undertake a review of the efficiency of the criminal justice system, exploring ways in which the operation of the system could be made more cost effective. His report was published in January 2015 (*see Box 5.24*).[19]

Box 5.24 Reform in progress

Lord Justice Leveson's review of efficiency in the criminal courts

In summary, he recommends:

- greater use of video and other conferencing technology across the system (including courts and prisons) particularly featuring remote hearings in the Crown Court, which would lead to a better service for all those involved and reduce both delay and cost;
- facilitating the use in court of evidence gathered by police on video cameras mounted on their bodies or helmets and a streamlined approach to other evidence

---

[19] More detail is in my blog, www.martinpartington.com, August 2014 and January 2015. The National Audit Office published a report on the costs of inefficiency in the criminal justice system in 2016: see www.nao.org.uk/wp-content/uploads/2016/03/Efficiency-in-the-criminal-justice-system.pdf.

Box 5.24 Continued

which has been captured electronically, such as interviews of child witnesses (achieving best evidence) and interviews with defendants;

- more flexible opening hours in magistrates' courts to accommodate those who cannot attend hearings during normal office hours;
- tighter case management by judges, including, in appropriate cases, the provision of timetables for evidence and speeches;
- that contracts awarded to those responsible for delivering prisoners to court should require greater efficiency so that prisoners appear on time and do not delay proceedings;
- that there should be funding available to pay for the inevitable cost of changing from the current systems to the more efficient ones.

In May 2015, the government announced it had accepted the bulk of these recommendations.

This has led to two initiatives currently on-going: *Transforming Summary Justice* for magistrates' courts; and *Better Case Management* for the Crown Court.

The Levenson report can be found at www.judiciary.gov.uk/publications/review-of-efficiency-in-criminal-proceedings-final-report/.

Transforming Summary Justice is at www.cps.gov.uk/publications/agencies/transforming_summary_justice_may_2015.html.

Better Case Management (BCM) is at www.judiciary.gov.uk/subject/better-case-management-bcm/.

These developments have informed discussions on the further reforms to the justice system envisaged in the Transforming Our Justice System programme (*see 4.2.2.2*). The criminal justice system is at the heart of this programme. The principal policy objectives relating to criminal justice are in *Box 5.25*.

Box 5.25 Reform in Progress

Transforming criminal justice

There are three principal objectives: (1) the criminal courts should be more flexible; (2) more should be done to address offender behaviour; and (3) the use of technology should be improved.

(1) *Criminal courts should be more flexible*—this will be achieved by:

    (a) Aligning the criminal courts: magistrates' courts and the Crown Court deal with different levels of criminal offence, but they must work better together to provide a more efficient service. Government and the judiciary are working on structural and procedural changes that will give the senior judiciary clearer oversight of, and flexibility to manage, judicial leadership in the criminal

Box 5.25 Continued

jurisdiction. The government plans to reform existing local justice areas, making it easier to transfer cases between the Crown Court and magistrates' court.

(b) Making it easier for vulnerable and intimidated witnesses (including victims) to give evidence: the greater use of pre-trial cross-examination in Crown Court trials will allow vulnerable and intimidated witnesses to pre-record their cross-examination. A pilot study found that this procedure meant witnesses gave evidence in half the time it would take at trial. The government believes that expanding this will reduce distress for victims and witnesses.

(2) *Doing more to address offender behaviour*—this will be achieved by:

(a) Introducing problem-solving courts: the government is already trialling this in parts of the country. It will explore the potential for expanding their use with the judiciary.

(b) Using out of court disposals: this is designed to help change offenders' behaviour at the earliest possible opportunity, with swift and certain consequences for offenders who do not comply with the conditions attached.

(3) *Improving the use of technology*—this will allow:

(a) Streamlining process: for example by removing unnecessary appearances in court (such as first appearances in magistrates' courts for cases which can only be tried in the Crown Court), introducing a more efficient process to allocate cases to the Crown Court or magistrates' courts, and allowing simple decisions to be made via a new online system.

(b) Making processes more efficient: the use of video link and telephone and video conferencing technology to make hearings easier and more convenient for all. The government wants to work with the police to hold bail hearings by video link from police stations to reduce the need for some offenders to be held in police cells overnight. In appropriate cases offenders will be able to plead guilty, be convicted, and be sentenced all on the same day by live video link from police stations.

(c) Introducing a new collaborative IT system: the Common Platform is already being developed to provide a single case management IT system for use throughout the Crown Court and magistrates' courts. Many current paper and court-based processes will be moved online, saving time and increasing efficiency for all court users.

(d) Enabling online convictions and fixed fines: for certain routine, low-level summary, non-imprisonable offences with no identifiable victim, the government is proposing to introduce a system which resolves cases entirely online. Defendants would log on to an online system to see the evidence against them before entering a plea. If they plead guilty, they can opt in to (and can always opt out of) the online system which allows them to view the penalty, accept the conviction and penalty, and pay their fine. Cases would be resolved immediately and entirely online, without the involvement of a magistrate.

Source: chapter 2: consult.justice.gov.uk/digital-communications/transforming-our-courts-and-tribunals/supporting_documents/consultationpaper.pdf.

5.7 The post-trial stages

5.7.1 Criminal appeals

Those convicted in magistrates' courts can appeal to the Crown Court, either against conviction or against sentence.[20] In 2016, around 10,000 appeals from magistrates' courts were made, 5,941 against verdict, the rest against sentence; 44 per cent of appeals against verdict were successful and 46 per cent of appeals against sentence resulted in a variation of the sentence.[21]

Appeals from the Crown Court can be made to the Court of Appeal (Criminal Division), but only with the permission of the court. In the year from October 2015 to September 2016, the Court of Appeal dealt with 1,247 applications for permission to appeal against conviction and 4,072 against the sentence imposed. Over 70 per cent of these applications were turned down. Of the 260 appeals against conviction (i.e. where permission to appeal had been granted) which were heard by the court, 94 were allowed. Of the 1,294 appeals against sentence which were heard, 924 were allowed.[22]

There is the possibility of a further appeal to the Supreme Court, but this needs the permission of the court, which is given in only a handful of cases.

5.7.2 Criminal Cases Review Commission

One of the most serious challenges facing the criminal justice system is ensuring that miscarriages of justice do not occur. Notwithstanding the opportunities for appeal and the outcomes of appeals, there will always be cases where the full facts have not emerged at trial or on subsequent appeal, possibly because there have been failures by the police or prosecution to put evidence before the court.

The Criminal Cases Review Commission was established in 1997 under Part 2 of the Criminal Appeal Act 1995.

It usually considers only those cases that have been through the normal judicial appeal process. It currently receives over 1,000 applications a year, but only a small number lead to a case being referred back to the Court of Appeal.

Reviews are conducted by case review managers. Decisions on the outcome of the work of the case review managers are taken by the Commission. The Commission has 11 members, appointed from a variety of backgrounds. Any decision to refer a case to the Court of Appeal is taken by a committee of at least three members.

The function of the Commission is to consider whether there would be a real possibility that a conviction, finding of fact, verdict, or sentence would not be upheld by the court, were a reference back to be made. In relation to reviews of convictions, there has to be either a legal argument or evidence that had not been raised at the trial or on

---

[20] For appeals in civil cases, *see* 8.12.

[21] See www.gov.uk/government/statistics/criminal-court-statistics-quarterly-april-to-june-2017 Main tables, table C8.

[22] Data from Court of Criminal Appeal, Annual Report at www.judiciary.gov.uk/wp-content/uploads/2017/02/cacd-lcj-report-2016-final.pdf.

appeal, or other exceptional circumstances; in relation to sentencing, again there has to be legal argument or information about the individual or the offence that was not raised during the trial or on appeal.[23]

5.7.3 Parole and the work of the Parole Board

Even though the court may have imposed a custodial sentence in a particular case, this does not mean that the convicted person will serve the whole period of the sentence. Sentences are subject to review by the Parole Board. This body was established under the provisions of the Criminal Justice Act 1967 and has been in operation since 1968. Its primary function is to make risk assessments that inform decisions whether prisoners can be released back into the community early. While protection of the public is crucial, the Board seeks to enhance the rehabilitative effect of prison in cases where that seems possible. The responsibilities of the Board vary, depending on different types of case. Important changes to the work of the Board were made by the Criminal Justice Act 2003.

5.7.3.1 Determinate sentence cases

Cases determined under the Criminal Justice Act 1991. Where a convicted person was sentenced to a fixed term of imprisonment on or after 1 October 1992, he or she becomes eligible for parole halfway through the sentence, backdated to include any time spent in custody on remand before the trial. (For those sentenced before 1 October 1992, the date of eligibility for parole arose one-third of the way through the sentence.) Thus a prisoner sentenced to four years on 2 January 1994, who had also spent six months in custody on remand, became eligible for parole on 2 July 1996—the parole eligibility date (PED).

Six months before the PED, Parole Board officers begin gathering information to enable a panel from the Parole Board to take an initial decision on whether the prisoner may or may not be suitable for parole. The prisoner may also be interviewed by a Parole Board member. In addition to written reports, the panel is required to take into account *directions* made by the Home Secretary. These give guidance on particular issues on which the panel must be satisfied before finding in favour of the prisoner. While the decision to grant parole is formally one for the Secretary of State, he has delegated his decision-taking powers to the Board in all cases where the prisoner was sentenced to a period of less than 15 years. At this stage the decision of the Board is a discretionary one; cases are referred to as *discretionary conditional release* (DCR) cases.

Whether or not prisoners are released following a Parole Board review, determinate prisoners are automatically released two-thirds of the way through their sentence. However, all those released either after a parole decision or under the automatic process remain subject to supervision by the Probation Service and are subject to recall

---

[23] A detailed account of the work of the Commission can be found in its *Annual Reports*. See www.ccrc. gov.uk/ for further detail.

either for reoffending or for other breaches of the probation supervision until 75 per cent of the period of the sentence has expired. (The recall rate is about 4 per cent of those serving determinate sentences who have been released on parole.) Although the supervision of the Probation Service ends at that point, the remaining 25 per cent of the sentence can be reactivated if the person is subsequently convicted for another criminal offence.

The Criminal Justice Act 2003 made recall to custody an executive decision—by the prison and probation services—rather than by the Parole Board itself. The offender has the right of appeal to the Parole Board and, even if the offender chooses not to exercise this right, the Parole Board scrutinizes all recall decisions to ensure they are fairly taken. By allowing the Parole Board to focus on assessing decisions of recall, the Act removed an anomaly whereby the Parole Board used to both advise on the decision to recall and act as the appeal body against those same recalls.

Cases determined under the Criminal Justice Act 2003. For these cases, prisoners are automatically released on licence once they have served half their sentence. They remain on licence until the end of their nominal sentence. Thus the Board is no longer involved in the initial decision to release. However, they retain a key role in deciding what should happen should a decision be taken to recall a prisoner for breach of the licence. The Parole Board now reviews such cases. The House of Lords held in the case of *Smith and West* [2005] UKHL 1 that those recalled had the right to make oral representations. The role of the Board has, therefore, become more like that of an administrative tribunal, less like that of a decision-taking agency.

5.7.3.2 Life sentences

The Parole Board also has important responsibilities in relation to life sentences. There are two sorts of life sentence: *mandatory* life sentences, where the judge must impose a life sentence (as in the case of a conviction for murder); and discretionary life sentences, where this was the sentence that the judge decided was appropriate because of the risk that the offender would commit another offence.

The starting point is a decision on the minimum term, now called *the tariff*. This is the minimum period that the prisoner must serve in prison. Under the provisions of the Crime (Sentences) Act 1997, the tariff for mandatory lifers was fixed by the Home Secretary, taking into account a recommendation of the trial judge. Following a decision of the European Court of Human Rights (*Stafford v United Kingdom*, Application No. 46295/99, 28 May 2002), the House of Lords declared that the imposition of the tariff was indistinguishable from sentencing, and thus in effect part of the trial process (*R v Secretary of State for the Home Department, ex p Anderson* [2002] UKHL 46). As Article 6 of the European Convention on Human Rights requires tribunals deciding criminal trials to be independent, the role of the Home Secretary was held incompatible with Article 6. The tariff in all cases is now set by the trial judge.

Three years before the expiry of the tariff, the case is reviewed by the Parole Board. It considers whether or not a prisoner is suitable to be moved to the more relaxed regime of an open prison. On expiry of the tariff, the Parole Board considers whether the prisoner is suitable for release on licence. If it decides to release on licence, the prisoner is still subject to supervision by the Probation Service for at least four years. At that point (or later) the Home Secretary may decide that the supervision requirements can be lifted. The prisoner remains liable to recall and for the balance of his sentence to be reactivated for the rest of his life, should there be reason for so doing, such as subsequent offending.

If the Parole Board concludes that, on the expiry of the tariff, release would not be appropriate, the case is reviewed, normally every two years.

5.7.3.3 Procedure

The process of reaching these decisions does vary. In the case of *mandatory* lifers, the decision-taking process is similar to that for determinate sentences. Reports are prepared; an interview is held by a member of the Parole Board with the prisoner; and a decision is reached on the papers. Mandatory lifer panels are specially constituted to include a judge and a psychiatrist. Again the panel is required to take into account *directions* prescribed by the Home Secretary. Originally, the actual decision was taken by the Home Secretary; the Parole Board panel could only make a recommendation. The Criminal Justice Act 2003 provides that the Board should take the decision.

For *discretionary* lifers, the process of review involves the compilation of a dossier of reports. But there is then a fundamentally important difference. An oral hearing (rather like a tribunal hearing) is listed before a discretionary lifer panel of the Parole Board (which includes a judge and a psychiatrist). The prisoner is entitled to legal representation at this hearing. At the conclusion of the hearing, the panel may recommend transfer to open prison conditions, or may in appropriate cases direct release.

5.7.3.4 Workload

The workload of the Board is substantial.[24] The key statistics are that in 2016–17, the Parole Board dealt with 25,204 cases on the papers, and held 7,377 oral hearings. Many cases dealt with on the papers ended by directing the prisoner to an oral hearing.

Following the decision of the Supreme Court in *Osborn, Booth and Reilly* [2013] UKSC 61 (which held that an oral hearing must be held where there is a dispute about the evidence between the prisoner and the Secretary of State), the number of oral hearings increased substantially—even in cases where there is no prospect of release. This led to significant delay in the holding of hearings by the Board, though delays are reducing.

5.8 The place of the victim

One of the ways in which the criminal justice system has been transformed in recent years is through increased recognition of the victims of crime. The position of the victim is fundamental to the whole criminal justice system since the victim's report that

---

[24] See www.gov.uk/government/publications/parole-board-annual-report for more detail on the work of the Board.

a crime has been committed is, save for the most serious offences, the key to further steps being taken in the criminal process. Further, the viewpoint of the victim is one of the factors taken into account by the CPS in reaching a decision whether or not to prosecute a case. There are respects in which sentencing policy reflects the impact the criminal activity may have had on the victim. Much of the activity in the youth justice system is designed to make the offender aware of the victim's perceptions of what he or she has done.

In recent years the place of the victim has been given greater statutory recognition. Many of the provisions in the Criminal Justice Act 2003, for example those relating to bail or the use of video links, are designed to assist victims and other witnesses to give evidence. More specifically, the Domestic Violence, Crime and Victims Act 2004 contained a number of provisions designed to ensure that the victim is kept informed about the progress of a case, and about the release of a prisoner.

Among the measures included are, first, it required publication of a statutory code of guidance for the treatment of victims, which must be endorsed by Parliament. In November 2015, this was replaced by the *Code of Practice for Victims of Crime*.[25]

Secondly, it provides that, where a court convicts a person (the 'offender') for a sexual or violent offence and imposes a prison sentence of a minimum of 12 months, the local probation board must take reasonable steps to establish whether the victim of the offence wishes to make representations about whether the offender should be subject to conditions on release (and, if so, what conditions), or wishes to receive information about those conditions. If the victim does express such a wish, the relevant local probation board becomes responsible for forwarding any representations the victim makes to the authority responsible for making the decisions about release. The board is also responsible for informing the victim whether the offender will be subject to any conditions in the event of release; for providing details of any conditions about contact with the victim or his family; and for providing any other information it considers appropriate. Similar provisions apply where an offender has been detained under the provisions of the Mental Health Act 1983.

Thirdly, the jurisdiction of the Parliamentary Commissioner for Administration is expanded so that he can investigate and report on complaints that a duty under the code of practice for victims has been breached. These relate to complaints that any person has failed to comply with a duty to victims relating to the need to keep victims informed. The Parliamentary Commissioner has the same powers to obtain evidence and examine witnesses as he has in relation to complaints of maladministration (*see 6.4.6.1*).

Fourthly, the Act provided for the creation of the post of Commissioner for Victims and Witnesses. The Commissioner's primary functions are: to promote the interests of victims and witnesses of crime and anti-social behaviour; to take steps to encourage good practice in their treatment; and to keep the code of guidance under review. The Commissioner is given various ways in which she can carry out these functions, including making reports to the Secretary of State, commissioning research, and making recommendations to an authority within her remit (a broadly defined group of those working in and around the criminal justice system). Further, the

Commissioner must provide advice on issues relating to victims and witnesses of crime and anti-social behaviour when requested to do so by any government minister. The authorities within the Commissioner's remit may also ask the Commissioner to give specific advice in connection with the information they provide, through whatever medium, to victims and witnesses. The post is currently held by Baroness Newlove.

Four further developments may be briefly noted: victim support schemes; the Victim Surcharge; the criminal injuries compensation scheme; and compensation orders.

5.8.1 Victim support schemes

There are now about 365 local victim support schemes with some 15,000 volunteers offering help to over 1.5 million victims. In the Crown Court, another 1,500+ volunteers help over 120,000 victims and witnesses who have to attend court. They do a great deal of work trying to reassure the victims of crime that they have not been targeted, but are simply the victims of opportunistic criminal activity. They also help victims and other witnesses cope with the stress and strain of appearing in court.

5.8.2 Victim Surcharge

The Victim Surcharge, introduced in April 2007, is an ancillary order imposed by a court. Following changes introduced on 1 October 2012, it is payable when an individual is sentenced to a conditional discharge, a fine, or a community or custodial sentence in relation to an offence committed on or after that date. Offenders under the age of 18 as well as adults will be ordered to pay the Victim Surcharge, although at lower levels than adults, to reflect the differences in sentencing principles between adults and juveniles. Revenue raised from the Victim Surcharge is used to fund victim services through the Victim and Witness General Fund.

5.8.3 The Criminal Injuries Compensation Scheme

This has been in operation for many years. This state-funded scheme was revised in 2001, 2008, and 2012. It is administered by the Criminal Injuries Compensation Authority.[26] During 2016–17, it received 31,563 applications, of which about half were unsuccessful. £143.3 million was paid in compensation to victims of violent crime. The scheme is limited to victims injured as the result of violent criminal activity directed towards them. Critics point out that other negative consequences of being the victim of crime are not thus compensated.

Two specific points may be noted. First, the amounts of compensation paid are defined in a statutory tariff; they are not assessed in the same way as damages for personal injury in civil litigation. This leads to complaints that the scheme under-compensates the victims of crime, particularly where they have suffered other than by way of

---

[25] See www.gov.uk/government/publications/the-code-of-practice-for-victims-of-crime.

[26] The 2016–17 Annual Report is at https://www.gov.uk/government/publications/cica-annual-report -and-accounts-2016–17.

physical injury. Secondly, as a result of amendments in the Domestic Violence, Crime and Victims Act 2004, it is now provided that the courts, when making a compensation order, can require sums obtained from the offender to be used to compensate the Compensation Injuries Fund (in cases where an award from the fund has been made).

5.8.4 Compensation orders

In addition to this statutory scheme, since 1972 the criminal courts have had power to order those convicted of crimes to pay compensation to their victims. These powers have been developed so that there are circumstances in which a compensation order may be imposed as the sole penalty. From 1988, the courts have been required to consider making compensation orders in defined groups of cases involving death, injury, loss, or damage, and to give reasons where an order is not made. Since 1991 the limits on the sums that magistrates may order as compensation have been increased.

The Legal Aid, Sentencing and Punishment of Offenders Act 2012 has created a duty on the courts to consider making a compensation order in such cases. These developments may be seen as more reparative forms of outcome for the criminal justice system.

5.9 Keeping criminal justice under review: the work of inspectorates

There is a lot of emphasis on the use of inspectorates to oversee the work of agencies involved in the criminal justice system (*see Box 5.26*).

Box 5.26 Legal system explained

Inspectorates in the criminal justice system

The current inspection regime comprises: Her Majesty's Inspectorate of Constabulary and Fire and Rescue Services (HMICFRS); Her Majesty's Crown Prosecution Service Inspectorate (HMCPSI); Her Majesty's Inspectorate of Prisons (HMI Prisons); and Her Majesty's Inspectorate of Probation (HMI Probation). Although constituted differently, they all predominantly ensure the safe and proper delivery of the services inspected and promulgate good practice:

- HMICFRC has a stated purpose to promote the efficiency and effectiveness of policing through inspection of police organizations and functions to ensure agreed standards are achieved and maintained, good practice is spread, and performance is improved. It also provides advice and support to the Home Secretary and police authorities and forces, and plays a role in the development of future leaders. These functions were extended to Fire and Rescue Services, when its role was expanded in 2017.
- HMCPSI has a stated purpose to promote continuous improvement in the efficiency, effectiveness, and fairness of the prosecution services within a joined-up criminal

Box 5.26 Continued

justice system, through the process of inspection, evaluation, and identification of good practice.

- HMI Prisons has a remit to inspect prison establishments and to report on the conditions of those establishments, the treatment of prisoners and other inmates, and the facilities available to them. The inspectorate also undertakes inspection of immigration removal centres and, by invitation, the military corrective centre.
- HMI Probation reports on the work and performance of the National Probation Service and of Youth Offending Teams (YOTs), particularly on the effectiveness of work aimed at reducing reoffending and protecting the public. It contributes to policy and service delivery by providing advice and disseminating good practice.

HMI Prisons and HMI Probation have a shared approach to inspection of offender management as it has been developed by the National Offender Management Service (NOMS).

The inspectorates undertake both single agency inspection and joint inspection:

- *Single agency inspection*: the statutory remit of each inspectorate requires it to inspect and report on the performance of its relevant organization (or, for prisons, the treatment and conditions of those in custody). This can be done via cyclical inspection of an area, risk-based inspection of an area, or thematic inspections on a particular topic. Given the current remit of the four inspectorates, their primary attention is on the safe and proper delivery of services within their separate organizations.
- *Joint inspection*: this can take the form of either routine or thematic inspections conducted by more than one inspectorate, on a particular topic involving more than one inspected organization. These can be done both within the criminal justice system and outside in areas such as education, health, or local services; for example HMI Prisons routinely inspects with OfSTED, the Royal Pharmaceutical Society, and the British Dental Board. Currently, joint inspections are resourced from existing budgets and must take into account the resource demands of single agency inspection. To facilitate cross-criminal justice system inspection, in 1998 the Chief Inspectors established a Criminal Justice Chief Inspectors Group (CJCIG) to undertake inspections within the criminal justice system on a joint basis. Since then the number of joint inspections has increased; initially they were thematic in nature, but since 2003 the inspectorates have combined to start inspecting criminal justice areas (or local criminal justice boards).

In 2005, a consultation paper argued that there was a need for institutional reform and that the four existing inspectorates should be brought together in a single 'super-inspectorate'. However, following the enactment of the Police and Justice Act 2006, the four inspectorates were given statutory authority to undertake joint work across the criminal justice system.

For further information on the joint working of the inspectorates, see www.justicein-spectorates.gov.uk/cjji/.

5.10 Key points

1. The criminal justice system embraces a huge range of agencies, which must be seen as a whole.

2. It is important to be aware of the different theories (not always consistent with each other) on which the criminal justice system as a whole, and sentencing policy in particular, are based.

3. Overall crime rates have been falling consistently for a number of years.

4. The police have significant powers to enable them to investigate crime.

5. Use of powers to stop and search individuals is particularly controversial.

6. Prosecutions policy is determined by the Crown Prosecution Service Code; not all cases investigated by the police are followed by a prosecution.

7. In both the magistrates' court and the Crown Court, the majority of cases are dealt with by a guilty plea; a trial is a statistical rarity.

8. The youth justice system is undergoing significant change.

9. Where a defendant is convicted by a jury, in over 80 per cent of cases the jury was unanimous.

10. The most commonly imposed penalty is a fine. But the use of community sentences is limited.

11. Governments are concerned about the cost of imprisoning people, particularly those sentenced to very short sentences.

12. The number of appeals, both against conviction and against sentence, is relatively small, but the success rate of appeals—particularly against sentence—is relatively high.

13. The place of the victim in the criminal justice system continues to be developed.

14. There is continuing concern about how members of the Black, Asian, and Minority Ethnic groups are dealt with in the criminal justice system.

5.11 Questions

Use the self-test questions in the Online Resources to test your understanding of the topics covered in this chapter and receive tailored feedback: www.oup.com/uk/partington18_19/.

5.12 Web links

Check the Online Resources for a selection of annotated web links allowing you to easily research topics of particular interest: www.oup.com/uk/partington18_19/.

5.13 Blog items

See Spotlight on the Justice System, at www.martinpartington.com/category/chapter-5-2/.

Suggestions for further reading

ASHWORTH, A., Sentencing and Criminal Justice (5th edn, Cambridge, Cambridge University Press, 2010)

ASHWORTH, A., and REDMAYNE, M., The Criminal Process (4th edn, Oxford, Oxford University Press, 2010)

ELKS, L., Righting Miscarriages of Justice? Ten Years of the Criminal Cases Review Commission (London, JUSTICE, 2008)

Other suggestions are made in the Further Reading listed in the **Online Resources**.

6

The administrative justice system

6.1 Introduction: administrative justice

Although the criminal justice system, discussed in *Chapter 5*, is institutionally extremely complex, the primary focus of the system—on regulating social behaviour, and dealing with those who break the rules—is relatively clear. By contrast, the very concept of 'administrative justice' is controversial, meaning different things to different people. Traditional analyses of the legal system, focusing on a straightforward distinction between criminal and civil law, fail to acknowledge a separate system of 'administrative justice'. Instead, it gets wrapped up in general discussion of civil justice.

In part, this reflects the continuing influence of the nineteenth-century writer A. V. Dicey, who argued against a separately identifiable body of *droit administratif* (administrative law). He thought that the creation of *droit administratif* would result in public officials being given legally preferential treatment and thus offend against the fundamental principle of the rule of law, that all should be equal under the law.

Over 100 years on, the reality is that the state plays a large part in the regulation of society; and there is a vast array of institutions employing people who provide public services. Although there may still not be a conceptually distinct branch of the law that may be described as administrative law, as there is in many countries in Continental Europe, any understanding of the modern English legal system must involve recognizing the distinct concept of administrative justice.

The primary focus of this chapter is on the institutions in which administrative law is practised. First, however, we reflect on the nature of administrative law and the role it plays in modern society.

6.2 The role of administrative law: authority and values

As just noted, one feature of the modern world is the significant role government plays in developing and implementing a vast range of social policies. Implementation of social policy depends on law. Administrative law:

- provides authority for public servants to deliver government policy, whose legitimacy is enshrined in the laws (primary, secondary, and tertiary—*see Box 3.6*) passed through the parliamentary system;

- authorizes the raising and expenditure of public funds;
- sets limits to the powers of public officials;
- creates the institutional mechanisms for calling public officials to account; and
- provides means for the redress of individual grievances or resolution of complaints by the citizen.

In addition to the functional attributes of administrative law, administrative justice embraces certain *values* or *principles* which should underpin good administration by those who deliver services on behalf of the state. These include: openness (or transparency); fairness; rationality (including the giving of reasons for decisions); impartiality (independence) of decision-takers; accountability; the prevention of the exercise of arbitrary power and the control of discretion; consistency; participation; efficiency; equity; and equal treatment (*see also Box 6.1*).

Box 6.1 System in action

Principles of administrative justice

In 2011, the Administrative Justice and Tribunals Council published its own statement of Principles of Administrative Justice. The Principles say that a good administrative justice system should:

- make users and their needs central, treating them with fairness and respect at all times;
- enable people to challenge decisions and seek redress using procedures that are independent, open, and appropriate for the matter involved;
- keep people fully informed and empower them to resolve their problems as quickly and comprehensively as possible;
- lead to well-reasoned, lawful, and timely outcomes;
- be coherent and consistent;
- work proportionately and efficiently;
- adopt the highest standards of behaviour, seek to learn from experience, and continuously improve.

While these may seem obvious, it is surprising how often these basic messages are forgotten. Their report also contains a self-assessment toolkit, which administrators can use as a template against which they can measure their organization. This is the sort of valuable work that has been lost now that the Council has been abolished (*see 6.6*).

As with the underlying values of criminal justice, the underlying values of administrative justice are not wholly consistent with one another. There may be circumstances in which openness should properly yield to confidentiality; where fairness of process may conflict with efficiency. Each of these values is contingent upon the context in which it is asserted. One of the challenges for those who govern, and for those who criticize government, is to achieve an appropriate balance between conflicting values.

The details of particular areas of substantive public law (e.g. rules relating to social security) are not for discussion here. Rather, the focus is on the mechanisms of accountability which exist to keep officials in check and which provide means of resolving disputes when things go wrong. But you should reflect on the tensions between the different values in administrative justice in the context of particular administrative activities—for example, the determination of asylum applications; or the collection of taxes; or the granting of planning permissions; or the payment of social security benefits.

6.3 The administrative justice system: an overview

A great variety of bodies and processes make up the system of administrative justice. They include:

- courts;
- tribunals;
- inquiries;
- ombudsmen;
- complaints procedures.

As with the criminal justice system, these employ thousands of people and cost millions of pounds to run. It is also necessary to consider the role of Parliament in this context, as well as the impact of the Freedom of Information Act 2000. Each of these is considered in this chapter.

6.3.1 The holistic approach

This way of conceptualizing the framework of administrative justice is not wholly orthodox. Practising lawyers tend not to think about administrative justice in the broad sense used here, but rather more narrowly about administrative law and in particular the special process available in the High Court known as *judicial review*. Academic administrative lawyers go beyond this court-focused approach to include in their analyses comments on other mechanisms for the resolution of disputes. But the treatment of topics other than judicial review tends to be somewhat superficial.[1]

There are perfectly good reasons for this:

(1) The *qualitative* importance of the law of judicial review is clear. It is in the reported decisions of judges in the Administrative Court (now also the Upper Tier Tribunal, *see Diagram 6.1*) and above that the jurisprudence of judicial

---

[1] There are honourable exceptions to this generalization: see e.g. Harlow, C., and Rawlings, R., *Law and Administration* (3rd edn, Cambridge, Cambridge University Press, 2009).

review has been developed. Fundamental principles—of procedural fairness, and limiting the exercise of discretionary power by officials—are the creation of the courts. The courts have also defined: who can bring proceedings by way of judicial review; the bodies and institutions which are subject to the principles of judicial review; and the grounds on which judicial review may be sought. The principles of judicial review provide the legal background to the administrative justice system. In doing this work, the judges assert that fundamental constitutional principle, the independence of the judiciary. The importance of this work has been expanded by the Human Rights Act 1998, which enshrines further principles against which official actions can be tested in the courts, in particular that UK laws must be compatible with the European Convention on Human Rights and that public authorities must act in compliance with the Convention.

(2) It is in the courts that practising lawyers earn good money and develop formidable reputations. With rare exceptions, legal aid is not available to pay for legal representation before tribunals or other dispute resolution/grievance handling fora. This reduces the incentive for legal practitioners to get to know about the wider world of administrative justice.

(3) The work of this wider range of bodies is often not the subject of formal published documentation. Legal scholars find it hard to access the material needed for a full review of the administrative justice system as a whole.

However, focusing on judicial review means that other procedures for the delivery of administrative justice are not paid the attention they deserve. In terms of the engagement that the citizen has with the administrative justice system, it is much more likely that a person will go to a tribunal than a court. The large number of ombudsmen that now exist handle thousands more cases in a year. A wide variety of complaints procedures deal with countless other grievances. *Quantitatively* tribunals, ombudsmen, and complaints procedures are far more significant than the courts. This account seeks to redress the balance.

6.3.2 Procedural variety

There are two important reasons for making this argument for a broad view of administrative justice, which arise not just from a desire to be different. First, what the administrative justice system—taken as a whole—offers is a vast test bed for the development and evaluation of new procedures:

- decisions being taken on the papers;
- decisions by a single judge;
- decisions by three- (or more) person tribunals;
- inquisitorial procedures;
- procedures using new IT technologies; and
- procedures involving the unrepresented and inarticulate.

It is one of the great wasted opportunities that those who have sought in recent years to introduce change into the civil justice system should have paid such scant attention to what goes on in practice in the administrative justice system. The latter has provided a rich source of ideas for how things might be done differently. Those who in the past may have looked down their noses at the institutions of the administrative justice system as 'not being proper courts' should think again. It is here that alternative procedures are to be found, often working extremely well.

6.3.3 Citizen redress

In addition, the failure to see the administrative justice system in a more holistic fashion prevents people from seeing the enormous variety of methods that exist for seeking the redress of citizens' grievances. This is a theme that was taken up by the National Audit Office (NAO) in an important report on citizen redress (*see Box 6.2*).

Box 6.2 Legal system explained

Citizen redress

A distinctive feature of public services is the arrangements for getting things put right, remedying grievances, or securing a second view of a disputed decision. 'Citizen redress' denotes all the administrative mechanisms that allow citizens to seek remedies for what they perceive to be poor treatment, mistakes, faults, or injustices in their dealings with central government departments or agencies. Of course, redress mechanisms may not find in favour of the citizens making complaints or bringing appeals. Indeed, in a well-run administrative system, the large majority of cases investigated should prove to be unfounded. Yet even in such cases the redress processes used should provide people with the assurance that they have been fairly and properly treated or that a disputed decision has been correctly made under the relevant rules.

The systems currently in place for the citizen to seek remedy when things go wrong have developed over time and for a variety of different purposes. Inevitably, this has resulted in complexity and variations in attitude and approach.

The main mechanisms for achieving redress currently are:

- customer complaints procedures;
- appeals and tribunals systems;
- references to independent complaints handlers or ombudsmen; and
- resort to judicial review (and other forms of legal action).

In cases where something is found to have gone wrong, one important outcome of such mechanisms may be the payment of compensation. The different redress mechanisms interconnect strongly. From the citizens' point of view they offer a range of different options and opportunities for trying to achieve very similar or connected outcomes. And from government organizations' points of view, the efficacy of some redress procedures may imply fewer cases running through other routes. For instance,

Box 6.2 Continued

good basic complaints-handling systems should minimize the number of cases referred on to ombudsmen or leading to legal actions.

Yet public sector redress systems have developed piecemeal over many years and have rarely been systematically thought about as a whole. Central government organizations make a strong distinction between complaints and appeals. Complaints concern processes and how issues have been handled. They have traditionally been considered as part of the internal business arrangements of departments and agencies. They are often thought about primarily in terms of customer responsiveness and business effectiveness. Appeals systems and tribunals concern the accuracy or correctness of substantive departmental or agency decisions. They conventionally form part of the administrative justice sphere. They are often considered primarily in terms of citizens' legal rights, natural justice, and a range of related quasi-judicial criteria. This bifurcated approach may have some advantages, but it is very distinctive to the public sector and has no counterpart in private sector firms. Rigidly separating complaints from appeals also means that many public service organizations are essentially providing two different basic systems of redress, which are set up and organized on different lines. And citizens also have to grapple with two very different concepts of redress, instead of a more integrated concept of 'getting things put right'.

Citizen redress procedures have an importance for the overall quality of public services that goes far beyond their direct costs. Complaints are an important source of feedback to central departments and agencies about where things are perceived by citizens as going wrong, a view also stressed by the Parliamentary Ombudsman. Hence they are a significant source of information on possible improvements in organizational arrangements. Similarly, the availability of appeals and tribunals options is intended to provide an effective incentive for officials to make considered decisions that are right first time. Providing a range of administrative procedures for citizens to seek remedies or redress is also a key area of civil rights, providing vital safeguards against arbitrary or ill-founded decision making by government organizations. So it is clearly essential that any changes made to citizen redress arrangements do not restrict established rights to independent review and an opportunity to state one's case.

However, it is also possible that the current workings of citizen redress institutions may not be optimally configured to deliver what the public most want. Current arrangements have built up over long periods, largely in separated ways, often specific to one policy sector or one government organization. So the existing ladder of redress options may not be as accessible or as useful to citizens as it could be. It also may well not deliver what citizens most want. Redress systems should be purposefully targeted to deliver valued benefits to citizens in a timely way, rather than just following through on established procedures whose added value for citizens remains unclear.

In the past there were separate channels in government for dealing with complaints, appeals, and ombudsmen processes. The complaints route has mostly been seen as a matter for departments or agencies to run in a decentralized way as they see fit, with only the general discipline provided by ombudsmen's comments. Appeals and

Box 6.2 Continued

tribunals confer important citizens' rights and are legally mandated and so in business terms are an inescapable cost. They were previously regulated in a separate, more legal manner by the then Lord Chancellor's Department with input from the Council of Tribunals. As a result, citizen redress arrangements have apparently not been monitored or costed in any systematic way by central departments (such as the Cabinet Office or the Treasury). The onus has been on departments and agencies to consider the effectiveness and efficiency of their own redress schemes as part of their wider drive to improve efficiency.

Source: Adapted and extracted from National Audit Office, *Citizen Redress: What citizens can do if things go wrong with public services* (HC 21, 2004–5) (London, The Stationery Office, 2005).

6.3.4 The costs of administrative justice

All dispute resolution procedures cost money to run. But many of them are currently provided free to the individual. It is important that government agencies understand the costs of the redress systems they are providing. Failure to do this will mean that resources may be wasted unnecessarily.

In its report on Citizen Redress, the NAO provided some first estimates of the costs of the administrative justice system, as broadly conceived here (*see Box 6.3*). It may be argued that, though significant, these costs are small compared with expenditure on public services taken as a whole. But this is not sufficient reason for not thinking critically about whether the present system could be made more efficient. A consequence of the failure to see administrative justice in the round is that it makes it hard to appreciate the amount of money spent on the provision of administrative justice systems.

Box 6.3 System in action

Cost of the administrative justice system

In 2005, research undertaken for the NAO estimated that nearly 1.4 million cases are received through redress systems in central government annually and are processed by over 9,300 staff at an annual cost of at least £510 million.

The overall public expenditure costs of handling complaints and appeals can be assessed very roughly as the cost per new case and research suggests the following data:

- complaints cost an average of £155 per new case;
- appeals cases cost an average of £455 per new case;
- the costs for independent complaints handlers and for ombudsmen vary a lot, ranging between £550 and £4,500 per case, but mostly around £1,500 to £2,000.

Box 6.3 Continued

There are very wide variations around these average numbers.

In addition to the direct administrative costs of complaints, appeals, and other redress systems, processing these cases can indirectly create substantial additional expenditures for some particular areas of the central government, via legal aid costs paid to those people eligible for this assistance. From information supplied by the Legal Services Commission, the NAO can say that these additional costs are a minimum of £198 million in central government (primarily in the area of immigration and asylum appeals), plus a small amount in welfare benefit appeals. A minimum additional £24 million is incurred in the National Health Service. The actual full costs involved here are likely to be much greater than this.

Cutting down the initial numbers of complaints or appeals, resolving more complaints and appeals more speedily and proactively, and improving the cost efficiency of current redress arrangements, could all make appreciable savings in public money, savings that could then cumulate with every passing year.

Source: Adapted from National Audit Office, *Citizen Redress: What citizens can do if things go wrong with public services* (HC 21, 2004–5) (London, The Stationery Office, 2005).

In recent years the cost of administrative justice, particularly tribunals, has not gone unnoticed by government. As a consequence, there has been a significant change of policy relating to the fees potential applicants to tribunals must pay. Significantly increased fees were applied to employment tribunal cases, which led to huge falls in the numbers of cases coming to these tribunals. (*See Box 6.4.*) A decision to impose large fee increases for cases before the First-Tier Immigration and Asylum Chamber, made in October 2016, was reversed in November 2016.

Box 6.4 Reform in progress

Employment tribunal fees

Until the coming into force of the Employment Tribunals and the Employment Appeal Tribunal Fees Order 2013, a claimant could bring and pursue proceedings in an Employment Tribunal (ET) and appeal to the Employment Appeal Tribunal (EAT) without paying any fee. The Order created a complex fee tariff in which different fees were paid, depending on the type of action being brought before the tribunal. In addition, a fee had to be paid at the start of proceedings, another when the case went to a hearing. Poor claimants who fell below defined income and capital limits could get their fees remitted.

The government's objectives in imposing the fees were said to be:

(i) Financial: to transfer a proportion of the costs of the ETs to users (where they can afford to pay);

Box 6.4 Continued

(ii) Behavioural: to encourage people to use alternative services to help resolve their disputes; and

(iii) Justice: to protect access to justice by getting a better balance between what the taxpayer funds and what the litigant funds.

An official review of the impact of the fee changes, published in January 2017 concluded that, broadly, these objectives had been achieved.

The Supreme Court has, however, reached a quite different conclusion. In *R (on the application of UNISON) (Appellant) v Lord Chancellor (Respondent)* [2017] UKSC 51, the Court concluded unanimously that the Lord Chancellor did not have the power to make the order and so quashed it.

There are at least three reasons why the judgments in this case are particularly interesting.

• First, in most cases where the validity of a statutory instrument is challenged in the courts, the argument turns on fairly precise questions of statutory interpretation— were the rule-making powers in an Act of Parliament sufficient to give the relevant minister the power to make the order being challenged? In this case a much broader, constitutional approach was adopted. Because the numbers of cases coming to both the ET and the EAT had fallen so dramatically since the introduction of the fees, the fees had had the effect of denying potential claimants access to justice. Lord Reed, in the principal judgment, referred back to a number of historic legal texts, including Magna Carta, to conclude that it is a constitutional principle, recognized in common law, that people should have access to justice.

• Second, the judgment relies heavily on a number of empirical studies to show that the effect of impact of the fees rules was quite disproportionate. The justices conclude that ordinary people on average earnings would have to forgo weeks if not months of expenditure on anything other than the most basic necessities to save the money needed to pay the relevant fees. The Court decided that the fees thus imposed are a quite disproportionate burden on those who might have an arguable case to take to the ET or EAT. The cosy conclusions of the impact review were totally rejected by the Supreme Court.

• Finally, Lord Reed makes a number of important observations about the rule of law and the functions of courts and tribunals in supporting the rule of law. 'Courts exist in order to ensure that the laws made by Parliament, and the common law created by the courts themselves, are applied and enforced. That role includes ensuring that the executive branch of government carries out its functions in accordance with the law. In order for the courts to perform that role, people must in principle have unimpeded access to them. Without such access, laws are liable to become a dead letter, the work done by Parliament may be rendered nugatory, and the democratic election of Members of Parliament may become a meaningless charade.' (See further paragraphs 66–85 of the judgment.)

The Supreme Court made it clear that it was not outlawing fees altogether; fees that achieved the goals set out in (i)–(iii) earlier would be lawful. The government will propose a new fees structure, but it has not yet been published.

Similar policies have also been developed in relation to the work of the civil courts (for further information *see Box 8.2*).

Before it was wound up, the Administrative Justice and Tribunals Council argued that other financial models should be considered. In particular it suggested that government departments against which successful appeals have been made should themselves make a contribution towards the costs of the appeal process (*see Box 6.7*).

6.4 The institutions of administrative justice

6.4.1 The Administrative Court and the Upper Tribunal: judicial review

The Administrative Court, part of the High Court, is at the heart of the administrative justice system. It is where the fundamental principles of *judicial review* have been developed. The essence of judicial review is straightforward. Public officials must act within the law.

The primary tasks of judges in judicial review cases are:

- *to interpret statutory provisions*: there are many situations, particularly after new legislation has been passed, when the law needs clarification. Deciding the limits of the law, and whether or not a person acted within the law, is clearly a judicial task;

- *to control discretion*: in some situations legislation is deliberately drafted to give officials flexibility in the application of the law. Where a statute states that the minister 'may' act in a certain way or reach a 'reasonable' decision, these are examples of discretionary power. The judges have developed the principle that the exercise of discretion must not be 'unreasonable' (*Associated Provincial Picture Houses Ltd v Wednesbury Corporation* [1948] 1 KB 223, CA);

- *to determine the validity of secondary legislation*: the UK Supreme Court does not decide, as does the Supreme Court in the United States, that particular items of legislation are unlawful; that would offend the principle of the sovereignty of Parliament. (This is currently subject to one exception, where UK legislation is contrary to the law of the European Union (*Factortame v Secretary of State for Transport (No 2)* [1991] 1 AC 603).) Under the Human Rights Act 1998, the courts have power to declare a provision in an Act of Parliament incompatible with the rights set out in the Human Rights Act 1998. The courts have long asserted the power to declare secondary legislation unlawful, on the basis that the statutory instrument was beyond the powers of the minister as established by the primary Act of Parliament (see e.g. *R (on the application of The Public Law Project) (Appellant) v Lord Chancellor (Respondent)* [2016] UKSC 39);

- *to determine the fairness of procedures*: the courts have also determined fundamental principles of fairness in the lower courts, in other tribunals, and in a range of other contexts in which decisions affecting the citizen are made. Where these principles apply, the person must know the basis of the case against her, and be given an opportunity to be heard;

- *to prevent bias*: in addition, judges have insisted that adjudicators in the courts and other fora must not be 'biased', in the sense that they must not have a personal interest in the outcome of any particular case; and

- *to provide a remedy*: where the court finds that the law has been broken, it has a range of remedies available to it (*see Box 6.5*). The courts can use one or more of them in their decisions. A particular feature of judicial review proceedings is that the courts have discretion whether or not to make an order or grant a remedy. They may find that there has been a technical breach of the rules, but will not make an order if the consequences of the breach are trivial, or the other side has behaved improperly.

Box 6.5 Legal system explained

Judicial review remedies

The remedies available to the courts include:

- *quashing orders*: the most commonly used remedy. The courts rarely make their own decision; they usually quash the decision and send it back to the original decision maker to retake;
- *prohibiting orders*: preventing a body from taking a decision it might be contemplating taking;
- *mandatory orders*: requiring a body to carry out a duty imposed by statute;
- *declarations*: clarifying the rights and obligations of the parties to proceedings;
- *injunctions*: an order to stop a body acting in a particular way; and
- (rarely) *damages*.

Source: Adapted from *Public Law Project Information Leaflet 5*, available at www.publiclawproject.org.uk/Publications.html.

6.4.1.1 Data on the use of judicial review

In 2000, there were 4,238 applications for permission to apply for a judicial review. By 2013, this number had risen to 15,594—a threefold increase. The huge rise in applications was largely down to an enormous increase in the numbers of cases involving immigration and asylum. Although only a tiny number go on to a full hearing, nevertheless all applications have to be decided. This imposed a considerable workload on the judiciary. The government has sought ways to reduce the flow of judicial review cases to the Administrative Court.

The most significant step was to divert the majority of immigration and asylum cases to the Upper Tribunal. This change was introduced in November 2013. It has had a significant impact on the Administrative Court. In 2016, there were 4,300 applications for judicial review, more or less the same as the 2000 figure. Of these, over half related to immigration and asylum. The bulk of immigration and asylum cases have not disappeared, however; there were 16,195 applications to the Upper Tribunal Immigration and Asylum Chamber in the year 1 November 2015–31 October 2016.

The government introduced other changes, including:

- increasing the fees payable for making an application;
- banning people from seeking a hearing in person if their initial written application has been ruled as being totally without merit;
- halving the time limit for applying for a judicial review of a planning decision from three months to six weeks; and
- reducing the time limit for applying for a judicial review of a procurement decision from three months to four weeks.

However, the government also took the view that the judicial review process is being used—they would argue abused—with the result that:

- it inhibits economic development by causing delay to major projects;
- it is used by campaign groups as a political tool; and
- it adds to the cost of implementing executive decisions.

Each of these arguments was hotly disputed by the opponents of reform. Nonetheless, the government developed further proposals for change to judicial review.

First, it decided that all planning decisions that were challenged by judicial review should be determined by a newly created specialist Planning Court (*see Box 6.6*).

Box 6.6   Reform in progress

The Planning Court

As part of the changes to judicial review, planning cases now go to the Planning Court. From April 2014, it deals with all judicial reviews and statutory challenges involving planning matters, including appeals and applications relating to enforcement decisions, planning permission, compulsory purchase orders, and highways and other rights of way. It forms part of the Administrative Court but is distinct from it. Cases can start at the following locations:

- The Royal Courts of Justice;
- Birmingham Civil Justice Centre;
- Cardiff Civil Justice Centre;
- Leeds Combined Court;
- Manchester Civil Justice Centre.

Planning Court cases are subject to tighter time limits than Administrative Court cases:

- Applications for permission to apply for judicial review are to be determined within three weeks of the expiry of the time limit for filing of the acknowledgement of service.

Box 6.6 Continued

- Oral renewals of applications for permission to apply for judicial review are to be heard within one month of receipt of request for renewal.
- Applications for permission under section 289 of the Town and Country Planning Act 1990 are to be determined within one month of issue.
- Substantive statutory applications, including applications under section 288 of the Town and Country Planning Act 1990, are to be heard within six months of issue.
- Judicial reviews are to be heard within 10 weeks of the expiry of the period for the submission of detailed grounds by the defendant or any other party.

Specialist judges, with planning expertise, sit in the Planning Court.

These changes are intended to reduce the delay that can sometimes affect planning decisions. For further details see www.gov.uk/courts-tribunals/planning-court.

Secondly, the Criminal Justice and Courts Act 2015 made further changes designed to reduce the use of judicial review (*see Box 6.7*). In making these changes, the government asserted that the principle that individuals can challenge the legality of government action is preserved. Nonetheless, public lawyers were very hostile to these changes.

Box 6.7 Reform in progress

Reforming judicial review

The Criminal Justice and Courts Act 2015 made changes to judicial review:

(1) Most important is section 84. Judges have always used discretion in deciding whether to give a remedy (*see Box 6.5*). If, despite the procedural or other error, the outcome of the original decision would have been the same, no order would be made.

Section 84 takes this further by providing that relief must not be granted and permission to seek that relief must not be granted where the court considers the conduct complained about would be *highly likely* not to have resulted in a substantially different outcome for the applicant. The historic discretion of the court is—under the new rules—limited by these stricter requirements.

However, the section gives back some discretion to the court. Where the court considers that it is appropriate to grant relief or permission for reasons of exceptional public interest, it may do so. If the court relies on this exception, it must certify that it has done so. These rules apply equally to the Upper Tribunal.

The unknown factor at the moment is the extent to which these new provisions will themselves generate litigation, in particular on the question of what is or is not 'exceptional public interest'.

(2) Sections 85 and 86 require the disclosure of the finances of those backing judicial review cases, even if they are not a named party, so that costs can be fairly allocated.

Box 6.7 Continued

(3) Section 87 provides that, unless a third party is invited by the court to intervene, there is a presumption that third parties who apply to join in a judicial review case as 'interveners' should normally be responsible for paying their own way—for example when a campaign group applies to become involved in a case already taking place between an individual and an authority. Before the change, other parties in the case could be ordered to cover the legal costs of the intervener.

(4) Sections 88–90 limit the use of 'cost capping orders', also called 'protective costs orders', to very exceptional cases of public importance. Such orders had come to be used quite widely to protect applicants for judicial review from having to pay the costs of the body against whom they were bringing proceedings where they (the applicants) lost their challenge. The effect of this was to alter the normal rule that the loser of a case pays the costs of the winning party. Since the bodies challenged by judicial review are public bodies, the government argued that this imposed an unfair burden on the taxpayer, who in effect has to pick up the cost. The new statutory provisions limit the circumstances in which such orders can be made.

(5) Finally, it has provided that grants of legal aid are limited to judicial review cases that 'have merit'.

Judicial review has not developed in a vacuum. It is a response to the fact that people no longer accept official decisions as readily as they once did. The reasons for this are complex: better public education; a more consumerist society; the development of this type of legal practice by legal practitioners. But government has also expanded its activities. It seeks to regulate large tranches of human activity. It is not surprising that use of judicial review, or the threat of such use, should now be part of the reality of modern public administration.

One consequence of the development of judicial review has been an increased use by pressure groups of the courts for testing the validity of legislation or its interpretation. The taking of test cases has become a part of contemporary legal practice.[2] The Human Rights Act 1998 provided a new focus for such work as challenges about the compliance of legislation and policy with the European Convention on Human Rights are made. It is too soon to tell how far practice has been altered by the changes made in 2015.

6.4.2 Tribunals

The vast majority of disputes between the citizen and the state get resolved, not in courts, but in tribunals. Some, such as the former General Commissioners of Income Tax, trace their history back to the late eighteenth century. Most are the creation of the twentieth century, reflecting increased involvement of the state in the lives of its citizens.

---

[2] See e.g. the work of the Public Law Project: www.publiclawproject.org.uk/.

For the first 20 to 30 years of that century, there was considerable concern about the use of tribunals as a mechanism for the resolution of disputes. It was argued that only courts had the constitutional authority to perform this function. (One of the advantages of the lack of a written constitution was that, despite this claim, there was no written constitutional principle that *required* all dispute resolution bodies to have the status of 'court'.) The development of tribunals was a pragmatic response to the problems caused for the court system when, at the end of the nineteenth century, jurisdiction to deal with disputes arising under the Workmen's Compensation Acts was given to the county courts. This resulted in those courts drowning in that work, preventing them from dealing effectively with other business. When the National Insurance Act 1911 was passed, creating the first social security benefits, appeals against decisions were not to the courts, but to a tribunal, the sportingly named *Committee of Referees*, with a further right of appeal to the equally sporting *Umpire*.

Criticism of the use of bodies other than the courts for resolving disputes led to fierce criticism, not least from the then Lord Chief Justice, Lord Hewart, who in 1929 published his famous polemic *The New Despotism*. This resulted in the establishment of the Committee on Ministers' Powers, under the chairmanship of Lord Donoughmore, which in 1932 reported that, in its view and subject to safeguards, tribunals were a necessary if not desirable part of the fabric of the English justice system.

The issue was revisited after the Second World War when, in 1955, another committee under Sir Oliver Franks was established to review tribunals and inquiries, following a scandal known as the Crichel Down affair. His committee reported in 1957. By this time many more tribunal systems were in existence. Franks accepted that, subject to basic principles of openness, fairness, and impartiality, tribunals should be acknowledged as a part of the adjudicative structure. Since that time, there has been no serious discussion about the need for tribunals. Indeed, their number has continued to grow (alongside other institutional developments, discussed later). The position of tribunals is even more secure following enactment of the Human Rights Act 1998, since Article 6 of the European Convention on Human Rights requires the existence of courts or tribunals to determine a person's civil rights.

6.4.2.1 Reforming the tribunals system

This is the background against which the Tribunals Service was created. In May 2000, Lord Irvine, the then Lord Chancellor, appointed Sir Andrew Leggatt (a retired Court of Appeal judge) to undertake a review of tribunals. His report, *Tribunals for Users: One System, One Service*, was published in August 2001. It set out a long list of recommendations, the central one being the creation of a unified Tribunals Service.

Publication of the report caused considerable consternation in the corridors of Whitehall. Government departments came to see that implementation of the review's proposals would involve some transfer of their functions to another department, never an attractive prospect. However, after protracted discussion, the Lord Chancellor announced early in 2003 that this central recommendation was accepted. The white paper setting out the government's intentions was published in the summer of 2004.

This not only set out the framework for the new service, but also argued that it was important to look at dispute resolution in the round. There should be clear and flexible pathways for the citizen to obtain redress when things went wrong.[3]

6.4.2.2 The work of the Tribunals Service

The new Tribunals Service came into being in April 2006. It started work using powers transferred to it by statutory order. The Tribunals, Courts and Enforcement Act 2007 gave the reform programme further impetus. The new structure began to operate in November 2008. On 1 April 2011, the Tribunals Service merged with the Courts Service to form Her Majesty's Courts and Tribunals Service (HMCTS).

The Act created two new, generic tribunals: the First-Tier Tribunal, dealing with the bulk of cases arising from official decision-taking; and the Upper Tribunal, hearing appeals from decisions taken by the First-Tier Tribunal, as well as judicial review cases referred to it by the Administrative Court. Tribunals are grouped into 'chambers'; pre-existing tribunals have been brought together in a practically functional way (*see Diagram 6.1*). New tribunal jurisdictions can be brought into this generic framework.

The Act created the post of Senior President, currently Sir Ernest Ryder. Following the creation of HMCTS, it was decided that the Lord Chief Justice, who is now head of the judiciary, should also be the formal head of the tribunal judiciary. This development was confirmed by the Crime and Courts Act 2013. However, the post of Senior President is retained so that he can continue to provide judicial leadership to the Tribunals Service.

The 2007 Act provided that legal members of tribunals have the title of judge. Tribunal judges can be assigned to more than one chamber. This development enabled the Judicial Appointments Commission to start thinking more strategically about the creation of a judicial career (*see 4.2.5*). Prospective judges can start in one jurisdiction, for example in the Tribunals Service, but then apply for appointment in other judicial contexts, for example the courts. This flexibility has been enabled by provisions in the Crime and Courts Act 2013. The current Senior President is determined to achieve even more flexibility in the deployment of judges across the administrative and civil justice systems.

To reduce the bewildering variety of practices and procedures of pre-existing tribunals, the tribunals now work to a single set of procedural rules, created by the Tribunals Rules Committee.

The Tribunals Service has a substantial caseload, but one that has reduced significantly within a very short time. Thus, in the financial year 2012–13, the total number of cases received was 881,388; of these, 501,131 related to social security and 191,541 were to the Employment Tribunal. Four years later, the overall total was down to 459,602, of which 228,645 related to social security.[4] The fall in numbers might be the result of officials and other parties taking better decisions first time—so reducing the

---

[3] See *Transforming Public Services: Complaints, Redress and Tribunals* (Cm 6243) (London, The Stationery Office, July 2004).

[4] Figures taken from tribunals statistics available at www.gov.uk/government/statistics/tribunals-and-gender-recognition-certificate-statistics-quarterly-january-to-march-2017.

Diagram 6.1 Structure of the tribunals system

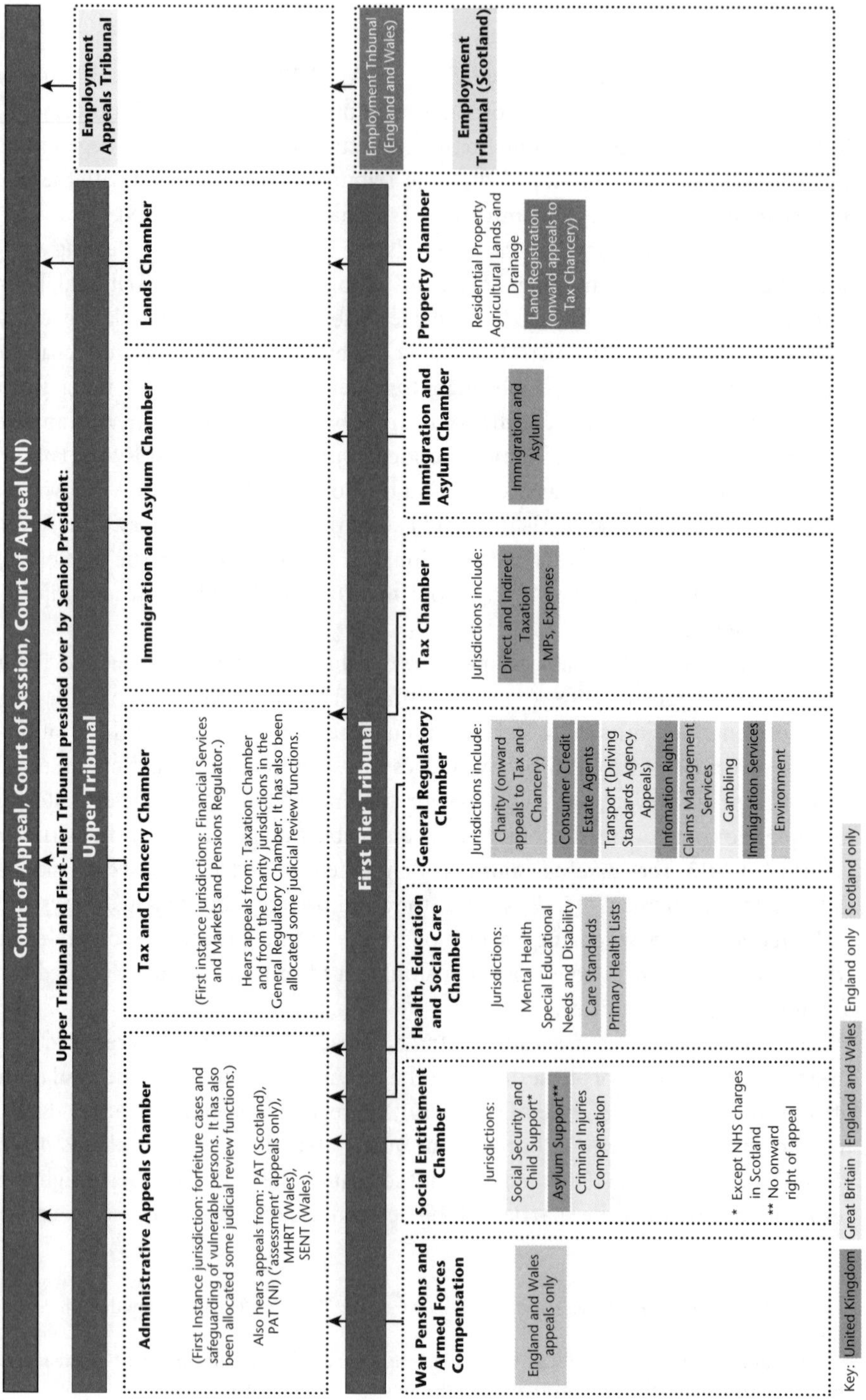

Court of Appeal, Court of Session, Court of Appeal (NI)

Upper Tribunal and First-Tier Tribunal presided over by Senior President:

Upper Tribunal

Administrative Appeals Chamber

(First Instance jurisdiction: forfeiture cases and safeguarding of vulnerable persons. It has also been allocated some judicial review functions.)

Also hears appeals from: PAT (Scotland), PAT (NI) ('assessment' appeals only)), MHRT (Wales), SENT (Wales).

Tax and Chancery Chamber

(First instance jurisdictions: Financial Services and Markets and Pensions Regulator.)

Hears appeals from: Taxation Chamber and from the Charity jurisdictions in the General Regulatory Chamber. It has also been allocated some judicial review functions.

Immigration and Asylum Chamber

Lands Chamber

Employment Appeals Tribunal

First Tier Tribunal

War Pensions and Armed Forces Compensation

England and Wales appeals only

Social Entitlement Chamber

Jurisdictions:

Social Security and Child Support*
Asylum Support**
Criminal Injuries Compensation

* Except NHS charges in Scotland
** No onward right of appeal

Health, Education and Social Care Chamber

Jurisdictions:

Mental Health
Special Educational Needs and Disability
Care Standards
Primary Health Lists

General Regulatory Chamber

Jurisdictions include:

Charity (onward appeals to Tax and Chancery)
Consumer Credit
Estate Agents
Transport (Driving Standards Agency Appeals)
Information Rights
Claims Management Services
Gambling
Immigration Services
Environment

Tax Chamber

Jurisdictions include:

Direct and Indirect Taxation
MPs, Expenses

Immigration and Asylum Chamber

Immigration and Asylum

Property Chamber

Residential Property
Agricultural Lands and Drainage
Land Registration (onward appeals to Tax Chancery)

Employment Tribunal (England and Wales)

Employment Tribunal (Scotland)

Key: United Kingdom   Great Britain   England and Wales   England only   Scotland only

Source: www.judiciary-gov.uk/about-the-judiciary/the-justice-system/court-structure/.

need for making an appeal; if so, these dramatic changes could be a sign of improved administration and decision-taking (*see 6.4.9*). But it is likely that other factors have played a much more significant role in these falls in numbers. They include:

- introduction of fees, particularly affecting the employment tribunal and the immigration and asylum chamber (*see Box 6.4. and 8.6.2*);

- reduction in rights of appeal, particularly affecting immigration case numbers;

- changes to procedures with the introduction of new rules relating to review and reconsideration of decisions, particularly affecting social security (*see 6.4.5*).

6.4.2.3 Special characteristics of tribunals

Tribunals have two distinctive characteristics: specialism and the 'enabling role'.

Most important is specialist expertise. The qualifications of tribunal judges and members should be appropriate for the cases they deal with. Thus, in addition to the legal qualifications of tribunal judges, other relevant professional expertise is used as well, for example from valuers or accountants or doctors. These are deployed in specialist contexts, such as tribunals dealing with health matters, tax matters, or property matters.

Secondly, tribunals make extensive efforts to deal with appellants who—as the result of a lack of legal aid—either have to represent themselves or have to rely on lay advocates. Unlike the adversarial approach of the courts, where the judges tend to take a back seat while arguments, for and against, are presented by advocates for both sides, members of tribunals take a more interventionist role, seeking to draw relevant information from the parties by appropriate questioning. Leggatt called this 'the enabling role' of the tribunal.

This is one example of the procedural innovation of the tribunal system. The courts—if they knew what went on in the best-run tribunals—would have much to learn from tribunals, particularly in dealing with 'litigants in person'. It is essential that the moves to make the deployment of tribunal and civil court judges more flexible do not result in the disappearance of these characteristics.

6.4.3 *Transforming Our Justice System*: administrative justice

The *Transforming Our Justice System* programme (*see 4.2.2.2*) is primarily focused on the work of the criminal and civil justice systems. Nevertheless it has identified some further initiatives it wants to see added to the reforms already made to tribunals.

These include:

(1) *Streamlining procedures and encouraging a balanced approach*: the government is seeking to simplify procedures and put entire services online where possible. It argues that many relatively straightforward tribunal decisions do not require full physical hearings, so where appropriate, judges will be making decisions based on written representations, hearings will be held over telephone or video conference, and specially trained case officers will help cases progress through the system.

(2) *Digitizing the Social Security and Child Support Tribunal*: this will be one of the first services to be moved entirely online, with an end-to-end digital process.

(3) *Simplifying panel composition*: the government wants to ensure that panels that make decisions in tribunals are designed to best suit the circumstances of the case. Most tribunals currently reflect historic arrangements. The government is proposing to revise the current arrangements for setting panel composition to make sure that that appropriate expertise is focused on those cases that need it.

(4) *Reforming employment tribunals*: employment tribunals deal with a substantial volume of claims every year—c. 88,400 in 2016–17. They work on similar principles to many other tribunals and the civil courts, but currently have an entirely separate structure, including a specific appeals tribunal. The government is considering whether the new approaches being adopted elsewhere in the justice system could be applied to the employment jurisdiction.

6.4.4 Inquiries

Historically, there was an important conceptual distinction between a tribunal and an inquiry. Whereas a tribunal usually had statutory authority to adjudicate a dispute and reach a final decision which, subject to any right of appeal, determined the matter, an inquiry gathered information, in the light of which a government minister would decide the issue.

In practice, this distinction became increasingly blurred. For example, Mental Health Review Tribunals (now in the First-Tier Tribunal), when dealing with mental patients who were detained in a mental hospital as a result of a court order, can only recommend to the Home Secretary that a patient should be released from hospital; it is the Secretary of State (or his officials) who takes the final decision. By contrast, many inquiries lead directly to a decision being taken, rather than a report to a minister which would form the basis for a decision.

6.4.4.1 Planning inquiries and related procedures

The principal use of the inquiry in the administrative justice system is found in the context of land use planning. In a geographically small country with a substantial population, it has long been accepted that the state has an interest in determining how land should be used. The planning process seeks to balance the competing interests relating to land use of urban dwellers, rural dwellers, farmers, industrialists, scientists, the pursuers of leisure interests, the providers of transport systems, and other utility providers (gas, electricity, water), to give just some examples. The bulk of planning decisions are taken by local authorities, acting as local planning authorities. Strategically important decisions—for example over the siting of a new airport—may be 'called in' for determination by the Secretary of State within central government.

Once a planning decision has been reached, rights of appeal are provided. In the planning context appeals are dealt with by planning inspectors. Originally, planning inspectors held inquiries and made recommendations to the Secretary of State in central government. These were inquiries in their original sense. As a result of changes in the law, planning inspectors now make the final determination in all but the most complex or important cases, where they still make recommendations to the Secretary of State. Thus, in most cases, the functions of the planning inspectorate are indistinguishable from the functions of a tribunal. Planning inspectors have three ways of proceeding:

- written representations;
- hearings; and
- inquiries.

Statistically, the inquiry is the least frequently used mode for determining planning appeals:

- *Written representations* are, as the name implies, a means of dealing with an appeal purely through written representations. This is the speediest and cheapest of the procedures and is particularly suitable for the determination of relatively small matters, for example an extension to a dwelling.

- *Hearings* involve the appellants and the local planning authority in a hearing before a planning inspector, but the process is consciously 'low-key'. Planning inspectors are trained to run hearings proactively to try to avoid the need for the use of expensive legal representation. The inspector shapes the hearing by assisting the parties to identify the issues that need to be addressed. Typically, the hearing is used in cases slightly more significant than those dealt with by written representation, but not as large scale as those going to inquiry.

- *Inquiries* are used primarily for major planning issues. Inquiries are also used to determine the shape of local planning authorities' local plans, which provide the background against which individual planning applications are decided. Inquiries involve hearing a wider range of persons with an interest in the decision—for example environmental groups or trade associations—than written representations or hearings. Procedurally, they are more formal, with the parties usually using barristers or solicitors to represent their interests. Inquiries can take a very long time and be very expensive; the public inquiry into the fifth terminal at London Heathrow Airport took over five years to complete. The inquiry into the third runway at Heathrow will also take a long time.

6.4.4.2 Particular and ad hoc inquiries

In addition to planning inquiries, which are held on a regular basis, other forms of inquiry are set up as the need arises; for example, inquiries into serious rail accidents or other disasters.

The government may also use an ad hoc inquiry to deal with the aftermath of a particular incident. Recent examples include the Leveson inquiry into the culture, practice, and ethics of the press and the Moore-Bick Inquiry into the Grenfell Tower fire. The Council on Tribunals issued advice on matters that government should take into account when establishing ad hoc inquiries.[5] Local authorities and other public bodies may also establish inquiries into a range of issues, as they arise.[6]

6.4.5 Review/reconsideration

Another form of redress of grievance is review—sometimes called reconsideration. This involves officials reviewing a decision to see whether new evidence should be sought, and whether or not the original decision was correct, or should be revised. In some cases, the reviewer is the initial decision-taker; in others, the reviewer is another official, usually more senior. Reviews may lack the independence that characterizes an appeal to a tribunal or an inquiry. But they can provide an easy and quick means of rectifying a decision where something has clearly gone wrong. Reviews are found in two basic forms: formal/mandatory and informal/discretionary:

- *Formal* reviews are those that are required by law to be carried out.[7]
- *Informal* reviews are not required by law but officials nonetheless carry them out as part of their routine administrative procedures. Before reconsideration of social security decisions became mandatory, any appeal by a social security claimant triggered an internal official review to check whether the decision appealed against was or was not correct. There is evidence that more cases are revised in favour of claimants at this stage than at the appeal stage.[8]

Reviews as a feature of the administrative justice system have been the subject of considerable criticism. In the same way that, in the context of criminal justice, decisions by the police to deal with suspects administratively—for example, by issuing a caution—are criticized for undermining the due process model of criminal justice, so too is review seen by some as undermining the due process model of administrative justice.[9]

Against this, others suggest that models of administrative justice should be based not just on due process but also on other values, such as cost-effectiveness and efficiency. This leads to the conclusion that review is not so objectionable, but is a sensible way of ensuring that mistakes are corrected without the expense and delay of a

---

[5] *Advice to the Lord Chancellor on the Procedural Issues Arising in the Context of Public Inquiries set up by Ministers*, July 1996 (HC 114) (London, Her Majesty's Stationery Office, 1996).

[6] Some of the issues are discussed in Law Commission, *In the Public Interest: Publication of Local Authority Inquiry Reports* (Law Com 289) (Cm 6272) (London, The Stationery Office, 2004).

[7] This now happens in relation to appeals concerning social security benefits. From 2013, all potential appeals are subject to mandatory reconsideration by the Department for Work and Pensions, before they can go to a formal appeal. For details see www.gov.uk/government/publications/appeals-process-changes-for-dwp-benefits-and-child-maintenance. The process was reviewed by the Social Security Advisory Committee in 2016.

[8] See Baldwin, J., and others, *Judging Social Security* (Oxford, Clarendon Press, 1992).

[9] Sainsbury, R., 'Internal Reviews and the Weakening of Social Security Claimants' Rights of Appeal', in Richardson, G., and Genn, H. (eds), *Administrative Law and Government Action* (Oxford, Clarendon Press, 1994).

tribunal hearing. Indeed, when well organized, reviews can have all the hallmarks of independence and due process.[10]

Experience suggests that the primary reason decisions taken by officials are later found to be wrong is not that the official has misunderstood the law to be applied to the case in question, but that the factual information on which the decision is based is in some respect wanting. It therefore makes sense to find ways of getting at the relevant facts other than by the relatively expensive and long-drawn-out process of a tribunal hearing. In this context, review can be helpful. However, if the way in which the review works is that no serious effort is made to see whether new evidence is forthcoming, or that those who may have a case to take to a tribunal become so disheartened that they fail to pursue their claims in full, then review may be criticized as not adding value to the administrative justice system.

Whatever the theoretical objections, review will remain a part of the administrative justice system. The question is not whether review should be part of the system, but rather, in what contexts is it or is it not appropriate.

6.4.6 Ombudsmen

6.4.6.1 The Parliamentary and Health Service Ombudsman

The Ombudsman concept was introduced into the United Kingdom from Scandinavia in 1967. The first Ombudsman was formally known as the Parliamentary Commissioner for Administration (PCA), though he is now described as the Parliamentary and Health Service Ombudsman (PHSO). The Ombudsman's original function was to investigate complaints and allegations of *maladministration* in UK government departments and related agencies that may have resulted in injustice. Over the years, the role has expanded to include the Health Service and the Victim's Code.

Two particular features of the PHSO's jurisdiction should be noted. First, members of the public are not entitled to complain directly to him (this does not apply to Health Service complaints). This so-called 'MP Filter' means that complainants get their complaint referred to the Ombudsman by a Member of Parliament (MP). MPs are not actually obliged to refer cases to her if they think they can deal with the matter themselves. The filter exists because, when the Ombudsman concept was introduced, some argued that it might undermine the primary responsibility of Parliament and its members to call ministers (and their officials) to account. The filter was not part of the original Scandinavian Ombudsman concept, where direct access by the public was permitted. In November 2011, the Ombudsman published a report recommending abolition of the MP filter.

Secondly, the PHSO cannot order that any particular consequence should follow a finding of maladministration. He can only persuade a government department, for example, to pay compensation to an aggrieved citizen. Again, in other countries,

---

[10] Harris, M., 'The Place of Formal and Informal Review in Administrative Justice', and Scampion, J., 'New Procedures', in Harris, M., and Partington, M. (eds), *Administrative Justice in the 21st Century* (Oxford, Hart Publishing, 1999).

the Ombudsman has power to enforce his decisions. This limitation emerged very clearly in the context of the decision in the Equitable Life case. There it was found that policyholders in the company had suffered as the result of official maladministration, but recommendations for financial compensation were for a long time resisted by government. The Coalition government decided that compensation should be paid.

In an important case decided by the Court of Appeal in 2008, *R (Bradley) v Secretary of State for Work and Pensions* ([2008] EWCA Civ 36), it was held that while rulings of the Ombudsman were not binding, a finding of maladministration should only be rejected if there were cogent reasons for so doing.

The Ombudsman has drawn up guidance on the principles to be adopted when considering what remedies should be offered to those who are found to have suffered maladministration. The range of remedies is much wider than those offered by the courts. They include: making apologies; offering explanations; taking remedial action; in some cases offering financial compensation.

As Health Service Ombudsman, he investigates complaints about failures in NHS hospitals or community health services, about care and treatment, and about local NHS family doctor, dental, pharmacy, or optical services. Members of the public may refer a complaint directly, i.e. there is no MP filter, though normally he pursues a complaint only if a full investigation within the NHS complaints system has been carried out first. He can only consider issues arising in the NHS in England.

Since April 2006, when the Victims' Code took effect (*see 5.8*), the Ombudsman has provided a complaints-handling service for victims of crime who have a complaint about the way in which any of the criminal justice agencies has carried out its obligations under the code. Such cases are subject to the MP filter. A statement from the Ombudsman in April 2013 argued that the Ministry of Justice should do much more to ensure that knowledge of the code amongst those who should be aware of it was improved.

Besides investigating and, where appropriate, redressing grievances, the Ombudsman sees its function as improving the quality of administration. Published reports contain guidance on good practice from which government or health departments should learn. In March 2007, a set of general principles of good administration were published. There are six:

- getting it right;
- being customer focused;
- being open and accountable;
- acting fairly and proportionately;
- putting things right; and
- seeking continuous improvement.

Though seemingly obvious, these basic principles are often ignored in practice.

Summaries of the Ombudsman's investigations are available on its website. So too are *Annual Reports*, as well as specific reports on particular issues. A report on the treatment of the elderly is a recent example. For the first time, in 2011, a review of complaints handling within government departments and other public bodies was published. Unsurprisingly, it found unacceptable variations in practice and procedure.

In 2005, there was a joint report covering both parliamentary and health service work. Issues particularly considered were: problems with the new tax credits system; the operations of the Child Support Agency; NHS funding of continuing care for people with long-term health care needs; and the need for a truly patient-focused NHS complaints procedure.

The *Annual Report* is considered by the specialist Public Administration and Constitutional Affairs Select Committee of the House of Commons, who interview the Ombudsman as well as senior civil servants from departments that have been criticized. Thus Parliament is kept informed about the Ombudsman's work and the impact it has had on government departments.

6.4.6.2 Local government and social care ombudsmen

The Ombudsman concept has been extended to local government. The Local Government Ombudsman covers all local authorities in England. His office investigates complaints against principal councils (not town, parish, or community councils) and certain other bodies in England, in particular, adult social care providers. By law, some kinds of complaint cannot be considered. Examples are personnel complaints and complaints about the internal running of schools.

As with other ombudsmen, the objective of the Local Government Ombudsman is to secure, where appropriate, satisfactory redress for complainants and better administration by local authorities. Since 1989, a number of guidance notes good administrative practice, drawing lessons from cases the office has handled, have been published. They include: setting up complaints procedures; good administrative practice; council housing repairs; local authority members' interests; the disposal of land; and remedies when things have gone wrong.

There has long been criticism that the division between the PHSO and the Local Government Ombudsman has meant unnecessary complications for the citizen seeking redress when things have gone wrong. In 2007, the government agreed that, where a complaint raises matters relating both to central and to local government, the two organizations could investigate it jointly (see the Regulatory Reform (Collaboration between Ombudsmen) Order 2007).

A draft Public Services Ombudsman Bill, which—if enacted—would merge the two schemes, was published in December 2016. Currently, however, this proposal is not being taken forward.

6.4.6.3 Public service ombudsmen in Wales and Scotland

If the idea goes ahead, England will be catching up with Wales and Scotland. In Wales, complaints originally went to four separate ombudsmen: the Commission for Local Administration in Wales; the Health Service Commissioner for Wales; the Welsh Administration Ombudsman; and also the Social Housing Ombudsman for

Wales. From April 2006, these were brought into a single scheme, the Public Service Ombudsman for Wales.

In Scotland there is also a generic Public Service Ombudsman. Established in 2002, he deals with complaints about Scottish public bodies previously dealt with by the Scottish Parliamentary Ombudsman, the Health Service Ombudsman for Scotland, the Local Government Ombudsman for Scotland, and the Housing Association Ombudsman for Scotland. He has also taken over the Mental Welfare Commission for Scotland's function of investigating complaints relating to mental health and complaints against Scottish Enterprise and Highlands and Islands Enterprise.

6.4.6.4 Other ombudsmen offices

Increasingly, more specialist Ombudsman or Ombudsman-type offices have been created. For example, an Office for Legal Complaints handles consumer complaints in respect of all bodies providing legal services, subject to oversight by the Legal Services Board (*see 9.4.2.2.c*); a Judicial Appointments and Conduct Ombudsman, created by the Constitutional Reform Act 2005, deals with complaints about judicial appointments and judicial conduct; the Independent Office for Police Conduct (the new name for the Independent Police Complaints Commission) deals with complaints against the police; a Prisons and Probation Ombudsman deals with complaints about the prison and probation service; and the Housing Ombudsman deals with complaints against (primarily) registered social landlords (housing associations). (From April 2013, his jurisdiction expanded to include council housing.) These are not considered further here, but more information is available on their websites, listed in the Online Resources.

6.4.6.5 The rise of private sector ombudsmen

Over the last 20 years or so, a distinctively British phenomenon has emerged. A considerable number of private sector industries have set up their own ombudsman schemes to deal with those customer complaints that cannot be resolved within a particular company. These include the Property Ombudsman, the Banking Ombudsman, the Insurance Ombudsman, and the Building Societies Ombudsman. By contrast with the PCA and the other public sector ombudsmen, where the levels of complaints have been relatively low, many of these private sector ombudsmen have large caseloads to deal with. They offer a 'mass-market' dispute resolution procedure, as opposed to the more 'Rolls-Royce' work of the PHSO.[11]

Following the Financial Services and Markets Act 2000, a Financial Services Ombudsman scheme brought together many of these private schemes. It operates under statutory rather than industry-determined powers. It has a substantial caseload and is able to award compensation up to £150,000. It has effectively replaced the courts as the forum for the resolution of consumer disputes with financial services providers.

---

[11] Williams, T., and Goriely, T., 'A Question of Numbers: Managing Complaints Against Rising Expectations', in Harris, M., and Partington, M. (eds), *Administrative Justice in the 21st Century* (Oxford, Hart Publishing, 1999).

6.4.6.6 Process

A common feature of all ombudsmen's procedures is that they operate on an 'inquisitorial' or 'investigative' basis. The complaint is made; the relevant ombudsman's staff investigates the complaint, taking further evidence both from the government department or other agency concerned and the complainant. In the light of the investigation a conclusion is reached on whether or not there was in fact maladministration. Many investigations result in a finding that the department or agency in question behaved perfectly responsibly, and the complainant was being unreasonable. Where there is a finding of maladministration, there is comment on whether the response of the department was appropriate. Many findings of maladministration lead to no more than the writing of a letter of apology, which is often all that the complainant wanted in the first place. Usually, there is no possibility of an oral hearing (though the Pensions Ombudsman is required to offer this).

6.4.6.7 The European Ombudsman

In addition to developments in England and Wales, the Ombudsman concept also extends to the work of the European Union. The creation of a European Ombudsman was approved in the Maastricht Treaty; the statute giving the Ombudsman his/her authority was agreed in 1994. The first European Ombudsman took up office in 1995; the third (and first woman), Emily O'Reilly, was appointed in 2013. They have been issuing annual reports on their work since 1996.

The Ombudsman operates on the basis of the *European Ombudsman Implementing Provisions*. These not only set out in general terms the principles on which the Ombudsman carries out their work, but also list the powers they have when determining cases: these include the possibility of making 'critical remarks' where no more general conclusions can be drawn from the case under investigation; and the making of a 'report with draft recommendations', where it appears that some more general lessons may be learned.

In addition, and unlike the national ombudsmen in England and Wales, the European Ombudsman has a very broad power to instigate his 'own-initiative' inquiries. One fruit of this, to date, has been the preparation of a set of draft recommendations, which have been put both to the European Commission and to the European Parliament and Council of Ministers, relating to the adoption of a *Code of Good Administrative Behaviour*. The reason for doing this was the result of reflecting on many of the individual complaints which had been received, which indicated that maladministration might have been avoided had clearer information been available about the administrative duties of Community staff towards its citizens. The code was approved by the European Parliament and published in March 2002.

6.4.7 Other complaints-handling bodies

It might be thought that, with the creation of ombudsmen to deal with issues at a high level and with the more recent development of a wide variety of complaints-resolution procedures in individual government departments, there were now adequate means for the redress of citizens' complaints. In fact, many other bodies and procedures have been created with more specific remits than the ombudsmen's but more general authority than an internal complaints procedure. Only a few examples are given here:

- The *Adjudicator* investigates complaints from people and businesses about the work of Her Majesty's Revenue and Customs, the Insolvency Service, the Public Guardianship Office, and the Valuation Office Agency. The Adjudicator does not look at issues of law or of tax liability, because tribunals resolve these problems. But she does look into excessive delay, mistakes, discourtesy of staff, and the use of discretion.

- The *Independent Complaints Reviewer* deals with complaints about an eclectic mix of government agencies, including (currently) HM Land Registry, the National Archives, the Children's Commissioner for Wales, and the Northern Ireland Youth Justice Agency.

- The *Independent Case Examiner* investigates cases where people feel they have been treated unfairly or are unhappy with the way their complaint has been dealt with by the business or agency which comes within her jurisdiction. They include: the Child Support Agency; Jobcentre Plus (including most work provider services); the Pension and Disability and Carers Services; the Child Maintenance and Enforcement Division (Northern Ireland); Northern Ireland—benefits and pensions only (Department for Communities) and the Independent Living Fund.

- The *Independent Adjudicator for Higher Education* operates an independent student complaints scheme to which all higher education institutions must adhere. The adjudicator handles individual complaints against those institutions, and may publish recommendations about how they deal with complaints and what constitutes good practice.

- The *Immigration Services Commissioner*, set up under the Immigration and Asylum Act 1999, is responsible for ensuring that all immigration advisers fulfil the requirements of good practice. His office is responsible for regulating immigration advisers in accordance with the Commissioner's Code of Standards (revised 2016), including taking criminal proceedings against advisers who are acting illegally.

The number and variety of these bodies has grown significantly over the last ten years and now looks very haphazard. There is considerable scope for rationalization.

6.4.8 'Collective' administrative justice: regulators of privatized utility providers

Another context for the resolution of disputes arises from the privatization of the main utility providers—water, gas, electricity, and telecommunications—whereby the provision of services by state monopolies was replaced by private companies. New regulatory offices—including OFWAT, OFGEM, and OFTEL (now OFCOM)—were established to regulate these new industries to prevent abuse of market power in the setting of prices, and to create the conditions in which other suppliers could come into the market to provide the competition essential for consumer protection. These regulatory offices have also had some responsibility for the development of procedures for dealing with individual customer complaints and complaints from others wishing to enter particular market sectors.[12]

This is not the place to consider the work of these industry regulators in detail. But their existence and the fact that they, too, play a part in the administrative justice system need to be noted.

6.4.9 Getting it right first time: putting people first

Notwithstanding all these dispute resolution procedures, there is a powerful argument that they would not be necessary if those who delivered public services were fully focused on delivering a high-quality service themselves. 'Getting it right first time' should be preferable to making the citizen complain, or appeal, or go to an ombudsman. This general issue has been a concern of government for many years. First was the concept of the Citizens' Charter. By contrast with the Ombudsman, where the concept moved from the public sector to the private, the Citizens' Charter (launched in 1991) involved private sector ideas about standards of customer care and service delivery being brought into the public sector.

Under the Blair government, the Office of Public Sector Reform defined four principles for public service delivery: national standards to ensure that people have the right to high-quality services wherever they live; devolution to give local leaders the means to deliver these standards to local people; more flexibility in service provision in light of people's rising expectations; and greater customer choice. Much of this was driven by the desire to enhance the use of information technology in the delivery of public services.

It is difficult to gauge the extent to which these principles have been delivered in practice. The nature of political debate and reports in the media is to focus on things that are not happening rather than on the positive developments that are occurring. There are often good reasons to think that progress is slower than ministers would like. In many parts of the country, public service pay levels make it hard to recruit staff of adequate quality. Some forms of public service are very stressful to deliver, which increases the problems of staff recruitment and retention. And some areas of social administration are very complex; however well staff do their jobs, there will be grounds for appeal or seeking reviews of decisions. Examples of services being delivered to much higher standards do not attract the same attention, though reports of the many official inspectorates suggest that good services are offered in many areas of government.

---

[12] See McHarg, A., 'Separation of Functions and Regulatory Agencies: Dispute Resolution in the Privatised Utilities', in Harris, M., and Partington, M. (eds), *Administrative Justice in the 21st Century* (Oxford, Hart Publishing, 1999).

There must continue to be a focus on the need for public services to deliver a better service to the public. Administrative justice should be based on a desire to ensure that official decisions are right first time. If officials get the initial decision right, then the consumers of public services should be better satisfied and have less need to use the myriad appeal and complaints mechanisms discussed in this chapter. (Indeed, one of the criticisms that can be made of many of the processes discussed earlier is that there is rather little institutional commitment to the idea of considering what general lessons might be drawn from the resolution of *individual* appeals or complaints. The very process of encouraging disputes to be resolved on an individual basis may disguise structural questions which, if addressed by the government department or other agency, might have prevented the problem arising in the first place.)

This was the subject of the 2011 report from the Administrative Justice and Tribunals Council, *Right First Time* (*see Box 6.8*).

Box 6.8 Reform in progress

Right first time

The Administrative Justice and Tribunals Council argued that there are too many successful appeals before tribunals, the result of poor decision taking within government. It argued that there should be more emphasis on 'getting it right'; and that departments that have unacceptably high levels of successful appeals should be made to help fund the tribunals and ombudsmen that sort incorrect decisions out. Public bodies could save money and improve the quality of service by making fewer mistakes and learning more from those they make.

Incorrect decisions impact significantly on the lives of those directly concerned. Compounding the problem is the repetition of these expensive errors. Too few public bodies have in place feedback mechanisms to ensure that the outcomes of appeals and complaints are understood throughout the organization.

'Right first time' means:

- making a decision or delivering a service to the user fairly, quickly, accurately, and effectively;
- taking into account the relevant and sufficient evidence and circumstances of a particular case;
- involving the user and keeping the user updated and informed during the process;
- communicating and explaining the decision or action to the user in a clear and understandable way, and informing the user about his or her rights in relation to complaints, reviews, appeals, or alternative dispute resolution;
- learning from feedback or complaints about the service or appeals against decisions;
- empowering and supporting staff through providing high quality guidance, training, and mentoring.

The report identifies the fundamentals of 'right first time' as leadership, culture, responsiveness, resolution, and learning. It also highlights practical steps that should

---

Box 6.8 Continued

be adopted and followed by leaders of public bodies when reviewing their services and attempting to establish a right-first-time approach. All such bodies should carry out a review of their systems, procedures, and decision-making structures to ensure that they are doing all they can to get decisions right first time.

The report argues that it is time to adopt a 'polluter pays' approach to help promote a right-first-time culture. Tribunals (including, but not limited to, those within the Tribunals Service) are currently carrying a heavy share of the financial burden caused by incorrect decisions. It recommends the development of funding models by which original decision-making organizations contribute to the cost of running tribunals through direct reference to the volume of successful appeals they generate.

To the extent that the range of institutional procedures considered in this chapter are needed, this may reflect the fact that standards of administrative justice are not as high as they should be.

6.4.10 Audit and quality control

The discussion of administrative justice has so far focused on the wide variety of procedures, ranging from courts to informal complaints-handling procedures, available to individual citizens dissatisfied with some aspect of public administration. Other mechanisms have also been introduced to try to ensure quality of performance and the provision of good public services that provide value for money.

Among alternative techniques used to try to achieve these more general objectives are:

- auditing: to ensure that value for money in the provision of public services is achieved;
- inspectorates: to ensure the quality of service provision;
- benchmarking: statistics to provide baseline data against which performance by public sector agencies may be measured; and
- public service agreements: designed to encourage the modernization of service delivery, support proposals for reform, and increase accountability by the setting of clear aims and objectives.

These techniques should also be seen as components of the administrative justice system.

6.5 Parliament

It has been argued in this chapter that our understanding of administrative justice should be seen as offering something more than the resolution of individual disputes between the citizen and the state. It should embrace other methods by which officials and other public servants are called to account. In this context, it must not be forgotten that Parliament—in addition to its legislative functions considered in *Chapter 3*—has important responsibilities. Three particular mechanisms may be noted here:

- MPs' questions;
- debates;
- select committees.

6.5.1 MPs' questions

The easiest way for an MP to try to get information or to get something done by a minister is to ask a Parliamentary Question (PQ). A small number of PQs are answered orally by the minister concerned; the vast majority of PQs receive a written answer. All answers—whether oral or written—are printed in *Hansard*, the official transcript of proceedings in Parliament. Although the issues on which questions are asked range very widely, many are designed to call ministers to account, and in that sense can be seen as within the landscape of administrative justice.

6.5.2 Debates

A great deal of parliamentary time is spent debating legislative proposals, as noted in *Chapter 3*. This use of parliamentary time is controlled by the government. But there are also opportunities for Parliament to debate other issues, not directly related to the law-making process, and some of these opportunities are outside the control of the government. They can be used by backbench MPs to raise issues about how government is working.

For example, at the end of each parliamentary day, there is a short 30-minute adjournment debate, introduced by a backbench MP. One innovation—introduced in November 1999—is that of *backbench debates*. Because of the amount of time the legislative process takes in the House of Commons, backbenchers had only limited opportunity to raise matters of more general concern. Three days each week are now available for backbench debates on matters not related to the legislative programme. Most of these take place not in the chamber of the House of Commons, but in Westminster Hall, which for these purposes is arranged in a horse-shoe formation—thought to be less confrontational than the familiar 'head-on' arrangements in the House of Commons.

The ability of backbenchers to control the issues considered in backbench debates has been increased by the decision to create a Backbench Business Committee, which has responsibility for scheduling the subjects for debates raised by MPs. The days available for this are controlled by the government. A number take place in the House of Commons; the rest in Westminster Hall. Around 35 days are available to the Committee.

6.5.3 Select committees

Parliament appoints a wide range of select committees to keep the work of central government departments under review. There are also a number of select committees that cut across departmental boundaries. These include: the Public Accounts Committee; the Public Administration and Constitutional Affairs Select Committee; and the Procedure Committee.

In addition to those in the House of Commons, there are also select committees in the House of Lords. They do not look at individual departments, but address more general issues. There are currently five major Lords Select Committees: the European Union Committee; the Science and Technology Committee; the Communications Committee; the Constitution Committee; and the Economic Affairs Committee.

Each select committee works by inquiring into topics which it selects for investigation. The committees work by gathering written and oral evidence, and in the light of this write a report which is presented to Parliament. They can call for named individuals (including ministers and civil servants) to attend the committee to be questioned. A particular feature of select committees is that many of them are chaired by MPs who are not members of the governing political party. For the most part, they seek to write unanimous reports, whatever the party political composition of the particular committee.

Select committees have become much more important in recent years as a mechanism by which MPs try to call government to account, although a lot of their detailed work is not well understood by the public at large.

6.5.4 Freedom of information

Lastly, note should be taken of the Freedom of Information Act 2000, which came fully into force at the beginning of 2005. The Act covers all central government departments, and a number of other bodies closely related to central government, including, for example, the Charity Commission, the Crown Prosecution Service, the Serious Fraud Office, and the Government Legal Department. The government produces regular statistical reports on the use of the Act. The most recent shows that between April and June 2016, 11,037 requests for information were received. This number has been relatively steady over the past two years.

The impact of this method of calling officials and other public servants to account can be extremely dramatic; the exposure in 2009 of information about the use (and abuse) of allowances by MPs was the result of investigative work undertaken through use of freedom of information requests.

6.6 Keeping the administrative justice system under review

From 1959, tribunals and inquiries were kept under review by the Council on Tribunals. It had a statutory responsibility to advise government on the work of the tribunals and inquiry systems under its jurisdiction; to comment on drafts of procedural regulations, on which the Council must be consulted; and to deal with such other matters as might be referred to it. In addition, the Council prepared a number of reports relating to general issues about the operation of tribunals and inquiries.

A particular feature of the Council was that its members had a statutory right to attend hearings. As a result of these visits many items of concern to the Council emerged, which translated into proposals for reform. They included:

- the need for training of tribunal chairmen and members;
- the importance of the role of the clerk and administrative support generally in ensuring the smooth running of tribunals; and
- the need for adequate levels of resource to enable the work of the tribunals to be done effectively.

The Leggatt review of tribunals saw the Council as a key part of the administrative justice system and recommended that its role should be enhanced.

From November 2007, the Council was transformed into the Administrative Justice and Tribunals Council. Details of the Council's powers were set out in the Tribunals, Courts and Enforcement Act 2007.

Notwithstanding this history, the Coalition government decided that, following its review of public bodies, the Council should be abolished. This happened in August 2013.

It was replaced by the Administrative Justice Forum. It was created to help the development of government policy. It took forward a number of issues identified as important by the former Council. These include:

- bringing coherence to the huge range of ombudsmen and complaints-resolution processes;
- determining who should pay for tribunals;
- dealing with the impacts of cuts in legal aid and general advice provision;
- developing more proportionate dispute resolution procedures.

One of its first tasks was to keep under review progress with the government's *Strategic Work Programme for Administrative Justice and Tribunals* (2012).

In 2017, the government decided that the forum should be wound up. A new body, the Administrative Justice Council, is to be established in 2018. It will be run by JUSTICE, with some financial support from the government, and will be chaired by the Senior President of Tribunals. At the time of writing, further details are awaited.

In addition to these government sponsored bodies, there is also the Ombudsman Association—a private organization founded by the ombudsmen in 1995 to ensure that only those bodies that subscribe to certain procedural standards use the label 'ombudsman'. In particular, they wanted to ensure that ombudsmen in the private sector of the economy, who are privately financed, are truly *independent* of their paymasters. It has also undertaken other activity, such as developing principles for the training and procedures to be adopted by individual ombudsman systems. One feature particularly worthy of note—and which it is surprising does not exist in other parts of the English legal system—is its link with the neighbouring common law jurisdiction, Ireland. (There would be advantage in thinking of other areas of the justice system where there might be opportunities for the British and the Irish to learn from each other.) However, it does not see its function as keeping the whole of the administrative justice system under review.

6.7 Key points

1. Administrative justice is central to the relationship between the citizen and the state.

2. Large numbers of bodies deliver administrative justice.

3. The Administrative Court plays a central role in developing the core principles of judicial review.

4. The average citizen is more likely to appear before a tribunal than a court.

5. The ombudsmen concept has expanded from dealing with public sector complaints into the private sector of the economy.

6. Tribunals are more flexible in their procedures than the courts.

7. Ombudsmen and complaints-handling procedures can offer different outcomes from those available in courts and tribunals.

8. Organizations are not as good at learning from the outcomes of complaints against them as they should be.

9. It is important to remember the role of Parliament in holding ministers and officials to account.

6.8 Questions

Use the self-test questions in the Online Resources to test your understanding of the topics covered in this chapter and receive tailored feedback: www.oup.com/uk/partington18_19/.

6.9 Web links

Check the Online Resources for a selection of annotated web links allowing you to easily research topics of particular interest: www.oup.com/uk/partington18_19/.

6.10 Blog items

See Spotlight on the Justice System, at www.martinpartington.com/category/chapter-6-2/.

Suggestions for further reading

CANE, P., *Administrative Tribunals and Adjudication* (Oxford, Hart Publishing, 2010)

HARLOW, C., and RAWLINGS, R., *Law and Administration* (3rd edn, Cambridge, Cambridge University Press, 2009)

Other suggestions are set out in the Further Reading listed in the **Online Resources**.

7

The family justice system

7.1 Introduction: law and the family

The role law should play in the regulation of family relationships is controversial. Some argue that law should have only a residual function, leaving people to structure their lives as a matter of private choice and personal morality. Others argue that society has a legitimate interest in family policy, particularly where children are involved. Furthermore, if support is not given to families, this leads to other undesirable social consequences, for example anti-social behaviour, youth crime, and teenage pregnancy.

The institutional framework within which family policy is developed has undergone considerable change in recent years. Ministerial boundaries have been redrawn and new agencies created. To give just three examples:

(1) Following the terrible case of Victoria Climbié, killed as the result of appalling physical abuse, in 2003 a Children's Minister was appointed within the (then) Department for Education and Science. The current Minister for Children and Families, within the Department of Education, is Robert Goodwill MP.

(2) The *Sure Start* programme aims to: increase the availability of childcare for all children; improve health and emotional development for young children; and support parents as parents and in their aspirations towards employment. Sure Start covers children from conception through to the age of 14, and up to the age of 16 for those with special educational needs and disabilities. One of the principal ways of delivering these objectives is through the creation of Sure Start Children's Centres. These bring together childcare, early education, health, and family support services for families with children under five years old.

(3) Under the Children Act 2004, the post of Children's Commissioner was created. Her function is to ensure that ministers are advised about the child's perspective in policy-making. Following a review, the Commissioner's functions were brought together with those of the Children's Rights Director, under the terms of the Children and Families Act 2014. The current postholder is Anne Longfield.

7.1.1 Law and the family

The principal functions of the law that relate to the family are:

(1) defining the rules for the validity of marriage and now civil partnerships;

(2) setting the bases on which marital relationships may be brought to an end through divorce or nullity;

(3) dealing with the consequences of divorce and other relationship breakdown, in particular questions of responsibility for children, financial support, and the division of property rights;

(4) providing a framework for the protection of children, including care and adoption;

(5) creating a framework for dealing with issues of domestic violence.

The last two are not dependent on the existence of a marriage; the first two are. The third is largely dependent on the existence of a marriage, though there is a limited though complex involvement of the law on the breakdown of *de facto* relationships.

The tension between law and morality came strongly to the fore over the last decade as first the Civil Partnerships Act 2004 and then the Marriage (Same Sex Couples) Act 2013 were passed, giving significant new rights to same-sex couples.

Underpinning much of the domestic law of England and Wales is an important international law dimension, particularly relating to the law that affects children. Although the International Convention on the Rights of the Child 1989 does not have direct impact on English law, it has considerable political significance. The effect of the Convention is kept under review by the Committee on the Rights of the Child, part of the United Nations Human Rights Commission. The role of the Children's Commissioner, mentioned earlier, is designed in part to reflect the government's desire to be able to report positively on the protection of the rights of children.

Four particular issues have emerged in the last 20 years as factors that have shaped the structure of the family justice system, and the roles that people who work within that system should perform:[1]

- First, there has been the important realization that if a marriage (or other long-term relationship) breaks down, the process of bringing that relationship to a formal end should—wherever possible—reduce the inevitable feelings of stress, rejection, and failure that accompany such a process, rather than add to them.

- Secondly, there is a clear acceptance in law that, as far as possible, the welfare of the child must be protected.

- Thirdly, there is much concern about the extent to which parents who have separated should be able to maintain contact with their children.

---

[1] Developments in the family justice system have been influenced by a considerable body of empirical socio-legal research. The Ministry of Justice has published occasional bulletins on this research, though none since www.gov.uk/government/uploads/system/uploads/attachment_data/file/485073/family-justice-bulletin-6.pdf.

- Fourthly, there is much greater awareness of the problem of domestic violence and other forms of abuse that occur in the family home. There have been important legal developments designed both to assist victims of abuse, and to send the broader educational message that such behaviour is not acceptable.

7.2 Family justice: the institutional framework

7.2.1 Creation of the family court

Until very recently, England and Wales did not have a family court. Instead, there were complex arrangements with different courts determining different issues that may arise in family law. Over a number of years, policy initiatives were taken which can be seen as steps towards the creation of a separate family justice system. These included:

- special care in the selection of judges;
- special training for judges;
- harmonizing rules of procedure;
- making the work of family courts more open.

Following these piecemeal developments, a more fundamental review of the family justice system was undertaken by David Norgrove. His *Review of Family Justice* was published in November 2011. The government has implemented the bulk of the changes he recommended.

First, the review decided that there should be a major institutional change. Until 2014, family law matters were divided between the High Court, county courts, and magistrates' courts (which were called family proceedings courts when dealing with family matters). Different levels of court could deal with different issues. Norgrove accepted that the time had come for the creation of a new stand-alone Family Court. The government accepted this recommendation, which was legislated for in the Crime and Courts Act 2013.

From April 2014, the Family Court has existed as a single entity with all family matters being commenced in the same place. In reality, much of the former division of work remains. Thus the more serious or legally significant cases still go to High Court judges who sit in the Family Court. County court and district judges who had been selected and trained for family work continue to do that work within the Family Court. And similarly, magistrates who used to do family work continue to do that work in the new court. But there is now a structural coherence that did not exist before.

7.2.2 Expert witnesses

Family cases, especially those involving children, often require the evidence of experts, e.g. social workers or child psychologists. Surprisingly, perhaps, there were no formal controls over the qualifications of these experts. In May 2013, the government launched a consultation on the standards that experts in family cases should meet. These have been brought into effect by the judiciary.

The standards, which were developed in partnership with the Family Justice Council (*see Box 7.2*), include making sure that the expert: has knowledge appropriate to the court case; has been active in the area of work or practice and has sufficient experience of the issues relevant to the case; is either regulated by or accredited to a registered body where this is appropriate; has relevant qualifications and has received appropriate training; and complies with safeguarding requirements.

7.2.3 Changing the culture of the family justice system

The Norgrove reforms were about more than structural change. He wanted to see a change in the culture of the courts. What particularly struck Norgrove were the delays in the system. He thought these could have very serious consequences, particularly where decisions relating to young children had to be made. He wanted all those who work in the family justice system to think critically about the contribution they make to it and ask themselves whether there were ways in which their role might alter to make the whole process more efficient. The package of reforms that Norgrove recommended was complex, but the government broadly accepted the recommendations. They were implemented by the Children and Families Act 2014 (*see Box 7.1*).

Box 7.1 Reform in progress

Reform of the family justice system: the Children and Families Act 2014

The Children and Families Act contains provisions that affect the family justice system. In respect of private family law (by which is meant the law about resolving disputes between family members—*see Box 7.3*), the Act includes provisions to:

- make it a requirement to attend a family mediation, information, and assessment meeting to find out about and consider mediation before applying for certain types of court order;
- send a clear signal to separated parents that courts will take account of the principle that both should continue to be involved in their children's lives where that is safe and consistent with the child's welfare, which remains the court's paramount consideration;
- introduce a new 'child arrangements order', replacing residence and contact orders;
- ensure that expert evidence in family proceedings concerning children is permitted only when necessary to resolve the case justly, taking account of factors including the impact on the welfare of the child, and whether the information could be obtained from one of the parties already involved in the proceedings;
- make changes so that when a child arrangements order is breached, the court can direct the parties to undertake activities designed to help them understand the importance of complying with the order and making it work;

Box 7.1 Continued

- streamline court processes in proceedings for a decree of divorce, nullity of marriage, or judicial separation (or, in relation to a civil partnership, for a dissolution, nullity, or separation order) by removing the requirement for the court to consider whether it should exercise any of its powers under the Children Act 1989. Arrangements for children can be decided at any time through separate proceedings under the Children Act 1989.

In respect of public family law, which relates to decisions about public authorities intervening to protect children (*see Box 7.3*), the Act includes provisions to:

- introduce a maximum 26-week time limit for completing care and supervision proceedings with the possibility of extending the time limit in a particular case for up to eight weeks at a time, should that be necessary to resolve the proceedings justly;
- ensure that the timetable for the case is child focused and decisions about it are made with explicit reference to the child's welfare;
- make it explicit that, when the court considers a care plan, it should focus on those issues essential to deciding whether to make a care order; and
- remove the eight-week time limit on the duration of initial interim care orders and interim supervision orders, and the four-week time limit on subsequent orders, and allow the court to make interim orders for the length of time it sees fit, although not extending beyond the date when the relevant care or supervision order proceedings are disposed of.

The changes to the family justice system are kept under review by the Family Justice Board, set up in 2012 and chaired by David Norgrove, and by the Family Justice Council (*see Box 7.2*).

Box 7.2 Reform in progress

Family Justice Council (FJC) and Family Justice Board (FJB)

The FJC was established in July 2004. It aims to:

- promote improved interdisciplinary working across the family justice system through improved coordination between all agencies;
- identify and disseminate best practice throughout the family justice;
- consult with government departments on current policy and priorities and secure best value from available resources;
- provide guidance and direction to achieve consistency of practice throughout the family justice system and submit proposals for new practice directions where appropriate;
- promote the effectiveness of the family justice system by identifying priorities for, and encouraging the conduct of, research.

Box 7.2 Continued

Source: Adapted from www.judiciary.gov.uk/about-the-judiciary/advisory-bodies/fjc.

The FJB was established in March 2012. Its purpose is to keep the programme of reform proposed in the Norgrove Report under review.

The FJB has three sub-groups to support its work:

(1) the Performance Improvement Sub-Group (PISG), which analyses the available performance information and galvanizes action to improve performance at the national and local levels;

(2) the Family Justice Council; and

(3) the Young People's Board, which supports the FJB's work and helps it to be child-centred by enabling young people to have a direct say in its work.

There is also a network of 46 local family justice boards (LFJBs), established to drive significant improvements in performance at the local level.

The FJB's strategic priorities are to:

(1) achieve the 26-week time limit for care and supervision cases;

(2) ensure that separating parents are encouraged and supported to resolve issues out of court, with mediation becoming established and effective practice;

(3) support and challenge all LFJBs to drive performance improvements and implement reforms effectively at the local level;

(4) ensure that the voice of the child is heard throughout the family justice system;

(5) improve outcomes for children who come into contact with the system; and

(6) ensure that research evidence influences and improves practice.

Source: Family Justice Board, *Action Plan to Improve the Performance of the Family Justice System* 2013–15, available at www.gov.uk/government/groups/family-justice-board.

Further information on changes to the family justice system since April 2014 is available at www.gov.uk/government/publications/whats-happened-since-the-family-justice-review-a-brighter-future-for-family-justice.

In addition to the work of these advisory bodies, the President of the Family Court, Sir James Munby, is taking a close personal interest in the programme to reform the family justice system. He issues regular newsletters on a wide range of procedural and substantive law matters.[2]

7.2.4 Court fees

I discuss the question of court fees further in *Chapter 8*. Here it may be noted that the fees for going to court on family law issues have recently been significantly increased. For example, the fee for seeking a divorce was increased from £410 to £550. Although

---

[2] To read his views, go to www.judiciary.gov.uk/publications/view-from-presidents-chambers/.

there are circumstances in which fees can be waived, the question arises of whether the level of fees charged is adversely affecting those who might be thinking of using the courts to resolve their family law issues, possibly deterring them from court altogether. This is an issue on which there will continue to be public debate.

7.2.5 *Transforming Our Justice System*: family justice

The cost of going to court also raises questions as to whether the current practices and procedures of the courts all need to be retained in their current form. The *Transforming Our Justice System* programme (*see 4.2.2.2*) does not actually have a great deal to say on the family justice system. Rather it acknowledges the fact that there have been massive changes in recent years which need longer to bed down.

One specific ambition of the transformation programme may, however, be noted in this context. This is that the application for and management of divorce proceedings should increasingly be done online. A trial scheme was launched nationally in January 2018. The President of the Family Court is very supportive of these developments, arguing that much can be done online. He would like to see further procedural change so that money matters—financial remedies (*see 7.6*)—are dealt with quite separately from divorce proceedings.

7.3 Children

One of the Family Court's heaviest responsibilities is taking decisions relating to the welfare of children. The principal source of law is the Children Act 1989, which puts 'the interests of the child' at the heart of any proceedings. The Family Court has to decide both public law cases and private law cases (*see Box 7.3*).

Box 7.3 Legal system explained

Public law and private law children cases

In relation to children, it is essential to distinguish between public law cases and private law cases.

- *Public law* cases are brought by public authorities—in particular the social services departments of local authorities—or the National Society for the Prevention of Cruelty to Children (NSPCC). They may be seeking orders from the court relating to the care, supervision, or emergency protection of children.
- *Private law* cases are those brought by private individuals, usually the parents of the child, seeking orders relating to the child in the context of a divorce or the separation of the parents.

One of the principal objectives of the Children Act 1989 was to ensure that the voice of the child was heard. Therefore, in most public law applications, the court appoints a

Box 7.3 Continued

children's guardian to assist the child, unless the court is satisfied that this is not needed to protect the interests of the child. The role of the guardian is to ensure that the court is fully informed of facts relevant to determining the best interests of the child. The guardian also seeks to ensure that the court is made fully aware of the child's feelings and wishes. Guardians are provided by the Children and Family Court Advisory and Support Service (CAFCASS), established in 2001 by the Criminal Justice and Court Services Act 2000. In defined cases, the guardian is also required to appoint a solicitor to act for the child, to ensure proper legal representation.

In private law cases, an analogous role is played by the Children and Family Reporter, also appointed by CAFCASS.

The caseload relating to both public and private law applications is significant.[3] 18,953 public law applications and 48,240 private law applications were made in 2016. Both figures are higher than the previous year, and are causing concern about the ability of the Family Court to deal with such numbers.

7.3.1 Orders

The Children Act 1989 provides for a wide range of orders that can be made by the courts in public law cases relating to children. They include:

- care/supervision orders;
- emergency protection orders; and
- exclusion requirements.

In addition, 'section 8' orders can be made in private law cases.

7.3.1.1 Care/supervision orders

These are made on application by either a local authority or the NSPCC (which is the only 'authorized person' under the Children Act 1989 able to bring such proceedings). Before an order may be made, the court must be satisfied either that a child is suffering or is likely to suffer significant harm, and that the harm or likelihood of harm is attributable to:

(1) the care given to the child; or

(2) the likelihood of the care not being what it would be reasonable to expect a parent to give a child;

or that the child is beyond parental control.

---

[3] Data in this chapter are derived from Ministry of Justice, *Family Court Statistics Quarterly* April to June 2017, available at www.gov.uk/government/statistics/family-court-statistics-quarterly-april-to-june-2017.

If the court is so satisfied, it may make an order:

(1) placing the child in the care of a designated local authority; or

(2) putting the child under the supervision of a designated local authority or probation officer.

Such orders cannot be made in relation to a child who has reached the age of 17 (16 if the child is married).

The effect of a *care order* is to impose a duty on the local authority to keep the child in care, to exercise parental responsibility over the child, and to determine the extent to which a parent or guardian may meet his or her parental responsibility towards the child. The effect of a *supervision order* is to impose a duty on the supervisor to advise, assist, and befriend the child, and to take the necessary action to give effect to the order, including whether or not to apply to vary or discharge it.

On average, it takes 27 weeks for such cases to be determined; 61 per cent are determined within the 26-week limit created by the Children and Families Act 2014.

7.3.1.2 Emergency protection orders

These are made where the court is satisfied that there is reasonable cause to believe that a child is suffering, or is likely to suffer, significant harm if not removed to accommodation provided by the applicant, or that the child should not remain in the place where she is currently living. Emergency protection orders may be sought where anyone, including a local authority, believes that access to a child is being unreasonably refused.

7.3.1.3 Exclusion requirements

From October 1997, the courts have had power to order the exclusion of a suspected abuser from a child's home, where ill-treatment of the child is alleged and either an interim care order or an emergency protection order has been made. A power of arrest can be added to the exclusion requirement, so that anyone in breach may be instantly arrested. Before an exclusion requirement can be ordered, the court must be satisfied that there will still be a person remaining in the premises with the child, and that that person has agreed to care for the child and has consented to the exclusion requirement.

7.3.1.4 'Section 8' orders

In addition to orders that can be made in public law cases, section 8 of the Children Act 1989 (as now amended by the Children and Families Act 2014) sets out the orders that can be made in private law cases. They are:

- *child arrangements* orders (which have replaced *residence* orders, determining where the child should live, and *contact* orders, deciding whom the child may see);

- *prohibited steps* orders, to prevent a defined action(s) taking place; and

- *specific issue* orders, dealing with particular aspects of a child's upbringing.

Annually, around 40,000 cases involving section 8 orders are started, the vast majority relating to residence and contact.

Problems with enforcement of these orders resulted in the government introducing new rules for dealing with parental separation. The Children and Adoption Act 2006 has two objectives.

First, it wants to promote the quality of contact between parent and child. The Act gives the court power to direct a party to take part in an activity that would promote contact with a child. Contact activities include attendance at programmes, classes, or counselling sessions designed to improve the quality of contact time, or to address a person's violent behaviour. This may occur during the proceedings, even if the court does not make a child arrangements order, or by making such activity a condition in a child arrangements order.

Secondly, it gives the court wider powers in cases involving breach of a child arrangements order by adding: a power to make enforcement orders imposing an unpaid work requirement; and a power to order one person to pay compensation to another for a financial loss caused by a breach. These powers are in addition to the court's powers relating to contempt of court and its ability to alter the residence and contact arrangements relating to a child.

7.3.1.5 A new approach—a problem-solving court?

One particular idea of which the President of the Family Court has become a strong supporter is that of 'problem-solving courts'. The theory is that many families get caught up in the care system because there are aspects of their life style—especially alcohol and substance abuse—which result in children coming to the attention of social service departments. The argument is that if you offer a programme of support for the parent(s) who are not coping well, to change their lives, this could result in fewer children being brought within the care system, with all the financial and emotional costs that this entails.

Some years ago, Judge Nicholas Crichton established a new type of court—the Family Drug and Alcohol Court (FDAC)—which sought to put these ideas into practice. In 2015, a FDAC National Unit was created, which seeks to promote the development of these courts in different parts of the country. In its first year it helped more than 15 such courts to come into existence. You can find out more about the FDAC, and the progress it has made at http://fdac.org.uk/.

7.4 Adoption

The other principal activity of the courts in relation to children concerns adoption, whereby the rights, duties, and obligations of a child's natural parents are legally extinguished and are vested, by order of the court, in the adoptive parents. It is essential that the court is satisfied that the adoptive parents are suitable and have consented to the adoption. Where possible it is also necessary to obtain the consent of the parents (including any guardian with parental responsibility), though this may be dispensed with if there is evidence that the natural parent has persistently ill-treated the child or that consent is being unreasonably withheld. Once again, the primary objective of the courts is to safeguard and promote the welfare of the child. This includes taking the views of the child into account.

Major changes to the law of adoption were made by the Adoption and Children Act 2002. The intention was, while continuing to protect children, to make it easier for those wishing to adopt children to do so, thereby increasing the number of adoptions currently sanctioned by the legal process. The Children and Families Act 2014 contains measures designed to increase the number of adoptions and to make the process less drawn out (*see Box 7.4*).

Box 7.4 Reform in progress

Children and Families Act 2014: provisions relating to adoption

The Act contains measures which:

- are intended to encourage local authorities to place children for whom adoption is an option with their potential permanent carers more swiftly, by requiring a local authority looking after a child for whom adoption is an option to consider placing them in a 'Fostering for Adoption' placement if one is available;
- are intended to reduce delay by removing the explicit legal wording around a child's ethnicity so that black and minority ethnic children are not left waiting in care longer than necessary because local authorities are seeking a perfect or partial ethnic match;
- enable the Secretary of State to require local authorities to commission adopter recruitment services from one or more other adoption agencies;
- are intended to give prospective adopters a more active role in identifying possible matches with children, by amending the current restrictions in relation to 'public inspection or search' of the Adoption and Children Act Register so that they can access the register directly, subject to appropriate safeguards;
- are intended to improve the current provision of adoption support by placing new duties on local authorities to provide personal budgets upon request and to give prospective adopters and adoptive parents information about their entitlements to support; and
- make changes to the arrangements for contact between children in care and their birth parents, guardians, and certain others and adopted children and their birth families, former guardians, and certain others, with the aim of reducing the disruption that inappropriate contact can cause to adoptive placements.

There was a rise in the number of adoption applications between 2011 and mid-2014, but since then the trend has been markedly downward. Recent figures show that during April to June 2017, there were 1,269 adoption applications, an 11 per cent reduction on the same period in 2016.

7.5 Matrimonial matters

The other principal work of the Family Court relates to the dissolution of marriages.

A marriage may be dissolved in two ways: divorce and nullity. *Divorce* is used in over 99 per cent of cases. To obtain a divorce, the petitioner must prove that the marriage has broken down irretrievably. This can be demonstrated by proof of: adultery; behaviour that the petitioner cannot reasonably be expected to live with; desertion for at least two years; two years' separation where the respondent consents; or five years' separation where there is no such consent. If any of these grounds is proved, a provisional measure, the *decree nisi*, is made. The divorce becomes final only after a final decision, the *decree absolute*. The existence of this two-stage process is to provide an opportunity, albeit rarely used, for second thoughts. Most cases are disposed of on the basis of paper evidence without the need for a hearing.

Where children are involved, the court must be satisfied with the arrangements for their welfare. These must be written down and, if possible, agreed between the parents. If agreement is not possible, the judge may order the parents to come to court so that the issues may be resolved. If the issues are uncontested at this point, the judge may issue a *section 8 order* (*see 7.3.1.4*).

The divorce caseload is substantial. Around 27,000 petitions for divorce were filed in April–June 2017 (down 10 per cent compared with the same quarter in 2016).

Nullity is the other mode of dissolving a marriage. However, this can be used only where there is proof that the marriage either was void in the first place (e.g. because one of the parties was under the age of 16 or was already married), or was voidable (e.g. because one of the parties was pregnant by someone else at the time of the marriage or the marriage was not consummated due to incapacity or wilful refusal). To obtain a decree of nullity, a two-stage process, similar to the divorce process, must be gone through.

Judicial separation is an alternative procedure for those who do not wish to or who for some reason cannot get divorced. It does not terminate the marriage, but legally absolves the parties to a marriage from the obligation to live together.

The use of these two procedures is very rare.

7.6 Financial remedy orders

Financial remedy orders (formerly called ancillary relief) are orders made by the court which are linked to divorce or other matrimonial proceedings. These relate to maintenance (periodical payments to an ex-spouse) and to lump sum payments or property orders (usually dealing with the matrimonial home).

The powers of the courts to deal with maintenance orders relating to the children of the marriage were to a certain extent taken over by the child support system. But plans that the Child Support Agency, created in 1993, should take over all this work foundered in the operational chaos that engulfed the Agency (*see 7.7*). The Family Court still makes a significant number of orders relating to the maintenance of or other financial provision for children. Between April and June 2017, 11,517 applications for financial remedy orders were made, 3 per cent down on the same period in 2016.

The large majority of applications are uncontested by the parties, requiring no court hearing.

Where the parties cannot agree, however, both sides are required to make the other party aware of how costs are mounting up, particularly if there is unnecessary delay in reaching a conclusion. In addition, the parties are required to undergo a financial dispute resolution appointment in which, with the assistance of a judge, an attempt is made to help the parties agree an outcome, rather than have a solution imposed on them by the judge.

7.7 Child support

One of the most controversial structural changes made to the family justice system was the creation of the child support system by the Child Support Act 1991. The principle behind the original scheme was straightforward. Far too many single parents, mostly women, found it impossible either to obtain an order for the maintenance of their children or, if they did obtain one, to enforce it. A consequence of this was that lone parents were heavily dependent on the provision of social security benefits for the financial resources needed to bring up their children, rather than being supported by the child's natural but absent parent. (In 1989, 23 per cent of lone parents claiming income support were receiving maintenance, compared to around 50 per cent in 1979.)

The child support system was intended to reverse this decline, by providing consistent rules for assessing maintenance liability and a readily accessible means for collecting and enforcing payment that was due, without the necessity for parents to use the courts. A system for getting absent parents to pay for their children had been introduced in Australia in the 1980s, apparently with great success. Thus, it was argued, a similar scheme could be introduced in the United Kingdom.

Administration of the scheme was the responsibility of the Child Support Agency. From the outset it was dogged by controversy. It never worked as intended, not least because the underpinning IT did not function properly. Over the following 20 years numerous measures that changed the rules and procedures were introduced. These included the creation of a new administrative body, the Child Maintenance and Enforcement Commission.

The current position is that families are encouraged to reach their own agreement. In order to assist parties to reach an outcome that is workable for them, the Department for Work and Pensions has established a Child Maintenance Service. It runs the Child Maintenance Options service, designed to give free and impartial advice to parties to help them negotiate their own agreement.

Where an agreement cannot be reached, the Child Maintenance Service can, in the last resort, impose an outcome on parents. A feature of the new service is that it imposes charges for using it. It is intended that these charges should be an incentive to parties to come to their own agreements.

A large number of historic cases that were originally determined by the Child Support Agency are in the process of being moved over to the new system. The intention is that this should be complete by the end of 2017.

Child support never worked as it was intended to do. Indeed, there is evidence that, notwithstanding the efforts in other parts of the family justice system to reduce tensions between former partners, child support actually exacerbated problems between them. Whether the latest arrangements will make any significant difference has yet to be determined; it must be said that past experience is not encouraging.

7.8 Domestic violence

Another way in which the family justice system has been transformed over the last 25 years has been the recognition of the problem of domestic violence and the need for the law and legal procedures to deal with cases swiftly and effectively (*see also Box 5.2*). There are now three principal items of legislation relevant in this context:

- Part IV of the Family Law Act 1996;
- the Protection from Harassment Act 1997; and
- the Forced Marriage (Civil Protection) Act 2007.

In addition, the Serious Crimes Act 2015 needs brief consideration.

7.8.1 Part IV of the Family Law Act 1996

This Act provides a set of remedies in domestic violence cases, which can be sought in the Family Court. Two types of order may be made:

- a *non-molestation order* to prohibit a person from behaving in a particular way towards another or which may seek to prohibit molestation in general; and
- an *occupation order*, which can define or regulate the rights of a person to occupy a home (irrespective of his ownership rights in that home).

Occupation orders are available not only to married couples, but also to cohabiting couples, others who live or have lived in the same household as the person seeking the order (though not tenants, boarders, or lodgers), certain relatives (such as parents, or brothers or sisters), and those who have agreed to marry. From July 2007, it has been a criminal offence to breach a non-molestation order.

If the court thinks that the respondent has used or has threatened violence against either the applicant or any child of the applicant, then the court must attach a power of arrest to the order, unless satisfied that the applicant or child will be adequately protected without such a power being attached.

In addition, the court may at the same time add an *exclusion requirement* to an *emergency protection order* or *interim care order* made under the Children Act 1989 (*see 7.3.1*), so that the suspected abuser (rather than the abused child) may be removed from the dwelling.

There is a substantial caseload arising from these provisions. Applications for non-molestation orders currently run at around 4,500 a quarter, with about another 1,000 applications for occupation orders.

7.8.2 Protection from Harassment Act 1997

This Act was initially introduced to combat the problem of stalking, but it applies more generally to the victims of harassment. Section 3 allows civil proceedings to be taken against anyone pursuing a course of harassment. The remedies available are an injunction—an order to prevent such behaviour in the future—and/or damages. Since September 1998, the courts have had power to make breach of an injunction enforceable by warrant of arrest. No information is available on the use of these provisions.

7.8.3 Forced Marriage (Civil Protection) Act 2007

This Act came into force on 25 November 2008. It enables the Family Court to make forced marriage protection orders to prevent forced marriages from occurring and to offer protection to victims who might have already been forced into a marriage. The number of applications and orders made is very small. In April to June 2017, there were 78 applications and 72 orders made.

7.8.4 Serious Crimes Act 2015: female genital mutilation protection orders

Following the enactment of the Serious Crimes Act 2015, a new order—the female genital mutilation protection order—has been available since July 2015 to protect young women who might be subject to FGM or who have been the victims of FGM. In total, there have been 163 applications and 147 orders made since their introduction up to the end of June 2017.

7.9 The practitioners

7.9.1 Lawyers and other providers

Given the fact that so many aspects of family life are regulated by law, in particular the issues relating to children, relationship breakdown, and other financial matters, it is inevitable that legal practitioners should be deeply involved in family law issues. This is a major area for legal specialism, with large numbers of lawyers offering family law services.

Practitioners have given considerable thought to their proper role in assisting the resolution of family disputes. For example, should they engage in heavily adversarial forms of litigation designed to advance their clients' interests, irrespective of the interests of the other party to the marriage or relationship and the children? Or should they adopt a more conciliatory approach?

The perception that lawyers often added to the problems of separating couples rather than helping their resolution led, some years ago, to the formation of the Solicitors' Family Law Association—now called Resolution. (There is an equivalent for barristers—the Family Law Bar Association.) It aims to bring a less hostile atmosphere to the resolution of family disputes.

Research suggests that, in general, solicitors have been rather successful at not exacerbating the conflicts between couples. Surveys of clients' responses to the legal services provided have, in general, been positive.

One of the ways in which practitioners have sought to develop the nature of their work with clients in the family law area has been through schemes of specialist training. For a number of years, the Law Society has run a Children's Panel, aimed particularly at solicitors who act for children in public law cases. Admission to the panel involves the lawyers demonstrating appropriate levels of qualification and experience.

In addition, during 1999, the Law Society established a Family Law Panel. The Solicitors' Family Law Association also established its own Family Law Panel and, in 1999, launched a scheme for the accreditation of those lawyers who sought to join the panel.

Those who practise family law have recognized the particular character of the work they have to undertake, dealing not only with the very considerable complexities of the law, but also the strong emotional context within which such work has to be carried out. As the need for special training of the judiciary has been accepted, so too has the importance of special training for practitioners been acknowledged.

It has to be noted, however, that—particularly in relation to divorce, where the parties are in agreement about their wish to divorce—there is now a considerable number of alternative providers offering online services to obtain 'quickie' or 'Do It Yourself' divorces at very low cost. This trend is likely to develop as online proceedings become more common.

7.9.2 Mediation and mediators

Notwithstanding the efforts of professional lawyers to shape the nature of family law practice to the needs of clients, successive governments have made changes to the ways in which family disputes are resolved, particularly cases paid for by the state. Government now takes the view that a preferable way of resolving family disputes should be through *mediation* outside the courts, rather than litigation in the courts.

Mediation is a form of assisted negotiation. Instead of a negotiation taking place just between the parties to the dispute and/or their representatives, mediation involves the intervention of an impartial third party, the mediator. The mediator's function is to try to help parties to a dispute reach an agreement acceptable to both sides. While the mediator cannot impose a solution on the parties, the presence of the mediator can contribute to the pressure to settle disputes.

In 2015, the Family Mediation Council introduced a compulsory accreditation scheme and new professional standards. All mediators and those working towards becoming a family mediator are required to be registered with the Council. The Ministry of Justice (MoJ) funded the preparation work and costs of implementing the new standards.

Mediation has been used to resolve family disputes for many years. Experience suggests that it is often successful in bringing the parties to an agreement. There is also evidence that it is liked by those who have gone through the process. Nevertheless, despite the enthusiasm of those who offer mediation services, only a small number of parties to family disputes voluntarily ask for their disputes to be mediated.

Despite this lack of enthusiasm, mediation is now central to policy on dispute resolution for family disputes (*see Box 7.1*). Reforms to legal aid, which came into effect in April 2013, made mediation central to the family dispute resolution process (*see 7.10*). From 3 November 2014, the first mediation meeting has been free to both parties, so long as at least one of the parties to the dispute is in receipt of legal aid.

7.10 Funding family law cases: the reform of legal aid

Under the Legal Aid, Sentencing and Punishment of Offenders Act 2012, major changes to legal aid came into effect in April 2013 (*see further Chapter 10*). Instead of legal aid potentially covering any matter of law, now only statutorily defined categories of work are within the scope of legal aid and therefore eligible for funding.

In the case of family matters, the only matters within the scope of the legal aid scheme are:

- public family law cases regarding protection of children;
- private family cases where there is evidence of domestic violence;
- private law children cases where there is evidence of child abuse;
- child abduction matters;
- representation for child parties in private family cases;
- legal advice in support of mediation;
- domestic violence injunction cases;
- forced marriage protection order cases.

Nothing else is fundable by legal aid, unless a case for exceptional funding is successfully made. (This is likely to hurt women particularly badly, as they were funded by legal aid more often than men.) Even for cases within scope, the focus is on funding for mediation rather than court proceedings—though this general principle does not apply in cases involving domestic violence or abuse.

Statistics from the Legal Aid Agency published in 2017 indicate that, despite the focus on mediation, legal aid payments for mediation are currently falling. By contrast, there has recently been a sharp increase in legal aid payments for family public law cases.[4]

---

[4] See https://www.gov.uk/government/uploads/system/uploads/attachment_data/file/647983/legal-aid-statistics-bulletin-apr-jun-2017.pdf.

The potential impact of these changes is enormous. For many years, practitioners reported that achieving profitability in legal aid practice was becoming increasingly difficult; there were signs that the now defunct Legal Services Commission (which used to run the legal aid scheme) had begun to share that concern. The fact is that a combination of the reductions in scope and significant reductions in the amounts of money legal aid now pays practitioners to deliver family law services has put enormous pressure on law firms. Without the development of innovative ways of delivering family law services, the levels of service which existed before the legal aid changes came into effect cannot be maintained.

7.11 Key points

1. Family law disputes involve extremely difficult issues which must be handled with particular care—especially where children are involved.

2. This is an area both of substantive law and of legal practice which has evolved considerably in recent years, and will continue to do so.

3. Ideas being developed in the wider civil justice system for the more efficient resolution of disputes (*see Chapter 8*) are also relevant to the family justice system.

4. It is an area in which the impact of research on the development of law and practice has been significant.

5. The use of mediation in resolving family disputes remains low but is likely to increase with more experience of how it works.

6. Looking to the future, many of the issues likely to come onto the agenda for the reform of family law—e.g. reform of grounds for divorce—will be very controversial.

7. Although governments may claim that they are happy for individuals to make their own choices about how they should structure their lives and relationships, a desire to get 'back to basics' and to promote 'family values' is one that successive Prime Ministers seem to find hard to resist.

7.12 Questions

Use the self-test questions in the Online Resources to test your understanding of the topics covered in this chapter and receive tailored feedback: www.oup.com/uk/partington18_19/.

7.13 Web links

Check the Online Resources for a selection of annotated web links allowing you to easily research topics of particular interest: www.oup.com/uk/partington18_19/.

7.14 Blog items

See Spotlight on the Justice System, at www.martinpartington.com/category/chapter-7-2/.

Suggestions for further reading

PARKINSON, L., *Family Mediation* (3rd rev. edn, Bristol, Jordans, 2014)

WIKELEY, N., *Child Support: Law and Policy* (Oxford, Hart Publishing, 2006)

Other suggestions are set out in the Further Reading listed in the **Online Resources**.

8

The civil and commercial justice systems

8.1 Introduction: civil and commercial justice

The scope of civil and commercial law is enormous; it embraces a wide range of issues relating to legal obligations and entitlements. It is in this context that many of the relationships between law and society considered in *Chapter 2* are seen to operate—particularly those relating to law and economic order. This is the part of the English legal system where the protection of property and other rights may be asserted, and where questions of the ownership of land, or intellectual property, or other forms of personal property are determined. So too are the consequences of breaches of contract and acts of negligence.

Much of the conceptual framework of the civil law has been shaped by the common law. The fundamental principles of contract, negligence, trusts, and property, and the principles of the law of equity, were all created by judges. These days, in response to social pressures, most common law principles have either been supplemented or replaced by legislation. Parliament has enacted measures, usually designed to protect the weaker party, which the common law was unable to do. Obvious examples are measures relating to the protection of consumers or tenants or employees.

There are constant pressures to add to the scope of civil justice. For example:

- As commercial interests become ever more complex and as the economy becomes more global, new demands for the protection of globalized interests arise.

- New forms of financial instrument have been created to take advantage of the internationalization of banks and other players in the capital markets, which need protection not only within English domestic law but also taking European and other foreign legal regimes into account.

- New technologies present major challenges. For example, there is much current debate about the legal implications of the use of the internet for commercial activity on principles of the law of contract. How are consumers and suppliers of goods and services provided through the internet to be protected? Issues have arisen about how to regulate use of the internet to spread defamatory statements, or pornography.

- The legal implications of new biotechnologies must be addressed. What can be patented? Which legal system should provide protection of the intellectual and other property rights involved? What are the legal implications of the human genome project?

In short, civil and commercial law cannot be divorced from their social and economic context.

The civil and commercial justice systems provide the institutional framework within which the rights and obligations found in civil and commercial law can be asserted. I use the word 'systems' in the plural deliberately.

The core of the civil justice system is found in the work of the county court. It is here that the bulk of the civil work that ends up in the courts is undertaken: dealing with the consequences of people getting into debt, or breaking their contracts, or suffering personal injury (negligence).

But there are also other more specialist areas of activity—for example relating to bankruptcy and the winding up of companies, or trade mark protection, or disputes arising out of construction contracts or shipping contracts or significant property matters—which relate to commercial activity, often with large amounts of money involved. Over the years a number of specialist commercial courts were created which have now been brought together under the general heading of the Business and Property Courts of England and Wales (*see 8.9*).

It is this development that leads me to argue that there are now two civil justice systems: a generalist one and a specialist commercial one.

The civil and commercial justice systems play a significant role, both in economic life and in the regulation of other social relationships, by seeking to ensure that bargains are kept, other rights are protected, and compensation for the adverse consequences of legally unacceptable behaviour is awarded to those who have been affected. Just consider what happens in those countries the rule of law to regulate social and economic behaviour is not accepted. It is extremely hard to attract investment into countries where there is no guarantee that contracts will be enforced or property rights upheld.

For many years, the civil justice and commercial systems have been changing, seeking—not always effectively—to adapt to external social and economic pressures. One key challenge has been how the English legal system should respond to globalization. The globalization of economic activity implies increased globalization of legal activity. At present, a great deal of international trade is made the subject of English law. International companies know that, if they have a dispute which needs to be litigated, this can be done in a system that is authoritative, expert and not corrupt. If those who seek the law's protection cannot find it in England, they will take their work elsewhere. This has been one of the main drivers in the creation of the Business and Property Courts—to send the signal that this country is the place in which serious commercial litigation can be properly and efficiently conducted.

8.2 Issues in civil and commercial justice

Before looking at the institutional framework of the civil and commercial justice system, I consider three important background questions.

8.2.1 Litigation and society: is there a compensation culture?

It is often said that modern society has become too litigious. It is asserted that people are too willing to rush to court when something has gone wrong; we have created a 'compensation culture'. This needs thinking about carefully.

It could be argued that, with better education, more people can now use the procedures and facilities that in the past were open only to the rich and powerful. Thus rather than being a bad thing, an increase in the use of litigation may indicate that ordinary people are no longer willing to accept things without question, as they might have done before. On that basis, an increase in litigation to assert legal rights may not only be expected, but to a degree welcomed.

Against this, it may be argued that there comes a point where the level of litigation suggests that something rather different has happened. People now seek to put the blame on others in situations where they should be taking responsibility themselves. This in turn may lead to unacceptable levels of resource—both cash and manpower—being expended on taking or defending cases in court which could be better spent in more socially productive activity. It may also lead to the view that the ability of the citizen to take sensible risks is being undermined.

In recent years, a number of developments have encouraged the view that a 'compensation culture' has been created in the United Kingdom. Particularly noteworthy are the television advertisements or the mobile phone messages encouraging those who have suffered personal injury or the mis-selling of insurance policies to make a claim.

Despite these developments, there is compelling empirical evidence that one of the key problems which continues to confront the civil justice system is that many people do not know how to assert their legal rights through the legal system, either through ignorance or through fear of the costs that may be involved. Thus the view that *any* rise in levels of litigation is by definition a symptom of a society ill at ease with itself should not be accepted uncritically. What is important is to support those with genuine and proper claims, while deterring those making claims that are wholly without foundation or merit. Achieving this goal is extremely difficult.

One way forward could be the provision of more and better public education about civil rights and obligations;[1] but, if taken seriously, this would be a huge and expensive task. A second possibility might be to limit legal liability, particularly for personal injury, so that claims would be admitted only where a defined percentage of injury has occurred; however, this is politically hard to deliver. A recent proposal to reduce the number of claims for 'whiplash' injuries in road traffic accidents is currently under consideration.

---

[1]   See *Legal Needs, Legal Capability and the Role of Public Legal Education*, Report from Law for Life: the Foundation for Public Legal Education (2015).

A third approach is to ensure that competition in the legal services market works to encourage innovation, drive up standards, and bring down costs (*see further 9.7*).

Over the last decade, large numbers of claims management companies were started which have used advertising to attract potential claimants with the use of 'no win, no fee' offers. However, the often aggressive business practices of some of these companies has led the government to regulate them more closely (*see 9.8.5*).

8.2.2 The provision of a civil justice system: is this a responsibility for government?

A second preliminary question that needs to be asked is: should the state provide a system of civil justice at all? Since disputes arising in this context are, by and large, private disputes between private parties, why should they not make arrangements for resolving those disputes themselves?

There are at least three reasons why the answer to this provocative preliminary question should be 'yes'. They all relate to the important constitutional role which the legal system plays in the overall system of government (*see 3.4*; *see also 6.4*).

(1) Our common law system requires the means to develop principles of the common law. This cannot happen without the senior courts and the authority that our constitutional arrangements give to the judges that sit in them to make and develop legal principle. Although the law-making functions of Parliament and other institutions are now far more significant than they were 100 years ago, modern statute law is still set in the common law context that has been shaped by the senior courts. Cases decided in the senior courts do not simply determine issues between parties to litigation; they have the wider public benefit of developing and interpreting the law for the future.

(2) The very fact that statute law is now a much more significant source of law means that there is a constitutional need for the court system to provide independent interpretations of the meaning of statutory provisions. All legislation has social and political objectives. Much modern legislation is designed to reduce imbalances in power, for example between landlords and tenants, employers and employees, or manufacturers and consumers. If the courts did not exist, much of this protective legislation—designed to achieve a wide range of policy objectives, including altering the nature of the relationships between parties—would be rendered even less effective than is often the case in any event.

(3) A third reason is more legalistic. Article 6 of the European Convention on Human Rights, incorporated into English law by the Human Rights Act 1998, provides that people should have a right to a fair trial for the determination of civil rights as well as criminal matters. A court system is necessary to satisfy this international obligation.

Notwithstanding these arguments, it is also the case that large numbers of disputes are dealt with outside the formal court system (*see 8.5*) and current policy proposals for transforming the civil justice system will lead to even more disputes being resolved outside the formal court system (*see 8.14*).

8.2.3 The purpose of the civil justice system: access for all or forum of last resort?

While the constitutional importance of the courts is clear, this does not mean that all disputes need to be resolved by the courts. The reality is that the vast majority of disputes are resolved without using courts—for example by negotiation, mediation, arbitration, or the use of other non-court procedures. Indeed, the rules of civil procedure, which regulate what goes on in court, have long contained incentives on parties to disputes to settle them without a formal trial.

There is, however, a paradox here. Lord Woolf's seminal review of civil justice, which kick-started 20 years of procedural reform in the civil justice system, was called *Access to Justice*. Yet Lord Woolf himself argued that the courts should be the forum of last resort. Important procedural reforms which resulted from his review reinforce this view (*see 8.4.8*). Nevertheless, he also argued that in those cases where there is no alternative to use of the courts and where it is essential that the courts are used, it is crucial that parties to a dispute have access to them. Some of the reforms he advocated—making rules of procedure more comprehensible for example—were designed to make it somewhat easier for potential litigants to start proceedings. But other changes have occurred, of which cuts in legal aid and increases in court fees are the most significant, which have made it harder for ordinary people to get access to justice. Thus, a question which needs to be borne in mind when reading this chapter and *Chapter 10* is: are the civil and commercial justice systems sufficiently accessible to those who need to use them.

8.3 Reforming the civil and commercial justice systems

For many years, it was widely recognized that the civil justice system had not been operating effectively. The main criticisms were that:

- court procedures were unnecessarily complex;
- the system was too slow;
- even if a court made a decision, it was very difficult to enforce it; and
- in general, the whole process cost far too much.

To try to deal with these issues, there have been three major reviews: the first, focusing primarily on procedural issues, by Lord Woolf; the second, focusing primarily on costs, by Lord Justice Jackson; and the third, on the structure of the civil courts, by Lord Justice Briggs. I discuss the first and third in this chapter; the second in *Chapter 10*.

8.4 Civil Procedure Rules 1998

8.4.1 Lord Woolf: *Access to Justice*

In 1994, Lord Woolf undertook a review of the civil justice system. His report, *Access to Justice*, was published in 1996. His vision was that those who wanted to bring cases to court should be able to do so efficiently, and at a cost proportionate to the amount in dispute. At the same time, the court should be the forum of last resort; every encouragement should be given to parties to settle their own disputes. At its most ambitious, Lord Woolf was seeking to change the culture of litigation by creating a framework within which both professional lawyers and those who wished to take their own cases to court (litigants in person) could do so, with their eyes focused on the issues which needed determination by a judge and setting aside matters that were not essential to the determination of the issue.

The Woolf report led to the enactment of the Civil Procedure Act 1997, which provides the statutory authority for the Civil Procedure Rules (CPR).

Before 1999, civil litigation was subject to two distinct codes of procedure:

- the *Rules of the Supreme Court* for cases dealt with in the High Court; and
- the *County Court Rules* for cases heard in county courts.

These were replaced by a single code, the *Civil Procedure Rules 1998*, which came into effect in April 1999. The new rules had a number of objectives.

8.4.2 Clearer language

A central aim of the new rules was that they should be easier to read and understand. The language of the rules was changed to make them more easily understandable. For example, those who bring cases to court are now 'claimants' rather than 'plaintiffs'; they swear or affirm 'statements of truth' instead of 'affidavits'; claimants now seek 'specified damages' instead of 'liquidated damages' or 'unspecified damages' instead of 'unliquidated damages'. The essential features of the case are set out in a 'statement of case' instead of 'pleadings'. There are numerous other examples. In short, the Rules sought to eliminate the Latin phrases and other old-fashioned terminology that made legal proceedings less comprehensible than they should be.[2]

Supplementing the rules are (1) practice directions; and (2) pre-action protocols.

8.4.3 Practice directions

Practice directions state how the rules are to be used in practice. Practitioners and other potential users of the civil justice system must be as aware of the directions and

---

[2] Of course, law students will still have to be aware of the old language, as an understanding of reported decisions made before the changes came into effect still depends on that knowledge. But, for the future, things should be clearer.

the requirements they impose as of the rules themselves. The mix of rules and practice directions, and the frequency with which they were amended following the launch of the new scheme, initially led to fears that it might result in the reintroduction of some of the complexity it was hoped the new system would eliminate. However, the pace of change has slackened and, although they are still updated regularly, the new rules and directions have been generally welcomed. They are available, free, at www.justice.gov. uk/courts/procedure-rules/civil.

8.4.4 Pre-action protocols

Pre-action protocols are guides to good litigation practice, setting standards and time-tables for the conduct of cases before court proceedings are started. They are negotiated and agreed by experienced practitioners, and approved by the Deputy Head of Civil Justice, a senior judge in the Court of Appeal. They are designed to ensure more exchange of information and fuller investigation of claims at an earlier stage so that potential litigants may be able better to assess the merits of a case and to ensure that proper steps are taken to resolve as many of the issues in dispute as possible, prior to the parties getting anywhere near a courtroom.

There are currently 13 protocols relating to defined classes of case: personal injury; clinical disputes; disease and illness claims; construction and engineering disputes; defamation; professional negligence; judicial review; housing disrepair; claims for possession based on rent arrears; possession claims based on mortgage or home purchase plan arrears in respect of residential property; dilapidations claims relating to commercial property; low value personal injury claims arising from road traffic accidents; and low value personal injury (employers' liability and public liability) claims. There is also a practice direction that sets out guidance as to pre-action steps in cases where there is no relevant protocol. The protocols are set out in the CPR.

8.4.5 Forms

Much work was done on the forms used to start and progress potential cases. Again this was designed to make it easier for the ordinary individual to use the courts, and to reduce professional costs by ensuring that particular documents do not always have to be specially drafted by professional advisers. The forms can be downloaded from the website of Her Majesty's Courts and Tribunals Service (HMCTS). Certain types of case can be conducted entirely online. At present these are limited, but the potential for expanding them is enormous and is a key part of the *Transforming Our Justice System* programme (*see 4.2.2.2 and 8.14*).

8.4.6 Use of experts

Lord Woolf wanted to limit the use of experts to one, who would be there to assist the court, rather than to represent the interests of either side. This was felt to be too draconian a step to take. Nevertheless, the CPR provide that experts have a duty to help the court on matters within their expertise. Furthermore, this duty overrides any obligation to the person by whom they have been instructed or by whom they are paid. Experts give evidence only if the court gives permission. Instructions to experts are no longer privileged, and thus their substance must be disclosed in their report. In practice, a single jointly appointed expert is becoming a common feature of civil litigation, save where the complexity of the issues warrants both sides having their own expert.

8.4.7 The overriding objective

Lord Woolf's main aim, expressed in the overriding objective in the CPR, was to tackle delay, and to try to ensure that the process (and its cost) is proportionate to the value and complexity of what is in dispute. To deliver this, the CPR have, at their heart, two key features—track allocation and active case management—designed to achieve this aim.

Track allocation depends on the size and complexity of the case. There are three tracks:

- a 'small claims track' in the county court for simpler, low value cases—currently up to £10,000 (£1,000 for personal injuries[3] and housing). Hearings tend to be informal, held in the judge's room (chambers) rather than in open court. Successful claimants do not usually get their costs in small claims cases;

- a 'fast track', also in the county court, for moderately valued cases (usually between £10,000 and £25,000), which can be tried within a day; and

- a 'multi-track', usually in the county court, but sometimes in the High Court, for the most complex cases.

From 2013, judges have had the power to transfer suitable business-to-business cases with a dispute value over £10,000 to the small claims track without requiring the consent of the parties. Judges also have the option of referring more complex cases with a case value below £10,000 to the fast track if that is considered appropriate.

Case management. Following allocation, the progress of the case is determined by judges managing the timetable for the case. Each county court circuit has a *designated* judge who has responsibility for ensuring that cases are actively managed. By giving judges clear powers to set the timetable for the litigation process, the Woolf reforms were also intended to ensure that adjudication of disputes was reached more speedily.

8.4.8 Incentives to settle

In line with his view that the courts should be the forum of last resort for civil and commercial disputes, Lord Woolf recommended increasing the incentives on parties

---

[3] The government announced in November 2015 that this limit would be increased to £5,000 for personal injury claims. Following consultation, the government decided in March 2017 that, while road traffic accident claims for less than £5000 should stay in the small claims track, the small claims limit for other personal injury claims should become £2000. It plans that these new limits should be in effect by October 2018.

to settle. Even before the Woolf reforms, the 'typical' dispute was resolved by negotiation and settlement, not by a trial in court. The civil and commercial justice systems are much more frequently used *indirectly* as part of the process of resolution, rather than *directly* with a case being tried before a judge.

There are huge incentives on parties to settle. Three may be particularly noted:

- *Cost.* The cost of litigation increases dramatically as the parties get closer to the courtroom door. It is at this point that the numbers of lawyers involved in a case tend to increase. Where barristers are used, their fees are significantly higher when they appear in court than when they are sitting in chambers providing written advice to clients. This is mitigated to a degree by the increasing use of fixed recoverable costs (*see 10.4.2*).

- *The indemnity principle.* This provides that, in the usual case, the loser of the case pays a large proportion of the costs of the winner. Given that clear-cut cases should not be coming to court at all, and that therefore there is always some uncertainty about the outcome of a trial (described by one legal academic as a 'forensic lottery'), this rule also helps to concentrate the minds of litigants.[4]

- *Payments into court and offers to settle.* The CPR provide that parties to proceedings may offer to settle a case or pay a sum of money into court. The formalities for making an offer or payment are set out in Part 36 of the CPR. If the offer or payment is not accepted, and the party who did not accept fails to do better at the end of any trial than the offer or payment in, then that party will be ordered to pay any costs incurred by the other side after the latest date on which such offer or payment could have been accepted without needing the permission of the court. The court has a discretion to depart from this principle where application of the rule would, in its view, be unjust. From 1 April 2013, if a claimant's offer is not accepted and at trial the claimant obtains a judgment at least as advantageous as the terms of his own offer, the claimant can claim an additional sum for damages in respect of a money claim or an additional sum for costs in respect of a non-money claim. The additional sum is 10 per cent on damages or costs up to £500,000 and 5 per cent on damages or costs above £500,000 up to £1 million. The maximum enhancement is £75,000.

8.5 Alternative dispute resolution and alternatives to courts

8.5.1 Alternative dispute resolution

The Woolf reforms embraced another development that has occurred over recent years—*alternative dispute resolution* (ADR) (*see Box 8.1*) or, as it is perhaps better

---

[4] The indemnity principle has now been restricted in defined cases through the introduction of qualified one-way costs shifting (*see 10.4.7*).

labelled, appropriate dispute resolution. This is an umbrella term describing a range of practices designed to assist parties to achieve a resolution of their dispute without the necessity of going to court for a full trial in a courtroom. Many of these techniques were developed in the United States where they are widely used. Their use in England has been less marked,[5] but is growing slowly.

Box 8.1 Legal system explained

Forms of alternative dispute resolution

ADR comes in a variety of forms. The principal ones are:

- arbitration;
- mediation; and
- early neutral evaluation.

Arbitration is a process whereby the parties to a dispute choose an arbitrator to determine their dispute. It is a private process. The arbitrator is often an expert in the matter which is the subject of the dispute, say a building contract. The parties are usually bound, contractually, to accept the decision of the arbitrator. It is thus like a court decision, an imposed decision, though, unlike with the court, the whole process takes place in private, out of sight of the general public. Indeed, confidentiality is one of arbitration's perceived advantages for many disputants.

Mediation is a technique whereby a third party—mediator—who is neutral so far as the parties to the dispute are concerned, attempts to explore the possibilities for the parties reaching an outcome which satisfies both of them. This is sometimes known as 'win–win', to contrast it with a court process, which may be characterized as 'win–lose'. This outcome will not necessarily be one which a court would have reached (or would have had power to reach), for example because the particular remedy—e.g. saying sorry—is not a remedy available in court. It has the advantage that the decision will be one at which the parties have themselves arrived, albeit with the advice and assistance of the mediator.

Early neutral evaluation is a process where someone with legal or other relevant expertise is given a preliminary view of the case and is asked to provide a frank appraisal of the likely outcome, should the case go as far as court. This may be used as a stage in attempting to reach a settlement by negotiation, rather than going to a full trial in court.

In the case of small claims, the court system itself has long used a form of ADR, as the district judges who determine these cases do so not in a formal trial but by an informal procedure, with only the parties to the dispute present and—usually—lawyers excluded.

An ADR scheme has been available in the Commercial Court (*see 8.9.2.1*) since 1993. An ADR scheme is also available in the Court of Appeal. The largest-scale experiment

---

[5] The use of mediation in the family justice system is discussed in *7.9.2.*

in the use of court-centred ADR took place in the Central London County Court, started in May 1996. A number of other courts have also developed ADR schemes. These were the subject of detailed evaluation by Professor Dame Hazel Genn.[6] The common feature of all these experiments is that, to date, their use has been modest. There is evidence that those who take advantage of ADR in general find it a helpful way of resolving their disputes. But the use of ADR is not as widespread as in other countries, particularly the United States, and certainly not as widespread as those who provide ADR services would like.

The post-Woolf civil justice system gives power to the judge, as part of their case management strategy, to stay a case for up to 28 days to give the parties a chance to use ADR where this seems to be appropriate. These powers have not been extensively used. However, the Court of Appeal has on a number of occasions stressed the importance of parties using ADR where they can. It has also indicated that unreasonable failure to do so may result in adverse rulings on the recovery of costs.[7]

The Ministry of Justice now actively promotes the use of ADR. It sponsors an online directory of accredited mediators, who provide mediation services for people in dispute on a civil law matter. Mediation is provided for a fixed fee, which varies according to the amount of money in dispute. The fees are set out on the first page of the website. It makes the process of finding a mediator very easy and is clearly designed to encourage use of mediation in the dispute resolution process.

There is also a free Small Claims Mediation Service. This is a telephone-based mediation service which has mediated over 15,000 cases in each of the last two years. The government wants all cases in the small claims track to be referred to the mediation service.

There are a number of difficult issues relating to the development of ADR that are currently unresolved. Among these issues are:

- *Compulsion.* At present no court can *require* the use of ADR.[8] Experience in the United States suggests that use of ADR does not take off until at least an element of compulsion is introduced. But is it right for the courts to require parties to a dispute to pay for something that may not resolve the matter but only add to costs and delay? For now, the consensus in England and Wales is that, while ADR may be encouraged, it should not be compulsory.

- *Standards.* Secondly, there is a question of how proper standards for those who offer ADR services are to be set and monitored. This has been addressed by the Civil Mediation Council, which has devised principles for the accreditation of ADR providers.

- *Costs.* Currently, government does not fund the provision of ADR services save for limited provision through the legal aid scheme (*see Box 10.5*) or through the

---

[6] Genn, H. and others, *Twisting Arms: Court Referred and Court Linked Mediation under Judicial Pressure* (London, Ministry of Justice, 2007).

[7] See the decision *PGF II SA v OMFS Company 1 Limited* [2013] EWCA Civ 1288.

[8] The position in the family justice system is discussed in *7.10.*

Small Claims Mediation Service. But ADR services must be paid for. If the costs are too high and nevertheless parties are required by the courts to use a process of ADR, may this not add to the cost of dispute resolution—something the Woolf reforms were attempting to reduce?

- *Outcome.* Will the fact that the parties may well be happier at the end of the ADR process than they might have been at the end of a trial compensate them for the expense of using ADR? It may well do. One of the most powerful claims for ADR is *not* that it is cheaper, but that it enables parties to disputes to retain control of the dispute resolution process, which may in turn enable them to move on with their lives more amicably than they might be able to do after a court hearing. But this will not always be the case. Indeed there will always be those who, on principle, want to litigate and refuse to use any form of ADR.

The *Transforming Our Justice System* programme clearly envisages that the use of ADR should increase in a modernized civil justice system (*see 8.14*). In October 2017, the Civil Justice Council published an important consultation paper on options for achieving this goal. (See my blog, www.martinpartington.com, October 2017.)

8.5.2 Alternatives to courts

The current squeeze on public expenditure is regarded by many as a major threat to the provision of legal services, in particular, dispute resolution services. However, there are those—including senior members of the judiciary—who see it as an opportunity to explore alternatives to current court processes, which would be both less costly to the state, and less costly for the individual to use. Indeed, there are already many alternatives available in specific contexts. Many of these are free to individual complainants. To give just a few examples:

- The Financial Services Ombudsman now deals with nearly all claims against financial institutions up to a value of £150,000.
- Tenancy deposit disputes are resolved by private arbitration schemes, underpinned by legislation.
- Many consumer disputes are resolved by trading standards officers, not through the courts.
- There are over 60 industry adjudication schemes already in existence in the United Kingdom, many of them not well understood, but resolving consumer disputes that otherwise might have gone to the courts.
- With prompting from the European Union, schemes have been developed for the increased use of ADR and online dispute resolution of consumer issues on a pan-European basis (*see 4.5.2*).
- Many law firms and other companies are developing alternative resolution processes for resolving particular categories of case, for example employment disputes.

These examples show that new processes are being developed in widely different contexts. What is noteworthy is that most of these initiatives are being driven by the private sector or by parts of government other than the Ministry of Justice. It is likely that the use of courts to resolve civil disputes will increasingly be limited to the most complex and valuable cases.

8.6 Civil and commercial justice: the institutions

Having considered the wider policy context within which the civil and commercial justice system has developed in recent years and noted the considerable changes that have already occurred and are still taking place, we now turn to the courts that do the work: the county court and the High Court. Three preliminary matters are considered first.

8.6.1 Generalist v specialist

One of the claims made for the courts in the civil justice system is that they are, and should be, generalist rather than specialist in nature. Certainly, any type of case that does not fall into any other of the jurisdictional categories considered in this book (criminal, administrative, and family) must be disposed of in the civil courts. While the claim that the courts are generalist in nature is still to some extent true, it should be treated with caution. There is now an increasing number of specialist courts that have been created, primarily because of the technicalities of the law and issues to be determined by those courts. This has happened particularly in areas of commercial and business law. A new Planning Court was created in 2014. The Business and Property Court was launched in 2017. The government has recently announced its intention to create a housing court. This raises the obvious further question whether there should be more specialist courts.

There are many arguments in favour of greater specialization. Specialist judges dealing with a specific range of issues would be better informed about the relevant law; thus the quality and consistency of decision making might be enhanced. (This is one of the strong arguments in favour of tribunals, which are presided over by people with specialist knowledge (*see 6.4.2.3*).)

Procedures could be better adapted to suit the users of the specialist courts and the types of issues to be dealt with in those courts. For example, special facilities might be available to deal with the particular types of emergency cases that might arise out of ordinary court hours. The practitioners who specialize in the areas of law concerned might be able to operate more efficiently by concentrating their resources in more specialized courts.

Against, it is argued that judges might become too narrowly focused, even bored with the tasks they were required to perform. Judicial manpower in specialist courts could not be used efficiently if the caseloads in those courts were insufficient to keep the relevant judges busy. However, this problem can be avoided by the flexible deployment of judges. Given recent trends, it seems inevitable that there will be more rather than less specialization in the years ahead.

8.6.2 Court fees: a self-financing system?

For many years, government policy has been that the civil justice system should be—broadly—self-financing.

Some argue that, on principle, 'justice' should be regarded as a 'free good', not subject to the principle of self-financing at all. Access to the courts for the determination of legal rights and entitlements is a constitutional right to which there should be no barriers—certainly not financial ones. Against that, others argue that the well-heeled, who may be fighting over financial matters worth thousands, perhaps millions, of pounds, should make—through the payment of fees—a contribution towards the running of the civil justice system.

Until 2014, although HMCTS set court fees (which claimants must pay before they can get their cases started and allocated to the appropriate track) at levels that were said to be designed to enable the court service to be self-funding, in reality this policy objective was not being met. Recent governments have decided that this was not sustainable.

Since April 2014, there have been significant increases in court fees which have transformed the fee landscape (*see Box 8.2*).

Box 8.2 Reform in progress

Court fees

The principal features of the current fee structure are:

- The maximum fee for money claims is now £10,000 for claims worth £200,000 or more. The government argues, with some force, that many of the claims brought for higher values involve large multi-national organizations or wealthy individuals. It therefore thinks it right to ask them to contribute more. In order to protect the most vulnerable, personal injury and clinical negligence claims are excluded from this higher cap, and fee remissions for those of limited means continue to apply.
- Fees in the Immigration and Asylum Chamber were increased significantly in October 2016, but this decision was reversed in November 2016. There are exemptions which are intended to protect the most vulnerable.
- The government has not applied fees to the Social Entitlement Chamber of the First-Tier Tribunal, where most applicants do not have the means to pay, or to the Mental Health Tribunal, which deals with especially vulnerable individuals.
- It introduced significant increases in the fees paid to access the Employment Tribunal and the Employment Appeal Tribunal, though these have recently been the subject of a successful challenge in the Supreme Court (*see Box 6.4*).
- In the first-tier property tribunal, it has introduced a range of fees at low levels for the majority of applications, while setting higher fees for leasehold enfranchisement cases, where there are often large sums of money at stake.
- It has also introduced fees to access the General Regulatory Tribunal and the Tax Tribunal.
- The government says its aim is to recover 25 per cent of the total cost of the service through fees, with taxpayers footing the rest of the bill.

Box 8.2 Continued

What is disappointing about these changes is that, in making their decisions, the government made no reference to the work done by the now defunct Administrative Justice and Tribunals Council, which suggested that discussion of income streams for providing the tribunals' service should also include consideration of what financial contribution those government departments against whom decisions are being appealed should make, particularly in cases where the department loses the appeal. The Council argued that the incentives on departments to get the decision right first time were not sufficiently strong (*see 6.4.9*).

8.6.3 Delivering the court service: local initiatives and centralized justice

The courts are managed by HMCTS. The day-to-day running of the courts is carried out on a regional basis through six *circuits*.[9] Supervision of the judicial work of each circuit is the responsibility of the *presiding judges*. These are judges of the High Court appointed—two for each circuit—by the Lord Chief Justice. They operate under a Senior Presiding Judge.

When Lord Woolf was preparing his *Access to Justice* report, he found that many courts had developed their own particular procedures for dealing with specific types of matter. This did not imply that the outcomes of cases would differ, but the ways in which the courts worked certainly did. Lord Woolf felt that it was important that someone appearing for trial in one town should be dealt with in essentially the same way as in any other. One of his hopes for the CPR was that this would encourage greater uniformity of process. Given the not inconsiderable discretion that is given to judges to manage cases, Lord Woolf's hopes in this respect have not been fully realized.

Indeed, a degree of procedural experiment is desirable, to see whether the work of the courts can be made more efficient. However, this should be as part of a controlled programme of pilot projects that can be properly evaluated by HMCTS, rather than the result of individual courts going their own way. It is also important that when new procedures are tested and found helpful, the results of good practice should be spread throughout the court system as a whole, not kept as a 'private custom' in a particular court or circuit. This will happen only if innovations are managed by HMCTS.

8.7 The county court

The county court is the work-horse of the civil justice system. It deals with the largest numbers of civil cases. Founded in 1846, it was designed to provide a forum for the

---

[9] Midland and Oxford, run from Birmingham; North Eastern, from Leeds; Northern, from Manchester; South Eastern, from London; Wales and Chester, from Cardiff; and Western, from Bristol.

resolution of what would these days be regarded as relatively modest consumer complaints. Over the years, its jurisdiction has expanded.

Today all civil actions can be started in the county court (*see Box 8.3*), save for a small number of cases where special statutory rules require proceedings to be started in the High Court. From time to time there have been suggestions that there should simply be a single civil court—effectively merging the county court and the High Court. But this option was not pursued by Lord Woolf.

There used to be 216 county courts, each with a separate building, throughout England and Wales. This number is now being reduced. It also used to be the case that, technically, each court was a separate court. This could lead to unnecessary complications about which court proceedings had to start in. The Crime and Courts Act 2013 created a single county court jurisdiction for England and Wales. The aim is to facilitate greater flexibility in the use of courts around the country and enable more proceedings to be issued from centralized online processing centres. Individual courts are now called hearing centres.

Each hearing centre is assigned at least one district judge, and some have at least one circuit judge. (Although circuit judges are full-time appointments, most do not spend all their time on civil matters, but sit as trial judges in criminal cases in the Crown Court.) District judges work full-time on civil issues (including some family justice matters). On 1 April 2017, there were 635 circuit judges in England and Wales, and 438 district judges.[10] They are assisted by 595 deputy district judges who are judges in training and who sit part-time. An overview of the work of the county court is in *Box 8.3*.

Box 8.3 System in action

Work of the county court

The county courts deal with all contract and tort cases, and all proceedings for the recovery of land, irrespective of value. From 2013, the financial limit below which non-personal injury claims may not be commenced in the High Court was increased from £25,000 to £100,000. In addition, some hearing centres deal with bankruptcy and insolvency matters, certain equity and contested probate actions (e.g. arising from alleged breaches of trust obligations or questions about the administration of a will) where the value of the trust fund or the estate does not exceed £350,000, plus any case which the parties agree can be heard in the county court. Straightforward money and possession claims can now be issued online.

The county court is a busy jurisdiction. In 2016, a total of 1,802,286 claims were issued (a rise of some 250,000 on the year before). However, the vast majority of money claims result in a 'default judgment', where the defendant did not defend the proceedings; a judgment by admission, where a defendant admits the truth of the

[10] These should be distinguished from District Judges (Magistrate's Court) who deal with criminal cases in the magistrates' court.

Box 8.3 Continued

claim; or a judgment 'by acceptance and determination', where the defendant made an offer which was accepted by the claimant.

Very few cases, under 3 per cent, end up in a trial. In those (rare) cases which actually go to trial, the average waiting time between the issue of the claim and the start of the trial is about 56 weeks. In a significant number of claims for damages for personal injuries, the costs that can be recovered by the winning party are now fixed (*see 10.4.2*).

Small claims take an average of 31 weeks to be heard. All cases allocated to the small claims track are offered the opportunity of mediation (*see 8.5.1*).

In addition, the court has power to make orders. The most important of these are possession orders where people have fallen behind with their mortgage or rent payments. The county court can also issue injunctions—orders for people to stop doing something such as harassment or anti-social behaviour. The county court can also issue freezing orders which freeze the assets of defendants to the hearing in the court.

Data drawn from *Civil Justice Statistics Quarterly, April to June 2017,* available at www.gov.uk/government/collections/civil-justice-statistics-quarterly.

8.8 The High Court

The High Court consists of three divisions. The Family Division, part of the Family Court, is considered in *Chapter 7*. The other two divisions are:

- the Queen's Bench Division; and
- the Chancery Division.

These courts handle cases both arising at first instance (i.e. cases being determined for the first time) and on appeal from courts lower in the hierarchical structure—the county court and a number of administrative tribunals. When sitting as an appeal court and when dealing with analogous matters such as judicial review, the High Court is known as the *Divisional Court*. Each division has a divisional court.

The Business and Property Courts framework was created in 2017 to bring together specialist branches of the Queen's Bench Division and the Chancery Division which deal with major commercial and property disputes (*see 8.9 and Diagram 8.1*)

8.8.1 The Queen's Bench Division

The Queen's Bench Division[11] is headed by the President of the Queen's Bench Division (a post created by the Constitutional Reform Act 2005). He is supported by around 70 full-time High Court judges, assisted by part-time deputy High Court judges, and

---

[11]   The work of the Administrative Court, also part of the Queen's Bench Division, is considered in *Chapter 6*.

circuit judges sitting as High Court judges. (High Court judges also go round the country 'on circuit' in order to hear the most serious criminal cases in the Crown Court.) The part-time judges deal with nearly 50 per cent of all trials.

The court deals primarily with common law business—actions relating to contract and tort. Torts (civil wrongs) embrace not only negligence and nuisance, but also other wrongs against the person, such as libel, or wrongs against property, such as trespass. Contract cases involve, for example, failure to pay for goods or services, or other alleged breaches of contract. Some fact situations give rise to actions both in tort and contract.

It is central to the philosophy of the post-Woolf era that only the most important cases should be dealt with in the High Court. As a result, only personal injury claims with a value of £50,000 or more may be started there. In other cases the claim must be for £100,000 or more. There are also a number of other types of proceedings which, by statute, must be started in the High Court.

8.8.1.1 Jury trial in civil proceedings

There is a right to trial by jury in civil proceedings for fraud, libel, slander, malicious prosecution, or false imprisonment. In other cases, a judge may in her discretion allow trial by jury; but this rarely happens. Where there is a jury, the jury will decide not only liability (e.g. whether the words used were libellous or not) but also the amount of any damages.

8.8.1.2 Workload

In 2016, 9,274[12] claims and originating summonses were issued in the Queen's Bench Division. Of these, just over 4,000 were issued in London, the rest in High Court District Registries around the country. Only 192 were disposed of after a full trial. As in other parts of the legal system, a full trial is the exceptional, not the typical, mode of disposal.

8.8.1.3 Divisional Court

Judges in the Queen's Bench Division usually sit alone; when they sit with others they are known as a Divisional Court. The Divisional Court of the Queen's Bench Division deals with judicial review cases (*see 6.4.1*), appeals by way of 'case stated',[13] *habeas corpus*,[14] committal for contempt of court committed in an inferior court, or appeals and applications under a variety of statutory provisions.[15] The bulk of the work is judicial review.

---

[12] Data in this section drawn from *Royal Courts of Justice Annual Tables, 2016* (part of *Civil Justice Statistics Jan–Mar 2017*).

[13] A process used e.g. by the Crown Court or a magistrates' court to obtain a ruling on a particular provision of criminal law.

[14] Where unlawful detention is alleged.

[15] E.g. under the town and country planning legislation.

8.8.2 The Chancery Division

The Chancery Division of the High Court is presided over by the Chancellor of the High Court, supported by 17 other High Court judges. They are assisted, as needed, by deputy High Court judges, who are either practitioners approved to act as such by the Lord Chancellor, or retired High Court or circuit judges. The extent of their use depends on the level of business before the courts.

Most of its work is now conducted within the framework of the Business and Property Courts (*see 8.9*). Uncontested probate matters are dealt with in the Family Division (*see Box 8.4*).

Box 8.4 Legal system explained

Uncontested probate matters: the Family Division

Uncontested probate matters are dealt with in the Principal Registry of the Family Division of the High Court, in any of the 11 district probate registries or 18 probate sub-registries in England and Wales. Grants of probate are made in cases where there was a will; letters of administration where there was not. There is a heavy workload. In 2015, well over 250,000 grants/letters were issued.

In 2016, a total of just over 9,500 claims and other originating proceedings were started in the Chancery Division; during the year, only 217 cases were disposed of following a trial. In addition, 4,305 bankruptcy petitions were issued, together with 3,148 other originating applications and 9,205 Companies Court proceedings. (This figure supplements the insolvency work of the county court.) The Divisional Court of the Chancery Division also disposed of a small number of appeals from the county court.

As with other parts of the civil justice system, the Chancery Division is very much the place of last resort for the resolution of disputes.

8.9 The commercial justice system: the Business and Property Courts of England and Wales

8.9.1 Introduction

Notwithstanding the reluctance of the judiciary to specialize, the fact is that in recent years both the High Court and the county court system have developed a range of specialist courts, designed to deal with a range of (primarily) commercial and company law matters. These have now been brought together and labelled the Business and Property Courts of England and Wales, which started work on 2 October 2017.

There are at least three important reasons why this has occurred. First, the development of this 'brand' is designed to send an international signal, that the courts of

England and Wales are *the* place for the expert resolution of high value commercial disputes. It is a logical development from the building of the Rolls Building in London as a modern, well equipped dispute resolution centre. These developments reflect the position of London in the global economy, and the need for the courts to provide appropriate levels of expertise in these specialist areas.

Second, the judiciary and policy-makers have been anxious to create centres of commercial expertise outside London. Thus the Business and Property Courts have also opened for business in Birmingham, Bristol, Cardiff, Leeds, and Manchester—cities outside London where there is also significant commercial activity.

Third, and perhaps the most important, the creation of the new court is designed to facilitate the flexible deployment of the specialist judges who have been appointed to the High Court and Chancery Division.

The structure of the Business and Property Courts is set out in *Diagram 8.1*.

Diagram 8.1 The Business and Property Courts of England and Wales

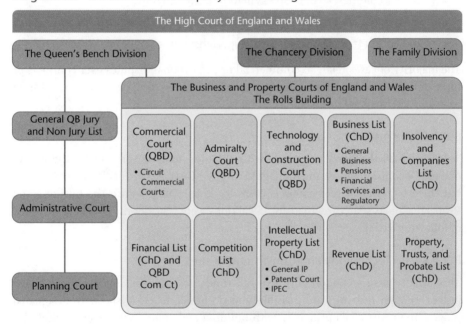

Source: https://www.judiciary.gov.uk/you-and-the-judiciary/going-to-court/high-court/

8.9.2 The constituent elements of the Business and Property Courts

The following paragraphs provide further information on the constituent parts of the Business and Property Courts.

8.9.2.1 The Commercial Court

This comprises two elements: the Commercial Court and the Circuit Commercial Courts.

The Commercial Court consists of 15 specialist judges who deal with a wide range of commercial matters, for example, banking, international credit, and the purchase and sale of commodities. They also deal with shipping matters not handled by the Admiralty Court—contracts relating to ships, carriage of cargo, insurance, as well as the construction and performance of mercantile contracts more generally. The Commercial Court also deals with questions that may arise from commercial arbitrations. In 2016, 830 claims were issued.

The Circuit Commercial Courts (formerly called Mercantile Courts) operate in regional centres throughout England and Wales as part of the Queen's Bench Division of the High Court. They decide business disputes of all kinds, apart from those which, because of their size, value, or complexity, are dealt with by the Commercial Court. As well as large cases, the Circuit Commercial Courts decide smaller disputes and recognize the importance of these, particularly to smaller and medium-sized businesses. These courts only deal with claims that:

- relate to a commercial or business matter in a broad sense;
- are not required to proceed in the Chancery Division or in another specialist court;
- would benefit from the expertise of a specialist judge.

The majority of cases relate to commercial or professional disputes over contracts or torts, or to issues arising from arbitration claims and awards. There are no maximum or minimum financial limits upon claims.

8.9.2.2 The Admiralty Court

This deals—as the name suggests—with shipping matters, principally the consequences of collisions at sea and damage to cargos. Most cases are dealt with in London, but there is power to refer suitable cases to other courts within the Business and Property Courts structure. In 2016, 159 actions were issued; only two were disposed of following a trial.

8.9.2.3 The Technology and Construction Court

This usually sits in London with five full-time *circuit* judges and two High Court judges, though hearings are possible outside London before specially designated judges. The court deals primarily with building and engineering disputes and also computer litigation. It can also deal with other matters such as valuation disputes and landlord and tenant matters involving dilapidations. It also handles questions arising from arbitrations in building and engineering disputes. During 2016, 359 proceedings were received; 180 trials were held in London. (Figures for cases dealt with outside London are not available.)

8.9.2.4 The Business List

The Chancery Business List includes a wide range of business disputes, often with an international dimension. Frequently these concern a business structure (company, LLP, LP, partnership etc.), claims against directors for breach of fiduciary duty, or disputes about contractual arrangements between investors. They also include claims in tort, such as conspiracy or fraud, claims for breach of contract, specific performance, rectification, and injunctive relief as well as other equitable remedies. The Business List also includes pensions claims, claims involving the Financial Conduct Authority, and cases involving regulators (other than the Pensions Regulator).

8.9.2.5 Insolvency and Companies List

Part of the Chancery Division of the High Court, this deals primarily with the compulsory liquidation of companies and other matters arising under the Insolvency Act 1986 and the Companies Acts. For example, a registered company that seeks to reduce its capital may do so only with the approval of the court. The bulk of this work is done in London. In 2015, 9,199 applications were filed in what was then known as the Companies Court, over half of which were winding-up petitions.

8.9.2.6 The Financial List

In 2015, judges in the Chancery and Queens Bench divisions decided that they would create a new Financial List for complex, high value financial cases. The list came into operation in October 2015.

The objective of the Financial List is to ensure that cases which would benefit from being heard by judges with particular expertise in the financial markets or which raise issues of general importance to the financial markets are dealt with by judges with suitable expertise and experience. Cases in the Financial List are managed and heard by specialist judges offering sophisticated dispute resolution of claims related to the financial markets.

8.9.2.7 The Competition List

As the name suggests, this handles complex competition issues, many of which arise for EU law. (There is some overlap between this list and the work of the Competition Appeal Tribunal, which sits outside the court system.)

8.9.2.8 The Intellectual Property List

This comprises three elements: a general intellectual property list; the Intellectual Property Enterprise Court; and the Patents Court.

The Intellectual Property Enterprise Court was created as a specialist court operating within the Chancery Division in 2013. It hears cases concerning patents, designs (registered/unregistered, UK/Community), trade marks (UK/Community), passing off, copyright, database rights, other rights conferred by the Copyright, Designs and Patents Act 1988, as well as actions for breach of confidence.[16]

---

[16] For a report on the work of the court, see www.gov.uk/government/uploads/system/uploads/attachment_data/file/447710/Evaluation_of_the_Reforms_of_the_Intellectual_Property_Enterprise_Court_2010-2013.pdf.

8.9.2.9 Revenue List (ChD)

This contains claims involving major points of principle where HMRC is a party. (This List does not include claims for the recovery of taxes or duties or where a taxpayer disputes liability to pay tax.)

8.9.2.10 Property, Trusts and Probate List

This list covers a large amount of Chancery work which is separate from the Business List and is not dealt with by the specialist Chancery Courts. The Property List deals mainly with land; the Trusts List with administration of estates and the execution of trusts, and with charities; the Probate List deals with complex matters relating to wills and the administration of estates.

8.10 Enforcement of judgments

Problems with the enforcement of judgments were one of the issues Lord Woolf sought to address. There is nothing more frustrating than taking a case to court, winning it, but then finding that it is well-nigh impossible to obtain satisfaction of the judgment. In situations where the loser has the backing of an insurance company, or (either private individual or company or other legal body) is extremely resource-rich, this is not usually a problem. But where the person against whom proceedings are brought is of moderate means or is a company with only limited resources, enforcement can be a major problem.

Both the county court and the High Court have powers to enforce their judgments (*see Box 8.5*). The government reviewed the procedures available to the courts for the enforcement of judgments, and in the Tribunals, Courts and Enforcement Act 2007 gave further powers to the courts to enforce judgments. In particular, courts now find it easier to discover what the financial position of a debtor is and to track debtors if they change employment.

Box 8.5 Legal system explained

Enforcement powers of the county court and the High Court

In the county court, the most common method of enforcing a monetary judgment is the warrant of execution against a debtor's goods. Unless the amount owed is paid, items owned by the debtor can be recovered by a bailiff acting on behalf of the court and sold. Large numbers of warrants are issued each year: 282,120 in 2016.

The county court's other powers to enforce its judgments include:

- attachment of earnings—where an employer is ordered to pay a defined part of the defendant's wages direct to the court, which pays it to the creditor;
- third party debt orders—where money owed by a third party to the defendant is seized and ordered to be paid to the judgment creditor;

Box 8.5 Continued

- charging orders, which are imposed on property to give security for the payment of a court order;
- administration orders, imposed where a person has got into serious debt, which enable regular payments to be made to the court, which then distributes the monies to the creditor(s); and
- orders for possession of land.

In the High Court, judgments may be enforced in many ways, including:

- writ of control (formerly the writ of *fieri facias* (fi-fa)) directing the High Court Enforcement Officer (the equivalent of the bailiff in the county courts) to seize and if necessary sell the debtor's goods to raise money to pay off the debt;
- writ of possession of land (with eviction if necessary to ensure that possession of property or land is recovered);
- writ of delivery of goods, an order to hand over specific goods;
- a charging order on land (this has the same effect as a mortgage, so that if the property is sold the amount of the charge (debt) must be paid out of the proceeds of the sale);
- a third party debt (formerly garnishee) order, which orders that a third party, normally a bank, holding money for the judgment debtor pay it to the judgment creditor direct;
- appointment of a receiver who will manage the judgment debtor's property or part of it in such a way as to protect the judgment creditor's interest in it.

An order to attend court for questioning (formerly an oral examination) is a procedure used in connection with enforcement. The debtor is required to attend court to give details of his earnings, expenses, savings, etc., so that the creditor can decide how best to enforce the judgment. In 2016, 71,105 enforcement proceedings were issued in the High Court, the vast majority being writs of control.

Source: Adapted from *Royal Courts of Justice Tables, 2016* and *Civil Justice and Judicial Review Statistics January to March 2017*.

The government also accepted that the rules regulating how bailiffs and enforcement agents do their work had become fragmented and archaic. Although Part 3 of the Tribunals, Courts and Enforcement Act 2007 gave the authority to reform the law, it was never implemented. The Crime and Courts Act 2013 amended the original provisions. The revised law is now operational. In particular, the new law clarifies: the power of bailiffs (enforcement agents) to enter premises; what goods they may take; and what fees they may charge.

Enforcement is an exceptionally difficult issue, particularly distinguishing between those who could pay but will not, and those who simply cannot pay. There would be considerable political opposition to a return to the Dickensian days of throwing debtors into jail.[17] Yet there is no doubt that, if the civil justice system cannot force those against whom awards of damages are made to pay up, users of the system see this as a serious weakness. In turn, this may encourage others not to pay.

8.11 Other courts and offices

In addition to the courts so far identified, there are a number of other offices that form part of the Senior Court. These include:

- *The Office of the Official Solicitor and Public Trustee.* The Official Solicitor operates under the authority of section 90 of the Senior Courts Act 1981. His primary duties are to protect the interests of children and mental patients, i.e. those who do not have full legal capacity to look after their own affairs. His department has a substantial workload. Among his responsibilities are child abduction cases. In 2001, the Official Solicitor took over responsibility for the *Public Trust Office.* The Public Trustee acts as executor or administrator of deceased persons' estates or trustees of wills or settlements where he has been named and has accepted the nomination.

- *The Court of Protection.* The Mental Incapacity Act 2005 provides for the creation of the Court of Protection. It is a superior court of record, able to sit anywhere in England and Wales, though the bulk of the work is done in London. For an overview of its work *see Box 8.6.*

Box 8.6 Legal system explained

The work of the Court of Protection

The Court of Protection makes decisions on financial or welfare matters for people who cannot make decisions at the time they need to be made (they 'lack mental capacity'). It deals with around 25,000 cases a year. Examples include:

- deciding whether someone has the mental capacity to make a particular decision for themselves;
- appointing deputies to make ongoing decisions for people who lack mental capacity;
- giving people permission to make one-off decisions on behalf of someone else who lacks mental capacity;
- handling urgent or emergency applications where a decision must be made on behalf of someone else without delay;
- making decisions about a lasting power of attorney (LPA) or enduring power of attorney (EPA) and considering any objections to their registration;
- considering applications to make statutory wills or gifts, and making decisions about when someone can be deprived of their liberty under the Mental Capacity Act.

---

[17] Even under present law, failure to pay certain taxes—a particular form of debt—can result in the imposition of a prison sentence.

Box 8.6 Continued

The court has powers to call for reports to assist in determining a case. Such reports can be commissioned from the Public Guardian (a statutory official), local authorities, National Health Service (NHS) bodies, or Court of Protection Visitors (replacing the former Lord Chancellor's Visitors). Local authority staff or NHS staff may already be providing services to the person concerned and be able to report to the court on the basis of their existing involvement. The Public Guardian or Court of Protection Visitor who is reporting to the court has access to health, social services, or care records relating to the person and may interview him in private. Where a Court of Protection Visitor is a Special Visitor (e.g. a registered medical practitioner or someone with other suitable qualifications or training), he or she may, on the directions of the court, carry out medical, psychiatric, or psychological examinations.

Responding to criticism that the Court of Protection was too secretive, a Pilot Practice Direction applies to new proceedings issued from 29 January 2016. The Practice Direction effectively changes the default position from one where hearings are held in private to one where hearings are held in public with reporting restrictions to protect identities. When an order has been made under the pilot, both the media and the public will be able to attend, unless a further order has been made which excludes them. It is intended that the Pilot Practice Direction, which was due to expire at the end of August 2017 should be made permanent by the end of 2017. A really interesting account of the complex issues that can come before the Court of Protection can be found in the lecture by Mr Justice Baker at https://www.judiciary.gov.uk/wp-content/uploads/2016/10/mr-justice-baker-shrieval-lecture-11102016-v2.pdf.

8.12 Appeals and the appeal courts

We have noted in passing that many courts have power to hear appeals in defined circumstances. Many appeals are satisfactorily disposed of in that context.

Some courts deal exclusively with appeals. They are particularly important in the English legal system, because it is through their reported judgments that the primary source of authority for the development of the common law and the interpretation of statutes is found (*see Chapter 3*). Arguably these appeal courts are the only truly generalist courts, in that they have the responsibility for dealing with whatever is presented to them by way of appeal.

8.12.1 Policy issues

In recent years, it has been suggested that there were too many avenues of appeal; and that the level of court at which an appeal is determined was not always the right one. Important changes were introduced by the Access to Justice Act 1999.

8.12.1.1 Permission to appeal

In order to bring an appeal in the Court of Appeal, it was always necessary for the appellant to seek the permission (formerly called the 'leave') of the court to bring an appeal. Under section 54 of the Access to Justice Act 1999, rules of court now require permission to appeal to be obtained for all appeals to the county courts, the High Court, or the Court of Appeal (Civil Division). There are limited exceptions; for example appeals relating to court orders that affect the liberty of the individual. There is no appeal against a decision either to give or refuse permission. Where permission is refused, there remains the possibility of making a further application for permission, either in the same or another court.

8.12.1.2 Second appeals

Once a county court or the High Court has decided a matter on appeal, section 55 of the Access to Justice Act 1999 provides that there is no possibility of a further appeal unless either the appeal would raise an important point of principle or practice, or there is some other compelling reason for the appeal to be heard. All applications for permission to bring a further appeal are dealt with by the Court of Appeal, irrespective of the court that determined the first appeal. If permission is granted, the Court of Appeal also hears the appeal.

8.12.1.3 Destination of appeals

Section 56 of the Access to Justice Act 1999 gave the Lord Chancellor power to vary, by order,[18] the avenues of appeal to and within the county court, the High Court, and the Court of Appeal. The general principle is that appeals should be determined by judges who are one level above the initial decision taker. Thus:

(1) for fast track cases heard by a district judge appeals lie to a circuit judge;

(2) for fast track cases heard by a circuit judge appeals lie to a High Court judge;

(3) in multi-track cases, appeals against interlocutory decisions by a district judge are to a circuit judge; by a master[19] or circuit judge to a High Court judge; and by a High Court judge to the Court of Appeal;

(4) in multi-track cases, appeals against final orders will be direct to the Court of Appeal, irrespective of the court making the initial decision.

8.12.1.4 Leapfrog appeals

In defined circumstances, an appeal may be brought direct from the High Court or the High Court in Northern Ireland, when sitting as a trial court. This is known as 'leapfrogging' and can occur where it is clear that the law in question needs clarification at the highest level, perhaps because there are inconsistent decisions from the Court of Appeal.

---

[18] See now the Access to Justice Act 1999 (Destination of Appeals) Order 2016, SI 2016/917, which came into force in October 2016.

[19] Masters are judicial officers of the High Court who determine interlocutory matters.

The power to allow cases which raise important questions of law to leapfrog direct to the Supreme Court has been expanded by the Criminal Justice and Courts Act 2015.

8.13 The appeal courts

The courts of appeal considered here are:

- the Supreme Court, which has taken over the judicial functions of the House of Lords;
- the Judicial Committee of the Privy Council; and
- the Court of Appeal.

8.13.1 The Supreme Court

On 1 October 2009, the Supreme Court took over the judicial functions of the House of Lords. There are 12 Supreme Court Justices. The President of the Supreme Court is Baroness Hale. The Constitutional Reform Act 2005 provides that new members of the Court are to be selected by a selection committee procedure. Membership is open not only to existing judges but also to those with long experience in practice. The first such appointment, of Jonathan Sumption QC, was announced in 2011.

The Court can, with permission, hear appeals from any orders or judgments of the Court of Appeal in England, the Court of Session in Scotland, or the Court of Appeal in Northern Ireland.[20] In addition, appeals may be taken, with permission, from the High Court when it has been sitting as a Divisional Court (i.e. as a court of appeal or when dealing with cases such as judicial review).

Permission may be granted either by the relevant Court of Appeal or, if that is not forthcoming, by the Supreme Court. (If a lower court grants permission, the Supreme Court cannot overturn that decision.) In practice, permission is granted by the lower courts very infrequently.[21] The right of the citizen to 'take her case to the highest court in the land' is in reality highly contingent, subject to considerable procedural constraint. The Supreme Court is a judicial resource that is sparingly used.

Most appeals are heard by courts of five Justices. Very significant cases may go to seven- or even nine-judge panels. (The *Miller* case concerning whether, following the Brexit referendum, Article 50 of the Treaty of the European Union could be triggered by the Executive using prerogative powers was determined by an 11-person panel, *see Box 3.2*.) Hearings are tightly time-controlled, lasting usually only two days. In 2016,[22] 210 applications for permission to appeal were presented; 75 were granted. In the same year, 73 appeals were heard by the Court; 30 appeals were allowed.

---

[20] Save, in the case of Northern Ireland or Scotland, where this is prevented by statute.
[21] It is not uncommon for the Criminal Division of the Court of Appeal to certify that a point of law of general public importance is involved in a case, but still to refuse permission to appeal to the Supreme Court.
[22] Data from *Royal Courts of Justice Annual Tables, 2016*.

Section 41 of the Constitutional Reform Act 2005 made specific provision as to the effect of decisions of the Supreme Court as judicial precedents. In essence, a decision made by the Supreme Court is to have the same effect as decisions of the House of Lords or the Judicial Committee of the Privy Council. So in the case of jurisdiction transferred from the House of Lords, a decision of the Supreme Court on an appeal from one jurisdiction within the United Kingdom will not have effect as a binding precedent in any other such jurisdiction, or in a subsequent appeal before the Supreme Court from another such jurisdiction. In the case of the devolution jurisdiction transferred from the Judicial Committee of the Privy Council, a decision of the Supreme Court is binding in all legal proceedings except for subsequent proceedings before the Supreme Court itself.

8.13.2 The Judicial Committee of the Privy Council

This remains the final court of appeal from those British Commonwealth Territories and four independent republics within the Commonwealth that have retained this right of appeal. It also determines constitutional issues arising from those independent territories that have a written constitution. The Judicial Committee also has jurisdiction over a number of domestic matters[23] and 'pastoral' matters (which relate to the Church of England). The statutory powers of the Committee derive from the Judicial Committee Act 1833, though the history of the Committee can be traced back to mediaeval times. The judges who sit in the Judicial Committee are (broadly) the same as those who sit in the Supreme Court, though they are on occasion joined by a senior member of the judiciary from the country whence an appeal has come.

Many find the jurisdiction of the Judicial Committee highly anachronistic—a throwback to a British imperial past that is long gone. Nevertheless, the Judicial Committee has a steady stream of work. In 2016, 75 appeals were entered. 59 cases were disposed of, 31 following a hearing, 29 without a hearing. Of the 31 appeals heard, 10 were allowed and 21 were dismissed. The issues it deals with are, by definition, of very considerable legal and social importance, not just for the country in question, but for the common law world in general.

8.13.3 The Court of Appeal: civil appeals

The Court of Appeal is divided into two divisions: the criminal and the civil. The Lord Chief Justice (who is also head of the judiciary) heads the Criminal Division;[24] the Master of the Rolls heads the Civil Division. They are assisted by 35 Lords Justices of Appeal. Other High Court judges assist, as required and as available, in the Criminal Division. Both the President of the Family Court and the Chancellor of the High Court sit in the Court of Appeal for part of their time. By comparison with the Supreme Court and the Privy Council, the Court of Appeal has a substantial caseload.

---

[23] Hearing appeals from a number of professional bodies, in particular under the Medical Act 1983 and the Dentists Act 1984. The Judicial Committee's powers to deal with devolution issues arising out of the passing of the Wales Act and the Scotland Act 1998 have been transferred to the Supreme Court.

[24] Information on criminal appeals is in *5.7.1*.

8.13.3.1 The Civil Division

The number of appeals coming to the Civil Division rose steadily during the early 1990s. They began to fall in 1996, and are now holding steady. During 2016, 1,029 appeals were disposed of; 329 of them were allowed. In addition 4,331 paper applications and 1,161 oral applications for permission to appeal were made.

8.14 Transforming our Justice System: Civil Justice

Despite the large number of changes that have been made to the civil justice system over the last few years, following the Woolf and Jackson reforms, many—including the senior judiciary—accept that the way it operates is not fit for the twenty-first century. Early in 2016, important reports from the Civil Justice Council and the pressure group JUSTICE fed into a review of the structure of the civil courts carried out in 2016 by Lord Justice Briggs (*see Box 8.7*).

Box 8.7 Reform in progress

The Briggs Review

Following on decisions relating to the reconfiguration of the court and tribunal estate, and the reinvestment of savings in IT to transform the efficiency of courts and tribunals (*see 4.2.2.3*) and decisions which seek to increase the income of the Courts and Tribunals Service through the levying of higher fees (*see 8.6.2*), Lord Justice Briggs was asked for his views on how to restructure the civil court system.

His principal recommendations were:

(1) A new *Online Court* should be created, designed to be used by people with minimum assistance from lawyers, with its own set of user-friendly rules. Briggs anticipated that it would eventually become the compulsory forum for resolving cases within its jurisdiction. It should start by dealing with straightforward money claims valued at up to £25,000. Briggs makes recommendations about how to help people who need assistance with online systems. He also recommends that complex and important cases, even of low monetary value, should be able to be transferred upwards to higher courts.

(2) *Case Officers*, a newly created body of court lawyers and other officials, should take over certain functions currently carried out by judges, such as paperwork and uncontentious matters. They would be trained and supervised by judges. Their decisions would be subject to reconsideration by judges on request by a party. They would operate independently of government when exercising their functions.

(3) As regards *Enforcement of Judgments and Orders (see 8.10)*, the county court should become the default court for the enforcement of the judgments and orders of all the civil courts (including the new Online Court). There would need to be a 'permeable membrane' allowing appropriate enforcement issues to be transferred to the High Court, and special provision for the enforcement of arbitration awards, in accordance with current practice and procedure.

Box 8.7 Continued

(4) As regards *Promotion of Mediation/ADR,* he recommends the re-establishment of a court-based out-of-hours private mediation service in county court hearing centres prepared to participate, along the lines of the service which existed prior to the establishment and then termination of the National Mediation Helpline.

Briggs also sets out a number of proposals for further restructuring of the civil courts. These include:

- a review of High Court divisions;
- a single portal for the issue of all civil proceedings, leading to the eventual abolition of District Registries;
- a review of whether procedural changes in the Court of Appeal should be applied to appeals to the High Court and to circuit judges in the county court;
- the possible convergence of employment tribunals and the Employment Appeal Tribunal with the county court.

He would also like to see the Family Court being given a shared jurisdiction (with the Chancery Division and the county court) for dealing with Inheritance Act disputes and disputes about the co-ownership of homes.

The government has now published its programme for transforming the justice system (*see 4.2.2.2*). The impact of this programme on the civil justice system could, if all goes according to plan, be dramatic. The principal features of what is now proposed are:

(1) *Introducing a new online process for resolving claims.* The government intends to create a new process to resolve many disputes entirely online, using innovative technology and specialist case officers to progress routine cases through the system, reserving judicial time for the most complex cases. A new Rules Committee will design this new system and keep the processes simple. When hearings are required, they may be held over the telephone or by video conference, focusing court resources on the most complex and difficult cases. The government hopes that in this way cases should reach a quicker resolution.

(2) *Encouraging parties to resolve disputes themselves where possible.* While not precisely adopting the Briggs recommendation for more court-based mediation, the government plans to increase signposting to mediation and alternative dispute resolution services to help people avoid court for minor disputes that would be better handled privately, without needing the court to intervene.

(3) *Extending the fixed recoverable costs regime.* This is discussed in *Chapter 10* (*see 10.4.2*).

(4) *Improving the civil enforcement rules.* The government intends to give the county court powers to issue attachment of earnings orders to the High Court to create a simpler, more consistent approach to enforcement, and make sure more people

can get the money they are owed. The government will also bring into force a scheme of fixed deductions from earnings to provide transparency and certainty on the rate of deductions from debtors' earnings to pay back their creditors.

(5) *Replacing statutory declarations in county court proceedings with a witness statement verified by a statement of truth.* This more detailed change will replace outdated and currently inconsistent procedures, which are inconvenient for people to use and resource intensive to administer, with a more modern digital approach, but keeping strong penalties where a statement of truth is found to be false.

The legislation needed to fully implement these reforms was initially contained in the Prisons and Courts Bill 2017; this was lost when the General Election was called in June 2017. A new Bill is currently awaited.

8.15 Key points

1. While popular rhetoric suggests that it is the right of every English person to have his or her day in court, in practice access to the courts is surrounded by barriers. There are substantial procedural and financial pressures on litigants to settle their differences outside the courts; and appealing against the decision of a court is subject to even more restrictions.

2. Judicial manpower is an expensive resource to be used only where really needed, particularly at the most senior levels. Much of the simpler case work is dealt with by part-time judges. There are also many occasions in which judges sit in a court of a higher level than the one to which they have been appointed—circuit judges in the High Court; High Court judges in the Court of Appeal, for example. There is thus considerable flexibility in how the available resource is used, though this begs the question—given the policy on court fees (*see 8.6.2*)—whether the public is actually getting the judicial service it thinks it is paying for.

3. There has been considerable frustration at the slow pace of investment in information technology in the civil justice system. Until this is remedied, the development of more efficient court procedures is very difficult, since much more civil work could be conducted electronically if the resources were available.

4. Increasingly, disputes affecting ordinary people are being dealt with outside the court system.

5. Delay and cost were the principal issues identified as in need of reform by Lord Woolf. The CPR have seen reductions in the time taken for a case to get to court, though the average time for even a small claim to be decided is far from speedy. Serious complaints about the costs of taking proceedings[25] ultimately led to

---

[25] See Goriely, T., Moorhead, R., and Abrams, P., *More Civil Justice? The Impact of the Woolf Reforms on Pre-action Behaviour* (Research Study 43) (London, The Law Society and Civil Justice Council, 2002).

Lord Justice Jackson's review of costs and his new work on fixed costs, which are discussed in *Chapter 10*. Despite all the changes that have been made so far, litigation in court remains generally an expensive undertaking.

6. The current government's transformation programme should lead to fundamental changes in the ways in which the courts work, how people access them, and where they are physically located, with an increasing shift of 'ordinary cases' away from courts into other dispute resolution procedures.

8.16 Questions

Use the self-test questions in the Online Resources to test your understanding of the topics covered in this chapter and receive tailored feedback: www.oup.com/uk/partington18_19/.

8.17 Web links

Check the Online Resources for a selection of annotated web links allowing you to easily research topics of particular interest: www.oup.com/uk/partington18_19/.

8.18 Blog items

See Spotlight on the Justice System, at www.martinpartington.com/category/chapter-8-2/.

Suggestions for further reading

BLAKE, S., BROWNE, J., and SIME, S., *The Jackson ADR Handbook* (2nd edn, Oxford, Oxford University Press, 2016)

BLOM-COOPER, L., QC, DICKSON, B., and DREWRY, G. (eds), *The Judicial House of Lords: 1876–2009* (Oxford, Oxford University Press, 2011)

DREWRY, G., BLOM-COOPER, L., and BLAKE, C., *The Court of Appeal* (Oxford, Hart Publishing, 2007)

GENN, H., *Judging Civil Justice* (Cambridge, Cambridge University Press, 2009)

JUSTICE, *Delivering Justice in an Age of Austerity* (2015) downloadable at justice.org.uk/our-work/areas-of-work/access-to-justice/justice-austerity/

LEGAL SERVICES RESEARCH CENTRE, *Causes of Action: Civil law and social justice. The final report of the first LSRC survey of justiciable problems* (2nd edn, London, Legal Services Commission, 2006)

Other suggestions are set out in the Further Reading listed in the **Online Resources**.

PART IV

THE DELIVERY AND FUNDING OF LEGAL SERVICES

9

Delivering legal services: practitioners, adjudicators, and legal scholars

9.1 Introduction: the providers of legal services

Conventional discussions about the delivery of legal services tend to focus on the role of the legal profession and its two branches: *solicitors* and *barristers*. Here a broader approach is adopted. In the same way that we have argued that the institutional framework of the English legal system can only be understood by referring to a wide range of institutions, not simply the courts, so too thinking about the full range of those who deliver services about legal rights and entitlements involves consideration of a much greater range of actors.

The purpose of this chapter is to provide an introductory account of the principal groups that provide legal services. It considers not only the professionally qualified, but also those who provide legal services without having legal professional qualifications. This is important, not least because there is a growing realization that the present model for the delivery of legal services, predominantly by lawyers working in private practice, is not sustainable.[1] The legal services market is undergoing rapid change. Those now starting to study law must—if they wish to do law-related work—consider a much wider range of career options.

While the bulk of the chapter focuses on those who deliver legal services directly or indirectly to clients, the chapter also includes consideration of those who provide legal services by adjudicating disputes. Lastly, the role of the legal academic is considered.

9.2 The practitioners

Three groups are considered in this part of the chapter:

- those professionally qualified as lawyers;
- those in professional groups allied to law; and
- non-legally qualified providers of legal services.

---

[1] See report from the Law Society *The Future of Legal Services* published in January 2016.

9.3 Professionally qualified lawyers: solicitors and barristers

According to the Legal Services Board,[2] on 1 April 2016 there were 145,059 solicitors; 15,288 barristers; 6,832 chartered legal executives; 1,283 licensed conveyancers; around 2,100 patent attorneys; and around 890 trademark attorneys.

Clearly solicitors and barristers dominate the legal services market. Their numbers have increased significantly over the last 25 years, the figures reflecting the increased demand for legal services associated with economic growth, the globalization of the economy, the UK's involvement in the EU, and other social and political changes placing greater emphasis on citizens' rights.

Three points are worth noting. First, there is a significantly improved gender balance of those entering the legal profession than there was 25 years ago. For a number of years now, more women than men have become solicitors. About a third of those in private practice at the bar are women. However, women are still not being appointed to the most senior roles in the numbers that should be expected.

Secondly, the ethnic balance of entrants, though far from satisfactory, has improved. Once again, those from the black and minority ethnic groups are not reaching senior legal positions in the numbers that would reflect a truly diverse legal profession.

Thirdly, there are clear indications that those from poorer backgrounds still find it harder to access jobs in the legal services market (*see further 9.11*). Both the regulators and the principal law firms state that they are committed to equality of opportunity. But it has proved hard to turn this theoretical commitment into reality.

9.3.1 What lawyers do

It is impossible to summarize the enormous variety of work that lawyers undertake. A long list would not be particularly enlightening. Much of the work of the large city firms relates to the commercial transactions of their clients, for example the headline-grabbing financial deals or takeover bids that shape economic and commercial life. Others offer services focused on the individual client, for example defending people accused of crime, dealing with the consequences of personal injuries particularly arising from road traffic accidents, buying and selling property, handling divorces, or winding up estates after death.

The focus of this chapter is on lawyers who work in private practice. However, the work of other significant groups of qualified lawyers should also be noted. Three specific examples may be given.

In-house counsel. Considerable and increasing numbers of lawyers work as in-house counsel, providing legal services for companies directly through their employment by the firms concerned. Most major companies have legal departments, staffed by professionally qualified lawyers, able to advise them on the legal issues that directly affect the company and its operations.

---

[2] Annual Report for 2016–2017. Figure 1.

Lawyers in central and local government. There are—broadly—two ways in which those professionally qualified as lawyers may be employed in central government. First, they may be specifically employed for their technical legal expertise: to draft legislation (Parliamentary Counsel), or to deal with the wide range of legal issues that arise in departments (the Government Legal Department). Large numbers of lawyers work in the Crown Prosecution Service. Many with law degrees and other legal qualifications are not employed as lawyers, but form part of the general Civil Service.

In local government, lawyers often hold senior positions in local authority administrations and play a very important role in ensuring that local authorities act within the scope of the powers given to them by Act of Parliament.

Lawyers in court administration. Qualified lawyers also play a very important part in the work of those courts and other dispute resolution bodies that do not use legally qualified adjudicators, for example justices' clerks in the magistrates' courts.

One of the great attractions of law is the enormous range of employment opportunities that the law provides for those who wish to practise or work in the legal system. There are also increasing opportunities to work in international agencies of various kinds.

9.3.1.1 Preliminary distinctions

When thinking about what lawyers do, two preliminary distinctions should be drawn between: (1) litigious and non-litigious matters; and (2) lawyers' services and legal services.

Litigious and non-litigious matters. A great deal of the work of lawyers is non-litigious—work designed to *prevent* litigation. This includes, for example, the provision of advice or the drafting of documents designed to ensure that people's affairs run smoothly.

By contrast, litigious work arises where things have gone wrong, where there are disputes that need to be resolved either between individuals or companies or between the citizen and the state. Rights to conduct litigation and to be heard in a court are subject to special statutory rules.

Legal services and lawyers' services. A second important distinction is between *lawyers' services*, services that can *only* be provided by professionally qualified lawyers, and *legal services*, which may, though do not have to, be provided by professional lawyers. One feature of the English legal system is that many people, other than those professionally qualified as lawyers, provide legal services which are required by members of the public and which deal with legal issues, for example advice about legal entitlements or the completion of legal transactions (*see Box 9.1* for examples).

Box 9.1 Legal system explained

Legal services and lawyers' services

Some examples of the distinction in practice are:

- The first source of legal advice for many people faced with problems about their employment ('have I been unfairly dismissed by my employer?') is a *Citizens' Advice Bureau* or a *trade union*. The person they see is trained to give the appropriate advice; the adviser

Box 9.1 Continued

may indeed recommend that the person should see a qualified lawyer. But the initial *legal service* does not usually come from a lawyer, but from a trained lay adviser.

- Similar points may be made in relation to advice sought by a tenant in dispute with her landlord; or to advice sought by a consumer where something has gone wrong with the provision of goods or services.
- Many people anxious to obtain advice regarding their legal entitlements to social welfare benefits are more likely to turn to the services of a *welfare rights officer*—again a lay person, albeit specially trained—rather than to professionally qualified lawyers.
- Those who buy or sell houses may use the services of a *licensed conveyancer* rather than a solicitor to complete their transaction.
- Many who want to make a will use will-writers who are not professionally qualified as lawyers.

Some legal services are provided by other professional groups. The most obvious example is that matters relating to individuals' legal liability to pay tax are typically dealt with, not by lawyers, but by *accountants*. In short, *legal services* are not provided exclusively by qualified lawyers.

Lawyers' services are a special sub-set of the total provision of legal services: they are services which either have to be provided by those qualified as lawyers (such as the provision of advocacy services in court—which are restricted to those who have acquired particular professional qualifications) or which, as a matter of practice, are provided by those qualified as lawyers. For example, it is inconceivable that large corporations would turn to lay advisers—however well trained—for advice on questions relating to a corporate takeover. Such clients want the expertise that professional lawyers hold themselves out as offering, and, should anything go wrong, the comfort of the insurance protection that is a part of professional responsibility.

Part 3 of the Legal Services Act 2007 has enshrined this distinction in legislation. It sets out a number of *reserved legal activities* (rights of audience, conduct of litigation, probate activities, notarial activities, the administration of oaths, and 'reserved instrument activities') that may only be performed by lawyers or others authorized to undertake such work. It is a criminal offence to undertake such work without authorization.

One example of the distinction between legal services and lawyers' services that has attracted considerable public attention is claims management (*see further 9.8.5*). The roles of paralegal staff and non-legally qualified advisers are discussed later in this chapter.

9.4 Regulation of the legal profession: the changing regulatory framework

Professional bodies like to regulate themselves. There are arguments in favour of self-regulation, in particular that only those within the profession can set and monitor proper professional standards. On the other hand, it is argued that self-regulation results in the creation of restrictive practices that work against the public interest by limiting competition and driving up prices. Over the last 50 years, there has been fundamental change to the ways in which the English legal profession is regulated, with much more intervention by government. Further change is on the horizon. I consider the changes in three phases: 1968–99; 2000–15; 2016–the future. I conclude this section with a short reflection on the relationship between the regulation of the legal profession and the independence of the profession.

9.4.1 Phase 1, 1968–1999: the attack on restrictive practices and the encouragement of competition

The attack on the restrictive practices of the legal profession began with a study by the Monopolies Commission, published in 1968. In evidence to the Commission, Professor Michael Zander provided a devastating critique of professional practices which, he argued, were not in the public interest.

When the Thatcher government came to power in 1979, Mrs Thatcher was determined to make the British economy generally much more competitive. The legal profession became caught up in a general attack on monopolistic power.[3]

9.4.1.1 Abolition of the conveyancing monopoly

The first, and most symbolically significant, change to lawyers' restrictive practices occurred in 1987, when the conveyancing monopoly was broken. Until then, only solicitors were entitled to charge for conveying the title in real estate from a vendor to a purchaser. Part II of the Administration of Justice Act 1985 enabled a system of licensed conveyancers, regulated by the Council for Licensed Conveyancers, to be established. The first licences under the scheme were granted in 1987. In addition, the practice of using fixed-scale fees for conveyancing was stopped.

9.4.1.2 Right to litigate and rights of audience

Next, fundamental changes were made to the right to conduct litigation and rights of audience. Before 1990, only solicitors could prepare cases for trial; only barristers had rights to be heard arguing cases in court. Under the Courts and Legal Services Act 1990, the government began to put these rights on a statutory footing. Instead of the professional bodies prescribing the rules relating to advocacy and litigation, as they had done in the past, the Act established a framework for authorized bodies (the Bar Council and the Law Society together with the Chartered Institute of Legal Executives) to set the rules.

The Access to Justice Act 1999 made further changes by enabling not only barristers but also solicitors and chartered legal executives to acquire the right to be heard in court. This is not an unqualified privilege; those who wish to act as advocates have to obtain prescribed qualifications.

---

[3] There is a tendency for all professional groups to feel that they alone are being picked on. In fact all professional groups have been subject to similar pressures.

9.4.1.3 Relaxation of restrictions on advertising

Third, rules on advertising were significantly relaxed so that firms of solicitors became entitled to advertise their services. While legal advertising in England and Wales may not have the flamboyance of lawyers' advertisements in the United States, nevertheless this development was also a significant break with the past. All significant legal practices now engage in a wide range of promotional 'practice development' activity.

9.4.2 Phase 2, 2000–2015: the Clementi Report and the Legal Services Act 2007

The changes of the 1980s and 1990s were far from the end of the story. In March 2001, the Office of Fair Trading published a report, *Competition in the Professions*, recommending that unjustified restrictions on competition should be removed. The government responded with a consultation paper and report into competition and regulation in the legal services market. It concluded that 'the current framework is out-dated, inflexible, over-complex and insufficiently accountable or transparent ... Government has therefore decided that a thorough and independent investigation without reservation is needed.'

9.4.2.1 The Clementi Report

In July 2003, Sir David Clementi was appointed to carry out this task. His terms of reference were:

- to consider what regulatory framework would best promote competition, innovation, and the public and consumer interest in an efficient, effective, and independent legal sector; and
- to recommend a framework that would be independent in representing the public and consumer interest, comprehensive, accountable, consistent, flexible, transparent, and no more restrictive or burdensome than is clearly justified.

In December 2004, Sir David published his report. The main recommendations, which the government broadly accepted, were:

- to establish a new legal services regulator, the Legal Services Board, to provide oversight regulation of frontline bodies such as the Law Society and the Bar Council;
- to set statutory objectives for the Legal Services Board, including promotion of the public and consumer interest;
- to prescribe regulatory powers that would be vested in the Legal Services Board, but with powers to devolve regulatory functions to frontline bodies (i.e. professional bodies), subject to their competence and governance arrangements;

- to ensure that the frontline bodies made new governance arrangements that would separate their regulatory and representative functions;
- to create a new Office for Legal Complaints—a single independent body to handle consumer complaints in respect of all members of frontline bodies, subject to oversight by the Legal Services Board;
- to establish alternative business structures that could see different mixes of lawyers and non-lawyers managing and owning legal practices.

9.4.2.2 The Legal Services Act 2007

The Legal Services Act 2007 put in place the regulatory framework envisaged by Clementi. The principal changes brought about by the legislation can be summarized as follows:

a. Separation of the representation and regulation functions of the professional bodies

Before the Legal Services Act became law, both the Bar Council (responsible for barristers) and the Law Society (responsible for solicitors) reorganized themselves so that their representative functions (sometimes referred to as their 'trade union' functions), designed to promote their members' interests to the wider public, were separated from their regulatory functions. While the Law Society and the Bar Council still retain some regulatory functions, primary responsibility for regulating solicitors now rests with the Solicitors' Regulation Authority (SRA), established in 2007 as the independent regulatory body of the Law Society. Similarly, barristers are now regulated by the Bar Standards Board, the independent regulatory body of the Bar Council. Other bodies, such as the Chartered Institute of Legal Executives, have also divided their representational and regulatory functions.

b. The Legal Services Board

Secondly, the Legal Services Board was established and became fully operational in January 2010. The regulatory structure created by the Legal Services Act 2007 is complex. The Legal Services Board undertakes its regulatory functions not directly with the legal professions, but indirectly through the profession-specific regulatory bodies, such as the Solicitors' Regulation Authority and the CILEX Professional Standards Board (*see 9.7.1*). This has led some to argue that the system is too expensive and cumbersome. The Legal Services Board wants to reduce the amount of regulation imposed on the legal profession. At one point, it stated that its ultimate goal was to do itself out of a job, with regulatory responsibility returned more directly to legal practitioners. More recently it has argued that it should be the sole regulator.

In addition to overseeing the regulatory activities of the professional bodies, the Board has a number of other tasks. For example it is required to increase public understanding of law and support the rule of law, tasks that had never before been set out in legislation (*see Box 9.2*).

Box 9.2 Reform in progress

Legal Services Board: the regulatory objectives

The Board must deliver eight regulatory objectives, set out in the Legal Services Act 2007:

- protecting and promoting the public interest;
- supporting the constitutional principle of the rule of law;
- improving access to justice;
- protecting and promoting the interests of consumers;
- promoting competition in the provision of services in the legal sector;
- encouraging an independent, strong, diverse, and effective legal profession;
- increasing public understanding of citizens' legal rights and duties;
- promoting and maintaining adherence to the professional principles of independence and integrity; proper standards of work; observing the best interests of the client and the duty to the court; and maintaining client confidentiality.

The Board has published its own commentary on these regulatory objectives. See www.legalservicesboard.org.uk/news_publications/publications/pdf/regulatory_objectives.pdf.

In 2014–15, its powers were expanded to regulate and license reserved legal activities beyond the traditional boundaries of the legal world. Thus the Institute of Chartered Accountants in England and Wales (ICAEW) was given the power to regulate and license its members to provide probate services, as was the Intellectual Property Regulation Board to provide services in IP. It has ensured that Chartered Legal Executives are able to deliver the same range of legal activities as barristers and solicitors.

c. Dealing with complaints: the Legal Ombudsman

Thirdly, the Office for Legal Complaints was established and the Legal Ombudsman appointed. This was the latest stage in a long process of trying to ensure that users of legal services had an effective way of resolving complaints and disputes against practitioners.

The approved regulators such as the SRA and the Bar Standards Board have responsibility for ensuring that their members have proper complaints-handling procedures in place. Initial responsibility for dealing with complaints lies with the firms or chambers of those professionals against whom complaints are made. If resolution is not possible at that stage, all unresolved complaints must be taken on to the Office for Legal Complaints.

The Ombudsman determines what further investigation is to be undertaken. The Ombudsman has power to award compensation of up to £50,000. The details of the Ombudsman's procedural rules are published on her website. In the first full year of operation (2011–12), the Office received over 75,000 applications. By 2015–16, this figure was down to 18,088, of which 7,033 were taken forward for investigation.

In addition, from January 2015, the Legal Ombudsman has had jurisdiction over claims management companies (*see 9.8.5*). In 2015–16, she received over 19,000 contacts relating to these companies; 2,438 were taken forward for further investigation.

9.4.3 Phase 3, 2016–the future: further changes to the regulatory framework

Despite all the changes that have taken place so far, more change is in the wind. There is an increasing sense that the changes that have been made have, so far, failed to deliver as much public benefit as they should have done. The key issues are argued to be:

- lack of innovation in the delivery of legal services;
- lack of competition in the provision of legal services;
- inadequate provision, especially for small businesses and poor individuals;
- lack of response to new commercial opportunities.

A number of ideas have already been put into the public arena, which while continuing to protect consumers of legal services are aimed at addressing these issues.

9.4.3.1 Review of the Legal Services Act 2007

In November 2015, HM Treasury published a policy paper: *A Better Deal: boosting competition to bring down bills for families and firms.* In addition, the government has promised a further review of how the regulatory structure created by the Legal Services Act 2007 is operating, with a view to making it more efficient. The Legal Services Board is clearly attempting to shape the debate on the future, arguing (in a 'vision' paper published in September 2016) for a single regulator across the whole of the legal services sector. The Solicitors' Regulatory Authority has already expressed concern about this idea.

9.4.3.2 Competition and Markets Authority (CMA) market study

The Competition and Markets Authority announced in January 2016 that it was going to take a close look at competition in legal services. Its final report was published in December 2016 (*see Box 9.3*). The regulatory bodies have broadly accepted the recommendations and are working on ways to respond to them.

Box 9.3 Reform in progress

Competition and Markets Authority report

The CMA found that competition in legal services for individual and small business consumers is not working as well as it might.

There was a lack of digital comparison tools to make comparisons easier for consumers. Lack of competition meant some providers can charge higher prices when substantially cheaper prices are available for comparable services.

Box 9.3 Continued

In response to these findings, the CMA set out a package of measures which challenges providers and regulators to help customers better navigate the market and get value for money. These changes were drawn up after discussions with key stakeholders, including the eight frontline legal regulators, and will be overseen by the Legal Services Board, which will report on progress.

They include:

- A requirement on providers to display information on price, service, redress, and regulatory status to help potential customers. This would include publishing pricing information for particular services online (only 17 per cent of firms do so at present).
- Revamping and promoting the existing Legal Choices website to be a starting point for customers needing help, information, and guidance on how to navigate the market and purchase services.
- Facilitating the development of comparison sites and other intermediaries to allow customers to compare providers in one place by making data already collected by regulators available. At present only 22 per cent of people compare the services on offer before appointing a lawyer.
- Encouraging legal service providers to engage with feedback and review platforms to ensure that customers can benefit from the experience of others before making their choice.
- Recommending that the Ministry of Justice looks at whether to extend protection from existing redress schemes to customers using 'unauthorized' providers.

In addition, the CMA considered the impact of legal services regulation on competition. The CMA found that whilst the current system is not a major barrier, it may not be sustainable in the long term. In particular, the framework is not sufficiently flexible to apply proportionate risk-based regulation which reflects differences across legal services which could harm competition. The CMA therefore also recommends that the Ministry of Justice reviews the current framework to make it more flexible and targeted at protecting consumers in areas where it is most needed.

See www.gov.uk/government/news/cma-demands-greater-transparency-from-legal-service-providers. Implementation of the recommendations is still in progress; at the time of writing, it does not seem that progress will be fast.

9.4.3.3 Regulation of claims management companies

In March 2016 an independent review of claims management companies (CMCs)[4] was published. At present, CMCs are regulated by a dedicated unit which operates within

---

[4] Details of the review are at www.gov.uk/government/uploads/system/uploads/attachment_data/file/508160/PU1918_claims_management_regulation_review_final.pdf.

the Ministry of Justice, rather than by a body more independent of government (*see also 9.8.5*). The review offered three options for the way forward:

(1) creating a wholly new external regulator;

(2) leaving things within the Ministry of Justice, while building on the reform programme currently being developed by the Unit; or

(3) transferring the function to the Financial Conduct Authority (FCA). The review favoured this option.

The government has announced that it will transfer this function to the FCA—but as this will require legislation, it will not take place before 2018. The Financial Guidance and Claims Bill 2017 was introduced into the House of Lords in June 2017.

9.4.3.4 Regulation of alternative business structures

In July 2016, the government published a consultation paper on what changes might be needed to the regulation of alternative business structures (ABS). When the Legal Services Board began the process of licensing ABSs in 2010 and in light of concerns raised about the potential risks of new and unknown business models, the legislative framework for the regulation of ABS businesses, set out in the Legal Services Act 2007, was made more onerous and prescriptive than that for traditional law firms (*see 9.6.1*).

Six years on, the government argues that experience suggests that ABS businesses have not been shown to attract any greater regulatory risk than traditional law firms. The Legal Services Board and front-line regulators have suggested that the current statutory requirements act as a deterrent and an unnecessary barrier to firms wanting to change their current business model to a more innovative one, as well as to new businesses considering entering the market. In light of this, the government is consulting on what changes, if any, should be made to the regulatory regime. A more recent (April 2017) research report from the Legal Services Board suggests that those who had been licensed as ABS did not feel deterred by the current regulatory framework.

9.4.3.5 Regulating unregulated providers of legal services?

Not all legal services are provided by lawyers or legal executives who are regulated by their professional bodies. There is a group of legal service providers who are not authorized and regulated under any legal sector-specific legislation, but who are providing legal services for profit. In 2016, the Legal Services Board published research on the work of this sector of the legal service market. The research looked in detail at will-writing, online divorce, and intellectual property.

The key findings of the research were:

- For-profit unregulated providers make up a small proportion of the legal services market. In the individual legal needs survey, they represented 4.5–5.5 per cent of cases in which consumers paid for advice or representation.

- Not-for-profit providers, most of whom are unregulated, accounted for approximately 37 per cent of all legal problems where advice was sought.

- Benefits for consumers include lower prices and greater price transparency compared to regulated providers, innovation and service differentiation, and competitive impact on regulated providers.

- The main risks to consumers relate to consumers not making informed choices and misleading advertising claims. The research did not assess the technical quality of the work of these providers.

- Consumer satisfaction with customer service is broadly comparable across regulated and unregulated providers—84 per cent versus 81 per cent respectively.

- More than half of consumers who instruct for-profit unregulated providers are aware of their regulatory status. Of those who do not check, a significant proportion do not do so because they assume that they are regulated.

- There is a limited potential market for voluntary regulation beyond existing trade associations given the size of the market and low appetite for such initiatives among providers.

For the time being, at least, the Legal Services Board concludes that the for-profit unregulated sector is smaller than expected, although in some segments these providers have gained significant market share. (For example, online divorce services are provided by just five major providers.) Consumers should be encouraged to check whether or not providers are regulated.

Thus there is currently no pressure to regulate this sector of the market. So long as the unregulated sector provides cost-effective services, with which consumers are satisfied, the lack of regulation is likely to continue. But if there is a highly publicized scandal, then the regulatory context could well change.

9.4.3.6 Conclusion

Given all these announcements it seems inevitable that in the coming years there will be yet more change to the regulatory framework affecting those who provide legal services. (As details emerge they will be noted in my blog: www.martinpartington.com.)

9.4.4 Maintaining the independence of the legal profession

Independence is a key attribute claimed for the legal profession. This is, constitutionally, an extremely important principle. It asserts that lawyers must have the right to give advice independently of the views of the government of the day, and to be protected if they do so. It also involves a professional obligation to take on cases that may be widely regarded as disagreeable or distasteful. The proposition that a person is innocent until proved guilty depends on lawyers being willing to develop and advance arguments on behalf of their clients, no matter how unpleasant those clients may be. The 'cab-rank' principle, whereby barristers are professionally obliged to take on whatever case comes to them next, is perhaps the clearest example of the operation of this principle.

The assertion of independence may also imply that the professions should be free to regulate themselves in accordance with their own rules of professional conduct, without interference from government. As we have seen, there has been significant erosion of the ability of the legal profession to regulate itself. The abolition of restrictive practices, and changes to legal aid and to modes of dealing with complaints about the quality of work, have all resulted from increased government intervention. The Legal Services Act 2007 took this process further. Yet more change is on the horizon.

Each example of government involvement may be justified, particularly in contexts where the legal profession has not been willing to reform itself in the public interest. However, the question how far government should go in regulating the legal profession is one needing constant attention if the role of the legal profession in assisting the individual, often against agencies of the state or other powerful bodies, is not to be compromised.

9.5 The changing nature of the legal profession

The regulatory changes of the last four decades, combined with much wider social and economic changes, have had significant impact on the legal professions. What follows is not a comprehensive account but lists some of the principal developments.

9.5.1 Growth and globalization

Most notable has been the inexorable rise in the numbers of lawyers, and the growth in the size of law firms and, for commercial firms, the increasingly global scope of their practices. Increased globalization of the world economy has been accompanied by globalization in the provision of legal services. British lawyers have responded in a variety of ways:

- Many large law firms in the City of London have gone through substantial programmes of merger and expansion.

- Significant groupings of leading firms in provincial commercial centres—for example Leeds, Birmingham, Bristol—have also developed, either through mergers and takeovers or the creation of networks of legal practices.

- Many of these firms have established presences in other key centres of economic activity, in Europe, the Middle East, the Far East, and the Americas.

- Mergers of English law firms with firms in other countries in Europe and the United States have resulted in the creation of new forms of international partnership.

- There has been a significant increase in the presence of overseas law firms, in particular US law firms, in London, which has added to the competitive pressures on British-based firms.

- There have been moves towards the creation of professional groupings that cut across traditional disciplinary boundaries—in particular, lawyers and accountants.

These trends are likely to continue.

9.5.2 The decline in high street practice and the rise in specialization

Generalist high street practices, found in smaller towns, suburban areas, and other locations, which have in the past provided a general service to private clients, have come under increasing commercial pressure and face considerable uncertainty. The ability to make a living from a mixed practice of some criminal work, some property transactions (such as conveyancing or probate), a little bit of family and divorce work, and some personal injuries work, which even ten years ago was quite common, is now very difficult. Many of the remaining sole practitioners and small firms fall into this category. The future of high street practice is under considerable threat, unless those who remain in this sector of the legal services market are prepared to rethink their commercial strategies.

One response has been a rise in the number of specialist/niche practices. Increasingly, smaller firms of solicitors and sets of barristers' chambers have come to specialize in particular areas—family law, criminal law, employment law, and housing law, to give some examples.

These developments have been supported in part by the legal professional bodies. For example, the Law Society has established a number of specialist panels, including the Children's Panel, the Mental Health Panel, and the Medical Negligence Panel.

In addition, members of the profession themselves have taken the lead in establishing specialist groups, many of which cross over traditional solicitor/barrister boundaries. There are now well over 40 such groups. They act in a variety of ways:

- They may be able to act collaboratively (within the competitive market) to promote the specialist services that they offer (thereby seeking to exclude non-specialists from their work).

- Some, such as the Solicitors' Family Law Association, have promoted new modes of legal practice, designed to provide a different form of lawyering for their clients—in the context of family law, a less confrontational approach designed to assist those whose relationships have broken down (*see 7.9.1*).

- Others, such as the Patent Lawyers' Association, have developed specialist programmes of advanced legal education and training designed to give their members special expertise and, thus, it is hoped, a competitive edge in the legal services market place.

- The specialist lawyer groups have also developed a very important influence in government. They can offer advice on how particular areas of practice may be affected by proposed policy changes in ways which the general professional bodies such as the Law Society or Bar Council may be unable to achieve.

9.5.3 Pay and conditions

The expectations of those entering the profession about the pay and conditions they should receive have also changed considerably over the last 40 years. A real problem in this context is that the financial rewards for those in some areas of legal practice, particularly the corporate sector, are hugely different from those in many specialist or niche areas, particularly those offering services to the less well-off groups in society. The emphasis on 'fat-cat lawyer' salaries in much legal journalism disguises the fact the many practitioners are not particularly well paid. Arguably, such stories are not in the interest of the legal profession taken as a whole (*see Box 9.4*).

Box 9.4 Legal system explained

Legal journalism and images of lawyers

One consequence of the changed context of legal practice, particularly the relaxation of restrictions on advertising, is that a significant branch of journalism has developed, devoted to the telling of stories about individuals and firms in the law and their doings. Some of the broadsheet newspapers have a weekly law section, much of which is concerned with what is in effect legal gossip. In addition there are specialist papers for the profession that focus in particular on the activities of law firms and sets of chambers. The 'free' paper, *The Lawyer*—which appears weekly—is supplemented by the expensive and glossy *Legal Business*, which focuses in particular on firms operating in the City and overseas.

One consequence of this new journalism is that public information about lawyers is to a large extent dominated by the stories which the PR departments of the large firms are able to place in this press. Stories about the impact and importance of the small high street firms find little place beside dramatic tales of takeovers, mergers, and other commercial/corporate activity. This creates at least three distortions:

- Those thinking of entering the law as a profession are denied the opportunity to consider the full range of legal careers open to them.
- They come to assume that the only type of lawyering worth undertaking is that which pays enormous salaries.
- The public assume that all lawyers act—and most significantly are paid—in ways suggested by the stories that appear in this press.

Much of the public hostility towards lawyers is, it may be surmised, the result of assumptions that legal services are very expensive and thus affordable only by the very rich. A more balanced picture would indicate that there are still many lawyers providing valuable services to the public for extremely modest fees.

9.5.4 The promotion of good practice and ethical standards

Historically, the provision of legal services was seen by members of the legal profession as a public service to which, in some rather mysterious way, commercial pressures somehow did not apply. The adoption of good practice and an ethical approach were, on this view, inherent in the provision of the service.

Whether there was ever any real justification for this belief, there can be no doubt that in the modern world the provision of legal services is quite clearly a business. If lawyers do not make a profit at the end of the year, they go bust. Legal practice must be subject to the disciplines of financial control, quality control, and efficiency that characterize all business activity. The emphasis on commercial and financial success has led the professional regulators to emphasize the importance of an ethical approach to lawyering, to ensure that practitioners do not take short cuts and forget the ethical principles that should underpin their work.

Over the years, the professional regulatory bodies have developed guidance on professional conduct, which includes a statement of the ethical framework needed for professional activity (as an example *see Box 9.5*).

Box 9.5 Reform in progress

The SRA Handbook

In October 2011, the Solicitors' Regulation Authority (SRA) brought into effect a new handbook on good practice and ethical practice which applies to solicitors in England and Wales. It adopts what is described as outcomes-focused regulation, which concentrates on the high-level principles and outcomes that should underpin the provision of legal services for consumers. The new handbook replaces a much more detailed and prescriptive rulebook. The intention is to establish a targeted, risk-based approach concentrating on standards of service that those regulated by the SRA should provide to consumers. However, the new approach allows greater flexibility to firms in how they achieve their outcomes (standards of service) for clients. The aim of the SRA is to set out a unified approach with the same standards applying to both traditional law firms and alternative business structures.

At the heart of the new approach are ten mandatory principles that apply to all. Those regulated by the SRA must:

- uphold the rule of law and the proper administration of justice;
- act with integrity;
- not allow their independence to be compromised;
- act in the best interests of each client;
- provide a proper standard of service to their clients;
- behave in a way that maintains the trust the public places in them and in the provision of legal services;
- comply with their legal and regulatory obligations and deal with their regulators and ombudsmen in an open, timely, and co-operative manner;

Box 9.5 Continued

- run their business or carry out their role in the business effectively and in accordance with proper governance and sound financial and risk-management principles;
- run their business or carry out their role in the business in a way that encourages equality of opportunity and respect for diversity; and
- protect client money and assets.

These principles are supported by more detailed notes indicating how they should work in practice. For further details, see www.sra.org.uk/solicitors/handbook/handbookprinciples/content.page.

The SRA is currently in the process of slimming the handbook down to make it 'simpler, shorter and sharper'.

The handbook for members of the Bar, including its code of conduct, is at www.barstandardsboard.org.uk/regulatory-requirements/bsb-handbook/?utm_campaign=203581_Regulatory%20Update%20November%202017%20unregistered%20Bar&utm_medium=email&utm_source=BSB%20Regulatory%20updates&dm_i=4HUI,4D31,20DKCS,H094,1.

Understanding these ethical principles is a crucial part of professional legal education, not least because failure to follow the guidance can result, in extreme cases, in loss of the right to practise. Courses for both solicitors' and barristers' professional examinations address these issues.

Notwithstanding these developments, many argue that instruction in and debate about the ethical issues facing the lawyer should be more comprehensive. A recent Legal Education and Training Review concluded, among other things, that from the outset, practitioners should have an understanding of the relationship between morality and law, the values underpinning the legal system, and the role of lawyers in relation to those values.

However cynically lawyers may be perceived, there are two particular respects in which the legal profession is able at least in part to demonstrate its ethical commitment: pro bono work; and test case litigation.

9.5.4.1 For free (pro bono) work

There has long been a tradition that lawyers offer free legal services to the poor. Before there was legal aid, there was a history of such provision in London and other major conurbations. In recent years, there has been a renewed emphasis on pro bono work, especially following major cuts to legal aid (*see Chapter 10*). Because the large commercial firms in the City of London and other commercial centres have been so obviously financially successful, there has been a renewed interest in the provision of free legal services by their staff in Citizens' Advice Bureaux and other agencies.

Some may regard this as little more than a token gesture. But, given the precarious funding position that many such agencies are in, it is work that makes a significant contribution to local legal service delivery. It is also true that the majority of those who offer pro bono services derive a great deal of professional interest and pleasure from the work they do.

Since 2008, when section 194 of the Legal Services Act 2007 came into force, it has been possible for successful litigants who are assisted on a pro bono basis to ask for some costs from the losing side. They do not get the money for themselves since, by definition, their case has been argued for nothing. But any pro bono costs that are awarded are paid to a nominated charity—the Access to Justice Foundation—which can then use the funds to promote other legal service activities. While the sums involved in no way compensate for cuts in the legal aid budget, it is a development which, while still at an embryonic stage, is helping to create new ways of providing at least some access to justice.

The professional bodies have taken a great deal of trouble to promote pro bono work over the last decade. Many important new initiatives have been taken, including an annual 'pro bono' week, with events being held around the country. There are 'pro bono' awards to lawyers who have developed outstanding examples of pro bono practice, both in the United Kingdom and in some cases overseas. This is an aspect of modern legal practice that should be much better understood.

9.5.4.2 Test case litigation

Test case litigation, sometimes called 'cause lawyering', is also often associated with lawyers being willing to take up broad general issues, particularly on behalf of more disadvantaged groups in the community. Historically, test case litigation in the United Kingdom has not had the same impact as, for example, in the United States, where legal provisions or policies were able to be tested for their constitutionality against the provisions of the Constitution of the United States. However, with ever greater involvement in Europe, both through the European Union and, in relation to human rights, through the Council of Europe, many challenges to English law have been mounted, in some cases with dramatic success. The Human Rights Act 1998 has generated more test case legislation, as provisions of English law are tested for their compatibility with the European Convention on Human Rights.

A number of legal charitable organizations participate in test cases by acting as interveners in cases before the Supreme Court. JUSTICE is the most frequent Supreme Court intervener.

9.5.5 The blurring of the distinction between solicitors and barristers

The organization of the practising legal profession in England and Wales differs markedly from that in many other countries. There is still an important distinction in professional identity between 'solicitor' and 'barrister'. However, because of the changed regulatory framework, the practical implications of the distinction are far fewer today than they were 40 years ago. Many of the services that used to be the exclusive preserve of one branch of the profession are now open to all.

In addition many restrictions on the tasks that people may perform within the legal system have been removed. The most important change in this context has been the adoption by statute of the principle that the highest judicial offices should be open to solicitors as well as to barristers (who formerly had a monopoly in relation to these appointments).

One question that these developments pose is whether the time has come for the two branches of the legal profession to fuse into a single profession, as happens in most other countries. Fusion has been debated on many occasions, though surprisingly not seriously in the last few years, despite all the developments that have occurred in recent years.

The arguments asserted by the Bar for its independence, in delivering both advocacy and other forms of legal advice, are actually very powerful—more powerful than some of the advocates for fusion allow. But in other countries with fused professions, the independence of the advocate is still strongly asserted. And the Bar's case must be weakened by the significant increase in the numbers of solicitor-advocates that are now practising. Other ways could be found to protect professional independence without the retention of a divided profession.

It seems inconceivable that this issue will not again become the subject of public debate.

9.5.6 Information technology and artificial intelligence

In common with everyone else, the legal profession has been increasingly affected by the development of new information technologies. Use of IT has transformed professional practice management. As legal information from government and the legal publishers and other sources becomes increasingly available in electronic form, and as court procedures become increasingly technology-driven, the impact of IT on legal practice has intensified. Legal practice, including litigation, will continue to change enormously in the next decade, reflecting both increased investment and further rapid technological change.

These developments are likely to have a significant impact not only on how those who deliver legal services interact with the courts and other agencies, such as the Land Registry (which has made it possible to register transfers of land online), but also on the organization of legal services, with much routine work being outsourced to other countries or away from London to locations where labour costs are lower.

In addition there is now considerable interest in the potential use of artificial intelligence to undertake routine legal tasks. There is much speculation about how far robots could take over core functions currently undertaken by lawyers and legal assistants. A lot of the stories which appear in the press on this subject come, I suspect, from AI developers wanting to generate interest in their products. I am sure that this will be a significant development in the coming years, but I also think that a revolution in how legal services are delivered will take longer than some of the rather breathless accounts which appear in the mass media.[5]

---

[5] A recent manpower survey, published by the Law Society in November 2017, suggests that by 2038, there could be a 20 per cent reduction in the number of posts, arising from the increased use of AI. See www.lawsociety.org.uk/support-services/research-trends/legal-services-sector-forecasts/.

9.6 Future trends

9.6.1 Alternative business structures

Historically, solicitors in private practice usually came together to form partnerships, though a substantial minority practise on their own as 'sole practitioners'. A recent development is that firms of solicitors have been able to form limited liability partnerships. Barristers in private practice work in 'chambers' but they are all self-employed within those chambers. Barristers were not permitted to form partnerships.

In his review of the legal services market, Clementi thought competition and efficiency would not be fully realized without alternative business structures allowing different combinations of lawyers and non-lawyers to own, invest in, and manage legal practices. He envisaged outside investors being brought into the market, as well as the possibility of lawyers establishing multi-disciplinary partnerships (with other professional groups such as accountants). Despite his proposals being strongly contested by the leaders of the professions, the government stood firm. The Legal Services Act 2007 made it possible for these developments to occur.

After much consultation, in 2011 the Legal Services Board agreed how approved regulators would be able to license alternative business structures (ABS). The first licence was issued by the Council of Licensed Conveyancers in October 2011. The SRA received approval to issue licences in January 2012. The Bar Standards Board was approved to issue licences in 2016, and began to do so in April 2017.

Since then, over 950 licences have been issued. At the end of March 2017, 892 of these were still active. The Legal Services Board published research in 2017 which indicated that firms with an ABS licence were more likely than others to make investments to enable them to expand their work; but the research also found that most such investments were coming from traditional sources (retained profits or bank loans) rather than major investment from external investors. The report said that external investors saw the legal services market as a 'sleepy' market, with great opportunities for investment returns. But the LSB concluded that unless and until there was a change of culture amongst legal service providers themselves, the incentives for innovation in the provision of legal services, including more provision at reduced cost, which could flow from increased external investment, were likely to be limited.

At the social welfare end of the market a number of providers of legal services have been contemplating how ABS might help them sustain their services, facing, as they are, huge cuts in publicly funded legal aid. For example, in April 2013 a legal advice charity in Leicester became the first not-for-profit organization to set up an ABS. The Community Advice and Law Service (CALS) won approval to launch Castle Park Solicitors Community Interest Company, whose profits will go to support the continuing work of the charity. A number of university law schools have also obtained an ABS licence to enable them to develop their legal advice activities.

It is hard to keep abreast of developments with ABS, but the website, www.legalfutures.co.uk/home, is an excellent place to start.

9.6.2 Innovation in the provision and marketing of legal services

In parallel with the creation of alternative business structures, practitioners have been developing innovative ways to provide and market legal services. To give just some examples:

- *'Virtual' legal services*: here, practitioners work largely from home. They may come into an office for meetings or to meet clients, but office space is kept to a minimum. Practitioners do not have their own rooms but hot-desk as needed. This enables practices to operate with greatly reduced overhead costs. One example is Virtual Law, offering business legal services. Another, offering principally legal services to individual clients, is Scott-Moncrieff & Associates. A third is Road Traffic Representation, an internet- and phone-based service offering advice to those charged with motoring offences.

- *Lawyers on demand*: a variation of the 'virtual' practice concept is the provision by a number of larger city firms of lawyers on demand. Sometimes referred to as an 'alumni service', lawyers who have worked full-time for a law firm, but who now wish to work more flexibly, are able to make themselves available for specific projects with commercial clients, often working in-house, but with all the professional support of their law firms. There are a number of examples of this: Lawyers on Demand at Berwin Leighton Paisner, Freshfields' Continuum, Allen and Overy's Peerpoint, and Pinsent Masons' Vario.

- *Franchises and networks*: new forms of legal franchising and networking are emerging, enabling individual law firms to continue to operate in their own right, but under the umbrella of the franchise/network operator which seeks to guarantee standards of service, control of fees payable by clients, and so on. One example is Quality Solicitors, whose members offer legal services in over 200 locations in England and Wales. Another is LawNet, a network of 67 medium-sized law practices based throughout the country. A new entrant, LawStore, opened four high street locations in 2015.

- *Direct public access*: in 2004, rules preventing direct access to barristers by members of the public were significantly relaxed. A number of examples of barristers offering legal services direct to the public, not from traditional chambers, have emerged over the years. One of the most long-standing is Clerksroom, originally based in Taunton, but now with a presence in a number of cities including London, Manchester, Birmingham, and Leeds. Recent reports suggest that barristers' chambers are increasingly promoting direct access.

9.6.3 Criminal advocacy practice

In October 2015, the government published a consultation paper on ways to enhance the quality of advocacy services in criminal trials. Among measures proposed are:

- the banning of referral fees in criminal cases;

- the creation of a special panel of criminal advocates to undertake publicly funded criminal trials in the Crown Court and above.

Final decisions on these proposals have not yet been made.

9.6.4 The internet: DIY law

There are also major developments taking place to enable ordinary members of the public effectively to undertake their own legal work, for example in drawing up wills, preparing divorce papers, or drafting standard commercial documents. At present, these initiatives are more developed in the United States. But companies such as Legalzoom are exploring how their services might develop for the UK market. Research into the potential for IT and the internet to deliver legal services in new ways is the subject of academic research in the ReInvent Law Laboratory in Michigan State University. This trend will be given a significant boost as the *Transforming Our Justice System* programme rolls out.

9.6.5 Unbundled legal services

A related development, which is already being seen in the legal services market, arises where people with a legal problem feel that they are able to do some of the work to resolve the problem themselves, but turn to a law firm for advice and assistance on issues which they do not feel capable of resolving. The consumer then only pays for the specific 'unbundled legal service' which he or she requires. In 2015, the Legal Services Board published research suggesting that this was an innovative way to deliver legal services to the less well-off, and made it clear that it would like to see more firms offering legal services on this basis.

9.6.6 The challenge of meeting unmet legal need

Despite all these changes, it is still the case that many individuals and small and medium sized companies do not have access to affordable legal services. This is an issue that concerns both the Legal Services Board and the Competition and Markets Authority. They both argue that more competition and innovation are needed to start to fill the gaps in provision. It is essential that both regulated and unregulated legal service providers continue to address the question of how to meet unmet need.

9.7 Professional groups allied to the legal profession

I noted earlier (*see 9.2*) that there are other professional groups allied to the legal profession. They provide many of the legal services that are not delivered by professionally qualified barristers and solicitors. The Legal Services Board already has oversight of a number of these groups.

9.7.1 Legal executives

Many staff employed in solicitors' offices are not formally qualified as solicitors, but nonetheless provide a great deal of legal service to the public. These are known collectively as 'legal executives'. Many of these are members and fellows of their own professional representative body, the *Chartered Institute of Legal Executives* (CILEX). CILEX organizes its own training programmes and examinations, which must be passed before a legal executive can call him- or herself a fellow of the Institute.

Legal executives play a central role in many legal practices, often being more knowledgeable in their areas of expertise than their fully professionally qualified colleagues. Legal executives who are fellows of CILEX are able, by taking additional courses and sitting additional examinations, to qualify as solicitors, and a number do so each year. Indeed they can go on to become partners in law firms and members of the judiciary.

CILEX has a Code of Professional Conduct, which is applied by the CILEX Professional Standards Board, an independent body created in October 2008 on a similar basis to the SRA, to ensure that CILEX members comply with their code. CILEX and the CILEX Professional Standards Board are both authorized regulators under the Legal Services Board.

9.7.2 Intellectual property attorneys

There are two specialist groups that operate in the intellectual property area: patent attorneys and trade mark attorneys. Each has a professional representative body, respectively the Chartered Institute of Patent Attorneys, and the Institute of Trade Mark Attorneys. Recently, they have established the Intellectual Property Regulation Board, to regulate both groups. All three bodies have become approved regulators under the Legal Services Board.

9.7.3 Licensed conveyancers

Licensed conveyancers came into existence following the ending of the solicitors' conveyancing monopoly. Their activities are regulated by the Council of Licensed Conveyancers, another approved regulator under the Legal Services Board.

9.7.4 Costs draftsmen

This group offers specialist legal services, drafting statements of lawyers' costs. They have a regulatory body—the Association of Law Costs Draftsmen—which is an approved regulator under the Legal Services Board.

9.7.5 Insolvency practitioners

Insolvency practitioners advise on, and undertake appointments in, all formal insolvency procedures—both personal (bankruptcies, sequestrations, individual voluntary arrangements, and trust deeds) and companies and partnerships (liquidations, company and partnership voluntary arrangements, administrations, and administrative receiverships). They also advise on, and act in, informal rescheduling of debts, reconstructions, and reorganizations for individuals and businesses facing financial difficulties. They belong to the Insolvency Practitioners' Association (IPA), a membership body recognized for the purposes of authorizing (licensing) insolvency practitioners under the Insolvency Act 1986. They are subject to oversight and inspection, not by the Legal Services Board, but by the Insolvency Service acting for the Secretary of State.

9.7.6 Accountancy firms

The Legal Services Board has approved the Institute of Chartered Accountants in England and Wales as a regulator of legal services. As a result, firms of accountants can now apply to establish ABS as part of their business offer.

It may also be noted that the Association of Chartered Certified Accountants is an approved regulator under the Legal Services Board in relation to reserved probate activities.

9.7.7 New professional groupings?

The changing face of legal service delivery is likely to mean more significant changes in the work undertaken in law firms and the professional groups that will undertake that work. Professor Richard Susskind, who has thought about this more than anyone in the United Kingdom, writes:

The emerging consensus is that traditional lawyers will still be needed for complex legal work in tomorrow's legal world but that routine, repetitive, process-based, and administrative work will be conducted through a variety of alternative sources—for example, by legal process outsourcing, near-shoring, off-shoring, sub-contracting to lower cost law firms, and so forth. When work is packaged and tackled in this way, new roles for legal professionals will emerge—the legal knowledge engineer, the legal process analyst, the legal project manager, and the legal risk manager, for instance.[6]

9.8 Non-legally qualified providers of legal services

9.8.1 Lay advisers/advocates

In addition to the formally qualified, there are substantial numbers of people who have not obtained legal qualifications, but who nevertheless deliver legal services. These include: the lay advisers who work in advice agencies, such as the Citizens' Advice Bureaux; welfare rights workers, often employed in local authority sponsored

---

[6] Extract from Susskind, R., *Provocations and Perspectives*, Briefing Paper 3/2012, paper submitted to the UK CLE Research Consortium (Legal Education and Training Review), October 2012, available at letr.org. uk/briefing-and-discussion-papers/index.html.

welfare rights offices; housing-aid workers working in housing advice centres; and many other lay advice workers working in a vast range of social, environmental, and other agencies.

9.8.2 Law Centres

One particular context in which the professionally qualified lawyer and the lay adviser come together is the Law Centre. The Law Centre movement started in the 1970s with the specific objective of targeting legal services to those who lived in deprived areas, principally in towns and cities. Historically, they have had a somewhat hand-to-mouth existence. Some have been funded by local authorities; others by private charities; one or two by central government. Agencies that satisfy standards set by the Legal Aid Agency are also able to obtain legal aid funding for defined categories of work (*see Chapter 10*).

9.8.3 Membership services

A number of membership organizations also provide legal services to their members. These services may either be general or related to the matters that arise from membership. Examples at the more general end of provision are the legal services provided as the result of membership of trade unions or other professional groups (e.g. the Medical Defence Union); more specific legal services are provided to members of, for example, the Automobile Association or the Royal Automobile Club.

9.8.4 Specialist agencies

A number of pressure groups also provide legal services. One motivation for this is to find appropriate test cases that might be brought to test the boundaries of statutory provisions. Examples include the Citizens' Rights Office, which is attached to the Child Poverty Action Group; the Public Law Project; Liberty (formerly the National Council for Civil Liberties); Shelter; and a number of environmental groups, such as Greenpeace. These agencies have been particularly successful in expanding the range of groups entitled to make representations to the courts in judicial review cases.

9.8.5 Claims management companies

Claims management companies emerged in the early 2000s, taking advantage of the possibility of claimants bringing actions on a conditional fee basis, often known as 'no win, no fee' (*see 10.4.4*). A regulatory regime was introduced in 2006, designed to ensure that non-lawyers who offered such services were authorized to do this work, and adhered to specified rules of conduct (*see Box 9.6*). There were many criticisms that such firms used intrusive marketing techniques, including unsolicited phone calls, and more recently unsolicited text messages.

Box 9.6 Legal system explained

Regulation of claims management

Under the Compensation Act 2006, persons providing a regulated claims management service must be authorized. The regulation applies to claims made for compensation in relation to personal injury, criminal injuries compensation, industrial injuries disablement benefit, employment matters, housing disrepair, and financial products and services.

Those who are already regulated (e.g. by being a solicitor, or under financial services legislation) are exempt from these requirements, as are certain other categories of persons or organizations, including charities, not-for-profit advice agencies, and some trade unions. The Act makes it an offence to operate without authorization, unless exempted. Detailed rules can be found in the Conduct of Authorised Persons Rules 2013 made by the Claims Management Regulator.

The following services are covered:

(1) advertising for, or otherwise seeking out (e.g. by canvassing or direct marketing), persons who may have a cause of action;
(2) advising a claimant or potential claimant in relation to his claim or cause of action;
(3) referring details of a claim or claimant, or a cause of action or potential claimant, to another person, including a person having the right to conduct litigation (but not if it is not undertaken for or in expectation of a fee, gain, or reward);
(4) investigating, or commissioning the investigation of, the circumstances, merits, or foundation of a claim, with a view to the use of the results in pursuing the claim;
(5) representation of a claimant (whether in writing or orally, and regardless of the tribunal, body, or person to or before which or whom the representation is made).

Among the requirements of the rules of conduct are:

(1) Cold calling in person is prohibited; other cold calling must be in accordance with industry codes.
(2) Referral fees paid must be disclosed.
(3) Certain information must be given to clients before they sign a contract.
(4) There is a 14-day cooling-off period after a contract has been signed.
(5) Where a contract is cancelled, any cancellation fee must be reasonable in the circumstances and reflect work done.
(6) There must be an internal complaints procedure.
(7) Where client money is held it must be held in client accounts that meet stipulated standards.

A team within the Ministry of Justice is currently responsible for regulating claims management companies. It issues annual reports on its work and other industry bulletins. Proposals to reform the regulation of CMCs are outlined at *9.4.3.3*.

Source: See generally www.gov.uk/government/groups/claims-management-regulator.

More recently, there were serious criticisms, where personal injury cases were involved, that the business model used by many of these companies relied on the payment of referral fees by, for example, firms of solicitors, insurance companies, or (in the case of motor accidents) garages who—for a fee—would receive the details obtained by the claims managers. In April 2013, referral fees in personal injury cases were outlawed. The latest information from the Ministry of Justice Claims Regulation Team suggests that a substantial number of claims management companies have gone out of business as a result of this ban.

9.9 Adjudicators and dispute resolvers

Much has been written about judges in the English legal system. As with other topics in this book, most accounts focus on a rather narrow body of the judiciary, namely those who sit in the High Court, Court of Appeal, and Supreme Court. There can be no doubting the influence of the judges who sit in these higher courts in shaping English law. But the chances of any member of the public appearing before one of these judges are remote in the extreme. Far more likely is an encounter with a district judge, a lay magistrate, a tribunal judge, a circuit judge, or one of the army of other dispute resolvers and complaints handlers that now exist. It is these adjudicators or dispute resolvers who are, in practice, the face of the judiciary, as seen by the public at large.

9.9.1 Definition

For the purposes of this book, adjudicators and dispute resolvers are all those who are empowered[7] to resolve disputes that have been brought to them. This definition includes all the senior judicial figures who sit in the High Court and other higher courts just mentioned. But it also includes:

(1) *circuit judges*, who determine civil cases in the county court, and criminal cases in the Crown Court;

(2) *district judges*, who determine civil cases, including small claims hearings, in the county court;

(3) *recorders*, who are, in effect, circuit judges in training;

(4) *magistrates*, both lay and professionally qualified,[8] who determine the vast majority of criminal cases that are dealt with in magistrates' courts;

(5) *arbitrators*, who determine a wide range of disputes referred to them under specially agreed arbitration agreements. Arbitrators are particularly used to resolve commercial disputes, both national and international;

---

[7] This definition could include those who determine disputes under purely private contractual arrangements, for example internal employment dispute resolution procedures or student disciplinary procedures, but they are not considered here.

[8] They are called *district judges (magistrates' courts) (see Box 5.11)*.

(6) *tribunal members and judges*, who deal with specific issues arising in defined legislative contexts: for example, disputes about entitlement to social security benefit, or disputes about employment matters;

(7) *ombudsmen*, as they appear in their various guises; and

(8) *mediators*, conciliators, complaints handlers, and others who offer alternative forms of appropriate dispute resolution (ADR).

9.9.2 Numbers

It is not possible to give a definite number for the people holding the various kinds of adjudicative office just listed. There are around 3,500 judicial office-holders, some 21,500 lay magistrates, and around 20,000 full- and part-time tribunal judges and members. The numbers in the other categories listed in *9.9.1* are not available. But it is a large total, going far beyond the numbers of people working in the courts.

9.9.3 Judicial independence and impartiality

The importance of judicial independence was considered earlier (*see Box 3.11*). An equally important practical consideration is the importance of judges and adjudicators being impartial. There have been cases where it is suggested that there may be judicial bias, in the sense that a judge may have some direct personal interest in the outcome of a particular case.[9] However, in general, the impartiality of the judiciary in England and Wales is largely taken for granted. Instances of judicial corruption familiar in some other countries do not seem to be a significant problem here.

9.9.4 Literature on the judiciary

With few exceptions, books about the judiciary have not in any strict sense been social scientific works. Drawing inferences about how judges think and thus come to decisions simply from the skewed sample of their work represented by reported decisions in the law reports is a wholly inadequate basis for serious analysis of how judges approach the judicial task.[10] Further, it is all too easy to assume that because someone is white, male, middle-aged, and public school- and Oxbridge-educated, he (less frequently she) brings attitudes to his (or her) judicial work that affect his (or her) decisions. Such links are not provable without detailed empirical study that has only rarely been taken into the judiciary.[11] There has, of course, been a problem, in that researchers who have sought access to the judiciary in order to conduct research into it have on occasion found such access difficult to obtain.

---

[9] A case where bias was found to exist is *R v Bow Street Metropolitan Magistrates ex p Pinochet* [1999] WLR 272, HL. See too *Locabail (UK) v Bayfield* [2000] 1 All ER 65, CA.

[10] Griffith, J. A. G., *The Politics of the Judiciary* (5th edn, London, Fontana, 1997); cf. Hodder-Williams, R., *Judges and Politics in the Contemporary Age* (London, Bowerdean, 1996).

[11] See Paterson, A., *The Law Lords* (London, Macmillan, 1982).

The stereotype of judges as white, male, of middle to late age, and from the (upper) middle class which is broadly, though by no means exclusively, applied to the higher judiciary is changing as a result of the recent emphasis on diversity in making judicial appointments. It is not at all accurate as a descriptor of the totality of judges/adjudicators/dispute resolvers in the vast array of fora that determine the disputes brought to them by ordinary members of the public.

9.9.5 Comment on adjudicators

A number of general points about those who perform dispute resolution functions in the legal system may be made:

- They are not all professionally qualified as lawyers. Some have other professional qualifications, such as accountants, surveyors, or doctors. Many have no specific professional qualification at all. In the same way that many legal services are provided by persons other than professionally qualified lawyers, so too many dispute resolution services are provided by those without legal qualifications.

- Many academic lawyers are embraced by this broader definition. The notion that somehow those with an academic background have no capacity to determine disputes in a fair and proper manner is simply not borne out by the evidence.

- The total number of dispute resolvers is considerably larger than traditional definitions of the judiciary suggest.

- Many appointments are full-time, but many more are part-time.

- Only the highest judiciary hold office 'on good behaviour'—a concept designed to enhance the fundamental independence of the judiciary by guaranteeing their right to remain a judge until the statutory retiring age, so long as they are of good behaviour. Most other groups, particularly part-timers, hold office on terms that can result in their being required to step down before the official retirement age.

- Only a limited number are able to take advantage of the attractive (non-contributory) pensions that are provided by government to full-time members of the judiciary.

- Many judges sit in more than one jurisdiction. For example a tribunal judge may also sit as a part-time district judge, thereby enabling him or her to acquire wider judicial experience. The Tribunals, Courts and Enforcement Act 2007 is encouraging even greater flexibility, which has enabled the Judicial Appointments Commission to develop the notion of a judicial career (*see 4.2.5*).

- Many judges now start to sit in their early forties, some even in their thirties. They are much younger than popular images of judges may suggest.

- There are more women holding judicial office than is often appreciated, though the numbers at the highest levels are still far too low. The numbers from ethnic minorities are significantly less impressive.

- Most judicial appointees now receive at least some training for the job through the Judicial College (*see 4.2.4.1*), though the amount of training decreases with the seniority of the post.

- There is still only a limited amount of monitoring of judicial performance. Such monitoring as does take place tends to be limited to performance by part-timers, and is often undertaken by those in full-time office. While too heavy monitoring could compromise judicial independence, certain factors, for example the ability to be civil to those appearing before them or to deliver written decisions within agreed timescales, would not seem impossible targets for assessment.

- There is a huge amount of procedural variation as between each of the adjudicative systems. The formal courts operate within a very detailed procedural framework, with a large number of rules of practice supplemented by yet more practice directions and protocols. Many other bodies have only the barest procedural outline prescribed by law, and instead operate with considerable discretion as regards procedural matters.

- By no means all tribunals operate on the basis that their 'typical' adjudication will involve a formal hearing of the parties. Many reach determinations on the basis of information presented in written form alone.

- While it is usual for tribunals that hold hearings to sit in public, in the sense that members of the public are entitled to attend hearings should they so wish, many do not, particularly where sensitive personal or financial information is being discussed.

- The dress of the judiciary is also much more varied than is often realized. The highly formalized process of the High Court, with impressive uniforms, dark wooden panelling, and advocates in wigs and gowns—the image of the television or film drama—is a statistical rarity. The vast majority of dispute resolvers operate with none of these formal trappings.

- Dispute resolvers work in a wide variety of locations. Many sit in court buildings or other specially dedicated accommodation. But there are many examples of adjudicative bodies sitting in local authority accommodation, or in hotels, or even on occasion in people's homes.

If one takes this broader view, it is seen that there is considerably more variety and flexibility of approach to dispute resolution than is often realized. Different procedures and practices have been developed to meet the specific needs of particular bodies.

9.10 The legal academics

Law claims to be a learned profession. Thus, a third group, delivering a rather different kind of legal service and one not given adequate recognition, should be noted, namely the legal academics and their work. Law teachers in the university law departments and in other locations where legal education is provided have a variety of functions. It is they who are responsible for the foundational stages in the professional formation of those qualified to deliver legal services.

First, law teachers provide basic education in law and legal principles, which provides new generations of lawyers with the fundamental intellectual tools to enable them to become lawyers. The leading university law schools also offer, through their law degrees, a traditional liberal university education, aiming to give students the capacity to think critically about law and its impact on society.

Secondly, law teachers deliver a wide range of professionally focused courses that transform the recent graduate from the preliminary academic stage to a person with the skills required to enter the world of practice. Some of these courses are offered within university law departments, but other providers, including the University of Law, and other private companies play a significant part in this market as well.

Thirdly, the law schools together with the private providers offer much of the advanced training in new developments in the law that is needed by legal practitioners to enable them to keep abreast of developments in the law and to break into new areas of law.

Lastly, law teachers—particularly those who work in the leading research universities—assist in the development of law and the legal system through the research they undertake, the books and articles they write, and the advice they give to governments and other agencies. The scope of legal scholarship has expanded enormously in recent years, again reflecting the growing complexity of the law, not only domestic law but also law coming from Europe and elsewhere. The impact of legal scholarship on practitioners is hard to gauge. Certainly the old rule that only dead authors could be cited in court has long been abandoned. Advocates now often refer to academic articles and books in their submissions, and in many reported cases the judgments adopt (or reject) the analyses of legal scholars. But this is the tip of the iceberg. Many practitioners developing a legal argument, or simply struggling to understand a particular legal doctrine, turn to the textbook writers for assistance. The importance of the work of the legal scholars in helping to shape legal arguments should not be underestimated. Their work is also central to the work of the law reform agencies, particularly the Law Commission.

A number of areas of practice that have developed in recent years have been the result of a combination of the work of legal scholars who helped to shape the areas and the practitioners who put them into practice. Examples include: the development of administrative law that arose from analysis of the principles of judicial review; the development of family law; and the law of restitution. A number of more specialist areas including private and public international law, housing law, and social welfare law have similarly been shaped by important academic contributions.

Notwithstanding these observations, there has been a surprising and disappointing reluctance by legal academics to get involved in the scholarly analysis of legal practice and procedure. Thus while endless books and articles are published offering systematic expositions and analyses of substantive law, it has been left to a very small number of legal scholars to focus on the questions of practice and procedure that are the life-blood of most legal practice, an understanding of which is essential to understanding law and the legal system.

In addition, alongside what is sometimes described as 'black-letter' legal research, focusing on the detailed analysis of legal doctrine, there has emerged over the last 25 years an increasingly rich body of 'socio-legal' scholarship, in which the law is analysed in an inter-disciplinary context, employing insights and methodologies from other social sciences, such as economics, social psychology, politics, and sociology. Much of this research is empirical in nature, and much has involved research into the practice of law. A number of areas of government legal policy have been significantly influenced by the outcomes of socio-legal research.[12]

9.11 Access to the legal profession—becoming a lawyer

Over the last 40 years, the legal profession became a largely graduate one. In the old days, professional qualifications could be obtained simply by apprenticeship in a solicitor's office or a barrister's chambers (and the passing of some not very demanding professional exams). Access to these opportunities often did not depend on formal, meritocratic selection processes, but on who you (or your family) knew. You also had to be able to pay the premium required by practitioners for taking on articled clerks/pupil barristers. These days are now long gone.

The massive expansion of university law schools over the last 40 years has opened up the opportunity for large numbers of young people to start the process of becoming lawyers. In addition, many of the graduates who enter the legal profession come with degrees other than in law. They obtain their legal qualifications through conversion courses undertaken following the obtaining of a first degree in another discipline. (This has been the subject of fierce argument between the legal professional bodies and the legal academics, the latter asserting that only the grounding of a good law degree gives potential entrants to the legal profession a real understanding of how law is made and fundamental legal principles.)

Two recent developments suggest that this may change. First, the huge increase in the costs of obtaining a university degree is making an alternative approach to obtaining a professional legal qualification by becoming a Chartered Legal Executive—where it is possible to earn while you learn—somewhat more attractive. Second, the present government is keen to promote apprenticeships. There are indications that at least a small number of entrants to the legal profession will come through the legal executive/apprenticeship routes.

The fact that law is now a largely graduate profession has been very important in enabling many, particularly women, to become lawyers. Nevertheless, the extent to

---

[12] The importance of investing in empirical research in law was reasserted in the Nuffield Foundation report, Genn, H., Partington, M., and Wheeler, S., *Law in the Real World: Improving Our Understanding of How Law Works* (London, Nuffield Foundation, 2006).

which people from different *class* backgrounds have been able to take advantage of these developments has not been as great as many would wish.[13] A number of initiatives have been designed to encourage potential students from less privileged backgrounds to contemplate university in general and the study of law in particular. For example:

- The Sutton Trust, founded in 1997 by Sir Peter Lampl, has for many years offered children from non-privileged backgrounds places on summer schools, designed to introduce them to university study.

- The Sutton Trust and the Legal Education Foundation (formerly College of Law) offer a *Pathways to Law* programme, run in partnership with 12 Russell Group universities supported by over 30 leading law firms. Some 300 places a year are on offer.

- The Social Mobility Foundation has, since 2005, been developing ways to support Year 12 school students in their university and professional choices. The Foundation works with law firms to provide internships. It also provides mentoring in association with the Diversity and Community Relations Judges, a group of volunteer judges from different parts of the country who work with schools and community groups to provide insight into the legal system and its workings.

- More generally, the judiciary have for a number of years encouraged school students to visit courts and have offered to visit schools.

- The Bar Council has taken a number of steps to promote the message that the Bar is open to anyone with the right aptitude and talent to become a barrister.

- The Law Society runs two access schemes offering assistance with legal practice course fees: the bursary scheme and the diversity access scheme.

- New proposals on professional legal education are currently under discussion by the professions. Proposed changes—to be introduced in 2020—are being driven, at least in part, by the desire of the professions to ensure that opportunities to become a lawyer should be open to all.

Despite all these initiatives, there remain concerns that the legal professions are not as open to all-comers as they should be. Recent decisions on the funding of higher education make many fear that opportunities to enter the legal profession may be reducing rather than expanding, with those from better-off backgrounds finding it easier to get started in the legal professions.

It is in this context that the law teachers bear a particular responsibility both to understand what is currently happening to the legal professions and to increase their awareness of the other career options—of which there are many—that should be considered by their students.

---

[13] The issue was considered in Chapter 3 of Alan Milburn's report (2012), see www.cabinetoffice.gov.uk/sites/default/files/resources/IR_FairAccess_acc2.pdf.

9.12 Key points

1. Professionally qualified lawyers work in a wide variety of contexts, including industry, central and local government, and private practices.

2. However, many people without formal legal qualifications also deliver legal services.

3. The holistic approach adopted here is fundamental to an appreciation of the enormous range of people who are engaged in delivering legal services.

4. The historic claim that the legal profession should be entitled to regulate itself has been discredited.

5. There is much more government involvement in the regulation of the legal profession.

6. The focus of the modern regulatory approach is to encourage competition and innovation in the delivery of legal services.

7. It is essential that the independence of the legal professions be maintained.

8. It is also important to remember the ethical requirements that must be adopted by those working as lawyers.

9. The consequences of the enactment of the Legal Services Act 2007 and the creation of the Legal Services Board are still far from clear; but there is enormous change affecting the legal professions.

10. There will be many more changes affecting the legal professions in the years ahead, many of which will come about very rapidly.

11. The holistic approach is also key to understanding the full range of adjudicators and dispute resolvers who work in the English legal system.

12. Legal academics play an important role in the professional formation of the new lawyer (as broadly defined).

13. They need to be fully aware of how the legal professions and legal services are developing and are likely to develop in the years ahead.

9.13 Questions

Use the self-test questions in the Online Resources to test your understanding of the topics covered in this chapter and receive tailored feedback: www.oup.com/uk/partington18_19/.

9.14 Web links

Check the Online Resources for a selection of annotated web links allowing you to easily research topics of particular interest: www.oup.com/uk/partington18_19/.

9.15 Blog items

See Spotlight on the Justice System, at www.martinpartington.com/category/chapter-9-2/.

Suggestions for further reading

ECONOMIDES, K. (ed.), *Ethical Challenges to Legal Education and Conduct* (Oxford, Hart Publishing, 1998)

JOSEPH, M., *The Conveyancing Fraud* (Harmondsworth, Penguin, 1975)

PATERSON, A., *Lawyers and the Public Good: Democracy in Action?* (Cambridge, Cambridge University Press, 2011)

SUSSKIND, R., *Tomorrow's Lawyers: An Introduction to Your Future* (2nd edn, Oxford, Oxford University Press, 2017)

SUSSKIND, R. and Susskind, D., *The Future of the Professions: How Technology Will Transform the Work of Human Experts* (Oxford, Oxford University Press, 2015)

TWINING, W., *Blackstone's Tower: The English Law School* (London, Stevens & Son/Sweet & Maxwell, 1994)

Other suggestions are set out in the Further Reading listed in the **Online Resources**.

10

Funding legal services

10.1 Introduction: funding legal services

Underpinning this book is the claim that law plays a central role in the functioning of our society (*see Chapter 2*). This role will, however, be limited if people potentially affected by law cannot take advantage of the rights and protections it affords. The overall effectiveness of the English legal system depends on services required by the public actually being available. Thus the final issue considered in this book is how legal services provided to the public can be paid for.

Implicit in *Chapter 9*, where the distinction between lawyers' services and legal services was drawn, is the fact that funding for legal services in the broad sense is provided in a variety of ways. Some services are paid for by clients themselves; others are provided free or at low cost from central or local government grants; some are provided free (pro bono) by the legal profession (*see 9.5.4.1*); others are paid for through membership of organizations such as trade unions or other professional organizations. Yet other services are funded by insurance companies out of premiums paid by their customers. There is a complex mosaic of funding streams for legal services in the broad sense used in *Chapter 9*.

This chapter does not consider the funding of legal services for the corporate sector or for wealthy individuals. For present purposes it is assumed that they can afford the services they require. This chapter concentrates on how legal services, in particular litigation, to the less well-off and the poor are paid for.

It is in this specific context that there is currently great upheaval and uncertainty. There is general agreement that going to court is too expensive; much less agreement on how policy on the funding of litigation should develop and whether there should be greater use of alternatives to litigation.

Currently the legal aid scheme and the bases on which civil litigation are funded are both experiencing major reform. When combined with the changes that are happening to the court and tribunal systems (*see Chapters 6 and 8*) and the legal profession (*see Chapter 9*), it is hard to offer a definitive account of their overall effect. What this chapter seeks to do is to make you aware of what has been done in the recent past and what is likely to develop in the future.

The discussion is in four sections:

- The first looks at the changing shape of *publicly* funded legal services.
- The second considers developments relating to the control of costs.

- The third looks at the *private* funding of litigation and other legal services.
- The fourth considers alternatives to litigation in the courts which could be appropriate for the resolution of disputes but much less costly.

10.2 Publicly funded legal services

10.2.1 The changing face of legal aid

When the modern Welfare State was created after the Second World War, one measure introduced by the then Labour government was the Legal Aid Act 1949. Initially, the scope of the legal aid scheme was limited to *civil legal aid*—the provision of legal representation in proceedings taken in the civil courts.

It subsequently developed to include:

- *criminal legal aid*—funding representation in criminal cases, eventually with a scheme for the provision of legal advice in police stations;
- a *'green form scheme'* designed to permit the provision by lawyers of legal advice and assistance on any matter of English law; and
- *'assistance by way of representation'* (ABWOR), which permitted in a limited number of circumstances the lawyer to extend assistance under the green form scheme to the provision of some representation.

Despite these developments, policy on legal aid was the subject of fierce debate:

- Notwithstanding its potentially wide coverage, in practice civil legal aid was used primarily to fund litigation on matrimonial matters and on personal injuries/accidents. Other areas of social law, for example housing or social welfare provision, were largely ignored by legal aid practitioners.
- The provision of legal aid was subject to means-testing—it went only to those falling below certain income and capital limits. When the first Legal Aid Act was passed it was estimated that nearly 70 per cent of the population was potentially entitled to legal aid. However, as the costs of legal aid increased, successive governments made the means tests meaner; the percentage of the population covered was severely reduced.
- There was no legal aid for proceedings before the majority of the tribunals established to deal with disputes between the citizen and the state (*see Chapter 6*).
- Governments found it hard to control public expenditure on legal aid. It was a 'demand-led' service. Thus, the government was committed to paying for all those cases in which the individual established an entitlement to legal aid.
- Any legal practice could offer to do legal aid work, irrespective of the level of expertise on the issue in question in the firm. This led to concerns about the quality of some of the work undertaken.

Successive governments tried to reform legal aid to deliver a wider range of services to the public, without public expenditure reaching unacceptable levels.

The first changes followed the Legal Aid Act 1988. Administration of the scheme was transferred from the Law Society to a new government agency, the Legal Aid Board. The Board tried to address the problem of quality by establishing a franchising scheme. Firms of solicitors could obtain a franchise only if they passed a special quality audit process. Under the scheme, solicitors were able to obtain a franchise in one or more of ten franchise categories.[1] At that time, some 2,900 firms of solicitors obtained at least one of the available franchises.

In addition, the Legal Aid Board began to test the viability of franchises being awarded to agencies other than solicitors' firms, such as advice agencies and law centres, which might provide legal advice and assistance to the same standards as solicitors' firms.

In 1997, the Legal Aid Board started to award contracts to franchised firms for the provision of defined categories of legal services. Firms with contracts were able to deliver legal services with reduced bureaucracy. Instead of having to submit claims for each item of legally aided work, they were able to deliver their services within the framework of the contract. A number of legal aid services had to be offered on the basis of a fixed fee, rather than the traditional method of charging by the hour.

These measures still did not go far enough. The cost to the state rose, without any significant expansion in the range of services funded by legal aid.[2] The Access to Justice Act 1999, which came into effect in 2000, made further changes. The Legal Aid Board was replaced by a new body—the Legal Services Commission. Legal aid was 'rebranded' as two new services: the *Community Legal Service* (CLS) and the *Criminal Defence Service* (CDS).

Despite these further changes, expenditure on legal aid still continued to rise. Even though the legal aid budget was no longer 'demand-led' but was capped, annual expenditure reached over £2.1 billion, a *per capita* level of expenditure well above that in other advanced countries.[3] In practice, the bulk of legal aid, around £1.2 billion, was spent on criminal legal aid; the rest went on civil legal aid—principally family legal aid.

The Cameron–Clegg Coalition government, seeking to make considerable savings in public expenditure, targeted legal aid for very significant cuts. These were provided for in the Legal Aid, Sentencing and Punishment of Offenders Act (LASPO) 2012.

Under LASPO, which came into force in April 2013, the Legal Services Commission was abolished. Administration of legal aid was transferred to a new Legal Aid Agency within the Ministry of Justice, headed by a specially designated Director of Legal Aid Casework.

---

[1] These included: criminal, family, personal injury, housing, and social welfare. A clinical negligence franchise was developed in February 1999.

[2] Although costs rose by 48 per cent in a six-year period, the numbers of people assisted rose by only 7 per cent. Indeed expenditure on civil and family legal aid rose by 42 per cent while the numbers of people assisted fell by 30 per cent.

[3] See www.justice.gov.uk/downloads/statistics/mojstats/international-legal-aid-comparisons.pdf.

LASPO has two principal features. First, the *scope* of the legal aid scheme, particularly civil legal aid, is seriously restricted (*see 10.2.2.2 and Box 10.3*).

The underlying principle on which LASPO is based is that there should be enough legal aid available to enable the government to meet its obligations under the European Convention on Human Rights, Article 6, which sets out the right to a fair trial. A number of politically sensitive matters are also to be covered by legal aid, in particular the protection of children and cases involving abuse and domestic violence. But apart from these, the citizen should bear the cost of legal advice and assistance, or seek advice that is available free. To mitigate potential hardship, in 2013, a scheme for the funding of exceptional cases was introduced (for a case study, *see Box 10.1*).

Box 10.1 System in action

Case study: exceptional case funding

LASPO provides that legal aid for civil cases can only be funded in statutorily prescribed classes of case (see LASPO section 9 and Schedule 1). However, section 10 of the Act provides that, in exceptional circumstances, civil legal services could be provided where:

(a) ... it is necessary to make the services available to the individual ... because failure to do so would be a breach of—
   (i) the individual's Convention rights (within the meaning of the Human Rights Act 1998), or
   (ii) any rights of the individual to the provision of legal services that are enforceable EU rights, or
(b) ... it is appropriate to do so, in the particular circumstances of the case, having regard to any risk that failure to do so would be such a breach.

The Lord Chancellor was clearly anxious to ensure that the existence of exceptional funding did not create a means for getting round the limitations he sought to impose on the legal aid scheme. Thus, in his initial guidance on exceptional case funding, published in 2013, it was stressed that, in reaching their decisions, case workers should understand that this funding 'is to be used for rare cases' only; 'limited resources' should be focused 'on the highest priority cases'. In relation to cases that might involve breach of Article 6 of the ECHR (right to a fair trial), the guidance stated:

The overarching question to consider is *whether the withholding of legal aid would make the assertion of the claim practically impossible or lead to an obvious unfairness in proceedings.* This is a very high threshold. (original emphasis)

Shortly before Christmas 2014, the Court of Appeal handed down its decision in the case of *Gudanaviciene.* The central issue was: was the Lord Chancellor's guidance lawful? It was argued, in effect, that the terms in which the guidance had been drafted imposed too high a threshold on applicants for exceptional funding, and that therefore the guidance went beyond the words of the Act, and was in consequence unlawful.

Box 10.1 Continued

The Court of Appeal agreed with this argument. In the course of a long judgment, it held, in part, that:

The fact that section 10 is headed 'exceptional cases' and that it provides for an 'exceptional case determination' says nothing about whether there are likely to be few or many such determinations. Exceptionality is not a test. The criteria for deciding whether an ECF determination should or may be made are set out in section 10(3) by reference to the requirements of the Convention and the Charter. In our view, there is nothing in the language of section 10(3) to suggest that exceptional case determinations will only rarely be made.

It therefore concluded that the Lord Chancellor's Guidance was unlawful.

The question for the government was: how to respond to this judgment? There were two options: take a further appeal to the Supreme Court; or reissue the guidance and hope that the revised guidance would comply with the Court of Appeal's interpretation of LASPO.

In the event, the government decided on the latter course. On 9 June 2015, the Lord Chancellor published revised guidance on how exceptional case funding decisions were to be made in future. While those who drafted the revised guidance are still concerned that the provision of exceptional case funding should be kept under control, the 'tone' of the document has softened. Now the emphasis, for case workers taking decisions on these matters, is whether—as the Act says—the provision of such funding is *necessary*.

To read the judgment of the Court of Appeal in the *Gudanaviciene* case, go to www.judiciary.gov.uk/wp-content/uploads/2014/12/gudanavicience-ors-v-dir-of-legal-aid.pdf.

To read the latest (2016) version of the Lord Chancellor's guidance on emergency case funding (non-inquest), go to www.gov.uk/government/uploads/system/uploads/attachment_data/file/477317/legal-aid-chancellor-non-inquests.pdf.

The second important consequence of LASPO is that the fees paid to lawyers, particularly in criminal legal aid, have been considerably reduced.

10.2.2 Civil legal aid

10.2.2.1 The importance of advice

Many people obtain initial advice on legal problems, not by going to see a solicitor, but by visiting one of the over 1,500 Citizens' Advice Bureaux, law centres, and other independent advice agencies that it is estimated exist in England and Wales.

These services often have lawyers or other professionally qualified staff attached to them. Around 6,000 people with a variety of qualifications work in these agencies, supported by nearly 30,000 unpaid volunteers. They deal with over 10 million inquiries each year and receive around £250 million from a wide variety of sources of public funding, from both central and local government.

The services that these agencies offer have developed haphazardly, often in response to specific local initiatives. Coverage throughout England and Wales is patchy. In some areas, there is under-provision, with no effective service at all. In others, there may be a number of agencies offering very similar services, with a consequent waste of scarce resources—both cash and manpower.

The Low Commission (*see Box 10.2*), which was established to consider the shape of legal services that should be provided following LASPO, urged that there should be greater investment in legal advice services, on the basis that good advice can help people solve their problems without resorting to litigation.

Box 10.2 Reform in progress

The Low Commission—responding to LASPO

The Low Commission was a private charitable initiative chaired by Lord Low. In its report, *Tackling the Advice Deficit: A strategy for access to advice and legal support on social welfare law in England and Wales*, published in January 2014, it set out a wide range of proposals for different ways of providing legal services to ordinary people. Their six overarching recommendations were:

• Public legal education should be given higher priority.
• Central and local government should do more to reduce preventable demand (e.g. by requiring the Department for Work and Pensions (DWP) to pay the costs of tribunal hearings where appeals were upheld).
• Courts and tribunals should review how they can operate more efficiently and effectively.
• The next UK government should develop a National Strategy for Advice and Legal Support in England for 2015–20, led by a minister, and preferably with all-party support.
• Local authorities, or groups of local authorities, should co-produce or commission local advice and legal support plans with local not-for-profit and commercial advice agencies.
• The next UK government should establish a ten-year National Advice and Legal Support Fund of £50 million per annum, to be administered by the Big Lottery Fund, to help develop provision of information, advice, and legal support on social welfare law in line with local plans.

The Commission believed that, by investing in a wider range of information and advice, with some legal help and representation, many of the undesirable consequences of LASPO can be avoided and will still save money. Apart from making courts and tribunals more efficient, there is no indication that the current government intends to respond positively to this report.

The full report can be read at www.lag.org.uk/media/147015/low_commission_report_final_version.pdf.

Similar arguments have been made in the 2017 report of the Bach Commission, *Right to Justice*, which is available at www.fabians.org.uk/wp-content/uploads/2017/09/Bach-Commission_Right-to-Justice-Report-WEB.pdf.

10.2.2.2 Scope of civil legal aid

Under early versions of the legal aid scheme, it was possible, at least in theory, to get legal advice and assistance on any matter of English law. This principle is now abandoned. Under LASPO, legal aid resources can be devoted only to those issues that are regarded by government as having sufficient priority to justify the use of public funds, subject to people's means and the merits of the case. The details are set out in Part 2 of Schedule 1 to LASPO (*see Box 10.3*).

Box 10.3 Legal system explained

Services excluded from civil legal aid

Schedule 1 Part 2 of LASPO excludes the following from legal aid funding:

- legal services provided in relation to personal injury or death;
- legal services provided in relation to a claim in tort in respect of negligence;
- legal services provided in relation to a claim in tort in respect of assault, battery, or false imprisonment;
- legal services provided in relation to a claim in tort in respect of trespass to goods, or in respect of trespass to land;
- legal services provided in relation to damage to property;
- legal services provided in relation to defamation or malicious falsehood;
- legal services provided in relation to a claim in tort in respect of breach of statutory duty;
- legal services provided in relation to conveyancing or the making of wills;
- legal services provided in relation to matters of trust law;
- legal services provided in relation to a claim for damages in respect of a breach of Convention rights by a public authority where the claim is made in reliance on section 7 of the Human Rights Act 1998;
- legal services provided in relation to matters of company or partnership law or arising in connection with a business;
- legal services provided in relation to listed social security benefits or in relation to compensation under the Criminal Injuries Compensation Scheme; and
- legal services provided in relation to changing an individual's name.

Source: Summarized from LASPO, Schedule 1 Part 2.

From April 2013, civil legal aid is still routinely available in civil and family cases where people's life or liberty is at stake, or where they are at risk of serious physical harm, or immediate loss of their home. This means, for example, that legal aid is retained for asylum cases, for debt and housing matters where someone's home is at immediate risk, and for mental health cases. It is retained for cases involving domestic violence or forced marriage. And it is retained for cases where people seek judicial review, for some cases involving discrimination that are currently in scope, and for legal assistance to bereaved families in inquests, including deaths of active service personnel. The extremely complex details are set out in Part 1 of Schedule 1 to LASPO (for more detail on family legal aid, see *7.10*).

10.2.2.3 Service levels

To ensure quality, all service providers must obtain a quality mark relevant to the type and level of service they are offering.[4] There are currently six service levels:[5]

- legal help;
- help at court;
- family help;
- help with family mediation (*see 7.10*);
- legal representation; and
- controlled legal representation.

The emphasis is on directing funding away from the provision of representation in court, towards the provision of legal advice services that do not require the use of lawyers in court. Indeed, legal aid also funds a civil legal advice scheme.[6]

10.2.2.4 Means test

Clients entitled to funded services must demonstrate that they are financially eligible—in other words they are subject to a means test.[7] Where applicants fall below a lower income threshold, they pay nothing. If they fall between a lower financial threshold and a higher one, provision of a funded service is subject to the funded client making a financial contribution towards the cost. Income above the higher level means they get no legal aid.

Following LASPO, all civil legal aid applicants, including those on welfare benefits, undergo an assessment of their available capital. Greater account is now taken of the equity in people's homes when assessing their capital means. A minimum £100 contribution to their legal costs has been introduced for all successful applicants with £1,000 or more disposable capital; higher contributions are required from those who are entitled to partial help with their legal costs.

In addition to the means test, where legal proceedings are designed to obtain an award of damages or other financial provision, any award of damages is subject to a 'charge' in favour of the Legal Aid Agency.

10.2.2.5 Merits test

The merits criteria are intended to reflect the kinds of rational judgements that would be made by a reasonable privately-paying person of modest means in deciding whether to bring or continue with litigation.

---

[4] For details, see www.gov.uk/legal-aid-agency-quality-standards.
[5] The details are set out in The Civil Legal Aid (Procedure) Regulations 2012.
[6] See www.gov.uk/civil-legal-advice.
[7] The provision of information and the provision of services for proceedings under the Children Act 1989 are outside this rule. Funding in family cases is discussed in 7.10.

Under the regulations, the merits criteria are divided into two main types: general merits and specific merits. The general merits criteria apply to all cases, save special cases where specific (less strict) merits criteria apply.

The general merits criteria comprise a number of tests to establish the merits of a case to be publicly funded. For example, where an applicant is seeking legal aid for full representation in court, the application is subject to a *prospects of success* test. Generally this means that the case must have a 50 per cent or more chance of succeeding. Less stringent prospects of success criteria apply to cases with certain features (e.g. cases with an overwhelming importance to the individual, cases which are of significant wider public interest, or cases where the substance of the claim relates to a breach of Human Rights Convention rights).

As noted, the specific merits criteria are generally less stringent than the general merits criteria. Some of the specific merits criteria consist of additional tests to ensure funding is targeted on appropriate cases. Others are tailored to specific types of case and employ criteria that would not have general application elsewhere. For example, in mental health proceedings the general merits criteria for legal representation do not apply; instead the Director must be satisfied that it would be reasonable in all circumstances for full representation to be available. These are less stringent criteria than the general merits criteria, given the potential consequences of the action for the applicant.

10.2.2.6 Very high cost cases

To prevent a large proportion of the legal aid budget being expended on a relatively small number of very expensive cases, a High Costs Civil Team controls the costs of such cases. Cases likely to exceed £25,000 in costs are referred to the Team. Special arrangements also apply to multi-party actions, where a large number of claimants are claiming loss from a single event or cause.[8]

10.2.2.7 Alternative dispute resolution

Alternative dispute resolution (*see 8.5* and *10.5.4*) is funded where this may be more effective than court proceedings. Where ombudsman schemes or complaints procedures or (*see 6.4.6, 6.4.7*)—which are generally free—are available that might be appropriate to resolve the problem in question, legal aid funding is not considered until these have been exhausted.

10.2.3 Criminal legal aid

The Criminal Legal Aid scheme comprises four principal elements:

(1) the provision of advice services in police stations and magistrates' courts through contracts with private-practice solicitors' firms operating through nationally provided duty solicitor schemes;

---

[8] More detail is at www.gov.uk/legal-aid-high-cost-cases.

(2) the provision of legal advice and representation in cases that go to court;

(3) the management of individual case contracts with defence teams for very high cost criminal cases; and

(4) the provision of services directly to the public through the Public Defender Service (PDS) (*see Box 10.4*).

Box 10.4 Legal system explained

The Public Defender Service

The Public Defender Service (PDS) was established in 2001 to offer an alternative to solicitors in private criminal legal aid practice. The service now operates out of four centres: Cheltenham, Darlington, Pontypridd, and Swansea. These offices operate as solicitors' firms but the staff are employed by the Legal Aid Agency, rather than paid fees by the Agency.

In 2014, the scope of the PDS was expanded by the creation of *PDS Advocates*, described as:

a team of 25 barristers and higher courts advocates including seven Queen's Counsel with experience at every level of the criminal justice system [providing] . . . independent, high quality, professional advice and representation to accused persons throughout England and Wales.

Amongst [the] team [are] advocates who specialise in murder, fraud, historic and serious sexual offences, terrorism and Very High Cost Criminal Cases.

[The team] can be instructed to carry out work by any solicitors looking for representation for their clients in the Higher Courts of England and Wales [and] are able to operate nationally.

This development occurred at a time when barristers were in significant conflict with the Ministry of Justice over rates of pay for criminal legal aid work and appears to have been a response to barristers refusing to take on some serious criminal trials.

For further details on the PDS go to publicdefenderservice.org.uk/.

By comparison with civil legal aid, the *scope* of criminal legal aid emerges from LASPO relatively unscathed. Criminal legal aid is retained for those criminal cases where it is currently available, in order to ensure that those accused of more serious criminal offences can access the representation required to provide a fair trial.

However, major changes have been made to the amounts that lawyers are paid. These include paying the same fee in respect of a guilty plea in the Crown Court regardless of the stage at which the plea is entered. In Crown Court cases that could realistically have been dealt with in the magistrates' court, a single fixed fee for a guilty plea is paid, based on fee rates in the magistrates' court. This complements other changes to the criminal justice system designed to encourage cases to be brought quickly and efficiently, thereby saving significant but avoidable costs. More generally there have been significant cuts in the rates of pay for criminal legal aid cases.

To contain the growth in costs of Very High Cost Criminal Cases (VHCCCs), the arrangements for solicitors in VHCCCs have been brought into line with those the previous government introduced for advocates. This means that more of these cases are paid within a graduated fee scheme where costs are more easily controlled.

In 2015, the government consulted on plans to introduce a panel scheme, whereby all publicly funded criminal defence advocacy in the Crown Court and above would be undertaken by advocates who are members of this panel. Membership of the panel would, it was hoped, reflect an assessment of the advocate's ability to conduct such litigation. However, these proposals are not currently being taken forward.

10.2.4 Legal aid: impact of LASPO

The impact of LASPO on the amount and cost of legal aid work is shown in quarterly statistical bulletins published by the Ministry of Justice (*see Box 10.5*).

Box 10.5 Reform in progress

The impact of LASPO; Legal Aid Agency Quarterly Statistics

The statistical bulletin for April–June 2017 shows that:

Criminal legal aid

Both workload and expenditure on *crime lower* (cases in the magistrates' courts, police stations, and prisons) have declined since the introduction of LASPO.
In *crime higher*, workload and expenditure on cases in the Crown Court also declined. (Much of this reduction is due to fewer cases being in the criminal justice system.)

Civil legal aid

The implementation of the LASPO Act in April 2013 led to large reductions in *legal help* workload and expenditure. Levels are now roughly one-third of pre-LASPO levels, though there is a continuing decline in both workload and expenditure.
Workloads in *civil representation* fell by a smaller proportion than legal help follow-ing the implementation of LASPO, and stabilized at around two-thirds of pre-LASPO levels. The number of certificates granted in April–June 2017 was actually 10 per cent higher compared to the same period of the previous year.
After sharp falls following LASPO, the number of *mediation* assessments rose in 2015, but has since fallen back.

Exceptional case funding (ECF)

In April–June 2017, 533 applications for ECF were made, of which 57 per cent were granted—the highest number since the scheme started in 2013.

Providers of legal aid

The Statistical Bulletin for January–March 2017 also shows that in the five years from April 2012 to April 2017, there was a significant fall in the number of provider offices for both crime and civil work. The fall was greater for civil (around a fifth) than for crime

Box 10.5 Continued

(down about 10 per cent) over this period. In the last year there was a 9 per cent fall in the number of civil providers and a 10 per cent reduction in crime providers.

Such figures would have led the former Legal Services Commission to ask itself whether there were enough providers in the system to provide a nationally based service, and if not, what might be done to arrest the decline.

Such questions are not raised by the Legal Aid Agency. Indeed, it is possible for the Agency to argue that, as there are still good numbers of providers applying for the various tenders for work that the Agency offers, there are still providers willing to do the work, and that therefore there is no problem. The Agency can still also argue that, by comparison with most other countries, per capita spending on legal aid services remains relatively generous.

What is missing from this analysis, however, is any consideration of the age profile of legal aid providers. It may plausibly be hypothesized that many legal aid providers have been doing the work for many years, remain committed to it, and will continue to do it as long as they can. But if no or only very little new blood is coming into the legal aid sector of the legal profession, then the medium to long-term future of the sector must be in some doubt. Such doubts will be reinforced by the continued cutting of the legal aid budget—which seems to be irreversible for the foreseeable future.

At the time of writing (November 2017) the government has announced that it will be undertaking a review of LASPO. It is still the case, however, that legal aid accounts for about 25 per cent of the total annual expenditure of the Lord Chancellor's Department. Major reversals of legal aid policy seem unlikely in the short term.

Source: www.gov.uk/government/collections/legal-aid-statistics which provides links to the quarterly bulletins.

Some of the service innovations introduced by the former Legal Services Commission have been retained. For example, it is already clear that telephone advice services will be extended to help people find ways to resolve their problems. Indeed, certain legal aid services can only be accessed through a telephone 'gateway'. The gateway is delivered by the Civil Legal Advice (CLA) advice helpline for England and Wales, paid for by legal aid. It provides, for people who qualify for civil legal aid, specialist legal advice, primarily by telephone, online, and by post, in relation to:

- debt;
- discrimination;
- special educational needs;
- housing; and
- family issues.

Clients who qualify for legal aid in the first three gateway categories listed above must usually receive any advice remotely. Clients who qualify in the other two categories of law have a choice about whether to receive any advice remotely or via a face-to-face provider.

Disappointingly, some of the more imaginative ideas developed by the Commission have been abandoned. In particular, I regret the abandonment of the pilots for new models for the delivery of legal assistance through Community Legal Advice Centres (CLACS) and Community Legal Advice Networks (CLANS). Research had shown that many people do not have single problems, but clusters of problems. The intention of the Advice Centres and Networks was that those requiring advice should, wherever possible, be able to obtain it from a single point of contact, rather than having to go to a number of different advice agencies. This was a very sensible approach, ended by the cuts.

The cuts raise more fundamental questions (such as those raised by the Low Commission). Have the ways in which legal advice and assistance been delivered in the past—with their emphasis on face-to-face meetings in offices—been as economically efficient as they could be? Cannot modern communication technologies be used more imaginatively to give legal advice to those who need it? Are the adversarial procedures currently used for determining particular types of dispute the best that can be devised? Are courts needed for all the processes that they currently undertake? Are there ways in which members of the public can be assisted to help themselves? How can we improve public legal education?

There are no easy answers to these and other questions that may be raised about the potential impact of cuts in legal aid expenditure. What may be asserted, however, is that the cuts should be a stimulus to thinking about new ways of delivering legal services to ordinary people. It is in this context that the future becomes very hard to predict. Re-engineering the ways in which the courts operate (*see Chapter 8*) and in which the legal (and related) professions organize themselves, following the Legal Services Act 2007 (*see Chapter 9*), is likely to combine with new rules relating to the funding of legal work, in particular litigation, to lead to types of legal service delivery quite different from what has been on offer in recent years.

10.3 Controlling costs

Changes to legal aid cannot be seen in isolation. It is important to note other ideas. Here we briefly consider recent developments relating to controlling the costs of litigation.

10.3.1 Controlling costs: the Woolf approach

As noted in *Chapter 8*, Lord Woolf saw reducing the costs of taking a case to court as a key objective in the reforms that he was proposing. There were two principal ways in which he envisaged that this objective might be achieved: making costs proportionate, and active case management.

10.3.1.1 Making costs proportionate

Before the Woolf reforms were introduced, the basic principle used to determine disputes about costs was that those charging the costs had to demonstrate that the costs they incurred were reasonable. Following the introduction of the Civil Procedure Rules (CPR), this principle was amended. The costs must be both reasonable *and* proportionate to the issue in dispute.[9] In cases where relatively small sums of money are involved, it might well be reasonable for a number of legal steps to be taken in preparing the case, but if the cost of taking those steps was substantial, the total costs, while reasonable, might still not be proportionate. A judge would therefore be required to disallow costs that, though reasonable, were not proportionate. The difficulties with this principle are obvious. What is reasonable? And what is proportionate?

10.3.1.2 Active case management

A second principle advanced by Lord Woolf and contained in the CPR is active judicial case management. This was designed to ensure that cases were dealt with more quickly. By preventing proceedings from dragging on, it was thought that the cost of litigation could be reduced. The problem here is that this objective is, to a significant extent, in conflict with other changes introduced in the CPR. Since the CPR also stresses the need for parties to put their cards on the negotiating table earlier than they used to, this means that cases which, prior to the introduction of the Woolf reforms, would have settled well before any trial was likely to take place, now require more work to be done at an early stage. This leads to a 'front-loading' of expense, which increases the costs of such cases.

10.3.2 Controlling costs: the Jackson approach

While there was broad support for the Woolf reforms, there was considerable evidence that the goal of cost reduction had not been achieved. In 2009, a new inquiry into the cost of civil litigation, led by the Court of Appeal judge Sir Rupert Jackson, was launched. The review was sponsored by the senior judiciary, who were particularly concerned about the impact of costs on access to justice. His final report was published in January 2010 (for some of the main findings, *see Box 10.6*).

Box 10.6 Reform in progress

The Jackson Review of the cost of civil proceedings

The report is extremely detailed and hard to summarize. The principal points he made were:

(1) *The importance of proportionality.* The costs system should be based on legal expenses that reflect the nature/complexity of the case. (Of course, the challenge remains of how proportionality is to be decided in particular cases.)

(2) *Greater use of fixed recoverable costs.* He proposed that the current regime of fixed recoverable costs should be considerably extended so that they should be set for all 'fast track' cases (those with a claim up to £25,000) to provide greater certainty.

(3) *Establishment of a Costs Council.* This would review annually fixed costs and lawyers' hourly rates, to ensure that they are fair to both lawyers and clients.

---

[9] The details are set out in CPR Part 44—general rules about costs.

Box 10.6 Continued

(4) *Changes to the conditional fees agreement (CFA) regime.*

(5) *Increasing general damages for personal injuries and other civil wrongs by 10 per cent.* This was to offset the effects of his proposed changes to CFAs for claimants.

(6) *'Qualified one way costs shifting'.* This would create an exception to the normal rule that the loser of an action pays the costs of the winner. Under his proposals, claimants whose claims are unsuccessful would only make a small contribution to defendant costs (as long as they had behaved reasonably). This would remove the need for them to purchase after the event insurance.

(7) *Scrapping of referral fees.* These are fees paid by lawyers to organizations that 'sell' damages claims to them but offer no real value to the process (apart from making the referrer better off).

(8) *Introduction of contingency fee agreements.* Jackson wanted lawyers to be able to enter into contingency fee agreements (as opposed to CFAs), under which, if a claim is successful, lawyers are paid a percentage of actual damages won, rather than a sum based on the cost of the work undertaken.

(9) *Much greater promotion of 'before the event' legal insurance.* This was to encourage people to take out legal expenses insurance, either on a 'stand-alone' basis or as part of another insurance purchase, such as household insurance.

Jackson argued that his proposed reforms should be seen as a whole and not 'cherry-picked', asserting that they provided a coherent framework whereby parties could enter into litigation with greater certainty about the costs involved. He argued that they would also assist in allowing for some claims to be resolved earlier with greater use of mediation.

Source: Adapted from *Final Report, Review of Civil Litigation Costs*, available at www.judiciary.gov.uk/publications/review-of-civil-litigation-costs/.

10.4 The Jackson Report: policy responses

Despite Lord Justice Jackson's plea that his reform proposals should not be cherry-picked, the government did just that. The following paragraphs set out ways in which the government hoped that the costs of litigation might be reduced, or structured in a way that enables those without significant resources to consider the possibility of asserting legal rights and entitlements through the courts.

10.4.1 Court fees

Before proceeding further, one issue to be considered in this context concerns the more commercial approach to court fees (*see 8.6.2*) which the government has been pursuing as part of its austerity agenda. It must be asked whether the level of fees now being demanded to access the courts is wholly consistent with the desire to control costs, particularly in litigating civil matters. One outcome of the increase in fees has been a reduction in the numbers of cases being brought to courts and tribunals. This poses the question whether increases in fees could actually be counter-productive. Serious falls in the numbers of cases will result in reductions in the income of the Courts and Tribunals Service, rather than the predicted increases.

10.4.2 Fixed recoverable costs (FRC)

One specific method for controlling costs is greater use of fixed costs for bringing cases to court. Jackson thought they were essential. The idea is not new.

During the 1990s, the Civil Justice Council, which advises the government on issues relating to the civil justice system, led a series of discussions with practitioners and the insurance industry to try to make some of the costs, particularly of routine litigation, more predictable. It was accepted, at least initially, that a fixed costs regime would not work in every litigation context. Nonetheless, the Council thought it right to explore whether there were situations in which fixed costs would be reasonable.

This led, in 2003, to the creation of a scheme for the use of fixed costs in relation to claims arising out of road traffic accidents for less than £10,000. These applied where liability for the accident was admitted, and where the only issue was the exact amount to be paid to settle the claim.

Lord Justice Jackson recommended that FRC be introduced for all fast track cases. The government did not go that far. But it amended the Civil Procedure protocols so that, from the end of July 2013, three classes of personal injury claims, for less than £25,000, where liability is admitted, must use a defined procedure which includes fixed costs. The classes of case are: those arising from road traffic accidents; those arising where employer's liability is involved; those arising where the liability of public bodies (e.g. local authorities) is involved. All such cases must be started online, using the Claims Portal.[10]

Jackson did not give up on the issue, and delivered a number of speeches, after he published his report, arguing for much greater use of FRC. His persistence was rewarded, when, in November 2016, he was asked to re-examine the issue. He published a supplementary report on the issue in the summer of 2017. (*See Box 10.7.*)

Box 10.7 Reform in progress

Lord Justice Jackson's Supplementary Report on Civil Litigation Costs

Jackson argues (as indeed he did in his first report) that there are two fundamental ways to prevent runaway costs:

(i) a general scheme of fixed recoverable costs (FRC), i.e. those costs that the winning party can claim from the losing party;

(ii) imposing a budget for each individual case ('costs budgeting')

---

[10] See www.claimsportal.org.uk/en/.

Box 10.7 Continued

In his Supplementary Report, Jackson makes the following recommendations:

1. FRC should be introduced for all fast track cases. The amount of costs which are recoverable would be laid out in a grid. Different sums would be permitted for different stages of proceedings.

2. Above the fast track, a new 'intermediate' track should be created for certain claims up to £100,000 which can be tried in three days or less, with no more than two expert witnesses giving oral evidence on each side. The intermediate track will have streamlined procedures and its own grid of FRC.

3. Clinical negligence claims are often of low financial value, but of huge concern to the individuals on both sides. The complexity of such cases means that they are usually unsuited to either the fast track or the proposed intermediate track. Jackson recommends that the Department of Health and the Civil Justice Council should set up a joint working party with both claimant and defendant representatives to develop a bespoke process for handling clinical negligence claims up to £25,000. That bespoke process should have a grid of FRC attached. This scheme would capture most clinical negligence claims.

4. Jackson states that it is essential that small and medium-sized enterprises should have access to justice. The Federation of Small Businesses argued that there should be an FRC regime for commercial cases up to £250,000; the costs levels must be reasonable; they must balance incentives and 'reduce the costs of going to law for small businesses'; there must be rigorous case management of cases subject to this regime; and there must be investment in modern IT systems to speed up court processes. Jackson did not think that all business cases require FRC up to the level suggested by the Federation. Instead he recommends a voluntary pilot of a 'capped costs' regime for business and property cases up to £250,000, with streamlined procedures and capped recoverable costs up to £80,000. If the pilot were to be successful, the regime could be rolled out more widely for use in appropriate cases.

5. Jackson recommends measures to limit recoverable costs in judicial review claims, by extending the protective costs rules which are currently reserved for environmental cases.

6. In relation to costs management, the budgeting process will continue to apply to proceedings falling outside the scope of FRC. One problem is that costs management cannot currently apply to costs incurred before the costs management process takes place. Jackson thinks that at some point further consideration may need to be given to setting a limit to these incurred costs, but that should not be considered further at this stage.

The response of government to these proposals is not currently available. Any changes would be subject to further consultation.

10.4.3 Abolition of referral fees

Jackson's recommendation on the abolition of referral fees was also taken forward. In personal injuries cases, these were abolished in April 2013 (*see 9.8.5*).

10.4.4 Changes to the rules on conditional fee agreements (CFAs)

CFAs were introduced by the Conservative government in 1990, long before Lord Woolf started his work. A CFA is defined in section 58 of the Courts and Legal Services Act 1990, as amended by section 27(1) of the Access to Justice Act 1999, as 'an agreement ... which provides for ... fees and expenses, or any part of them, to be payable only in specified circumstances'—in effect 'no-win, no-fee'.

The importance of CFAs was significantly increased by the Access to Justice Act 1999. It became a principle that legal aid should not be provided in cases where alternative funding (including CFAs) was available. (CFAs cannot be entered into in relation to criminal and most family proceedings.)

CFAs allow solicitors to take a case on the understanding that, if the case is lost, they will not charge their clients for all or any of the work undertaken. But the client also agrees that if the case is successful, the solicitor can charge a *success fee* on top of the normal fees, to compensate for the risk the solicitor has run of not being paid all or some of her fees in cases that are not successful. The success fee was calculated as a percentage of the normal fees and the level at which the success fee is set reflects the risk involved. Regulations provided that the 'uplift' of the success fee could be no more than 100 per cent of the normal fee.

Until 1999, the success fee was paid out of damages recovered. In 1999, the law was amended so that the success fee had to be paid by the party against whom a costs order has been made (in essence the losing party) in addition to any damages that may have been awarded. The same party also had to pay the costs of any after the event insurance (ATE) premium.

The party who lost an action thus faced the prospect of considerable costs. Since most of those represented under CFA agreements do not have the resources to pay those costs, ATE insurance was designed to cover them. This change to the funding of litigation meant that where a person covered by insurance lost, the insurance company was liable not only to meet the costs of the other side, but also the 'success' fee and the ATE premium.

While CFAs arguably provided a means for enabling people to go to court who might not otherwise have been able to contemplate such a step (and in this sense increased access to justice), they were open to a number of forms of abuse, which were identified by the late Lord Bingham in his judgment in *Callery v Gray* [2002] 1 WLR 2000 at [5], HL:

(1) Lawyers may charge excessive costs knowing that their own client will not have to pay them; the costs burden thus falls quite disproportionately on the losing party. Where that party is an insurance company, this has the effect of forcing up insurance premiums.

(2) Lawyers may set the success fee at a level that is grossly disproportionate to any fair assessment of the risk involved in the case.

(3) Insurers may charge premiums grossly disproportionate to the risk being underwritten.

All these problems were acknowledged by Lord Justice Jackson. He recommended that success fees and after the event insurance premiums should no longer be recoverable from the losing party. He saw them as being the greatest contributor to disproportionate costs.

The government adopted Jackson's recommendations, which were implemented by the Legal Aid, Sentencing and Punishment of Offenders Act 2012. From April 2013, the successful claimant has to pay the lawyer's 'success fee' in CFAs; this is capped at 25 per cent of the damages recovered, excluding damages for future care and loss. This gives the claimant an incentive to control his lawyer's fees.

To compensate for these changes, general damages for non-pecuniary loss (e.g. for pain and suffering) were increased by 10 per cent. The details are in the Court of Appeal's judgment in *Simmons v Castle* [2012] EWCA Civ 1288. The increase applies to cases which settle or where judgment is given after 1 April 2013, unless there is a funding agreement, such as a CFA, which pre-dates 1 April 2013.

10.4.5 Litigation funding agreements

Section 28 of the Access to Justice Act 1999 introduced a new concept, the *litigation funding agreement*. This allows a party to be funded by a third party (rather than the solicitor), for example a trade union or other prescribed group. In these cases the funder pays the solicitor's normal fees. However, where the case was won, the funder was entitled to be paid the success fee by the losing side and was able to retain that element of the fee to cover losses on cases that are not won. As with CFAs, the recoverability of success fees has been capped and the recovery of ATE insurance premiums from the losing side has been prohibited by LASPO.

10.4.6 Damages-based agreements (DBAs)

DBAs under which lawyers may take a percentage of damages awarded—known in other jurisdictions as 'contingency fee agreements'—were also recommended by Jackson. LASPO amended the law to allow lawyers to enter into such agreements. The amount that the lawyer can take from the damages recovered by the winning side to meet her costs is limited in personal injury cases to 25 per cent, excluding damages for future care and loss. In other cases, the limit is set at 50 per cent. (Special rules apply to DBAs used for proceedings before the Employment Tribunal, which had been permitted since 2010.)

Use of DBAs has been very limited because the detailed rules which regulate their use are extremely complex. The Ministry of Justice has drafted proposals for amending the regulations. It was also agreed that the Civil Justice Council should take a specialist look both at the draft revised regulations and wider policy issues. Its report on both these matters was published at the beginning of September 2015.

Revised draft regulations have been published which, when brought into effect, should clear up some of the issues which worried litigators.[11]

---

[11] For more information go to www.martinpartington.com/category/chapter-10-2/ (September 2015) and follow the links.

10.4.7 Qualified one way costs shifting

Following Jackson, a new regime of 'qualified one way costs shifting' has been introduced in personal injury cases, which caps the amount that claimants who lose their case may have to pay to defendants. Claimants who lose, but whose claims are conducted in accordance with the rules, are protected from having to pay the defendant's costs.

10.4.8 Promotion of private before the event legal insurance

Jackson noted that many people have bought before the event legal insurance, often as part of another insurance policy such as household contents insurance or motor insurance. The government does not seem minded to do anything about the recommendation that it should promote legal expenses insurance. This would seem to be a commercial decision for insurance companies to take.

But it is arguable that one of the consequences of cuts to legal aid is that the potential market for private legal expenses insurance has increased and might provide a commercial opportunity for insurance companies. Of course, the very poorest would not be able to take advantage of any new products that insurers may develop, but that should not stop insurers from engaging in the legal expenses insurance market more actively than they currently do.

10.4.9 Proposal for a Costs Council

This was not taken forward by the government.

10.5 Other ideas for meeting the costs of litigation

In addition to Jackson's report and the reforms he promoted, other ideas for finding alternative ways to fund litigation have been developed or considered. I mention three here.

10.5.1 Third party funding

Another idea advanced by the Civil Justice Council is *third party funding*. Here an investor buys the right to conduct litigation on behalf of a claimant or, more usually, a group of claimants. This gives the claimant money without having to await the outcome of an often protracted litigation process. The funder recovers the cost of the investment by taking the case forward and, it hopes, receiving an award of damages greater than the sum it has already paid out, from which it takes an agreed percentage. This process, sometimes called 'claim-farming', has been developing in a number of other jurisdictions, notably in Australia.

The legal services industry itself has taken forward proposals for the third party funding of litigation. An industry group—the Association of Litigation Funders—has devised a code of conduct to which litigation funders must adhere. This is proving to be an important source of finance for major commercial litigation.

Jackson identified a number of concerns in relation to third party funding: for example, funders needed to have an adequate capital base to provide their funding; funders should not be entitled to withdraw funding during the proceedings; the ability of funders to influence litigation and settlement of proceedings should be restricted and defined with clarity. The industry subsequently developed a code of practice which deals, adequately in Jackson's view, with all these matters. See associationoflitigation-funders.com/.

10.5.2 Crowd funding

While third party funding is relevant for large heavyweight commercial litigation, it does not really assist the individual or small litigant. For this sector of the market, a more recent innovation has been the introduction of a scheme for crowd funding litigation. This has been used with some success to fund, on a modest level, cases of social importance, such as environmental issues or social care. Whether this can fill a long-term gap in the funding market remains to be see. But it is an interesting idea. More detail is at www.crowdjustice.co.uk/.

10.5.3 Supplementary Legal Aid?

In 2009, the Civil Justice Council published an important advisory paper urging that consideration be given to a number of ideas for additional funding. Among these was a recommendation for the creation of a *Supplementary Legal Aid Scheme*, based on a model developed in Hong Kong, which provides legal aid to a wider group of people than the current scheme. This requires those who have received assistance from legal aid to pay a levy into the scheme either from the damages they recover or the costs they recover, which can then be used to fund further activity.

A somewhat similar idea has been developed by the Bar Council for a Contingent Legal Aid Fund, under which funds would be provided for advancing a case, and where—if the case was successful—a percentage of damages secured would be returned to the Fund.

Jackson was in favour of this idea, but it is not yet one that has found favour with government.

10.5.4 Re-engineering the system: alternative procedures

So far the discussion has considered ways in which the cost of using courts to resolve disputes might be reduced. This assumes that adversarial proceedings in the courts are the only proper way to resolve disputes. This view needs to be challenged. Already there have been a number of important policy initiatives that have effectively taken the potential for litigation away from the courts and provided an alternative, and much cheaper, procedure for the resolution of disputes.

The most notable example is the Financial Services Ombudsman, which now resolves—at no cost to the complainant—the vast bulk of disputes concerning the private customers of financial institutions, up to a value of £150,000—considerably more than many of the cases that come before the courts.

In a different context, the scheme for tenancy deposit protection established by the Housing Act 2004 offers a free dispute resolution service where landlords and tenants are in dispute about how a tenancy deposit should be divided at the end of a tenancy.

Large numbers of consumer disputes are resolved either by the complaints departments of large companies or through the work of different trade associations representing various providers of goods and services. Some of these bodies are entirely self-regulated; others are underpinned by statute (*see 8.5.2*).

Similarly, mediation as an alternative form of dispute resolution (*see 8.5.1*) has been promoted at least in part on the basis that it offers a less costly way of resolving disputes. Many of the dispute resolution processes, such as tribunals, ombudsmen, and complaints handling, discussed in the context of administrative justice (*see 6.3*) could be adapted for use in the proportionate resolution of private disputes.

The lesson here is that effective ways of avoiding much of the expense of going to court can be achieved by the creation of procedures that take place outside the court context. The common feature of all these alternatives is that they are provided either free or at very low cost for those who seek to use them. The *Transforming Our Justice System* reform programme offers the possibility of new much cheaper processes within the courts' system.

10.6 The response of the legal profession

Clearly there are those in the legal profession who realize that the reduction of costs paid by clients is likely to mean that their income will be reduced. At the same time, many lawyers acknowledge that the cost of many of the legal services currently provided is too expensive. There is evidence that the legal profession is responding to the challenge of the cost of providing legal advice and dispute resolution.

Thus the profession is moving away from its traditional reliance on hourly charge-out rates to offer legal services on a more pre-determined basis. There is market pressure to deliver more for less. It is delivering legal services in new ways, more cost effectively (*see 9.6.2*).

In addition, the pro bono activity of the legal profession should also be mentioned (*see 9.5.4.1*). This has been driven by many lawyers acknowledging that they have done extremely well out of the ways in which legal services are currently delivered. They accept there is a good moral case for them to give something back to the community; this has been promoted by the leaders of the legal profession.

In the same context, it is worth noting that many law-teaching institutions have developed different forms of clinical legal education, which offer legal advice and assistance to members of the public. One of the most long-standing is the Free Representation Unit promoted by young barristers and student barristers. The main professional law course providers, such as the University of Law and BPP, now offer pro bono options, which large numbers of law students participate in. A number of university law schools run law clinics that take in cases from members of the public. In addition, Street Law is a project developed in the United States, but now brought to the United Kingdom, in which law students in a large number of universities offer information about legal rights to community groups and members of the public.

There is still much more to be done to reduce costs and improve efficiency. There is no prospect of replacing the legal aid that has been lost in the last few years. So it will be up to the lawyers and the others who provide legal services, urged on by the demands of the professional regulators (*see Chapter 9*), to develop imaginative alternatives to address the problem of meeting needs for legal services an affordable way.

10.7 Key points

1. Access to justice is essential if the claim to have an efficient legal system is to be sustained. We have seen in this chapter that the availability of legal aid, particularly in civil matters, is currently being seriously cut back.

2. Debate on legal aid was, in the past, dominated to a large extent by the legal profession. The legal aid scheme was largely designed and developed by the Law Society. While there should be no doubt that those who undertook this work were determined to create a scheme that delivered a needed service to the public, it is also the case that the legal profession was the principal beneficiary of it. The injection of over £2 billion of public money into the legal profession was not trivial. The rate of growth of public expenditure in this area—despite rhetorical claims that 'justice is without price'—could not be sustained.

3. Put another way, if policy-makers had started the legal aid scheme from scratch with a budget of over £2 billion, would they have devised the legal aid scheme that eventually developed? Those who accept that the answer to this question is 'no' must then think what the shape of any alternative might be.

4. Civil legal aid, which had been the most innovative area for the development of legal services, has been badly hit. This has already led to a number of suggestions for different ways of delivering legal services on civil legal matters.

5. Although the *scope* of criminal legal aid was left more or less unscathed, the fees payable under the scheme have been significantly cut back.

6. Although legal aid expenditure has fallen (to around £1.5bn) it is still a significant amount, about a quarter of the MoJ's annual expenditure.

7. It looks inevitable that the balance between funding by the state and other private sources of funds will alter.

8. How newly emerging alternative business entities offering legal services will respond to the new environment is, at present, impossible to foretell. However, it is worth noting that there have been many occasions in the past on which lawyers, having failed to preserve some then current practice (e.g. the conveyancing monopoly), have, once they realize that they have lost the argument, responded

in imaginative and unexpected ways to regain ground that would otherwise be lost to other providers.

9. It is likely that there will be much greater use of different forms of insurance to spread the risk of litigation while ensuring that there are income streams available to fund litigation.

10. At the same time, and although this will be resisted fiercely by legal practitioners and the judiciary, there is likely to be much greater emphasis on the individual undertaking dispute resolution without the benefit of professional legal assistance. This can only be achieved if there is continuing support for the provision of legal advice.

11. This could lead to a sharp debate about whether the adversarial litigation process which is currently at the heart of the English legal system will continue to be a viable feature of the system, save for the most significant cases that need to be adjudicated in this way.

10.8 Questions

Use the self-test questions in the Online Resources to test your understanding of the topics covered in this chapter and receive tailored feedback: www.oup.com/uk/partington18_19/.

10.9 Web links

Check the Online Resources for a selection of annotated web links allowing you to easily research topics of particular interest: www.oup.com/uk/partington18_19/.

10.10 Blog items

See Spotlight on the Justice System, at www.martinpartington.com/category/chapter-10-2/.

Suggestions for further reading

LEGAL SERVICES RESEARCH CENTRE, *Causes of Action: Civil law and social justice. The final report of the first LSRC survey of justiciable problems* (2nd edn, London, Legal Services Commission, 2006)

REGAN, F., and others, *The Transformation of Legal Aid: Comparative and Historical Studies* (Oxford, Clarendon Press, 1999)

Other suggestions are set out in the Further Reading listed in the **Online Resources**.

PART V

CONCLUSION

11

The transformation of the English legal system: pressures and challenges

11.1 Introduction

The study of law is not just about learning rules. It is about thinking about the law, and asking questions. Whose interests do particular rules of law serve? Do they make sense? How do they operate in practice? Should the law be reformed?

Throughout this book, I have been raising questions which need to be asked when thinking about the English legal system. What are law's functions? How is law made? What are the contexts in which it is practised? Who are the different actors in the legal system? How are legal services funded? Is the legal system in a fit state to achieve its apparent purposes?

One of the images of law which, I suggest in my blog,[1] many of those coming to study law may have is that the legal system is rather traditional, conservative, reluctant to change. The present reality is totally different.

The English legal system is undergoing a process of transformation that will radically alter how the legal system and those who work within it will function. So rapid is the pace of change that by the time you graduate and start looking for employment, the world you will enter will be significantly different from the one that currently exists.

Who has been driving these changes? Why are these changes occurring? What challenges do all these changes throw up? What follows does not answer all these questions. The aim is to get you to think about what is happening and what the implications for the future may be.

---

[1] www.martinpartington.com/about-the-book.

11.2 The pressures for change

The main sources of pressure that have led to the current process of change and transformation can be grouped under two broad headings:

(1) Government.

(2) Other pressures:

- the economic recession;
- information technologies;
- competition from other professional groups.

11.2.1 Government

Over the last 20 years, there have been substantial institutional changes to the English legal system. They have fallen, broadly, into two phases:

- first, those inspired by the modernization agenda of the former Labour administrations led by Tony Blair and Gordon Brown (1997–2010);
- secondly, those introduced by the Coalition/Conservative administrations led by David Cameron and Theresa May (2010–present).

Many of the changes in *Phase 1* have been noted in context in earlier chapters. They include:

- the creation of the Ministry of Justice (2007);
- the transfer of responsibility for offender management services (prisons and probation) from the Home Office to the Ministry of Justice (2007);
- the creation of the Legal Services Commission, to run legal aid and pioneer new approaches to the delivery of legal services to the poor (2000), now replaced by the Legal Aid Agency (2013);
- the creation of the Supreme Court (2009), replacing the judicial functions of the House of Lords;
- the creation of the Tribunals Service (2007) subsequently merged with the Courts Service (2011);
- the creation of the Judicial Appointments Commission (2006);
- the establishment of the Legal Services Board to regulate the legal professions and to promote innovation in the delivery of legal services (2007);
- the creation of the Legal Services Ombudsman and rationalizing procedures for dealing with complaints against lawyers (2007);
- the establishment of the Sentencing Council (2009) to advise on sentencing policy;
- the implementation of major reforms to civil procedure, with the new emphasis on active case management by the judges (1999).

In *Phase 2* institutional change included:

- the abolition of local police authorities and their replacement by elected Police and Crime Commissioners (2012);
- the creation of the College of Policing (2012);
- the creation of the National Crime Agency (2013);
- reform of the county court (2013);
- the creation of the Family Court (2014);
- the creation of the new list for hearing high value commercial disputes (2015) and the Business and Property Courts of England and Wales (2017);
- improving the efficiency of the criminal justice system (2015);
- launching the *Transforming Our Justice System* reform programme (2016).

There have also been changes driven by the desire of government to involve private and third sector bodies in the work of the justice system. Private sector prisons were first created in 1992, a development continued under the Blair and Brown Labour administrations. The principle was extended in 2014, through the creation of a new Probation Service, including private and third sector providers (2014) replacing the previous entirely public sector probation service.

An overriding policy imperative in *Phase 2* has been the desire to reduce public expenditure. This has had a significant impact on the English legal system.

The most obvious effect has been on the legal aid scheme. In this context:

- the scope of the legal aid scheme has been restricted;
- the Legal Services Commission was wound up and replaced by the Legal Aid Agency, operating within a much tighter legal framework;
- legal aid practitioners' pay has been significantly reduced.

In addition:

- There have been major changes to the fees that potential litigants must pay to get a case started in court, and in many tribunals.
- There is currently a major reshaping of the courts and tribunals estate.
- A big investment in IT for the courts is in progress.
- There has been a reduction in the number of legal advice agencies.
- The Crown Prosecution Service has had its funding reduced, which may be leading to an increase in the numbers of private prosecutions.
- More litigants in person are appearing in the civil courts.

The response of many practitioners to these developments is to deplore them and to demand the restoration of reduced funding. I take a more provocative starting point.

Cuts in public expenditure are not necessarily a bad thing. If current practices waste resources, there is no good reason why change should not be introduced to improve efficiency as well as reduce cost. Those who simply want earlier levels of public expenditure to be restored are not facing political reality and, more importantly, show a lack of imagination.

11.2.2 Other pressures

Other important sources of pressure can be briefly noted. Each of the following has had a major impact on the ways in which legal practices—particularly those in the City of London—organize and run their businesses.

11.2.2.1 The economy: recession, recovery, and Brexit

While the major economic recession of the late 2000s may have passed, it has had a significant impact on the legal system, not simply in the UK but in other countries as well. Many large corporations that pay the bills of the large corporate law firms are now taking a much closer and more critical look at their expenditure on legal services. This has put significant pressure on corporate law firms in particular to look at their business models and develop ways of working that are more efficient and deliver better value for money to their clients. The prospect of Brexit is causing the major commercial law firms to think hard about how they can respond to the new business contexts that Brexit will create.

11.2.2.2 Information technologies

The legal professions have been investing significantly in information technologies (IT), again in order to drive efficiency and enable them to reduce their overheads. There is now serious debate about the prospect of various forms of artificial intelligence taking over routine lawyering functions within the foreseeable future.

11.2.2.3 Competition from other professional groups

Lawyers are increasingly facing competition in the provision of their services from other professional groups, in particular accountancy practices who are starting to take advantage of the rules for the creation of alternative business structures created by the Legal Services Board.

11.3 The challenges of change

What challenges to the English legal system do these pressures for change present?

An effective and efficient legal system is essential for the promotion of the rule of law. Everyone, not just the rich and powerful, should have access to the legal system. The reality is that the rich and powerful will be able to continue to hire lawyers and take legal proceedings more or less as before. It is the needs of the less well-off and less powerful that must particularly be borne in mind. The overriding challenge is to ensure that ordinary people (and small businesses) can get access to justice when they need to assert their legal rights. Here I suggest a number of developments which, if developed energetically and imaginatively, could help to achieve the objective.

306 INTRODUCTION TO THE ENGLISH LEGAL SYSTEM

This will not be easy. It will require strong leadership from legal professionals, government policy-makers, and the judiciary. Some decisions already taken may need to be re-examined to see whether their impact has been disproportionately negative—e.g. the massive increases in court and tribunal fees or cuts in legal aid.

11.3.1 Expanding use of information and communication technologies

While investment in information and communications technology (ICT) by practitioners has been enormous, changing considerably how lawyers work, investment in ICT in courts and tribunals has so far been pitifully slow. Use of ICT should go much further to increase access to justice.

There are interesting examples already operating of the extremely effective use of technology to resolve disputes. They allow people to bring cases online, to upload evidence, and to have the cases dealt with over the phone or remotely through video conference or just on the files as submitted without any hearing. The dispute resolution procedures adopted by the Financial Services Ombudsman, the Parking Adjudicators, and the Dispute Service are the most quoted examples.

Some categories of civil case, in particular money claims and possession claims, can currently be started online. But these are very modest examples of what could be delivered by HM Courts and Tribunals Service by the creation of portals that structure the information that needs to be provided by parties to a dispute to enable decisions to be reached by an independent judge or assessor.

The use of ICT has transformed the provision of consumer services, and indeed government services. By contrast, the use of ICT in the legal system has lagged behind. There is no reason why ICT cannot be developed to improve access to justice by enabling more people to do their own litigation and obtaining other services from the court by using online applications. (It may well be that courts and tribunals will need to employ special advisers who can assist members of the public with their interactions with newly developed claim portals.)

ICT could also be widely used to create 'virtual' courts or tribunals, in which parties could engage with the judge online or by phone, rather than having to be present before him/her. This would not be suitable in all cases; but there is no reason why many more routine cases could not be dealt with this way.

Imaginative use of ICT could also enable specialist judiciary to be used more flexibly. For example, judges with housing law experience could determine cases remotely, without the need to have a housing specialist in every court.

11.3.2 Making a greater commitment to customer service delivery

It is a cliché that 'justice delayed is justice denied'. While active case management—introduced following Lord Woolf's reforms to civil justice procedure and now introduced into the family and criminal justice systems—has reduced delay, the courts and tribunals service still fails to embrace fully a commitment to service standards which the public ought to expect.

A government website (open.justice.gov.uk/home/) proudly proclaims, for example, that a small claim will usually be decided within 31 weeks. Is this something to boast about? Other more complex cases take much longer. Active case management has helped. But much more needs to be done. Strong judicial leadership, combined with the imaginative use of ICT proposed in the last section, ought to enable the courts and tribunals service to deliver a much more efficient and speedier service to the public than is currently on offer.

It might also be necessary to consider the hours during which courts and tribunals sit. There is much discussion about doctors offering a seven days a week service. While not going that far, how about Saturday morning hearings? The Parking Adjudicators already offer this. At present, it is possible to obtain emergency orders from judges at any time. And courts have been known to sit at weekends, in particular after major incidents of public disorder. But are current opening hours of courts (10am to 4pm, Monday to Friday) enough?

11.3.3 Using more specialist courts

The creation of the Courts and Tribunals Service has, surprisingly, not led to any serious discussion about whether the non-criminal courts should become more specialized.

The traditional view has been that, in general, courts should be generalist, not specialist in nature. It is up to the advocates appearing before the courts to instruct the judges on the law that needs to be applied in the particular case. From the judges' point of view, this means that they have a variety of work which keeps them interested. But is this the best way to organize the judiciary?

Consider the present position:

- All tribunals have a specialist jurisdiction, with judges who are specifically trained in the relevant area—social security, employment, immigration, child support, housing, and the like.

- The Family Court operates with specially trained judges.

- For commercial disputes, there is a whole raft of specialist jurisdictions, for example Technology and Construction, Patents, Admiralty, Companies, Commercial. A new list with specialist judges to determine high value commercial disputes has recently been established in London. These have recently been combined into the Business and Property Courts of England and Wales.

- A specialist Planning Court was established in 2014.

- Currently there is a consultation on how housing disputes should be distributed between the (generalist) county court and the (specialist) Lower Tier Property Chamber. The Secretary of State for Communities and Local Government announced in September 2017 that a new housing court would be established, though no details are currently available.

A consequence of specialization is that judges become familiar with the particular area of law under consideration, and—where needed—can provide at least some assistance to an unrepresented party to identify relevant issues and relevant evidence. The 'enabling role' of the judge has long been acknowledged in tribunals; it should equally be accepted in civil courts.

I think there should be a serious discussion about abandoning the principle of a generalist civil court, and creating further specialist jurisdictions, for example, a specialist consumer affairs court/tribunal; or a specialist personal injury court/tribunal.

As suggested earlier, imaginative use of ICT could enable specialist judges to deal with cases remotely. It would not be necessary for every court to have its own specialists.

The danger of judges becoming stale or bored as a consequence of dealing with a more limited variety of cases would be resolved by creating opportunities for training in new jurisdictions—as has already started to happen with the appointment of tribunal judges who subsequently move into other judicial contexts.

11.3.4 Thinking about the judicial function

Not enough time has been spent in recent years thinking about the role of judges in courts and tribunals. This may be because the functions are regarded as self-evident. Surely, people would say, the judges' task is to:

- hear the evidence presented;
- find the facts in the light of that evidence;
- understand and if necessary rule on the law relevant to the issue to be decided;
- reach a decision in the light of these exercises;
- having reached a decision, communicate this to the parties.

These assumptions raise a number of questions which should be considered more fully, particularly for non-criminal issues.

First, how important is it for the judge to hear evidence as opposed to read it—in particular where there is a great deal of documentary evidence? To what extent should the oral tradition in hearing cases be retained? There are already many types of case which proceed entirely on the papers. Can this principle be extended further?

Secondly, in how many cases is a ruling on a point of law really crucial? In many routine cases the law is clear. It is the facts that are unclear. If this is correct, then once the facts are determined, the result follows pretty easily from those findings. If this is right, then is current use of (expensive) judicial time justified? Could cheaper alternatives be considered, as JUSTICE recently argued in its paper *Delivering Justice in an Age of Austerity*?

Thirdly, is the practice of judges in the civil courts and in some tribunals giving long judgments really necessary? Much time and trouble could be saved if judges initially limited themselves to stating the outcome with perhaps brief reasons—only writing a full judgment if needed for an appeal.

11.3.5 Promoting alternative dispute resolution (ADR)

Despite enormous encouragement to use ADR by both the judges and government, the use of ADR techniques to resolve cases still remains limited. It seems that, despite official and judicial pressure, many practitioners find it hard to develop a business model that enables them to make money from using ADR. There is therefore little incentive for them to encourage their clients to go down the ADR route.

There is some evidence from other common law jurisdictions that making ADR compulsory is an essential step that must be taken if there is to be a more general change in litigation culture and practice. Although undoubtedly controversial, this is an issue which should be revisited. The 2017 paper by the Civil Justice Council has made a start on this.

Consideration should also be given to much greater integration of ADR into the services provided by courts and tribunals. This would mean that setting out towards a court hearing would not be the only option for those starting civil proceedings. The court service itself could offer alternative destinations for the resolution of disputes.

11.3.6 Funding access to justice

Big money is being invested in major commercial litigation to fund the enormous costs of bringing such cases. What are the options for the non-wealthy?

Assuming that there is no increase in the levels of legal aid funding, which is clearly not on the agenda at the moment, there is a range of possibilities. Many of these have been considered in Chapter 10 (*see 10.3*) and will not be repeated here. In addition, a coordinated strategy, on the lines set out in the Low Commission Report (2014) (*Box 10.2*), would, I think, make a big difference.

But there are two other, related, matters which I think deserve much more attention: treatment of legal issues in the mass media; and public legal education.

11.3.7 Improving treatment of legal issues in the mass media

Apart from the drama of the big criminal trial or a scandal involving a miscarriage of justice, discussion about law in the mass media is very limited. There are notable exceptions: the BBC radio programme, *Law in Action*; the weekly law pages in some of the broadsheet newspapers; and related online blogs, together with a number of consumer programmes that touch on aspects of the law, may be mentioned. However, there is little rounded discussion about law-making, the practice of law, or the impact of law on the citizen. Unlike other aspects of our intellectual life, such as history, science, or medicine, law is not regularly the subject of mainstream media programming.

Yet the centrality of law to different social orders suggests that the media neglect of law and legal issues is extremely unsatisfactory. Programme makers may feel that law is too complex a subject to make it attractive for mass programming. But this failure simply contributes to the mystique of law and enhances the power of the lawyer in society, at a time when arguably opportunities for greater general understanding of and access to law should be growing.

There are signs that this may change a little. In 2010 there were two excellent TV programmes on the new Supreme Court. Sky News offers live coverage of Supreme Court proceedings. And the Coalition government started the broadcasting of some proceedings in the Court of Appeal.

However, there are no plans to televise criminal trials, which happens a great deal in the United States and other countries. There was a notable experiment in the United Kingdom a number of years ago when some criminal trials in Scotland were shown in edited form on television. While such a step might give the appearance of greater openness of the legal system to the public, it should be remembered that televising trials may merely serve to exacerbate current images of law—that the typical legal process is a criminal one, in which there is a lengthy trial of the case for and against the accused. We know from *Chapter 5* how *untypical* such cases are.

There is no discussion about televising cases in the administrative justice, family justice, or civil justice arenas; or programmes dealing with the vast majority of cases that are resolved without a full-scale trial.

Part of the reason public discussion of legal issues is so limited may be that those who operate within the legal system themselves have shown only limited interest in presenting their work to a wider audience. Much professional legal activity is conducted on the basis of confidentiality, which may result in a lack of individual enthusiasm to enter the public eye. Furthermore, there are those in the legal profession who think that it goes against the professional grain to seek publicity for their work. However, a consequence of such attitudes is that the law and its practitioners tend to hit the headlines only when things have gone wrong.

Lawyers and other practitioners should be willing to shape a more educational public information agenda, and to work with the media to develop opportunities for a fuller understanding of law and the legal system in all our lives. The difficulties of making a wider range of programmes about law may be substantial. Nevertheless, the challenge remains to provide a new, more informed treatment of legal issues in the mass media. This could play an important part in the shaping of public perceptions about the legal system and those who work in it, which could in turn contribute to making the legal system function more effectively.

11.3.8 Increasing public legal education

The proposition that ordinary citizens can in any real sense be assumed to know the law that governs their lives is just not tenable. While it may not be realistic to complain that there is too much law, the challenge for law-makers and others involved in working the legal system is to provide better information about law and its processes. The now defunct Legal Services Commission started to invest in the provision of such information on the internet. Other agencies are also increasingly using websites to provide information. But lack of usable information remains a serious weakness in the current institutional arrangements of the legal system. As with the challenge of providing better general information about law through the mass media, there is still a considerable challenge to be faced, particularly within government, about the use of new information and communication technologies to make information about citizens' rights available to a much wider public than is presently the case.

Important initiatives are being taken on public legal education.[2] But these are not generously funded. Public legal education is much better developed in some other countries (e.g. Canada or Australia). Their example should be strongly emulated in the United Kingdom.

I think that the universities could play an important role in this development. All universities are now required to ensure that their work has public impact. In a number of disciplines, notably the sciences, Chairs have been created for the development of the public understanding of the area in question. But there is no equivalent Chair in the Public Understanding of Law. Some might decry such a development as 'dumbing down'. I disagree. A Professor of the Public Understanding of Law could draw together interdisciplinary teams that would not only look at how information could be presented in ways that ordinary people could understand, but also—crucially—study the channels for the effective communication of information to members of the public in a way and at the times when this information would be useful.

The fact that the Legal Services Board has public legal education on its statutory list of tasks is a welcome recognition of the importance of this issue. But they are not taking it seriously. They should promote it much more actively.

11.4 Final comment

Many of the developments of the last 15–20 years occurred piecemeal; there was little sense of an overall policy strategy (save perhaps reducing public expenditure). The new emphasis on efficiency in the criminal courts and on transformation in the civil courts and tribunals suggests that there is now emerging an overarching framework for justice policy that seeks to make the system work better for its users, at reduced cost and with greater efficiency. Effective delivery of these policies will depend on continuing strong leadership from both the judiciary and the Ministry of Justice.

Whatever happens, the English legal system will continue to be very dynamic. It is a system within which those with energy and new ideas will have much to contribute.

Those starting the study of law today need to be open to new ideas and to take advantage of and indeed help to shape the opportunities that will undoubtedly exist in the modern English legal system. Above all, you need to keep a close eye on what is happening and ask yourself how you are going to fit into this rapidly changing world.

---

[2] www.lawforlife.org.uk/. Also noteworthy is the fantastic 'Democracy Live' part of the BBC News website; it is an amazing source of information about developments in all four UK governments and the European Union. See www.bbc.co.uk/democracylive/.

11.5 Web links

For one consultant's view of this rapidly changing environment, see Furlong, Jordan, Your Travel Guide to the New Legal Landscape, available to download free at www.lodlaw.com/aboutus?view=reports.

You can also keep up to date through my blog, www.martinpartington.com.

11.6 Blog items

See Spotlight on the Justice System, at www.martinpartington.com/category/chapter-11-2/.

Index